ABRAHAM LINCOLN
The Year of His Election

ABRAHAM LINCOLN

The Year of His Election

By

ALBERT SHAW

☆☆

*Profusely Illustrated
with Contemporary Cartoons
Portraits and Scenes*

NEW YORK
THE REVIEW OF REVIEWS CORPORATION
1929

Copyright, 1929
Albert Shaw

Made in the
United States of America

CONTENTS

vii

CONTENTS—*Continued*

CONTENTS—*Concluded*

ABRAHAM LINCOLN AS HE BECAME A NATIONAL CHARACTER

From a photograph taken by Brady when Lincoln visited New York in February, 1860, to make the Cooper Union address.

THE AMERICAN EAGLE IN DANGER

UNCLE SAM: "What are you doing to that bird of mine. He doesn't belong to either of you. Look sharp, or he'll give you a taste of his claws!"—From *Frank Leslie's Illustrated Newspaper*.

CHAPTER I

Opening Scenes of a Political Year

Democrats gather in convention at Charleston—Lincoln from his Illinois home observes events—The cultured and self-sufficient Charlestonians scorn the Northern and Western Douglas delegations

THE LAST YEAR of James Buchanan in the White House, ending on March 4, 1861, was in many respects the most critical and disturbing twelvemonth, except for years of actual war, in the history of the United States. We find the events of the year succeeding one another like the progressive scenes of a stupendous political drama. Notable personages crowd the stage, and the sharpening antagonism of the sectional dispute between North and South becomes the distinct motive of a contest that rapidly assumes the aspects of tragedy. Parties are rearranging themselves, and the presidential campaign is going forward under four separate banners.

At the beginning of the year Buchanan is somewhat expectant of Democratic support for a second term; but soon he finds his further leadership rejected alike by Northern and Southern factions, with Mr. Bennett of the New York *Herald* almost alone in upholding him. Stephen A. Douglas and Jefferson Davis have become the undisputed champions of the rival wings of the Democratic party.

Meanwhile, the Republicans are gathering strength from all factions and elements in the North; and William H. Seward of New York confidently expects the presidential nomination at the hands of the convention that is to meet at Chicago. At the same time Abraham

I

Lincoln, returning to the West from a successful introduction to Eastern audiences, assumes the rôle of a receptive candidate, planning to succeed, in case of Seward's failure, through the well-known strategy of compromise.

Within this thrilling political year Lincoln is successful in the ordeal of the Republican convention, and at the end of the electoral campaign we find him in the envied position of President-elect, with Buchanan directing the Government for another period of four months. Lincoln and the Republicans look on with anxiety, because their triumph at the polls is promptly met by the defiant note of Southern secession. Buchanan shifts his attitude, reorganizes his Cabinet, tries in vain to stem the rising tide of revolt, and on March 4, 1861, he turns over to his successor a central Government not of thirty-three States, but of only twenty-six.

I do not think that readers of our day should find it tedious to study in some detail the situations and occurrences of that time of change and of dire menace. In devoting all the chapters of this volume to that single year of political and governmental turmoil, I have found it necessary to condense rather than to expand or elaborate. My object has been the simple one of making the politics of 1860, and the governmental situations of 1860-61, seems as vivid and as real as those of our own day. The free use of the cartoons of that year, and of portraits and other illustrations, will, I believe, help the reader to breathe the atmosphere of a strenuous era of party strife and sectional division.

On the morning of March 4, 1860, a year to the very day before his ride in state with President Buchanan through military guards up Pennsylvania Avenue for his inauguration at the Capitol, Abraham Lincoln was taking an affectionate leave of his son Robert Todd Lincoln at Exeter, New Hampshire, where the youth was a pupil in Phillips Academy.

Lincoln had spoken impressively at Cooper Union in New York on Monday, February 27th; had made a speech at Providence, Rhode Island, the next day; and after other addresses had arrived at Exeter on Saturday. A volume by Elwin L. Page, published in 1929, reminds us that Lincoln's New England visit deserves the research that the author has bestowed.

The most agreeable chapter in Mr. Page's book is the one that tells the story of Abraham Lincoln's Sunday with Robert and a group of his companions at the Academy. I do not remember any similar incident in Lincoln biographies. Listening to banjo music and telling stories, Lincoln made himself agreeable in the most natural fashion. Lads who had less than three months to wait for the thrilling news of the Republican nomination at Chicago, and only eight months until their friend's election as President was announced, were never to forget that they had actually seen Lincoln at close quarters and in a happy mood.

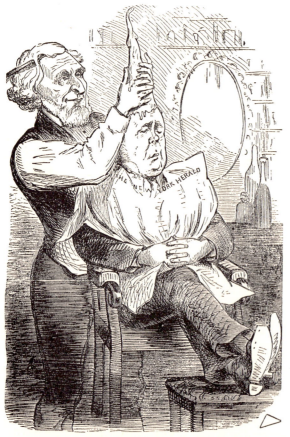

"THE MAN FOR CHARLESTON IS BUCHANAN"

President Buchanan sits in the chair, the barber "soaping him" being James Gordon Bennett, editor of the New York *Herald*. Characteristic of the President, exaggerated by the cartoonists, was an arrangement of his hair that made it rise to a point over the forehead. The caricature reproduced above, published as the Democratic convention was about to meet, was inspired by the *Herald's* endorsement of Buchanan for a second term.

We find Lincoln spending another week in making notable speeches before his departure from New England; and his dated correspondence shows that he was at home again in Springfield, Illinois, not later than March 14th. He was now occupying himself with the political situation, realizing that the question of Republican success was involved in the results of the convention of the Democratic party that was to open in Charleston, South Carolina, April 23rd. The date of the Republican gathering at Chicago had been fixed for May 16th, and Lincoln was now a candidate.

The proceedings at Charleston, about which I am proposing to write at some length, were filling the newspapers. By this time the press was making liberal use of telegraphic facilities. Every politician in the country was following with intense interest the struggle at Charleston between the Northern supporters of Douglas and the coalition of anti-Douglas delegations from the Slave States. Referring to a letter from Senator Lyman Trumbull, Lincoln wrote: "I have postponed answering it, hoping by the result at Charleston to know who is to lead our adversaries before writing. But Charleston hangs fire, and I wait no longer." He admitted that he had the presidential fever in a mild form, and he intimated that if Douglas were nominated he himself might be the one Republican who could carry Illinois against the "Little Giant."

In his letters of May 1st Lincoln is assuming that Douglas will be nominated by the remnant of the regular convention at Charles-

APRIL 23, 1860.]

VANITY FAIR.

THE CHARLESTON SOLILOQUY

"To be or not to be, that is the question."

HAMLET, *his last appearance in this character.*   J—s B—ch—n
POLONIUS, *by request, with the favorite song,*
"The Man for Charleston is J. B."   J G B—n—tt

Late in the year 1859 a new periodical began publication at New York, called *Vanity Fair*. It was admittedly an imitation of the London *Punch,* in size, general appearance, and above all in the style of its leading cartoons. These were the work of Henry Louis Stephens. As the reader will discover for himself, Stephens produced the most striking cartoons from that time until Thomas Nast appeared on the scene in 1861. In this cartoon, Hamlet is President Buchanan, and Polonius is James Gordon Bennett, editor of the New York *Herald.*

ton—which, as our narrative proceeds, the reader will know was destined not to happen. On May 2nd, Lincoln was writing very capable political letters, taking a practical—and upon the whole a cheerful—view of his own prospects. With so much concerning the observer at Springfield, Illinois, as the convention season of 1860 had opened, we may now turn our attention to the meeting of the Democratic clans, from the thirty-three States then existing, at the designated convention city.

SOUTH CAROLINA INSTITUTE, WHERE THE DEMOCRATIC
CONVENTION MET IN APRIL, 1860

Charleston was proud of this building, which was dedicated to the promotion
of mechanical and agricultural arts. Adjoining it was the Circular Church
(Presbyterian). During the eleven-day convention devout Charleston folk met
in their churches daily.

With sectional feeling on both sides so intense as to foreshadow secession and war, why
did the Democratic party decide to hold its
national convention of 1860 in South Carolina? No convention of any party had ever
before been held farther south than Baltimore
or Cincinnati. Charleston was not a large
city, having then only about twenty-three
thousand white people, with seventeen thousand slaves, and several
hundred "free colored." It
was not even the capital of
the State, Columbia having
been accorded that honor in
the year 1790 when as yet it
was nothing more than a
clearing in the forest wilderness. Charleston for almost a century and a half had
been the provincial and State
capital, and it continued without rival in its region as a
center of political influence.
More than any other place in
the entire South, it had
always represented the dis-
tinctively Southern and
"state-rights" point of view.

With the exception of Boston, Charleston was the most
self-sufficing community in
the United States, in its sense
of intellectual and social superiority. It did not look beyond its own borders to test
the value of any of its creeds
or doctrines. Its public men
were orators and logicians of
the highest order of talent
and training. Its women
were accomplished, intelligent and devoted. In its long
history Charleston had stood
apart — a brilliant, isolated
community, idealistic, uncompromising, ready at any
time to sacrifice property and
risk life itself for convictions of right and justice.

The dogmas of Nullifica-
tion and Secession had been drifting up and
down the Atlantic seaboard from the very beginning of the American Union. Charleston
under the leadership of its greatest thinker
and orator, John C. Calhoun, had induced
South Carolina to declare the tariff of 1832
null and void, on the ground of its harmful
discrimination against the interests of this
typical Southern seaport. Charleston and its

A RAILROAD TRAIN OF THE SIXTIES

There were many unconnected local railways, with tracks of varying gauges,
and therefore no "through" trains. This illustration is reproduced from a large
colored lithograph, exceedingly rare, loaned by Robert Fridenberg.

THE CITY OF CHARLESTON, SOUTH CAROLINA, IN 1860
Situated on a narrow peninsula formed by the Ashley and Cooper rivers, as they empty into the bay
and the ocean, Charleston had long been the principal port on the South Atlantic seaboard. It
had a population of only 40,500 in 1860, but it had been the center of the Nullification movement in
1832, and was to take the lead in the program of Secession, later in the year 1860.

tributary country were flourishing by reason of the European demand for cotton and other Southern products, and it was advantageous to import cargoes from Europe at the lowest possible rates of duty.

President Jackson denounced nullification. He proposed to deal with it by force. But it was Henry Clay's compromise tariff, promptly introduced and passed by Congress, rather than Jackson's threats, that induced South Carorina to rescind its nullification ordinance. In the opinion of Charleston it was not Jackson but Calhoun who had won in that contest. A versatile biographer of the new school, writing the lives of Jackson, Calhoun and Clay in succession, with intervals for mental re-adjustment, might make each one of these three statesmen the hero and the victor in his several versions of this nullification crisis.

The doctrine that any individual State, while remaining in the Union, could pass for itself upon the desirability of a federal law and nullify it at pleasure, was made to seem convincing in the subtle reasoning of Calhoun and Rhett and other South Carolinian leaders. But it gained no hold upon the country, and Jackson's political stand and his personal aggressiveness were generally approved.

It was otherwise, however, with the doctrine of Secession. If the Union was a voluntary partnership of a group of sovereign States, with a central government of limited powers acting merely as the agent of these associated sovereignties, it was easy enough for disaffected Southern communities to accept the line of reasoning that made Secession morally and legally justifiable. All of these States proclaimed their intense devotion to the Union and the national flag, and declared that nothing—except the menace of policies at Washington clearly ruinous to their interests —could induce them to take practical steps in the direction of their abstract right to secede. In the very nature of things, Charleston continued to be a foremost exponent of the extreme sentiment of disaffection.

STARTLING AND HEART-RENDING NEWS
This is a New York cartoon, picturing consternation among New York Democrats of a certain type upon receiving news from Charleston that board would
be $50 per day—in advance. Plug-uglies, they were called, hired to supervise
cheering in the galleries in the interest of a favored candidate.

compromised by choosing the diplomatic and inoffensive Mr. Buchanan, whose absence as United States Minister at London had kept him out of recent controversies. Douglas, as a much younger man, had gracefully waived all privileges under the two-thirds rule, and instructed his followers to make the Buchanan nomination unanimous. His leadership of the Democratic party was so fully taken for granted, and his future prospects were so bright, that he was entirely ready to concur in the proposal to hold the Democratic convention at Charleston in 1860. The Dred Scott Decision had been accepted by the Democratic party, and had reassured the South. The choice of Charleston,

With bitterness so intensified by the Kansas troubles, the John Brown raid at Harper's Ferry, and such books as "Uncle Tom's Cabin" and Helper's "Impending Crisis," it was truly a strange and hazardous political experiment to hold a national presidential convention at Charleston. The whole country felt that it was an ominous proceeding; and indeed it proved to be the most stubbornly divided party convention of our entire history. The answer to the question why the Democrats should have gone to Charleston instead of meeting again at Cincinnati as in 1856, could therefore, be so framed as to involve almost everything in our political and constitutional history. But it may also be explained fairly well in a few brief paragraphs.

It happened that the decision to go to Charleston had been made four years earlier at the Cincinnati convention. Harmony was the Democratic note at the beginning of the Buchanan régime. Douglas was in high favor, and the principle of squatter sovereignty was regarded in the South as of distinct advantage to slave interests. The Cincinnati convention, declining to give President Pierce his desired renomination, had

TRAINING FOR THE CHARLESTON CONVENTION
The former Mayor of New York, Fernando Wood, takes boxing
lessons in preparation for the Charleston convention. There had
been a split in the Tammany organization, and Wood was temporarily out of power. He went to Charleston at the head of a
rival delegation, which was not seated though it attracted much
attention. Later in this year 1860 Fernando Wood was again in
control of Tammany, and was elected Mayor of New York City
for the third time.

then, was to signify party harmony and the triumph of South Carolina's views, as understood in 1856.

Unfortunately, however, the surprising but creditable opposition of Douglas to the fraudulent Lecompton Constitution, under which Kansas would have been admitted as a Slave State, had plunged the harmonious party into discord increasingly harsh and resounding. Factions were now boldly defined. Douglas stood out as the leader of the Northwest, while Jefferson Davis of Mississippi emerged as the recognized successor to Calhoun, a leader of the true South Carolina type, the interests of Alabama and Mississippi being now regarded as quite identical with those of South Carolina and Florida.

Douglas was a man of courage. He had been defied and taunted in the Senate, and, so far as we are aware, he had no serious thought of trying to induce the National Democratic Committee to change the place of the convention. Jefferson Davis and Stephen A. Douglas did not themselves go to Charleston, for

MIDNIGHT IN CHARLESTON

Exhausted delegates, and others, occupy every nook and corner. Enter two of the Unterrified from New York. "Hello, Jim, where's them beds of our'n we paid $5 for in advance? This won't do. I think we'll have to clean this ranch out." And Jim replies: "Sail in!"

Congress remained in session until June 25th, and they were occupied in the Senate. But they were, of course, well represented by their respective adherents.

The trains to Charleston had been crowded with delegates from different States who talked politics excitedly all the time, as their wood-burning locomotives bore them through the swampy Southern pine forests, and as they stepped to Mother Earth at intervals while

DELEGATES LEAVING THE CHARLESTON HOTEL FOR THE DEMOCRATIC CONVENTION, ON THE OPENING DAY
From a contemporary drawing.

pauses were made at convenient wood-piles or water-tanks. The present-day Northern visitor to charming Georgian and South Carolinian cities, or to the fascinating winter resorts of Florida, patronizes a luxurious train without change of cars. But a political reporter who accompanied the delegates to Charleston in 1860 noted the fact that he and his fellow-travelers had to change from one train to another six times, in some instances having to drive across a town from one station to another. The era of union stations, of consolidated railway systems, and of through trains had not arrived before the Civil War.

Not only were most of the railroads limited in extent to particular States, but their tracks were of varying gauges. Some American roads used the standard English gauge of 4 feet 8 inches. The New York State railroads were 4 feet 8½ inches and in Pennsylvania a variety of gauges existed. New Jersey, like most of Ohio, had adopted the 4 feet 8 inch standard. The larger number of railroads in the Southern States at that time used a 5-foot gauge. Certain mid-western roads were laid with 5 feet 4 inches between rails. The old Erie road and several others were known as broad gauge, that is, a full 6 feet. The Missourians came out of their State to make connections for the conventions of 1860 on roads having a gauge of 5 feet 6 inches. Sleeping cars had been introduced, but were not much patronized. Dining cars had not been thought of, and at certain stations trains stopped "twenty minutes for refreshments," and passengers crowded wildly into railway eating houses adjoining the so-called "depots."

For virtually all of the Northern delegates the trip to Charleston was like a strange adventure into some far distant country, about whose manners and customs the reports had been altogether conflicting. There were pro-slavery men from Massachusetts, led by Caleb Cushing and Ben Butler. There were men of mercantile interests from New York, concerned about the maintenance of Southern trade and the collection of outstanding accounts. There were Tammany men who could not appreciate Charleston culture, but who had not the slightest objection to the reopening of the African slave trade.

The great majority of the Northern delegates, however, especially those of the new States west of the Alleghanies, had one fixed purpose and point of view. They were going to Charleston to nominate Stephen A. Douglas. I have spoken of conditions of travel because all this had much to do with the political trends and movements of that period. There had been little inter-blending of colonial life before the Revolution. But the common struggle for independence, through a term of

seven years, had thoroughly nationalized Virginians like Washington and New Englanders like John Adams. The Northern States one by one were eliminating slavery in that early period, and the Southern States fully expected to do the same thing, as soon as they could find the convenient time and the feasible method. But with the unsettled conditions of the country, the great distances that separated the capitals of States, and the diverse industrial and agricultural systems that prevailed, everything was soon tending towards the intensifying of local life and interest.

Ohio, for instance, in the forty years before 1860 had become a notably independent area of self-initiated thought and action. It had some trade with the East, and Cincinnati was dealing with the South by virtue of steamboat traffic. But interstate life was a slight influence, as compared with the vigor and the adequacy of the strictly local life of particular States or smaller areas.

And if this was strikingly true as regards the West, circumstances had made local concentration still more complete in the South. Washington, as the Federal Capital, afforded a common meeting ground. But the statesmen came together in Senate and House somewhat as leaders of European countries now meet in the Council and Assembly of the League of Nations at Geneva. The new States of the South—Alabama, Mississippi, Louisiana, and Arkansas—had been settled from the old South almost exclusively. They cherished the traditions of the Revolution, and were intensely loyal to the Constitution as they understood it. But they had no feeling of fraternal intimacy with the people of the North.

The unorganized national domain that extended to the Pacific had been acquired through Southern statesmanship, following the annexation of Texas, the events of the Mexican War, and the California adventure. It was not so much that individual Southern men were actually eager to go to the arid lands of the Apaches and other hostile Indians in order to set up slavery. But they could not conceive of any good reason why they should not have the right to take slaves to this new country if they so desired. In the intensity of their sec-

THE POLITICAL ZOYARA.

[M'LLE ELLA DOUGLAS IN THE GREAT PIROUETTE ACT.]

GENTLEMAN FROM THE SOUTH.—Looks a good deal like it, and yet——
GENTLEMAN FROM THE NORTH.—Waäl, I donno; guess it's rayther doubtful.

The question uppermost at the Charleston convention was whether Senator Douglas of Illinois would or would not be nominated. The cartoon represents him as Zoyara, around whose sensational performance in the circus there was unsolved mystery as to whether the rider was a woman, as she appeared to be, or a man. The two men in the audience—one a Democrat from the North, the other from the South—are speculating in similar fashion about Douglas's chances in the convention.

tionalism, so slightly influenced by contact with the intellectual and economic trends of the modern world, they had unconsciously fallen away from the broad viewpoints of Washington and Jefferson.

As we study now the character and lives of typical Southern leaders of that day, we can understand how they came by degrees to represent local feeling and sectional interest. Their attacks upon the protective tariff were for reasons obvious enough. Their desire to annex Cuba, also, is easy to understand. But a certain quality of bitter intolerance showed their lack of a true sense of proportion. Perhaps the best explanation of it is to be found in the corresponding bitterness and intensity of the Northern anti-slavery men. The more carefully and impartially one studies the movements of 1860, the more evident it becomes

that John Brown's raid, in its effect upon sectional consciousness, was an incident fraught with profound significance.

Historians of our own day, in the South and in the North alike, have been studying with open mind and with as little prejudice as possible the sectionalism that shattered the Democratic party in 1860 and precipitated the war in 1861. They are all agreed that slavery was a bad thing, especially for the white race in the South; and they are practically unanimous in finding that both sections, through appeals to prejudice and passion, were contributing to a solution by clash of arms that ought to have been reached by peaceful and generous agreement among civilized men and women, all of whom professed high ethical and religious standards.

The delegations to Charleston included

over six hundred members, although each State was allowed only the number of votes in the convention that corresponded to its membership in the electoral college, the total being 303. The newer parts of the country, beyond the Alleghanies and north of the Ohio River, were developing with great rapidity. They were national in spirit, modern in their economic structure, and naturally opposed to slavery as a permanent institution. They were inclined to respect the Constitutional rights of the old Slave States, but they were opposed to the extension of slavery in the new national domain, and were out of sympathy with the growing demands of the Southern leaders.

The delegates from those western States knew little or nothing about slavery from their own personal experiences. They were curious about Charleston, and when not sitting in the stormy sessions of the convention, they were alternating between the slave market with its novel and unwelcome scenes and the open churches, where each day the devout Charlestonians were gathered in earnest supplication for the triumph of the Southern cause in the convention, and the abasement of Douglas.

Charleston had always been an intensely religious place. It had gradually accepted slave labor as indispensable to its prosperity, and had adopted codes of social ethics that seemed to reconcile material welfare with the dictates of Christianity. The planters and their wives held it as a sacred duty to give religious instruction to their Negroes; and missionary societies were in existence to promote that view. The Douglas delegates were not socially acceptable to the fastidious Charlestonians, and

WILLIAM L. YANCEY

The leading orator of the Democratic convention at Charleston. An Alabama lawyer, journalist, and former Congressman, he stoutly opposed any compromise with the North on the question of slavery. Yancey was in the forefront of those responsible for the failure of Douglas to receive the presidential nomination.

the situation was too tense and serious for festivity or agreeable hospitality.

The reader interested in practical politics must keep in mind the simple fact that the results of 1860 turned upon the hopeless cleavage in the Democratic party. In 1912 the Democrats won the election of Woodrow Wilson with ease, because of the split between the regular Republicans who renominated President Taft and the Progressive Republicans who persuaded Mr. Taft's predecessor, Mr. Roosevelt, to head their ticket. These circumstances had their conclusive bearing upon our part in the happenings of the World War. My object in this allusion is to remind the reader that parties—and especially their quadrennial conventions—have since Jackson's time been a vital factor in our system of government. Lincoln, Douglas, Davis, and the other leaders of 1860, can only be understood in the light of party politics.

We have ample information in newspaper files of the political movements of 1860, and from no other sources can much information be derived. Fragments are to be found in the correspondence of statesmen, and in public speeches. Industrious and accurate historians like Mr. Rhodes have relied upon these newspaper files. The most colorful and complete account of all the half-dozen conventions was that of Mr. Murat Halstead, who attended them as a correspondent of the Cincinnati *Commercial*. His letters and dispatches were promptly compiled and published in book form for convenient reference during the campaign. He included in the volume much official and tabulated information, using the day-by-day records of the newspapers of the four convention cities, Charleston, Chicago, Baltimore, and Richmond. He opened his record with the following statement which gave the key to the whole situation:

The Hon. Stephen A. Douglas was the pivot individual of the Charleston convention. Every delegate was for or against him. Every motion meant to nominate or not to nominate him. Every parliamentary war was *pro* or *con* Douglas.

On the route to Charleston, delegates and others who were proceeding to attend the convention, talked about Mr. Douglas. The questions in every car and at every station, were: Would he be—could he be—should he be nominated? Could he get a majority of the convention? Could he get two-thirds? Would the South support him if he should be nominated? Would the Administration acquiesce if he were nominated?

In the North the distinction between the views of Douglas and those of Seward, or even of Lincoln, was not regarded as a vague or ill-defined matter. On the other hand, intra-party differences between Douglas and Jefferson Davis were less understood in the North. It appeared, however, as Mr. Halstead at once discovered, that many delegates from the lower South would not admit at all that Douglas could be the candidate of an undivided Democratic party. They regarded Davis as a patriot and Douglas as a traitor—little better than Seward himself. They repelled the patronizing assumption that the Southern cause could be promoted by putting Douglas in the White House. The most conspicuous leader of the Southern faction was the Hon. W. L. Yancey, of Alabama, whose fame had spread throughout the country, and who was known in the North as the "prince of fire-eaters." On his arrival at Charleston, Mr. Halstead described him in the following terms:

He is a compact, middle-sized man, straight limbed, with a square built head and face, and an eye full of expression. He is mild and bland in manner as Fernando Wood, and has an air of perfect sincerity which Wood has not. No one would be likely to point him out in a group of gentlemen as the redoubtable Yancey, who proposes according to common report to precipitate the cotton States into a revolution, dissolve the Union and build up a Southern Empire. The strong point made against him by the Douglasites is that he is a disunionist. It will not frighten him, nor his Southern friends, however, to apply that epithet to him. I very much doubt whether the Douglas men have a leader competent to cope with him in the coming fight. It is quite clear that while the North may be the strongest in votes here, and the most noisy, the South will have the intellect and the pluck to make its points.

This was written three days before the convention opened, with Charleston in political ferment.

A CARTOON THAT FORESHADOWED EVENTS

(Senator Douglas, Democrat, and Senator Seward, Republican, were the leading candidates of their parties for the presidential nominations. The cartoon was published in *Frank Leslie's Illustrated Newspaper*, a New York weekly, in February, 1860, two months before the first of the nominating conventions was to assemble.)

DOUGLAS: "Well, Billy, what are you driving at now?"
SEWARD: "I am peddling books—anything to get a living. Shall I put you down for 'The Impending Crisis'?"
DOUGLAS: "No, thank'ee, Billy. The impending crisis will put us both down, I reckon."

THE DEMOCRATIC CONVENTION IN SESSION AT CHARLESTON, SOUTH CAROLINA

More than six hundred delegates assembled in the hall of South Carolina Institute from April 23rd to May 3rd. There were sharp sectional differences over slavery declarations in the platform, and nearly all the Southern delegates withdrew. The convention adjourned, to meet at Baltimore on June 18th.

CHAPTER II

Hopeless Division at Charleston

The convention splits over a Squatter-Sovereignty platform—Douglas leads through fifty-seven indecisive ballots—Bolters adopt the Davis pro-slavery planks—Shifting the scene to Baltimore

THE DOUGLAS MEN had come to Charleston boastful and confident. On April 22nd, the day before the convention opened, the prospects seemed favorable for Douglas. His supporters were working quietly to diminish antagonism. But his opponents were conjuring up everything distasteful to the South in his record, and above all they held against him the unpardonable offense of his association with Seward and the "Black Republicans" in defeating the Lecompton Constitution, under which they had tried in vain to admit Kansas as a pro-slavery State.

It was no secret that the delegates from seven Southern States were pledged to withdraw if Douglas should be nominated. The retort of the Douglas men was that in case of such a split, Northern sympathy would so strengthen Douglas that the Republicans would lose all along the line. Thus Douglas would be chosen President by Northern electoral votes, the South having been left to a desperate fight, within its own States, between extremists and moderates.

Senator Slidell of Louisiana, a conspicuous opponent of Douglas in the Senate, had suddenly decided to come down to Charleston from Washington, arriving just before the convention. Mr. Halstead describes Slidell as "a gentleman with long, thin, white hair, through which the top of his head blushes like the shell of a boiled lobster. The gentleman has also a cherry-red face, the color being that produced by good health and good living joined to a florid temperament. His features are well cut, and the expression is that of a thoughtful, hard-working, resolute man of the world. He is a New Yorker by birth, but has

PROMINENT CANDIDATES FOR THE DEMOCRATIC NOMINATION IN 1860

Of the eleven men in this group only three were Northerners—Douglas of Illinois, Lane of Oregon, and Pierce of New Hampshire. A deadlock among the delegates prevented the Charleston convention from selecting a candidate, and later resulted in the nomination on rival tickets of two of the men whose portraits appear in this group, Douglas and Breckinridge. Lane was selected as running-mate for Breckinridge. Within a year, also, two others, Davis and Stephens, were to be President and Vice-President of a seceding Confederacy. Our illustration is reproduced from a double-page spread in *Harper's Weekly*, published two days before the convention assembled. The artist had based his sketches upon portraits made by Matthew Brady, the famous photographer, who operated studios in Washington and New York.

made a princely fortune at the New Orleans bar. He is not a very eloquent man in the Senate, but his ability is unquestioned, and it is universally known that he is, with the present Administration, the power behind the throne greater than the throne itself. Mr. Buchanan is as wax in his fingers. The name of this gentleman is John Slidell. His special mission here is to see that Stephen A. Douglas is not nominated for the Presidency."

Senator Pugh of Ohio, the only Democrat in the Senate who now stood with Douglas, spoke in answer to the florid convention speech of Mr. Yancey. "It had not the silvery music, the grace and polish that distinguished the oration of Mr. Yancey, but it was keen, shrewd, and telling." Mr. Pugh "insisted that the Southern demand for peculiar protection of their peculiar property in the Territories had no warrant in the Constitution."

In the work of the convention three rules were more or less in conflict with one another. The ordinary rule of the majority was applicable to the adoption of a platform and other matters of business. The two-thirds rule was again agreed upon as requisite to the nomination of candidates for the presidency and vice-presidency. The rule of one delegate from each State in the make-up of standing committees was also adopted, this, like the other two rules I have cited, being accepted as belonging to time-honored Democratic con-

CALEB CUSHING (1800-79)
The chairman of the Democratic convention at Charleston
was a Massachusetts lawyer, a Harvard graduate, who
had been Attorney General in the cabinet of President
Pierce. He had also served in the House of Representatives, and as United States Commissioner to China had
concluded the first treaty with that country in 1844. In
the war with Mexico, Cushing was made a Brigadier General but saw no active service. Though pro-Southern in
1860, he became a strong supporter of President Lincoln
in 1861; and for many years he survived as a distinguished
international lawyer and diplomat.

vention procedure, rather than for reasons of
immediate strategy at Charleston.

There was no dispute about organization;
and a shrewd Massachusetts lawyer, Caleb
Cushing by name, strongly pro-Southern in
his sympathies, was made permanent chairman. It was decided to deal with the crucial
question of the platform, before proceeding
to name the ticket. The Southern element had
determined to make the nomination of Douglas impossible by the adoption of a platform
upon which he could not consistently stand.

For this purpose there were at hand the
resolutions that Jefferson Davis had introduced in the Senate. It had been planned to
secure the approval of the Democratic Senators, and thus to give prestige and standing to
a series of statements and expressions that
could be transported to Charleston, and there

adopted as the principal articles of faith for
the party's campaign against the Republicans.

Every Democratic Senator had adhered to
these resolutions, as finally drafted early in
March, except Douglas himself and his friend
Senator Pugh of Ohio. The platform committee at Charleston consisted of thirty-three
members, this being the number of States in
the Union at that time. California and Oregon, dominated by federal patronage under
Buchanan's influence, sent delegations that co-
operated with the South. Otherwise, the
Northern delegations were supporters of
Douglas, and opponents of the Davis dogmas.

If Oregon, for example, had acted with the
Douglas States, leaving California to act with
the South, the Douglas men would have had
seventeen as against sixteen. But when California and Oregon both acted under the leadership of Jefferson Davis and the South, the
platform committee stood seventeen to sixteen
in favor of the Davis resolutions.

The convention had assembled and organized on Monday, April 23rd. The platform committee worked until Saturday, while
the convention waited in suspense for its report. But it could not agree; and majority
and minority platforms were presented. I am
dwelling somewhat upon this situation because
it was one of the approaches to a definite split
in the Democratic party which, in turn, made
Republican victory practically certain and
Southern Secession inevitable.

The minority or pro-Douglas report on platform simply reaffirmed the Cincinnati resolutions of 1856. It accepted the Dred Scott
Decision, and was as conciliatory as possible
towards the South; but it maintained the
Douglas view of the right of Territories to exclude slavery. The majority report, embody-
ing the Davis resolutions, took aggressive
ground as regards the right of slaveholders
to carry their property anywhere within the
territories or the unorganized domain that belonged to the United States. It asserted the
right of slaveholders to be protected everywhere by the federal government itself, calling
for special legislation to that end.

Hon. Henry B. Payne, of Ohio, presented
the minority report, and spoke with excellent

OUR POLITICAL SNAKE-CHARMER.

DOUGLAS: "You perceive, ladies and gentlemen, that the creatures are entirely under my control. (Aside) I hope the brutes won't bite."

The supporters of Senator Douglas had come to Charleston confident that he was the outstanding leader of his party. More than that, they believed that positions Douglas had taken in the Senate, over a long period, made him the one man likely to receive support from outside the party ranks. These snakes which Douglas tries to charm represent Republicans, Old Line Whigs, and members of the American party, as well as regular Democrats and anti-Lecompton Democrats.

feeling and earnest protestations of good will toward the South. The advocate of the majority report was Mr. Yancey of Alabama, who stood foremost in the ranks of the Southern orators of that day. His impassioned eloquence was the despair of a whole school of rhapsodists who cultivated his theatrical style. This picturesque and torrential manner of speech was preferred to the more calm and restrained method of Northern orators of the classical Websterian school.

Mr. Yancey denounced the Northern Democrats because in the background of their positions lay the admission that slavery was a thing intrinsically wrong in itself. He held that, on the contrary, slavery was right and not wrong; and that, if the Northern Demo-

crats had espoused that view, the anti-slavery movement would have been completely discredited, whereas it had grown from feeble and despised beginnings until it now had become dominant. "When I was a schoolboy in the Northern States," said Mr. Yancey, "Abolitionists were pelted with rotten eggs. But now this band of Abolitionists has spread and grown into three bands—the Black Republicans, the Free Soilers, and the Squatter Sovereignty men—all representing the common sentiment that slavery is wrong. I say it in no disrespect, but it is the logical argument that your admission that slavery is wrong has been the cause of this discord."

The answer to Mr. Yancey was made by Senator Pugh of Ohio, who was one of the few members of either branch of Congress who had left Washington to attend the convention. As I have already said, he was the only member of the Democratic party in the Senate who had remained a faithful follower and supporter of Douglas. All the other Democratic Senators had deserted the brilliant leader who had, only two or three years before, been recognized by his fellow members as the party's autocratic chieftain and the dominating figure in the Chamber.

Mr. Pugh, as quoted by Murat Halstead in his contemporary report of the national political conventions of 1860, thanked God that a bold and honest man from the South had at last spoken and told the world the truth regarding Southern demands. As to Mr. Yancey's assertions that Northern Democrats must say that slavery is right and ought to be extended, Mr. Pugh answered, with emotion: "Gentlemen of the South, you mistake us—you mistake us; we will not do it."

JAMES A. BAYARD
When the Southern delegates withdrew from the main gathering at Charleston and held a convention of their own, Bayard presided over their four-days' sessions. He was a distinguished constitutional lawyer, a member of the United States Senate from Delaware. His father had been a Senator, and his son and grandson in due time were to serve Delaware in that chamber.

On Saturday, the sixth day of the convention, Senator Bigler of Pennsylvania, representing his intimate personal friend, President Buchanan, moved that both platforms be sent back to the committee for re-study, with a view to reporting on Monday, when the convention should proceed to vote. There was protracted parliamentary confusion over this suggestion, but in effect it prevailed. Mr. Rhodes, commenting upon this deadlocked situation, holds the view that the South might have waived its platform preference if it could have named the candidate. He observes that not a single Northern State could have been carried on the Davis platform proposed by the majority of the committee, and further that no candidate holding the extreme Southern view would have been successful in Northern States, no matter what the platform might have declared.

Douglas and his platform were inseparable, and no compromise, from their standpoint, would have been effective. The Cincinnati platform which contained implied acceptance of the Dred Scott Decision, and which made strong protests against Northern nullification of the Fugitive Slave Laws, represented the full measure of concession that Northern Democrats could make to the South. If the South had been willing to accept such a platform, it should also have acquiesced in the nomination of Douglas, who alone could carry the necessary Northern States. But with Southern sentiment now so aggressive and so arrogant as unfairly to stigmatize Douglas and his supporters as Abolitionists, it was clearly seen on both sides that there was no basis for agreement.

At this stage Mr. Halstead reported:

JOHN SLIDELL
New Yorker by birth and New Orleans lawyer by profession, Slidell served in the United States Senate from 1853 until Louisiana withdrew from the Union in 1861. As an opponent of Douglas in the Senate he had come to Charleston to see that the presidential nomination went to someone else. He was a foremost Secessionist.

I am not stating the case over-strongly, when I say that there is a general consciousness that the Convention is making so bad a record, its deliberations are becoming of so little importance, that it will be impossible to defend any conclusion likely to be reached, before the country. The Democratic party has here furnished to its enemies the ammunition that will enable them to annihilate the preposterous pretensions which it has for some years put forth. The scenes around me are those of dissolution of the Democratic organization.

The Northwestern delegates are disheartened.

They see that it will be impossible for them to drag through the coming campaign so cumbersome a mass of antagonisms as have been presented here.

I have several times this morning heard the remark, "The President will be nominated at Chicago."

In other words, there was a pessimistic feeling at Charleston that the party split would result in Republican victory, although this was not a universal opinion or a foregone conclusion.

And so on Monday the voting began, and the Douglas platform prevailed by a majority of 165 to 138. The South had the majority of States, but the Douglas delegations averaged larger. Several delegates from Massachusetts, New Jersey, and Pennsylvania, known as "Northern men with Southern principles," joined Oregon and California in making a total of 30 anti-Douglas votes from Free States. Of the 165 pro-Douglas votes, only 12 came from States (mostly on the border) where slavery existed. In short, the split was practically

DANCING FOR EELS IN THE CHARLESTON MARKET.
DOUGLAS IN HIS CELEBRATED BREAKDOWN.

Douglas, as usual, is given the central place in this group of candidates before the Democratic convention. His rivals in the foreground are President Buchanan (left) and Jefferson Davis (right). In the rear, left to right, are: ex-President Pierce, Governor Wise of Virginia, and R. M. T. Hunter, also of Virginia.

upon the sectional line. President Buchanan had done his utmost in behalf of the Southern view, and had been chiefly responsible for the Oregon and California delegations.

The declaration of the vote on platform was followed by protests and announcements of withdrawal. The delegations from Alabama, Mississippi, Louisiana, South Carolina, Florida, Texas, and Arkansas left the convention hall, after a series of brief speeches in justification. Secession from the convention was not without more or less open threat of secession of Southern States from the Union. Georgia, much less eager, reluctantly followed the other departing States. It should be said

that some of the delegations had been instructed in advance by their State conventions, and could not have done otherwise than withdraw as they did.

It should further be explained that two delegates from Louisiana, three from South Carolina, three from Arkansas, two from Delaware, one from North Carolina, and several from Georgia had refused to go out, leaving something like 258 official votes, to be cast by a considerably larger body of delegates.

It was held that the nominee must secure 202 votes, this being two-thirds of the legally complete convention. On the first ballot, Stephen A. Douglas received 145½, R. M. T.

Hunter of Virginia 42, James Guthrie of Kentucky 35, Andrew Johnson of Tennessee 12, Daniel S. Dickinson of New York 7, Joseph Lane of Oregon 6, Isaac Toucey of Connecticut 2½, Jefferson Davis of Mississippi 1½, Franklin Pierce of New Hampshire 1.

This voting for a candidate continued through three days, 57 ballots having been taken without final result. The Douglas strength gained six or seven votes, and remained to the end at about 152. There was no chance for any other candidate, Guthrie of Kentucky reaching 65½ at the expense of the other minor candidates. By a vote of nearly four to one the convention on the 3rd of May (this being its tenth day) decided to adjourn and to meet at Baltimore on June 18th, recommending that other delegates be chosen to replace those who had withdrawn from certain States. Douglas had received a clear majority vote of the whole convention including the seceded delegates; but the two-thirds rule had intervened to prevent his nomination.

It remains to be said that the bolters from the main convention had taken another hall in Charleston, where they occupied themselves for four days with oratory, while the larger body was vainly seeking to nominate a candidate. The chairman of this smaller body was the Hon. James A. Bayard of Delaware. The adoption of the Jefferson Davis resolutions—that is to say, the majority platform—was a prompt and unanimous action. This minor body, postponing the question of a candidate, adjourned to meet at Richmond, Virginia, on the 11th of June, where they could, by a week, anticipate the assembling of the Douglas convention at Baltimore. It seemed likely enough that there would be still another split, with the prospect of an agreement between the Charleston seceders and the Baltimore seceders upon a pro-Southern ticket of their own.

The Douglas men of the North, and the supporters of Hunter, Guthrie, and other Border-State candidates, left Charleston with no memories of a pleasant sojourn. They had been compelled to stand their ground at the cost of a breach that was altogether likely to result in Democratic defeat and in the victory of the Republican party, with the further imminent danger of a secession movement far more serious than the mere factional division of a political party.

The adjournment of both factions until the middle of June, allowing an interval of six or seven weeks, was decided upon in the forlorn hope that something might be done by the Republican convention—which was to meet at Chicago in the middle of May—that would so affect the national situation as to bring the Democratic groups closer together, as they sensed the common menace that could be successfully met only by a reunited front.

In his graphic description of pre-convention scenes, Mr. Halstead had gone the rounds of hotels and headquarters during the evening of April 22nd, a few hours before the opening of the convention. He had found a group of Administration Senators luxuriously established in a large, old-fashioned building in King Street. One of these was Senator Jesse D. Bright of Indiana, a bitter personal enemy of Douglas. "The rosy gentleman with the farmer-like aspect, slightly inclined to be just fat enough to be sleek, and whose countenance is so placid that you would not imagine that he had ever been crushed by Douglas in debate . . . . . is the Hon. William Bigler of Pennsylvania." Here also was Senator John Slidell of Louisiana, "seated at a round table upon which books, newspapers, and writing materials are scattered about."

The following is Mr. Halstead's description of the gentleman who presided over the seceding minority that walked out on April 30th: "The full-faced gentleman without a vest, sitting on the corner of a chair, and smoking a fragrant cigar in the contemplative style—the gentleman with long brown curling hair parted in the middle——is Senator Bayard of Delaware, a distinguished lawyer and a Democratic partisan of long standing. He could do his State some service by helping her to get rid of slavery, but he is a pro-slavery man. He is a descendant of the illustrious Chevalier Bayard, the knight without fear or reproach. Senator Bayard is a handsome, courtly gentleman, who is personally a goodly man to know."

Mr. Bayard made an elaborate speech at the opening session of the bolting group, which, on motion of Mr. Yancey, styled itself "the Constitutional Democracy." Mr. Yancey further proposed "that the platform adopted by the Democratic party at Cincinnati be confirmed, with the following explanatory resolutions"— these proving to be simply the sum total of the majority platform that had been reported to the main convention, but had been voted down by the Douglas men. The platform as proposed by Mr. Yancey, and unanimously adopted, thus consisted of the Cincinnati platform of 1856, plus the Jefferson Davis resolutions, formulated by the Democratic Senators at Washington. It is to be noted that in correcting the journal the word "seceding" was rejected, as was the word "withdrawing," and the word "retiring" was adopted.

The main convention at Institute Hall was now deserted by the spectators representing the intellect, beauty, and fashion of Charleston, and the theatre where the bolters met was crowded with visitors of those classes. A prominent member of this convention in the theatre, Judge Meek of Alabama—"a very powerful public speaker, whose height was variously estimated between 6 feet 4 inches and 6 feet 8 inches—was in favor of nominating a ticket which should consist of Jefferson Davis and Mr. Bayard." "What the present convention had really desired," Judge Meek said, "was to have put forward a great historical name that would have commanded confidence and respect all over the world—I allude to Jefferson Davis of Mississippi." On May 4th Senator Bayard, who felt that secessionist tendencies began to appear too openly in the speeches of delegates, made a typically eloquent speech for the maintenance of the Union of the States, and then retired from the convention, thus achieving a second bolt.

Both conventions adjourned late on May 3rd, the Northern delegates and visitors at once setting out for Washington. Charlestonians were not sorry to see them go, and were apparently more relieved than apprehensive as regards the political crisis.

MEETING OF THE SOUTHERN SECEDERS FROM THE
CHARLESTON CONVENTION

When the Democratic convention had been in session for a week, most of the delegates from Southern States withdrew and held a meeting of their own, in St. Andrew's Hall. They went no farther than to adopt the platform that had been rejected by the Douglas delegates in the main convention (known as the Southern platform), and then adjourned to meet later at Richmond. In the end they endorsed the Breckinridge-Lane ticket, nominated at Baltimore by another group of Democratic seceders.

CHAPTER III

Guiding Minds at the Capitol

*The Davis-Douglas disagreement weakens the Democrats—An eye-
witness describes the two leaders and their Senate debate—Seward and
Chase, on the Senate floor—Aspirants for the Republican nomination*

FOR THE PURPOSES of the newspaper correspondents the convention dates were conveniently distributed. The Whigs and Americans, with their National Constitutional Union, were to meet at Baltimore on May 9th, and the formal opening of the Republican convention at Chicago was set for May 16th. Washington was now the center of political intrigue and excitement, with Congress still in session, and with the foremost political leaders actually members, at that time,

THE SENATORIAL TAPSTER.

CUSTOMER: "I notice you draw your ale very mild now, William."

LANDLORD SEWARD: "Yes, this is a new tap. My customers thought the Rochester ale was rather too strong."

As Senator Seward's pre-convention campaign for the presidential nomination progressed it was noted that his utterances in the Senate became less radical than the famous "Irrepressible Conflict" speech at Rochester in 1858.

of the United States Senate. Senator Bigler of Pennsylvania had returned from Charleston to make his confidential reports to President Buchanan.

Senator Bayard, "a courtly gentleman whose romantic ancestry and name, as well as his long curls, and fine features, and distinguished air, were admirably adapted to concentrate the gaze of the ladies," was now on hand to explain to his fellow Senators his successive retirements at Charleston. Senator Pugh of Ohio was giving his version to Senator Douglas, with whom, undoubtedly, he was contriving party strategy in anticipation of the adjourned Democratic convention that would meet in June. Senator Slidell, on the other hand, was planning with the pre-eminent leader from the lower South, Senator Jefferson Davis, for the maintenance, without compromise, of the firm and sincere stand that the Southern delegates had made at Charleston under the Yancey-Slidell leadership.

The debates on the floor of both Houses were political and sectional, with ordinary public business claiming little attention. Concerning themselves especially about the party conventions of that year, historians have somewhat ignored the contemporary proceedings at Washington. The famous Davis resolutions, which were intended to read Douglas out of the party, had been endorsed by Democratic Senators, with only Douglas and Pugh to oppose them. It was after the break-up of the Charleston convention that the great debate between Douglas and Davis took place on the Senate floor. This was a memorable situation because it staged the climax and marked the end of the activities in that chamber of several of the most brilliant figures in all the records of the Senate. In his "Life of Jefferson Davis," Prof. William E. Dodd sums up the situation at Washington, in the interval of suspense between conventions, with the following account of this historic debate:

The quarrel between Davis and Douglas, begun on the 9th of December, 1857, had come to a dramatic conclusion. The intense interest attaching to the two senators during these weeks and months of exciting discussion, was due to their representing so truly the aims and wishes of the great sections of their party, still in possession of the Administration, and with many chances of success at the next election but for this threatening dispute. After the break-up of the Charleston convention, Davis urged a vote on his resolutions in the Senate. Douglas opposed them in a speech which lasted the better part of two days, and which was a severe arraignment of the Southern wing of the Democracy. He charged Davis with forcing the Yancey program on the party, which must either disrupt it or commit it to the expansion of slavery under the protection of the national government. This was a true indictment.

Davis retorted, with unbecoming *hauteur,* that the South demanded only what the Constitution guaranteed it, and cited the Supreme Court's decision in the Dred Scott case as a final verdict in his favor. He also reviewed the history of the party and of the country since the introduction of the Wilmot Proviso in 1847. The issue had been joined, he said, on the question of dividing the spoils of war in 1847, had been temporarily settled in 1850, renewed in 1854 by Douglas himself, and now, he continued, "we are confronted again with it on the plains of Kansas and in every hamlet throughout the Confederation. It has now become the one subject of dispute in the Democratic party and it behooves us to say what shall be done."

After two days of bitter arraignment of Douglas and his followers, Davis closed this, his most remarkable speech in the Senate. His manner throughout was condescending and contemptuous, which not only did not injure his opponent, but did much harm to his own cause. The influence of this discussion penetrated every social gathering in Washington during these last days of the old Congress. Ladies and gentlemen of the different sections were

JEFFERSON DAVIS: A WAR-TIME CARTOON
The Senator from Mississippi was the South's candidate for the Presidency in 1860. A year later he was chosen President of the Confederate States.

under constant restraint, when they happened to meet in polite society, lest they should refer to the one subject uppermost in the minds of all. The representatives of the people of a common country mingled with one another as if under rules of an armistice.

Waiting for the Whig convention a few miles away at Baltimore, Mr. Halstead was a close observer of these scenes in the Senate. His description of personalities supports felicitously the exaggerated portraiture of the cartoonists, whose contemporary caricatures of such leaders as Douglas, Seward, and Davis are so abundantly reproduced in these pages.

Mr. Davis, bearing a great strain of public responsibility, and fully aware that circumstances had made him the undisputed leader of the Southern cause, had been greatly handicapped by ill health. He would have been in retirement, either sojourning at his beautiful home in Mississippi, or resting at Saratoga or at a seacoast resort, but for his high spirit and his sense of duty. Mr. Halstead, whose habit it was to write as he observed, and who was doubtless sitting in the Senate press gallery on May 8th, gives us a pen picture that is well worth bringing to light again:

The crowd has filled the galleries of the Senate Chamber, expecting to hear Jeff Davis's speech; and there are expectations that Douglas will reply. The hands of the Senate clock approach the points indicating the hour of one, and the people are weary of the monotonous reading of bills and petitions by title, and the presentations of the miscellany of deliberative bodies in audible tones. Ah! Here he comes. The crowd in the galleries gives a buzz of relief, and everybody tells his right hand man—"here he comes—that's Jeff Davis."

And can it be possible that he proposes to make

MURAT HALSTEAD (1829-1908)

The accounts of the national conventions of 1860, written by Halstead in daily dispatches to the Cincinnati *Commercial* and later brought together in a book, are among the best sources for the political history of that eventful year. During and after the Civil War the author had a long and brilliant career as correspondent and editor of the *Commercial* and the *Commercial-Gazette*. In his later years he was editor of the Brooklyn *Standard-Union*, and in the Spanish-American War he visited the Philippines and Cuba, publishing his observations in those islands. The portrait is of the 1860 period.

a speech? You are surprised to see him walking. Why, that is the face of a corpse, the form of a skeleton. Look at the haggard, sunken, weary eye— the thin white wrinkled lips clasped close upon the teeth in anguish. That is the mouth of a brave but impatient sufferer. See the ghastly white, hollow, bitterly puckered cheek, the high, sharp cheekbone, the pale brow full of fine wrinkles, the grisly hair, prematurely gray; and see the thin, bloodless, bony, nervous hands! He deposits his documents upon his desk, and sinks into his chair as if incapable of rising.

In a few minutes the Vice-President gives his desk a blow with his ivory hammer, calls for profound order, and states that the Senator from Mississippi has the floor. Davis rises with a smile. His speech was closely reasoned, and his words were well chosen. Once in a while he pleased his hearers by a happy period; but it was painfully evident that he was ill.

This was the man who was soon to lead in the formation of the Southern Confederacy, and the creation of a government with its executive, legislative, and judicial departments, and with its seat at Richmond only 100 miles from the federal capital at Washington. He was to appoint, promote, and set aside commanders of great armies, and to speak the final word in deciding strategic movements. He was to have full authority in the financial measures for the prosecution of a great war. He was to appoint diplomatic agents, seek the support of European interests, secure recognition of belligerent rights, and maintain his position against almost overwhelming odds through four long years of historic conflict.

Jefferson Davis, in centuries to come, will stand out more clearly than in these days, while his memory is still darkened by the shadows of failure and defeat. Those who would glorify Lincoln should not disparage or belittle the rival President at Richmond. Rather, Lincoln's personal achievements, and his typical and representative qualities, are the better appreciated when we take his measure in comparison with all the American leaders of his generation, placing the most generous estimate upon the motives and the abilities of each one.

Thus it is only when we have set full value upon the intellectual and moral leadership of Seward, Chase, and the other Republican chieftains, that we can realize the full stature of Abraham Lincoln. In like manner it is necessary to do justice to Stephen A. Douglas if one would rightly appreciate the slow but inevitable rise of Lincoln to the mastery of men and of sentiment in Illinois. The statesmen of Europe, looking on at the campaign of 1860 and the approach of the crisis of Secession, saw in Jefferson Davis a brilliant and accomplished statesman, and in Douglas they saw an idolized popular leader of extraordinary talent and capacity. In Seward, Sumner, and Edward Everett they saw cultured and widely traveled American publicists, cosmopolitan in experience, versed in the diplomatic and international history of the United States. These were the equals of the foremost statesmen of Europe. But Europe was yet to learn that the self-educated pioneer from the Illinois prairies had attained an intellectual balance,

and a measure of wisdom in practical affairs—
along with natural gifts of leadership, and the
"humble and contrite spirit" that rejected all
the impulses of selfish ambition—that set him
deservedly in a place above all his contemporaries at home or abroad.

The personality of Stephen A. Douglas bore
no resemblance to the conventional pattern of a
Senator. Mr. Halstead's description, written
on that same day, in May, 1860, unconsciously
interprets for us some of the caricatures that
are reproduced in my chapters as evidence of
current sentiment:

And here, coming from the cloak-room on the
Democratic side, is a queer little man, canine head
and duck legs—everybody knows the little Giant—
he looks conscious of being looked at; and he is
pointed out by a hundred hands, as he makes pre-
tentious strides of about eighteen inches each, toward his chair. Two or three of his admirers in
the gallery are disposed to applaud, but you hear
merely the rattle of a single boot-heel. . . . . . The
little Giant wears his black hair long, but it is getting thin, and is not the great tangled mass we saw
on his neck a few years ago. And, O Little Giant!
It grows gray rapidly. Now he proceeds to twist
himself down in his chair as far as possible, and
places his feet in his desk; and thus his admirers
in the gallery look upon the prodigious little man,
squirming flat on his back. He doesn't feel very
elastic this morning, that is evident. He requires
a large vest—and large as he is about the chest, his
waist is becoming still more extensive. But he has
an immense head—in height, and breadth and depth
—in indications of solidity and force, you cannot
find its equal in Washington. There is power under
that massive brow, and resolution in that grim
mouth; no doubt at all of that.

The scene that Mr. Halstead describes, as he
gives these sketches of Davis and Douglas,
was that of the elaborate speech of the Mississippi Senator in support of his resolutions.
He was expounding the right of any citizen
to take his slave property into the common
territories, and to have protection for it, regardless of the intentions or preferences of the
territorial inhabitants. In this speech, Davis
reviewed the successive positions of Douglas,
in order to prove his opinions and his votes to
have been unsound and heretical. It was a

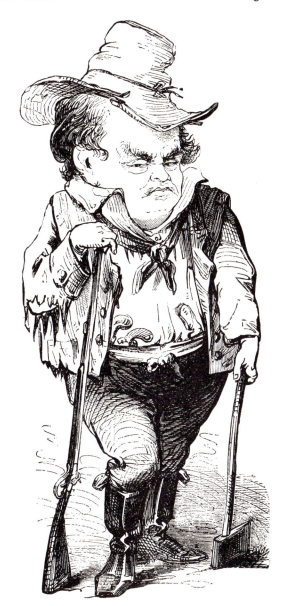

AN 1860 CARTOON OF DOUGLAS
"Squatter sovereignty" was a term which had been applied with some sarcasm as a substitute for the phrase
"popular sovereignty" which Douglas had used to charac-
terize his plan of leaving it to the settlers of a Territory
to decide whether it should become a free or a slave State.
This caricature of Douglas presents him as the original
squatter sovereign.

speech on high grounds as regards its manner
and its freedom from offensive personal attack; but it was intended to destroy the standing of Douglas as a presidential candidate.

It was several days later that Douglas replied in his two days' speech. As one of his
biographers remarks: "It was addressed less to

SENATOR SEWARD AS THE CARTOONIST SAW HIM
He had been a member of the upper branch of Congress for eleven years, and had previously been Governor of New York. In 1860 he expected to be the Republican choice for the Presidency.

and through the press. Cass, he said, the author of the now deadly doctrine of popular sovereignty, was nominated in 1848. The compromise of 1850 embodied that principle. The Kansas-Nebraska struggle was settled by expressly adopting it. The Cincinnati platform, on which all Democrats had stood for four years, distinctly affirmed it. The Charleston convention, within a few days, had reaffirmed it. His own speeches showed that he had adhered to it constantly from the beginning of his career. The change was not in him but in the Southern wing of his party. He protested that he did not desire the nomination, and only permitted his name to be used that he might be vindicated against the presumptuous efforts of a little coterie to cast doubt upon his Democracy, and their attempt to proscribe him as a heretic might be rebuked."

As a conclusion of this memorable Senate debate, it is to be noted that Davis bluntly asked Douglas whether, if elected President, he would sign a bill to protect slave property in States, Territories, or the District of Columbia. Douglas declined to answer, holding that it would be inappropriate for him to declare in advance what he might do if he were in the White House.

We should have only the faintest notion of the intense interest that had been awakened in these political personalities during that period of suspense in the month of May, if we could not readily imagine the galleries of the chambers of Congress crowded day by day. Visitors were eager to see Davis, Douglas and the other notables of the Senate, with only less interest in the men who were prominent at the other end of the Capitol. The Senate was still strongly Democratic, while the House, by virtue of the election of 1858, was narrowly Republican. In the Senate, the Davis resolutions were finally adopted, one by one, by votes of 36 to 20. The fourth and most critical of these resolutions read as follows:

Resolved, That neither Congress nor a territorial legislature, whether by direct legislation or legislation of an indirect and unfriendly character, possesses power to annul or impair the Constitutional right of any citizen of the United States to take his

the Senate than to the adjourned Charleston convention. He exhaustively proved the soundness of his Democracy, and repelled the charge of heresy by rehearsing the history of Democratic conventions and platforms since 1848, quoting the declarations of the party and its leaders in convention, on the platform, slave property into the common territories and there hold and enjoy the same while the territorial condition remains.

This was passed by a vote of 35 to 21, Mr. Douglas being ill and absent, and his friend Pugh of Ohio joining the Republicans in voting against it.

Thus ended the era of Democratic harmony so piously proclaimed by President Buchanan in his inaugural address as based upon the doctrine of Squatter Sovereignty. The Republican minority led by Seward was profoundly interested, because the position of the leaders at Washington made it fairly certain that there could be no reconciliation at Baltimore in June. This Democratic rupture pointed with assurance to a Republican victory, and made the nomination at Chicago eminently worth while for any man who had the courage to cherish presidential ambitions, in a national situation that had become so desperate.

Mr. Seward and Mr. Chase, both in the Senate, were dauntless men who aspired to the nomination, with Seward expecting to win by sheer pre-eminence of long standing, and Chase encouraged by his friends to believe that he might be selected as a compromise candidate in a contest between Seward and "the field." It is worth while, therefore, as the Chicago convention was only a few days deferred, and as there was keen interest in the New York Senator, to quote Halstead's portrayal of Seward in the Senate chamber:

And now an individual appears on the other [Republican] side of the House who at first sight seems to be rather a comical person. He has the most singular head in all the assortment before you. It rises above the ears like a dome, and looks not unlike a straw stack in shape and color. His nose— a high sharp beak—strikes out below the strawy hair that thatches the dome. Can you imagine a jay-bird with a sparrow-hawk's bill—the high tuft of feathers towering above the eyes—the keen hook below? There is a quaintness in that high head and high, sharp nose. You are anxious about the forehead. You are sure that must be a man of talent, and he must have a forehead. But to save you, you cannot tell which is hair and which is forehead. All is of the same parchment hue. You seem, once in a while, to catch a glimpse of a lofty mountain range of ideality, according to the maps of the phrenologists. This tall and peaked and pallid head

WILLIAM H. SEWARD, OF NEW YORK

For thirty years, though not continuously, Seward had held public office. In 1830 he had been elected to the State Senate; from 1838 through 1842 he was Governor; and since 1849 he had served in the Senate at Washington, first as a Whig and then as a Republican. Throughout the Presidency of Lincoln, Seward was his Secretary of State.

is perched upon a body that is active and restless. It moves about with school-boy elasticity. It walks with a slashing swagger. It strikes off with a rollicking gait from one point to another, and is in and out of the chamber by turns.

There is an oddity in the dress in harmony with the general queerness of the thing. The pantaloons have a dingy, oaken appearance. You would not be surprised to see breeches of that color in Oregon, but in the Senate chamber they are without a parallel. And did you ever see so much tail to a frock coat in your life? There is certainly a grotesque amount of coat-tail. Now after making the round of the Republican side of the chamber, about twice in ten minutes, he offers from the chair a petition in a hoarse, croaking voice; and when the Vice-President recognizes the Senator from New York there is a stir in the galleries, and a general stare at the gentleman with the top-knot, and beak, and voice. He sits down, takes a pinch of snuff, and presently you hear a vociferous sneezing, and the high headed, straw-thatched gentleman is engaged upon his beak with a yellow silk handkerchief. And you remember that Seward takes snuff, and has ruined his voice by the nasty habit.

THE HEAD OF THE NATION
Buchanan possessed two characteristics which the cartoonists seized upon. One was an upstanding forelock, here shown protruding through his hat. The other was a pug nose, easy to caricature.

a distinguished career before him as a Republican editor of independent convictions. One might well judge from these bits of boyish description of the political characters of 1860 that young Halstead was a reader of Dickens, whose friend he afterwards became. We may therefore quote a few more lines from Halstead's offhand descriptions, all of that same date:

In the Republican corner of the Senate chamber is a familiar face and form—you recognize the portly person and massive intellectual developments, the thin, frizzly hair and oval brow of Salmon P. Chase. Next to him is Governor Dennison. Seward comes up to them and seems to be guilty of some good thing, for they laugh violently but quietly, and Seward rubs his oaken breeches with his hands and then gives his nose a tremendous tweek with the yellow handkerchief. He is wonderfully affable. He acts as though he would kiss a strange baby. Ah, he is a candidate for the Presidency.

Popular biographies of Mr. Seward were at that time in wide circulation, and hundreds of thousands of copies of his recent speeches, had been distributed, giving a less radical impression than those earlier ones that had emphasized the "higher law" while predicting the "irrepressible conflict." Mr. Seward slipped away from Washington to remain at his home in Auburn, New York, just before the Chicago convention assembled, fully expecting to be nominated and elected, and regarding his long Senatorial career as definitely concluded.

Mr. Halstead, while still in college at Cincinnati, had paid his way by writing for newspapers, and he was in his element as a political reporter. He was soon to make a reputation as one of the ablest of war correspondents, with

THE PRESIDENT'S HOUSE, WASHINGTON
From an early engraving

CHAPTER IV

A Genuine Middle-Ground Party

The Constitutional Unionists include Whigs, moderates, and lovers of harmony—Bell and Everett, two sterling candidates—Their Baltimore convention denounces sectionalism and ignores the slave question

WHILE THE FREE SOIL party was evolving rapidly, from its starting-point in the Wilmot Proviso of 1846 to its merger with the new but permanent Republican organization in 1856, there remained certain political elements, especially in the Border States, that stubbornly refused to go with the lower South on the one hand, and with the anti-slavery North on the other. These remnants were for the Union first, and for the settlement of the slavery question at some future time through natural economic changes or through the kind of statesmanship that had been dealing with slavery elsewhere in the world. What was left of the old Whig party in the Border States and the lower South had come to be known as the American party; and in New York and elsewhere the so-called "Know-Nothing" party, representing old Americanism as against the new alien elements, was inclined to act with these Border State Whigs.

Col. A. K. McClure observes that the American or Know-Nothing party "had gravitated from the original Native Americans of 1844 into the Order of United Americans and had coalesced with the remnants of the Whig party and with the anti-administration Democrats in most of the Northern States. It had reached about its highest measure of strength in 1855, chiefly because of its strong hold in the South. In New England and the far western States the Americans had been very generally absorbed in the Republican organization when the battle opened for the Presidency in 1856."

This movement had, as I have explained in the earlier volume, presented ex-President Fillmore as the head of its third-party ticket, in the campaign of 1856, with Andrew Jackson Donelson of Tennessee, the adopted son of Gen. Andrew Jackson, running for Vice-President. There had been drifting fragments of the old Whig party assembled in a separate convention at Baltimore in 1856, with Edward Bates of Missouri presiding; and this convention had ratified the ticket of Fillmore and Donelson. There had been, in some States, a coalition electoral ticket in order to unite the Republican support of Frémont with the American support of Fillmore, to defeat the Buchanan ticket.

Edward Bates had now in 1860 become a Republican, and was Greeley's choice for the Presidency; and many others who had

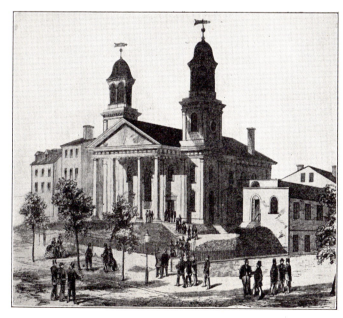

WHERE THE UNION CONVENTION WAS HELD

The old First Presbyterian Church of Baltimore had recently been converted into a courthouse, and it proved to be the most convenient place for the assembling of a third-party convention made up of remnants of the Whig-American groups. The auditorium, we are told, was tastefully fitted up, and a full-length portrait of Washington was placed behind the president's chair.

supported Fillmore in 1856 had now headed toward the party of Lincoln, Seward and Chase. Although it was only in Maryland that this Fillmore ticket prevailed, by a plurality over the Buchanan and Frémont tickets, the popular vote was large elsewhere, especially in the South. It held the balance between the two major parties in a number of States. And in 1860 there were many moderate men, North and South, who believed that — more than ever — there was need to keep alive the "Union" movement.

It was natural enough, therefore, that these same unassimilated political elements should in 1860 feel it their duty to present a ticket of their own that might secure the support of Union-loving men, especially in the upper tier of Slave States, and thus lessen the danger of a violent break. While the Democratic factions were watching one another, and were especially concerned in following the movements of the Republicans who were about to gather at Chicago, these Whig-American groups came together in a convention at Baltimore on the 9th of May, now calling themselves the Constitutional Union party.

The convention was less strict in apportionment of delegates than those of the larger parties, but it drew members from two-thirds of the States, and it represented a movement that was genuine and far from insignificant, both in character and in extent. Among the ten or twelve names of capable public men for whom votes had been cast in the convention that nominated Fillmore

THE PARAGON, EDWARD EVERETT, OF MASSACHUSETTS

Orator, preacher, educator, and statesman, he was unanimously named for the Vice-Presidency in 1860 on the Constitutional Union ticket. In all our history, Everett was perhaps the finest example of the scholar in politics. Our portrait is reproduced from an engraving by Sartain.

in 1856 were those of the picturesque Sam Houston of Texas and the reliable John Bell of Tennessee. When this convention of 1860 proceeded to ballot, votes were cast for ten men, all of them of excellent repute, and at the head of the poll were the steadfast John Bell and the patriotic Samuel Houston. Next came John J. Crittenden of Kentucky, Edward Everett of Massachusetts, John McLean of Ohio, William A. Graham of North Carolina, William C. Reeve, John M. Botts and William L. Goggin (all three of Virginia), and William L. Sharkey of Mississippi. At least half of these men belonged to the first rank of American statesmen of their generation.

It was a highly respectable convention; and Sam Houston was obviously too unpolished a frontiersman to gain the votes of the Northern element. It was deemed best on all accounts however to take a Southern candidate, and on the second ballot the nomination went to John Bell of Tennessee, with Houston still a strong second. For geographical balance, Edward Everett of Massachusetts was unanimously chosen to complete the ticket.

There had been agreement on a platform, this consisting of a preamble and one resolution. The preamble declared: "Experience has demonstrated that platforms adopted by the partisan conventions of the country have had the effect to mislead and deceive the people, and at the same time widen the political divisions of the country by the creation and encouragement of geographical and sectional parties."

The resolution following this sage remark declared that "it is both the part of patriotism and of duty to recognize no political principle other than the Constitution of the country, the Union of the States, and the enforcement of the laws." The rest of the resolution merely pledged the Constitutional Union party to "these great principles of public liberty and national safety against all enemies at home and abroad, believing that thereby peace may once more be restored to the country, the rights of the people and of the States re-established, and the Government again placed in that condition of justice, fraternity, and equality which under the example and Constitution of our fathers has solemnly bound every citizen of the United States to maintain a more perfect union, etc."

These, of course, were fine words, and they were adopted with sincerity. But they were not likely to impress the militant movement of Jefferson Davis and his friends that was sweeping the South. Certainly the Whigs could not expect the Douglas Democrats to turn away from following their chosen leader; and least of all could they check the rising tide of anti-slavery Republicanism that now saw victory assured through the division into three parts of all the elements opposing it.

Under the circumstances, the Constitutional Union party gave a good account of itself in the ensuing campaign. Its candidate, John Bell, was born in February, 1797, near Nashville, Tennessee, and he died in that State in 1869 in his seventy-third year. While still a minor, he was a practising lawyer and was elected to the State Senate. He went to Con-

JOHN BELL, OF TENNESSEE
The presidential candidate of the Constitutional Union party in 1860 had been a member of the House (serving two years as Speaker) and of the Senate; and he had also been Secretary of War in 1841. He was among the founders of the Whig party. The Bell-Everett ticket received the electoral votes of Kentucky, Tennessee, and Virginia. Bell advised Tennessee's secession in 1861.

gress in 1827, and remained there for fourteen years. He had been a free-trader, but became a strong protectionist and was a leading opponent of South Carolina's nullification. He favored the United States Bank, and deserted President Jackson and the Democratic party, becoming a prominent Whig, which led to his election as Speaker of the House in 1834, James K. Polk of his own State being his Democratic rival. He had the courage as speaker to deal favorably with petitions for the abolition of slavery in the District of Columbia.

In 1841 John Bell became Secretary of War in President Harrison's cabinet. With most of his colleagues, he left the cabinet on account of disagreements with Harrison's successor. Soon afterwards he was elected to the United States Senate, where he opposed Douglas's Nebraska Bill of 1854, while with Douglas he opposed the Lecompton Constitution of 1858. After the election of 1860 he retired from public life, and died in 1869. He was one of numerous public men of extraordinary experience, ability, and high character in public and private life, whose well-earned reputations became obscured by the abnormal conditions that resulted in the catastrophe of civil war.

Mr. Bell figures conspicuously in the cartoons and illustrations of the political movements of 1860, and it is wholly appropriate at this time to pay some tribute to his unblemished record as a public man of high type, a presidential nominee who would under normal conditions have served honorably and ably if elected to our highest office.

As for Edward Everett, he was the true type of American scholar in public life. He was the country's most finished and eminent orator. He had graduated at Harvard in 1811, with all possible prestige, at the age of seventeen, becoming at once a tutor, and making his mark as a theological writer when still in his teens, while also gaining a reputation as a brilliant Boston preacher. At the age of twenty he was appointed Harvard's professor of Greek, and went abroad for study in Germany, France, England, Italy, and Eastern Europe, meeting scholars and famous men everywhere, and coming back after some four years, as the most accomplished American of his day. He carried on his professorship while preparing Greek text-books; edited the *North American Review;* and wrote scores of articles. After five years he entered in 1824 upon a congressional career of five terms, during all of which he served as a member of the Committee on Foreign Affairs. He was regarded as in some

KEEPING QUEER COMPANY

"Strange, these girls never will profit by example! There was poor Silva Grey, who let herself be deluded by that Democrat fellow in 1856; and now Belle Everett's following in her footsteps, never heeding that awful warning!"

Politics indeed arranged peculiar combinations in 1860. Within a year Bell was helping to take Tennessee out of the Union, while Everett was a loyal Massachusetts supporter of President Lincoln, whom he had opposed in the campaign. The reference to the Silver Greys recalls a nickname that had been applied to a conservative element of the Whig party, "grey-haired respectables."

sense a successor to John Quincy Adams, in the character of an expert in the field of American foreign relations.

In 1835 Mr. Everett was elected Governor of Massachusetts and three times re-elected. When the Harrison administration took office in March, 1841, he was sent as Minister Plenipotentiary to England, under Daniel Webster as Secretary of State. Our relations with England were at that time seriously strained; first, because of the long unsettled question of the Northeastern boundary; second, by reason of certain shipping and naval controversies, several American vessels having been seized by British cruisers on the African coast; and third, there were issues relating to the Oregon boundary, with still others having to do with claims, and differences affecting fisheries. Mr. Everett's services at London were eminently valuable.

Coming home again after four years, he was chosen President of Harvard University, in 1846, and he entered upon various literary labors of importance. The death of Daniel Webster occurred in October, 1852, and Mr. Everett was at once appointed Secretary of State, holding that office during the remaining four or five months of President Fillmore's administration. Even in that brief period his diplomatic achievements were remarkable. His next public post, immediately following his brief service as Secretary of State, was that of United States Senator from Massachusetts. Like Mr. Bell, he opposed vigorously the repeal of the Missouri Compromise and Douglas's Kansas-Nebraska Bill. Temporary illness led him to resign from the Senate in 1854. For two or three years he lectured on George Washington, for the benefit of the fund that acquired Mount Vernon for preservation as a national memorial.

He was engaged in similar enterprises of philanthropy and patriotism when, in 1860, he was nominated with John Bell in the Constitutional Union convention at Baltimore. Edward Everett was an American scholar and statesman of such superiority in training, experience, and qualities of character and of public spirit, that his memory will in due time be fully rescued.

POLITICAL "BLONDINS" CROSSING SALT RIVER.

The exploit of Blondin, who crossed Niagara on a tight-rope in 1859, furnished a new idea for the cartoonists. Three of the four rival presidential candidates are here trying to cross the chasm between North and South. The fourth candidate, John Bell, with his running-mate, Edward Everett, stands on the Constitutional Bridge—"built by Washington, Jefferson, and the patriots of '76." Lincoln is attempting to cross on a rail, with the ineffective aid of Horace Greeley. Douglas is losing his balance through the dead weight of the Squatter Sovereignty end of his balance pole. Breckinridge, on the shoulders of his running-mate, Lane, feels his Slavery Extension rope parting under his feet.

With his philosophical mind and wide experience, Everett was able to see the slavery question in historical perspective. He abhorred the thought of civil war over a problem that intelligent and cultured gentlemen of Charleston and Boston should have been able to solve amicably upon lines of statesmanship. He recognized, as did too few of his Massachusetts friends, the full truth regarding the national and international nature of an institution which had made the South its unwitting victim, rather than its fortunate beneficiary.

If men as broad-minded as John Bell and Edward Everett could have been made joint dictators, with power to enforce their policies, we should have solved the slavery problem to the credit of the North and South alike, and to the great advantage of both races and all classes. The Constitutional Union party, therefore, as it emerged in 1860, deserves hon-

orable mention, although its only hope lay in acting as some sort of buffer between the intensely serious and implacable cohorts of slavery and the hardly less excited and determined hosts of anti-slavery men who had read "Uncle Tom's Cabin," Helper's "Impending Crisis," Seward's speech on the Irrepressible Conflict, and Lincoln's orations on the House Divided Against Itself. These fervent Northerners were anticipating the verdict of posterity, and were already idealizing "old John Brown" as one of the world's immortal heroes.

Edward Everett and John Bell, not to mention other conservative and moderate men of 1860, certainly were not surpassed in the qualities of personal courage, humanitarianism, and unselfish zeal for the public welfare by a zealot like John Brown. But the world does not choose men of patience and ripe wisdom for its gallery of heroes unless, as in the case of Lincoln, a career of poised judgment and discretion ends suddenly in a blaze of triumph, instantly followed by the shock of martyrdom, with no long years of later controversy to form an anti-climax and confuse the record.

Undoubtedly the Constitutional Union convention contained a higher degree of mellowed wisdom than those of the two great parties. The historians are inclined to pass over this gathering at Baltimore with a few meager lines; and there is the more freshness and novelty in the colorful pages of Mr. Halstead's story, with its racy humor and its keen political insight. Touching the convention as a whole, we are told that there were "many distinguished men on the floor, but they are mostly 'venerable men' who have come down to us from a former generation of politicians, and whose retirement from the busy scenes of public life has been rather involuntary than otherwise." For enthusiasm, unanimity, and constant and prolonged applause, no convention had ever surpassed this one.

The convention was called to order by Mr. Lincoln's old friend, the respected Kentucky Whig, John J. Crittenden, who named Washington Hunt, a former Governor of New York, as temporary chairman. Mr. Hunt was made permanent presiding officer, and served well through the two days of the convention's proceedings. Conspicuous as orators in the convention were Erastus Brooks, editor of the New York *Express,* and George S. Hillard, an editor of the Boston *Courier*. The speakers all criticised the Democrats and the Republicans alike as inconsistent and sectional. They were in full agreement on everything that was said and done, and Mr. Halstead thought there was too much unanimity to be interesting. "Everybody is eminently respectable, intensely virtuous, devotedly patriotic, and fully resolved to save the country. They propose to accomplish that political salvation, so devoutly to be wished, by ignoring all the rugged issues of the day."

Their avoidance of a platform of specific planks, and their failure to mention the word "slavery" throughout the whole convention, did not seem a frank facing of realities. "What this element proposes to do," said Mr. Halstead, "can be stated in one way in the South and another way in the North, and thus our excellent friends will have all the advantages of an ambiguous platform, and will not encounter any of the disabilities attendant upon a written standard of orthodoxy."

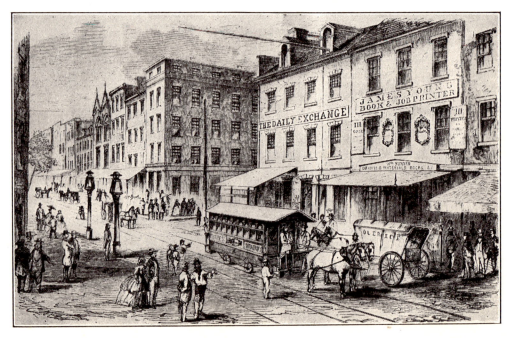

THE FIRST STREET CAR IN BALTIMORE, IN JULY, 1859

THE POLITICAL GAME OF BLUFF

This cartoon of May 12, 1860, is based upon a newspaper quotation, as follows: "As neither section of the Democratic party will make any nomination at present, the Republicans, instead of seeing their enemy's hand, have first to show their own." The Republican convention had been called for May 16th, more than three weeks after the date fixed by the Democrats. But the adjournment of the Democratic convention at Charleston, to meet again at Baltimore in June, had placed the Republicans in the position of having to launch their ticket first.

CHAPTER V

The Republican Convention at Chicago

Rapid rise of a Western metropolis—The lower South is not represented by delegates—A gathering of striking personalities—Various elements in the new party—Organizing the convention

ONE IS TEMPTED to dwell upon the contrasts and parallels of the tragic year 1860. In the complacent mood of 1856 the Democrats had gone to Cincinnati to nominate Buchanan rather than Douglas. This was actually a travel adventure for most of the delegates, but not a hazardous or unpleasant one. Franklin Pierce had been nominated at Baltimore in 1852, and the old Maryland town had seemed the natural meeting place for Northern and Southern Democrats in quadrennial council. After their disastrous pilgrimage to Charleston, they were looking again to the more familiar and congenial environment of Baltimore in the hope of reconciliation. Cincinnati in the '50s had become known as the "Queen City of the West," when it was without a rival in the upper Mississippi valley. It was accessible by numerous railroads, and by steamboats from the new States of Minnesota and Iowa, as well as from the States farther South. If Cincinnati rather than Charleston had been the convention city again in 1860, it is quite possible that the Democratic party might have been held together, with some concessions and compromises.

33

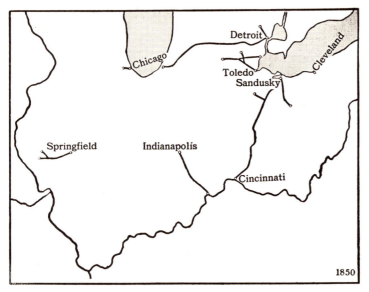

A RAILROAD MAP OF OHIO, INDIANA, AND ILLINOIS IN 1850

gates at the Chicago convention were old enough to remember reading about the seven thousand Pottawatomie Indians who were gathered there only twenty-seven years earlier, in 1833, to take part in the ceremony of transferring their lands, on the point of their departure for a new home west of the Mississippi. These questions of Indian title and settlement had been playing their part in the economic and political controversies suggested by the territorial names of Kansas and Nebraska.

The statement has been much repeated that Abraham Lincoln had never seen the metropolis of his own State and of the Northwest until long after he had served his term in Congress. The intention of writers who have accepted this unverified tradition has been to emphasize their view of Lincoln's strictly local acquaintance and standing, until a short time before his nomination in the Chicago convention. A mere comparison of dates suffices to show that when Lincoln came of age and settled in Illinois, in 1830, Chicago

In great part it was the success of the River and Harbor Convention at Chicago that had encouraged the Republicans to foregather in the new town on Lake Michigan that was soon to surpass Cincinnati as the business center of the Middle West. Twenty years earlier, in 1840, Cincinnati was ten times as large as Chicago in population, and probably fifty times as important in its trade relations. In 1850 Cincinnati was about four times as large, and Chicago had become a focus of Lake traffic and an important point in the planning of prairie railroads. By the census of 1860, Cincinnati had 161,000 people, and Chicago 112,000. Three years later Chicago had fully caught up, and was soon thereafter outdistancing all possible rivals. St. Louis had grown so fast between 1850 and 1860 that it was well ahead, not only of Chicago, but also of Cincinnati; but its pre-eminence was temporary, yielding to Chicago as river traffic declined and as the "Granger" railroads grew in mileage and traffic volume.

A great majority of the dele-

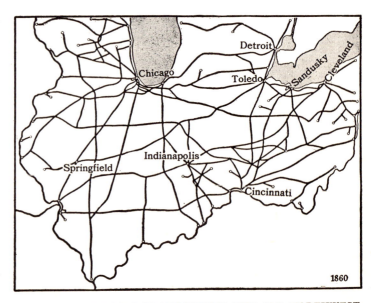

HOW THE RAILROADS TRANSFORMED THE OLD NORTHWEST
Compare this map of railroads existing in 1860 with the one reproduced above. Together they give an impression of the rapidity with which western railroad building had proceeded within the decade before the Civil War.

CHICAGO, THE CONVENTION CITY, AS IT APPEARED IN 1860

The city at the southern end of Lake Michigan had grown with extraordinary rapidity during the previous decade; and it was already destined to be the metropolis of the West. The large building in this illustration is the Tremont House, from the balcony of which Lincoln and Douglas had spoken in July, 1858, during their senatorial contest. In this hotel, also, Douglas died on June 3, 1861.

had no existence. It was not until five years later that it was a straggling village in the swamps, of less than 1,000 people.

It had not grown to a total of much more than 4,000 people when Lincoln was taking his active part in the Harrison campaign of 1840. St. Louis was much the older city, and was the natural metropolis for southern Illinois in the early days, since traffic sought the rivers. Lincoln had active business connections in St. Louis, which was no ragged village but a real city. Chicago was a scattered hamlet of bottomless mud in wet weather, and of dense clouds of black dust in days of drouth and ceaseless winds. But now in 1860 Chicago had in its turn also assumed city airs, more than four-fifths of its population having arrived within less than ten years. With indomitable energy and faith in the future, the people of Chicago were raising the central district, block by block, to a new level; paved streets were appearing; and far-reaching plans

were in view for this interior metropolis.

I have not presented these statistics casually as mere items of information; but rather because of their vital bearing upon the political problems of 1860. The fame of Chicago's mushroom growth had made it possible for Mr. Judd to persuade his Republican colleagues—who had met under the shadow of Independence Hall at Philadelphia when they nominated Frémont in 1856—to ordain the romantic excursion to the breezy Northwest, there to witness the building of some hundreds of new frame houses, and the auctioning of some thousands of town lots, during the three or four days of the convention.

It was this amazing Western progress that was giving reality and power to Republican views of national destiny. It was also making possible the choice of a Western candidate. While Southern Illinois had been Democratic and Central Illinois had been Whiggish and moderate, Northern Illinois, and especially

Chicago with its new population largely of New England origin, had for several years been a Republican stronghold. In its capacity as a booming young metropolis, with real-estate speculation as a leading interest, there was great and unanimous enthusiasm, regardless of party lines, over the opportunity to entertain the Republican convention. Although aspiring to everything worth while, Chicago could not pretend to rival the intellectual culture of Boston, or the social refinement of Charleston. It was too raw to have assumed the urbanity of New York, Philadelphia, or Baltimore. But what it lacked of finish and charm was offset by its optimism and energy.

This hopeful mood was the more striking and commendable because the West as a whole had been swept as by a hurricane by the panic of 1857, and was recovering only through hardship and distress. There had been one of those recurring periods marked by the collapse of land values, the failure of banks, the low prices of farm products, and the consequent failure of thousands of farmers to meet mortgage obligations, with widespread bankruptcy of merchants. Those buoyant State policies of almost unlimited support for canals and railroads that Lincoln had advocated, had sorely strained the credit of Illinois, as of other Western States.

The South was looking on at the progress of the new Northwest with some apprehension, because of the future political bearing of these trends of population and wealth. This alone was enough to explain the almost desperate Southern demand for the extension of slave territory. But apart from this wider forecasting of sectional conditions, the South was rather disdainful, in view of immediate facts. The South in 1860 was aboundingly prosperous, while the West was toiling so painfully to recover from its speculative collapse. The direct trade of the Cotton States with Europe was important enough to account for the contrast in the economic status of the two sections. This also is of primary consequence, because if the circumstances had been reversed—Southern business being prostrated, and the North and West at the very peak of a prosperous era—there would have been too little self-confidence to have made a secession movement possible.

I do not know how to cite any evidence of this Southern state of mind that could be more conclusive than a few sentences from a letter written by a leader of distinction and experience, Hon. James H. Hammond, then one of the two Senators from South Carolina. The letter is the more convincing because it was written privately to a personal friend, the eminent scholar and publicist, Dr. Francis Lieber, and it was not published until long afterwards. It was written at the time of the failure of the Charleston convention, in order to explain the Southern position to a great political scholar who had gone from the University of South Carolina to a new post at Columbia University, New York. The confidence with which a leader like Senator Hammond dared to expound the Southern position makes it easier to excuse men of lesser mentality or experience.

Strange as it might seem, the Cotton States utterly failed to grasp the stern economic realities that confronted them. The emer-

THE REPUBLICAN WIGWAM AT CHICAGO, IN WHICH
LINCOLN WAS NOMINATED

The Republicans of Chicago raised $7,000 and built, for convention purposes, an auditorium, known as the "Wigwam," with a seating capacity of 10,000. It stood at the corner of Lake and Market Streets, near the Chicago River and within a third of a mile of the heart of the city. From the roof of the Wigwam a cannon salute announced Lincoln's nomination.

AN HEIR TO THE THRONE,
OR THE NEXT REPUBLICAN CANDIDATE

Barnum's Museum in New York was established in 1857, but it had been closed for some time and was reopening with great hullabaloo in 1860. Among its attractions was a strange creature whom the Great Showman had named "What Is It?" The cartoon disparages Lincoln's candidacy by suggesting that Barnum's freak would be nominated by the Republicans four years later. Horace Greeley introduces the "illustrious individual" as combining all the graces and virtues of Black Republicanism. Lincoln accepts the "intellectual and noble creature" as his own worthy successor, who will prove to the world the "superiority of the Colored over the Anglo-Saxon race."

gence of a new center like Chicago had been so rapid that they had not learned to measure its significance as against a Charleston, a Savannah, a Mobile, a Vicksburg, or even a New Orleans. Senator Hammond told Dr. Lieber in a patronizing tone that he would sustain the Union of States as long as he could, although he regarded it as cramping the South, which would have many advantages to gain from separation and independence. The following sentences from the Senator's letter throw a flood of light upon decisions in which, within a few months, South Carolina was to take the unhesitating lead:

"I firmly believe that the slave-holding South is now the controlling *power* of the world—that no other power would face us in hostility. Cotton, rice, tobacco, and naval stores command the world; and we have sense to know it, and are sufficiently Teutonic to carry it out successfully. The North without us would be a motherless calf, bleating about, and die of mange and starvation."

Not all men in the South, of course, were blinded as was Senator Hammond. There were many who were practical enough to waive the extreme view of theoretical rights, rather than face a hopeless conflict in which their vaunted prosperity would disappear as if a cyclonic storm had swept from Virginia to Texas. Such men of sound judgment were now welcoming and supporting the Bell-Everett ticket, which was destined to carry the three Slave States of Virginia, Kentucky, and Tennessee, and to poll a considerable vote in the farther South.

But the majority, following the lead of men like Hammond, Yancey, and Jefferson Davis, were the victims of delusion as to the relative efficiency of the material resources of the Cotton States, when compared with those of the corn and wheat belt of the North and West. The magical growth of Chicago was but an expression of the recent transition of the western wilderness with its wheat and corn farms, its herds of cattle on the prairies, and its lumber camps in the pine forests of Michigan, Wisconsin, and Minnesota. The upper Mississippi Valley, with the Lake region added, had become stronger in men and resources than the lower valley, with Texas thrown into the scales, in spite of the world demand for cotton and other Southern products.

To head the Republican campaign in 1856 had seemed a forlorn venture, and the results had justified Seward's avoidance of a premature nomination. He had thought it well to let Frémont make the run, while he held himself in reserve for the more favorable opportunity that was likely to come in 1860. The split at Charleston seemed now to make Republican success well-nigh certain. The Republicans, therefore, assembled with a feeling of strength and unity, scenting victory in the air. All this was making the Republican convention as different as possible in its atmosphere from the unhappy, reproachful, and painfully discordant gathering of the Democratic clans at Charleston. Republicans had been fortunate in the State elections of 1859 throughout the North, having been largely victorious, while losing by only slight margins where they had failed to achieve a plurality.

There was another marked contrast between Chicago and Charleston. At the Southern city every State of the Union had a full delegation, and some, like New York, had two. At Chicago, there were, of course, delegates from

all the Free States, but there were none whatsoever from North Carolina, South Carolina, Georgia, Florida, Alabama, Mississippi, Louisiana, Arkansas, and Tennessee. On the other hand, there were delegations from five border States in which slavery existed, these being Delaware, Maryland, Virginia, Kentucky, and Missouri. There was also a scanty and irregular delegation from Texas, although when the election occurred in November Texas had no Republican electoral ticket in the field and not a single vote in that great State was reported for Lincoln.

The convention was called to order at noon on Wednesday, May 16th, in the Wigwam that Chicago citizens had built for the purpose, by Hon. Edwin D. Morgan, in his capacity as chairman of the National Republican Committee. Mr. Morgan was at that time Governor of the State of New York, in which post he served until 1862, after which he sat for six years in the United States Senate. He proceeded at once to read the call that had been issued by the National Committee in December. To quote this cumbrously worded call is to set forth at once the basis upon which the new Republican party had been gathering its support from the earlier Free Soilers, Abolitionists, "Americans" and Know-Nothings, anti-slavery Democrats, and Free-State Whigs.

The call was extended to everybody "willing to co-operate with Republicans in support of the candidates who shall be nominated, and who are opposed to the policy of the present Administration, to federal corruption and usurpation, to the extension of slavery into the territories, to the new and dangerous political doctrine that the Constitution, of its own force, carries slavery into all the Territories of the United States, to the opening of the African slave trade, to any inequality of rights among citizens; and who are in favor of the immediate admission of Kansas into the Union, under the Constitution recently adopted by its people, of restoring the federal administration to a system of rigid economy, and to the principles of Washington and Jefferson, of maintaining inviolate the rights of States, and defending the soil of every State and Territory from lawless invasion, and of preserving the integrity of this Union and the supremacy of the Constitution and laws passed in pursuance thereof, against the conspiracy of the leaders of a sectional party, to resist the majority principle as established in this government even at the expense of its existence."

This indeed was a long sentence; but it summarized the attitude of the Republican party in opposing not only the views of the Southern Democratic faction led by Jefferson Davis, but also those of the Northern Democrats who were followers of Senator Douglas. I quote it as a convenient way of showing in what spirit the Republicans assembled. Those who favored such views were invited to send two delegates from each Congressional District, and four delegates - at - large from each State.

Mr. Morgan presented Hon. David Wilmot of Pennsylvania as temporary chairman, whose brief speech denounced "the new dogma . . . . that the Constitution was established to guarantee to slavery perpetual existence and unlimited empire." In calling the roll, the names of all the States were pronounced in order to emphasize the absence of nine. The permanent chairman of the convention was the veteran George Ashmun of Massachusetts, who had been a Whig member of Congress but was now an ardent Republican. He criticized President Buchanan, and complimented the convention upon its spirit of harmony.

In the routine proceedings of organization Mr. Halstead remarks upon the great applause with which the names of "Greeley of Oregon," Carl Schurz, and Francis P. Blair, Sr., were

GEORGE ASHMUN

Permanent chairman of the Republican convention at Chicago, a former Whig member of Congress (1845-51). He was a Yale graduate and distinguished lawyer of Springfield, Massachusetts. He was the last person to visit Lincoln at the White House, on the evening of the assassination.

received. Alluding to the report of the Committee on Permanent Organization, Mr. Halstead remarks: "The Hon. Geo. Ashmun, the presiding officer, was escorted to his chair by Preston King and Carl Schurz, the one short and round as a barrel and fat as butter, the other tall and slender. The contrast was a curious one, and so palpable that the whole multitude saw it, and gave a tremendous cheer.

CARL SCHURZ

Involved in the German revolutionary movement of 1848, Schurz had come to America in 1852 and settled in Wisconsin four years later. In 1860 he headed the Wisconsin delegation at the Chicago convention, and aided powerfully as a speaker in the campaign that elected Lincoln.

"Mr. Ashmun was speedily discovered to be an excellent presiding officer. His clear, full-toned voice was one refreshing to hear amid the clamors of a convention. He is cool, clear-headed and executive, and will despatch business. He is a treasure to the convention, and will lessen and shorten its labors. His speech was very good for the occasion, delivered with just warmth enough. He was animated, and yet his emotions did not get the better of him. In conclusion he referred, as if it were an undoubted fact, to the 'brotherly kindness' he had everywhere seen displayed."

This afforded the irrepressible Halstead no little amusement, because around the hotels the pro-Seward and anti-Seward men were talking with almost as much heat and recklessness as had been shown at Charleston between the pro-Douglas and anti-Douglas men.

If the Republican party had not faced conditions with a sense of reality, and with courage for the emergencies of the period, this convention of 1860 would now have little importance for us in the retrospects of American politics. But as it happens, the Democratic convention at Charleston, and the Republican convention at Chicago, of the year 1860, were by far the most memorable and significant voluntary gatherings of American citizens acting in party organizations in the entire history of the country. Both conventions were made up of men who, for the most part, were influential leaders in their respective States or Congressional districts.

To study the lists of delegates to either of these conventions is to discover scores of men who were either already prominent by reason of their leadership in national affairs, or else were destined to take responsible parts in the struggle of the following five years. Some of them were to be conspicuous in the annals of our public life for two decades after the war was over. As one reads the list of delegates to the Chicago convention he may well be surprised to find how many names are those of men afterwards prominent in the history of their States, and also how great a number were assured of a place in such a future work as the "Dictionary of American Biography."

John A. Andrew, who became the eminent War Governor of Massachusetts, headed the delegation from his State. William M. Evarts, a later Secretary of State, came as spokesman of the powerful delegation from New York to support the candidacy of William H. Seward. The three other delegates-at-large from New York were Preston King, John L. Schoolcraft, and Henry R. Selden. Gideon Welles, who became a member of Lincoln's Cabinet. headed the Connecticut delegation. David Wilmot, foremost of Pennsylvania Republicans, had as a colleague Thaddeus Stevens, perhaps the greatest parliamentarian who ever sat in Congress. Another Pennsylvanian was William D. Kelley, foremost champion of protective tariffs. The famous Francis P. Blair headed the Maryland delegation, with his son, the equally well-known Montgomery Blair (who became Lincoln's Postmaster-General) as a colleague.

The anti-slavery leader, Joshua R. Giddings, was a member of the Ohio delegation that included many able and influential men, with Hon. D. K. Cartter as chairman. A delegate-at-large from Indiana was Caleb B. Smith, who became a member of Lincoln's Cabinet. Lincoln's friend, N. B. Judd, headed

the Illinois delegation that also included Lincoln's old law partner, S. T. Logan of Springfield. Carl Schurz of Milwaukee, the most influential of the educated Germans who had come to America after the revolutionary movement in Germany of 1848, headed the delegation from Wisconsin. The Iowa delegation included a remarkable list of men who became eminent in our later history, among them William B. Allison, James F. Wilson, W. P. Hepburn, John A. Kasson. From Missouri came Francis P. Blair, Jr., and B. Gratz Brown. In the Oregon delegation we find included the name of Horace Greeley of New York, the most famous of American editors, who, as inveterately opposed to the nomination of Seward, had been excluded from the list of New York delegates. Arriving at Chicago, he had been invited to sit in the convention as a member of the Oregon group.

The first business before the convention had to do with the question upon what numerical basis the nomination of candidates should be made. A majority of the Committee on Rules held that since the Republican party was national in character, and since its convention was to be organized upon the lines of the Electoral College, the requisite majority should be one that ignored the absence of delegations from nine Southern States. Mr. Kelley of Pennsylvania presented the views of the majority of the committee with great eloquence, giving reasons also for seating a delegation from the Territory of Kansas and one from the District of Columbia. The argument was directed toward making the necessary majority larger than it would have been if a simple majority of those present and voting should suffice to make the convention's decisions.

The minority report was presented by Mr. A. B. James of the New York delegation. Mr. Kelley had said: "We looked at the call of the convention and we found that it invited not only the people of the Northern States—not only the people of the Border States—but the people of the United States; and if any State is not represented, whether it be by accident or design, we count her as here." Mr. James, for the minority, not attempting to compete with the eloquence of Mr. Kelley, merely stated that the Credentials Committee had fixed the number of voting delegates in the convention as 466. "You will thus see the difference," said Mr. James, "between the two reports; one is substantially a 'two-thirds rule.' If there are 466 votes, 311, I believe, is two-thirds of that vote, and this rule requires 304. Therefore it is only 7 short of the two-thirds rule, which has been adopted by the Democratic party in the management of their conventions."

"I am not aware," continued Mr. James, "that any such rule was ever adopted by any party in opposition to that party, and I am not aware that that party ever adopted that rule until 1836, and again in 1844, when it became necessary for the interest and purposes of slavery that the minority should rule the majority. For that reason I am opposed to that rule. I have sufficient confidence in the integrity and judgment of this convention to trust the nomination of its candidate to the majority of the delegates here. If the minority report is adopted instead of the two-thirds rule, the result will be left to the wisdom and patriotism of a majority of the convention."

The minority report was adopted on a roll call of the States, by a vote of about four to one. While the controversy was brief, and the result was accepted in perfect good temper, the difference was regarded as having a very decided bearing upon the prospects of Mr. Seward as the leading candidate. Under the majority rule, as proposed by Mr. Kelley, his success would have required an almost two-thirds vote of the actual convention. Under the rule as adopted he could have been nominated by a much smaller number.

At the end of the first day Mr. Halstead noted that the Republicans were all divided into two classes known as the "Irrepressibles" (pro-Seward) and the "Conservatives," and he proceeded to remark that "the favorite word in the convention is 'solemn.' Everything is 'solemn.' In Charleston the favorite was 'crisis.' Here there is something every ten minues found to be solemn. In Charleston there was a *crisis* nearly as often. I observed as many as twenty-three in one day."

He concluded by informing his Cincinnati

COTTON IS KING

A Senator from South Carolina, quoted in this chapter, painted a glowing picture in 1860 of the slaveholding South as the controlling power of the world. This New York cartoon, of a period not much later, suggests that the real strength of the South was the Negro race.

newspaper that "the Ohio delegation continues so divided as to be without influence. If united it would have a formidable influence, and might throw the casting votes between candidates, holding the balance of power between the East and the West."

The Ohio State Republicans had favored Governor Chase as a candidate, but had not instructed the delegation to act as a unit. If the Ohio group had been as determined and ardent as that of Illinois it might indeed have failed to secure the nomination of a leader so positive and radical in convictions as Salmon P. Chase. But it might have worked decisively for Seward. On the other hand, it might have dictated the convention's compromise choice.

Thus far Mr. Thurlow Weed, the strategist-in-chief of the Seward forces, was doing exceedingly well, and Horace Greeley was correspondingly anxious.

CHAPTER VI

Abraham Lincoln Is Nominated

*A platform reflecting the growth of anti-slavery sentiment is adopted
unanimously—Crisp nominating speeches present favorite sons—
Seward against the field—Lincoln victorious on third ballot*

THE ROUTINE PROCEEDINGS of a convention are fascinating, always, to the politically educated. In the year 1860 the fate of the nation was bound up in decisions that could be reached only through the more or less tedious parliamentary methods of these representative party assemblies. The present chapter will recount the principal occurrences that belong to the story of the three-day Republican convention that made Abraham Lincoln the party's presidential nominee.

A convention must first be organized (1) with approval of the credentials of its members, (2) by adopting rules of procedure and appointing standing committees, and (3) by the election of its temporary and permanent officers. These things having been done at Chicago, the report and adoption of the platform was the next business in order.

The document, promptly produced, was amended in only one particular after discussion on the floor, and was adopted unanimously amidst scenes of tremendous enthusiasm in the Wigwam. The chairman of the platform committee was Judge William Jessup, of the Pennsylvania delegation. The chairman of the Ohio delegation, Mr. Cartter of Cleveland, moved the previous question upon the adoption of the platform, without debate or opportunity for amendments. This was defeated chiefly at the instance of Mr. Giddings, an anti-slavery leader, who

Old Santford

A "RAIL" OLD WESTERN GENTLEMAN

The fence-rails that Lincoln split in his youth became symbols used in his campaign, and were so received throughout the North. Added significance attaches to this cartoon because it bears the signature of Frank Bellew, who had just come to America to pursue a career that had begun as a member of the staff of the London *Punch*. To him such symbolism must have seemed far-fetched.

desired to amplify a resolution alluding to the Declaration of Independence, the Constitution, and the Union, by quoting from the Declaration those clauses which declare "that all men are created equal; that they are endowed by their Creator with certain inalienable rights; that among these are life, liberty, and the pursuit of happiness; that to secure these rights, governments are instituted among men, deriving their just powers from the consent of the governed."

Although the Negro race was not mentioned in the brief discussion of the proposed amendment of Mr. Giddings, it was plain that his purpose was not merely to amplify phraseology. He had distinctly in mind the recent Dred Scott Decision, and was proposing to strengthen the foundations of the Republican edifice. Ultimately, Mr. George William Curtis of New York, orator and man of letters, brought this quotation from the document of 1776 into a rewritten second plank, and the convention accepted it. "I rise simply," said Mr. Curtis, "to ask the gentlemen to think well before, on the free prairies of the West in the summer of 1860, they dare to wince and quail before the men who in Philadelphia in 1776—in Philadelphia in the Arch Keystone State, so amply, so nobly represented on this platform today—before they dare to shrink from repeating the words these great men enunciated."

THE REPUBLICAN CONVENTION OF 1860 IN THE CHICAGO WIGWAM

When the doors were opened on May 16th, the first day of the convention, every seat was taken and even the standing room (space for 4,500 persons) was promptly filled. The galleries had seats for 3,000, to which gentlemen accompanied by ladies were admitted. In this convention, organized cheering was an important device. Lincoln's managers made the most of this. Every gain in balloting won by the Illinois candidate met with a thundering response from the galleries. The "Irrepressibles" (Seward men), whenever possible, vied with the Lincoln men in demonstrations.

The platform as a whole was, therefore, accepted with a completeness of accord and genuineness of enthusiasm that had never been surpassed in any large political convention. I place emphasis on this statement because of the contrast between the unity shown at Chicago, with the lack of any sharp disagreement whatsoever, and the violent platform dissensions that had torn asunder the national Democratic party in the convention at Charleston. That Southern gathering had tried in vain to find a basis upon which harmony of doctrine and unity of leadership might be maintained. As for Chicago, the convention though national in form was sectional in fact and in sentiment. The Southern delegates attending it represented mere shreds and remnants, the Republican party having no actual foothold south of the Mason and Dixon line and the Ohio River.

The platform began with a statement of the propriety and necessity of the formation of the Republican party, and proceeded to declare, after quoting from the Declaration of Independence, that "the Federal Constitution, the rights of States, and the Union of the States must and shall be preserved." The third plank denounced Southern threats of disunion as constituting "an avowal of contemplated treason which it is the imperative duty of an indignant people sternly to rebuke and forever silence." The next clause upheld as inviolate "the right of each State to order and control its own domestic institutions according to its own judgment exclusively," and it then proceeded—obviously referring to the John Brown raid, for which the Republican party as such had, from the first, disavowed all responsibility—to declare that "we denounce the lawless invasion, by armed force, of the soil of any State or territory, no matter under what pretext, as among the gravest of crimes."

Paragraph Five arraigned the Buchanan administration in terms of general and specific disapproval, and the next clause charged the Administration with reckless extravagance and systematic plunder of the public treasury by favored partisans. It referred to "the recent startling developments of fraud and corruption at the federal metropolis." Next, in several resolutions, the platform dealt with the latest phases of the slavery issue. It denounced "the new dogma that the Constitution, of its own force, carries slavery into any or all of the Territories of the United States." It declared that "the normal condition of all the Territories of the United States is that of freedom." It branded "the recent reopening of the African slave trade, under the cover of our national flag, aided by perversions of judicial power, as a crime against humanity and a burning shame to our country and age," and it called upon Congress to take "prompt and efficient measures for the total and final suppression of that execrable traffic."

The next paragraph struck directly at the Douglas doctrines; and since these were to be involved in the campaign we may quote the brief plank in its entirety: "That in the recent vetoes by their Federal Governors of the acts of the legislatures of Kansas and Nebraska, prohibiting slavery in those Territories, we find a practical illustration of the boasted Democratic principle of Non-Intervention and Popular Sovereignty embodied in the Kansas-Nebraska Bill, and a demonstration of the deception and fraud involved therein." The immediate admission of Kansas under its Free State Constitution was next demanded.

The twelfth plank called for protective tariffs, and policies for promotion of internal prosperity. Then followed a demand for the enactment "of the complete and satisfactory Homestead Measure which has already passed the House." (It will be remembered that President Buchanan and the Democratic Senate were not in accord with the Republican House in promoting a liberal western land policy that would build up more rapidly the Free States of the Northwest). The fourteenth clause supported a liberal treatment of foreign-born citizens. The next advocated appropriations for river and harbor improvements, while the sixteenth declared "that a railroad to the Pacific Coast is imperatively demanded by the States of the whole country; that the Federal government ought to render

immediate and efficient aid in its construction; and that, as preliminary thereto, a daily overland mail should be promptly established."

The platform ended with an appeal for the support of all citizens who are in substantial agreement with its principles, regardless of their previous affiliations. It was adopted in the afternoon of the second day of the convention, and there was a call to proceed at once to ballot for a presidential candidate.

There were many delegates, however, who desired more time for the strategy and tactics of this crowning business for which the convention was assembled; and it was decided to adjourn until ten o'clock on the following day. Upon assembling on the morning of May 18th, the clergyman who opened the session with prayer concluded his brief supplication in the following phrases: "We entreat thee, that at some future but not distant day, the evils which now invest the body politic shall not only have been arrested in their progress but wholly eradicated from the system. And may the pen of the historian trace an intimate connection between that glorious consummation and the transactions of this convention. Oh Lord, our God, Thou art in Heaven and we on earth, therefore should our words be few. Our prayer is now before Thee. Wilt Thou hear, accept and answer it, for the sake of our Redeemer!"

It was a drastic process by which the evils to which the Rev. Mr. Green thus referred were eradicated from the system of the body politic. Certainly the subsequent historian has been justified in finding intimate connection between the transactions of that convention and the treatment to which the body politic was about to be subjected. Certain minor interruptions, due to the adjustment of credentials from certain States, principally Maryland, Virginia, Oregon, and Texas, served only to illustrate the remarkable efficiency and harmony of the convention; and the main order of business was not appreciably delayed.

The urbane Mr. Evarts of New York now addressed the chairman as follows: "As the convention has decided by its vote to proceed to ballot, you may be assured that I do not rise for the purpose of making a speech. I rise

PROMINENT CANDIDATES FOR THE REPUBLICAN PRESIDENTIAL
NOMINATION IN 1860

This illustration is reproduced from a double page in *Harper's Weekly* of the day before the convention assembled. Conspicuous over all is the portrait of New York's candidate, Senator Seward. Opposite the portrait of Lincoln is that of John Bell of Tennessee, who had just accepted a presidential nomination from the Union convention at Baltimore. The other candidates whose portraits appear in the group are (at the left): Edward Bates of Missouri, who became Lincoln's Attorney-General; William Pennington of New Jersey, Speaker of the House; Salmon P. Chase, Governor of Ohio and Lincoln's Secretary of the Treasury; and John C. Frémont, Republican nominee in 1856 and a Major-General in the Civil War. At the right are: Nathaniel P. Banks, Governor of Massachusetts and later a Major-General; John McLean of Ohio, Associate Justice of the Supreme Court; Simon Cameron of Pennsylvania, Lincoln's first Secretary of War; and Cassius M. Clay of Kentucky, appointed by Lincoln to be Minister to Russia.

simply to ask, Sir, whether it is in order to present names in nomination." The president of the convention replied: "The Chair is of the opinion that under the execution of the order adopted, it may be in order to put in nomination such persons as you desire, without debate."

Whereupon Mr. Evarts—setting, in my opinion, a good example, that has been painfully disregarded in many subsequent conventions—proceeded with the following nominating speech: "In the order of business before the convention, Sir, I take the liberty to name as a candidate to be nominated by this con-

vention for the office of President of the United States, William H. Seward." Whereupon the amiable presiding officer permitted the convention to relax, and to indulge in prolonged applause.

Mr. Judd, chairman of the Illinois delegation, then arose and made the following speech: "I desire, on behalf of the delegation from Illinois, to put in nomination, as a candidate for President of the United States, Abraham Lincoln, of Illinois." It is noted that after Mr. Judd sat down there was "immense applause, long continued."

Mr. Thomas H. Dudley of New Jersey next

in order addressed the chair: "Mr. President, New Jersey presents the name of William L. Dayton," after which there was applause but no riotous enthusiasm.

Andrew H. Reeder of Pennsylvania then took the floor and spoke as follows: "Pennsylvania nominates as her candidate for the Presidency, General Simon Cameron."

After the decent interval allowed for cheering, Hon. D. K. Cartter of Ohio declared: "Ohio presents to the consideration of this convention, as candidate for President, the name of Salmon P. Chase." (Applause).

Hon. Caleb B. Smith of Indiana in his turn claimed the floor: "I desire on behalf of the delegation from Indiana to second the nomination of Abraham Lincoln, of Illinois." (Tremendous applause).

Francis P. Blair of St. Louis, with a real candidate to offer, made the following state-

ANOTHER "TWO-SHILLING" CANDIDATE

First Colored Person: "Abe, is yese gwine to guv up de wite washin' perfession?"

Second Colored Person: "Yes, deed I is. Gwine to split rails now. Bobbolitionists make um President, p'raps!"

There was much disappointment in the East, and particularly in New York, when Seward failed to receive the Republican nomination for the Presidency. An editorial in *Vanity Fair,* from which this cartoon and the one on the opposite page are reproduced, alluded to Lincoln's appearances on the lecture platform for a 25-cent admission fee (which was later denied), and dubbed him "a characterless candidate, supported by an aimless party," who possessed "certain characteristics which, if there is any power in newspaper fun, will go far toward defeating him."

ment: "I am commissioned by representatives of the State of Missouri to present to this convention the name of Edward Bates as a candidate for the Presidency." The name of Mr. Bates received applause to which a man of his high repute was entitled.

Then arose another Blair, namely the Hon. Austin Blair of Jackson, Michigan, who announced: "In behalf of the delegates from Michigan, I second the nomination for President of the United States of William H. Seward." (Loud applause).

The Hon. Tom Corwin of Ohio next made a speech in which he offered the name of a well-qualified but somewhat time-worn candidate. "I rise, Mr. President, at the request of many gentlemen, part of them members of this convention, and many of them the most respectable gentlemen known to the history of this country and its politics, to present the name of John McLean."

Next Mr. Carl Schurz seconded the nomination of William H. Seward, on behalf of the Wisconsin delegation, and Mr. John W. North of Northfield, Minnesota, speaking for his delegation, also seconded Seward, and William A. Phillips of Lawrence, Kansas, followed with the statement, "I am commissioned, not only by the delegation from Kansas, but by the people of Kansas, to present the name of William H. Seward of New York."

The next man to catch the chairman's eye was Hon. Columbus Delano of Ohio, who said: "I rise on behalf of a portion of the delegation from Ohio to put in nomination a man who can split rails and maul Democrats —Abraham Lincoln."

Mr. William M. Stone of Iowa stated: "Mr. President, I rise in the name of two-thirds of the delegation of Iowa to second the nomination of Abraham Lincoln." Delano and Stone were heartily applauded, when they nominated Lincoln, by the crowd in the Wigwam that was made up of local supporters of the Illinois candidate.

In a spirit of exuberant hospitality towards the candidates and the party at large, one of the Illinois delegates arose and declared: "Mr. President, in order or out of order, I desire to move that this convention, for itself and this vast audience, give three cheers for all the candidates presented by the Republican party." Whereupon the dignified President of the gathering calmly stated, "The gentleman is out of order."

And then arose the chairman's fellow citizen of Massachusetts, John A. Andrew, who made a speech of eight words, instead of one of eight hundred, which would have been deemed sufficiently curt and laconic in a typical convention of these later times. Mr. Andrew said: "I move you that we proceed to vote."

The whole number of votes cast was 465, and the number necessary to a choice was 233. The result of the first ballot was as follows: William H. Seward, 137½; Abraham Lincoln, 102; Edward Bates, 48; Simon Cameron, 50½; John McLean, 12; Salmon P. Chase, 49; Benjamin F. Wade of Ohio, 3; William L. Dayton, 14; John M. Reed of Pennsylvania, 1; Jacob Collamer of Vermont, 10; Charles Sumner of Massachusetts, 1; John C. Frémont of California, 1.

Seward's vote was made up principally of the larger half of the Maine delegation, all but four of the twenty-five Massachusetts men, New York's entire 70, Michigan's 12, Wisconsin's 10, and the entire small delegations from California, Minnesota, Kansas, and the District of Columbia.

Lincoln on this first ballot had 19 New England votes, 4 from the large Pennsylvania delegation, 14 from Virginia, 6 from Kentucky, 8 from Ohio, 26 from Indiana, 22 from Illinois, 2 from Iowa, and 1 from Nebraska. Seward would have needed Pennsylvania and

VANITY FAIR.

JUNE 9, 1860.]

SHAKY.

DARING TRANSIT ON THE PERILOUS RAIL, · · · · · Mr. Abraham Blondin De Lave Lincoln.

This was *Vanity Fair's* first cartoon of Lincoln, published shortly after the nomination. Blondin had crossed Niagara Falls on a tight-rope, 1100 feet long, stretched 160 feet above the water; and he was performing similar feats in other parts of the country. The fence rail upon which Lincoln walks is decayed and broken. From the bank, Horace Greeley, worried lest the Negro's interests should be neglected in Lincoln's canvass, calls out: "Don't drop the carpet-bag!"

Indiana; but out of Pennsylvania's 54 he received only 1½, most of the delegates voting for Cameron, who otherwise received only 3 scattering votes.

The 48 cast for Bates included Missouri's 18, Oregon's 5, Delaware's 8, with 8 from Maryland and 7 from Connecticut, besides a scattering vote or two. The McLean support was merely nominal and scattering. The vote for Wade was casual and tentative. Dayton's vote was nothing more than a complimentary first-ballot gesture, from his own State of New

Jersey. A like thing was true regarding Vermont's 10 votes for Collamer.

It was plain, therefore, that the nomination of any one of the candidates would have to come as the result of regroupings, based upon the following of Seward or that of Lincoln. When the second ballot was announced it was found that William H. Seward had 184½ votes, a gain of 11, and Lincoln had 181 votes, a gain of 79. It became evident, also, that Pennsylvania's vote for Cameron on the first ballot had been merely complimentary, inasmuch as there was only one vote for him on the second ballot, with 48 Pennsylvania votes for Lincoln and 2½ each for Seward and Mc-Lean. The same thing proved true of the Vermont vote, which went solidly for Lincoln on this second ballot, together with all but one of the New Hampshire vote. Massachusetts did not abandon Seward, and Michigan and Wisconsin held firmly with New York; but Iowa gave Lincoln 5 and Seward 2. Chase on this second ballot held 29 of the Ohio votes, but the original 8 for Lincoln had increased to 14 Ohio supporters on the second ballot.

Without delay the third ballot was ordered, and this was the last that was taken. As the delegations actually voted, Lincoln's total reached 231½, as against 180 for Seward, the number necessary for a choice being 233, as already stated. With only 1½ votes necessary to insure the nomination, and before the result of the vote was made known, Mr. Cartter of Ohio rose to announce the change of 4 votes from Mr. Chase to Abraham Lincoln.

This of course was final and conclusive, and

HANNIBAL HAMLIN, OF MAINE

When chosen for the Vice-Presidency, on the ticket with Lincoln, Hamlin was serving his second term in the Senate. At first he had been an anti-slavery Democrat, but he joined the Republican party soon after it was formed. Hamlin presided over the Senate until March 4, 1865. Later he sat again in the Senate for twelve years, and subsequently for a time was Minister to Spain.

the members of delegation after delegation through their chairmen declared their desire to correct the vote from their States. This movement resulted in shifts to Lincoln that practically included the entire convention, with Mr. Evarts, as the Seward spokesman, promptly moving to make it unanimous.

The Seward support had been firm and consistent, without much variation. It had produced 173½ on the first ballot, 184½ on the second, and 180 on the third. The swing of a large block of Ohio ballots to Lincoln had brought Pennsylvania, Ohio, Indiana, and Illinois into line, and with the majority of the delegates of Kentucky and Virginia for the Illinois candidate (these States giving him 27 as against 14 for Seward) it was plain that no combination could be formed that would bring victory to the Republican leader of New York, whose friends had gone to Chicago with such confidence.

How and why Seward was defeated, and how Lincoln was nominated are matters of political history about which the present generation is not sufficiently informed. If Seward had been nominated, it is held possible though by no means certain, that the course of American history would have been completely changed. There are two reasons for this suggestion, one being that the Democrats might have won the election, and the other being that Seward's views on the question of resistance to secession were not those of Lincoln.

Thus it was by no means a question of rivalry between two excellent and competent leaders that was determining the choice of the Chicago convention. There were principles at stake, and for the sake of those principles the

THE RAIL CANDIDATE.

Rails that Lincoln had split thirty years earlier played a prominent part in the demonstration at
Chicago and throughout the campaign. Horace Greeley, in the cartoon above, remarks to Lincoln:
"We can prove that you have split rails, and that will insure your election." Lincoln replies that
this rail—the Republican platform—is the hardest stick he ever straddled. The Negro proclaims:
"It's awful hard work carrying Old Massa Abe on nothing but dis ere rail!"

party was endeavoring to name the candidate
whose chances of election might be best. There
was applause for all the candidates, and no
disparagement of any one of them. I shall
comment upon Seward's defeat and Lincoln's
nomination in two subsequent chapters.

It remains to speak of the selection for the
Vice-Presidency. The delegates had heard
the nominating speeches, taken the ballots,
nominated Abraham Lincoln, listened to a
number of eloquent speeches of acquiescence
and endorsement, all in a single session of the
convention's third day. Adjournment was
taken to a five-o'clock session, which opened
with the presentation of candidates for the
second place on the ticket. The nominating
speeches were each limited to one brief sentence. Mr. Wilder of Kansas presented the
name of John Hickman of Pennsylvania. Mr.

Cartter of Ohio named United States Senator
Hannibal Hamlin of Maine.

Mr. Boutwell of Massachusetts had a name
to present that survives in political and military
history, and speaking for the Massachusetts
delegation he said: "On behalf of a great majority of the people of that Commonwealth
and New England, I present the name of the
'iron man' of Massachusetts, Nathaniel P.
Banks." Caleb B. Smith of Indiana announced: "I present the name of the gallant
son of Kentucky, Cassius M. Clay." Mr.
Lowry of Pennsylvania nominated Andrew
H. Reeder, a Pennsylvanian who was then
territorial governor of Kansas, and prominent
in the news of the day.

Two ballots were taken. On the first the
vote stood Hannibal Hamlin 194, Cassius M.
Clay 101½, Mr. Hickman 58, Governor

Reeder 51, General Banks 38½, with a few scattering votes including six from Texas for General Sam Houston. A second ballot settled the matter conclusively by giving Hamlin 357, Clay 86, and Hickman 13. A friend of Cassius Clay hastened to move that the vote for Hamlin be made unanimous; and after some brief concluding items of business the convention adjourned and the evening was devoted to a triumphal street parade, followed by a ratification meeting in the Wigwam. The President, Mr. Ashmun, made an appropriate farewell speech, complimenting Mr. Lincoln and Mr. Hamlin, with both of whom he had served in Congress.

Mr. Halstead, describing the closing scenes, writes: "Now that the business of the convention was transacted, we had the usual stump speeches, and complimentary resolutions, and the valedictory from the chairman, and the 'three times three' upon adjournment for the candidate."

The convention dissolved after voting its thanks to the citizens of Chicago.

"The city was wild with delight," states Mr. Halstead: "The 'Old Abe' men formed processions, and bore rails through the streets. Torrents of liquor were poured down the hoarse throats of the multitude. A hundred guns were fired from the top of the Tremont House. The Chicago *Press and Tribune* office was illuminated. That paper says:

'On each side of the counting-room door stood a *rail*—out of the three thousand split by 'honest Old Abe' thirty years ago, on the Sangamon River bottoms. On the inside were two more, brilliantly hung with tapers'."

So ended the second of the two most signi-ficant political conventions that have thus far been held in the history of the United States.

The convention had lasted three days. Chicago had done its best to entertain the delegates. Steamship excursions had been offered them on the Great Lakes, and all who chose to remain after adjournment were taken upon free trips over new Western railroads; to inspect the canal connecting Lake Michigan with the Mississippi; to go down the river to Quincy or St. Louis, and to return by other routes to Chicago or to their Eastern destinations. Chicago had appreciated the advertising it had received from the Waterways Convention of 1849, mentioned in our first volume, and the Republican convention had now provided for the city its second great national occasion, and the first of the many political gatherings that it was destined to entertain.

Mr. Halstead, describing the return of the delegates to their home States, writes:

I left the city on the night train on the Fort Wayne and Chicago road. The train consisted of eleven cars, every seat full and people standing in the aisles and corners. I never before saw a company of persons so prostrated by continued excitement. The Lincoln men were not able to respond to the cheers which went up along the road for 'old Abe.' They had not only done their duty in that respect, but exhausted their capacity. At every station where there was a village, until after two o'clock, there were tar barrels burning, drums beating, boys carrying rails; and guns, great and small, banging away. The weary passengers were allowed no rest, but plagued by the thundering jar of cannon, the clamor of drums, the glare of bonfires, and the whooping of the boys, who were delighted with the idea of a candidate for the Presidency who thirty years ago split rails on the Sangamon River—classic stream now and for evermore—and whose neighbors named him "honest."

THE BARK OF STATE, WITH "LONG ABE" AT THE HELM

"THE IRREPRESSIBLE CONFLICT".

OR THE REPUBLICAN BARGE IN DANGER.

Published by Currier & Ives.   152 Nassau St N.Y.

Senator Seward is being thrown overboard from the Republican barge, by the other leaders of the
party. In his struggle he cries out that he had built the boat and he alone could save it. Uncle Sam
on the bank (a younger man than the cartoonist's modern conception) expresses his opinion that the
crazy craft cannot be saved by throwing the pilot overboard. Lincoln, at the rudder, boasts that he
has "steered a *flat* boat before." Horace Greeley is the leader of those who are casting Seward from
the boat, while others who may be recognized are Edward Bates (afterwards Lincoln's Attorney-
General) sitting next to Greeley; Francis P. Blair, editor of the Washington *Globe,* grasping Seward's
foot; and James Watson Webb, editor of the New York *Courier and Enquirer,* in the bow.

CHAPER VII

Why Seward Was Not Available

*His earlier radicalism had left prejudices—Criticism of his record as
Governor—Greeley's enmity, Weed's friendship—Pennsylvania turns
the scales, and Illinois, by skillful management, reaps the benefit*

WILLIAM H. SEWARD and Abraham
Lincoln had by no means been rivals.
In Illinois the careers of Lincoln and
Douglas had been parallel, with many co-
incidences and sharp contrasts for the greater
part of thirty years. Each of these two State
figures had been growing into a position of
admitted leadership, as the shattered fragments of earlier parties had rearranged themselves, emerging as the Republican and Democratic parties of the period from 1854 to 1860.

But Lincoln had not, even in a limited sense,
been a national figure until he had made the
Cooper Union speech in New York. Seward
had long been the most conspicuous leader of
the movement that took practical form in
1860. He was a political figure of the first
rank, belonging intellectually in the class of
John Quincy Adams, Webster, and Clay, upon
the careers of all of whom he had pronounced
eulogies that may be read today as among the
best examples of biographical interpretation.

51

That Seward would be nominated at Chicago was regarded as wholly probable. The Democrats had adjourned their stormy and discordant sessions at Charleston partly in the hope that Seward's expected nomination at Chicago would so affect national sentiment as to make possible a healing of the breach between the followers of Jefferson Davis and those of Stephen A. Douglas.

The path to the presidency is beset with many pitfalls. Pre-eminence among party leaders has usually been gained through experiences that have made enemies as well as friends. The crisis of 1860, however, was too serious for the indulgence of mere prejudice or personal preference or selfish ambition. The candidates proposed at Chicago were all men worthy of confidence, and any one of them in normal times would have made a creditable nominee, who if elected would doubtless have proved to be a capable President.

There are no explicit specifications by which to judge and measure candidates for high office. It is not true, as sometimes asserted, that the presidency in the nature of the case seeks second-rate men and rejects the most highly qualified. But our system of State representation in party conventions, and in the electoral college, results in complications that render it impossible to predict results with any confidence as regards particular men. The political system in England inevitably brings to the position of Prime Minister men who are accepted heads of parties; and we find administrative control in the hands of a Palmerston, a Russell, a Gladstone, a Disraeli, a Salisbury, a Balfour, an Asquith, a Lloyd George, or a MacDonald. In the United States a Webster, a Clay, a Calhoun, a Crawford, a Benton, a Seward, a Douglas, a Chase, a Blaine, or a Bryan may fail to reach the presidency to which he has aspired. In England such leaders are likely in their turn to have attained the premiership. The list of our Secretaries of State includes the names of a number of statesmen who in other countries would have held a higher office.

It does not follow that their failure to achieve the presidency was due chiefly in any case to the fact that an undiscriminating democracy preferred to put second-rate men in the White House. In several cases, however, a leading candidate has failed of nomination because his career has identified him too positively with certain views and positions.

Thus Buchanan had been nominated by the Democrats in 1856 largely because he had been absent from the country as Minister to England, and had taken no active part in the repeal of the Missouri Compromise. As a Pennsylvanian who could carry his own State, he was eminently desirable. He was acceptable also to the South, because he had been identified with the Ostend Manifesto that had proclaimed our intention to acquire Cuba. Douglas was keeping his hold upon the Northern Democracy as an aggressive leader; and since he had not become repugnant to the South, he might have been nominated and elected in 1856. But in 1860 his candidacy was splitting the Democratic party, because the South had turned against him.

Horace Greeley, editing the most influential organ of the Republican party, and showing incessant energy as a party journalist, was opposed to the nomination of Seward; and therefore he was not accorded a seat in the New York delegation. But he had recently traveled in the far West, where the weekly New York *Tribune* was the lesson-book of Republicanism, and he was made a member of the Oregon delegation. He had until 1854 been a warm friend and supporter of Seward, and—with Thurlow Weed, of Albany, an almost equally famous journalist—he had been one of a triumvirate headed by Seward that had supervised party affairs in the earlier stages of the evolution of the Republican party in the State of New York, and the East at large.

But the old firm of Seward, Weed, and Greeley had been broken up. Thurlow Weed remained with Seward, as the most skillful political manager of his time. Living at Albany, Mr. Weed's relations with the legislature and the State government were close, and he was one of those "practical" politicians always to be found in both leading parties, who have for more than a hundred years practised the peculiar arts of machine politics in the State of New York.

Mr. Weed was reputed to have ample money at his disposal, the better to facilitate his efforts on behalf of Seward, and he was in a position, also, to make pledges and compromises looking to appointive posts. The New York delegates, therefore, with Weed as Seward's personal representative, went to Chicago with complete confidence in the success that awaited them.

As Lincoln's Secretary of State, during a period when our foreign relations were of such vital consequence, Seward was destined in the next five years to make the record that has given him enduring fame as the first-named member of the War Cabinet. The present-day reader is familiar with Seward's name only because he became a member of Lincoln's political and administrative family. Readers naturally prefer to concentrate their attention upon the life of Lincoln, and only the more thoughtful students of history are fully aware of the relative position of public men previous to 1860. It may be well at this point, therefore, to recall in a few sentences the earlier record of a statesman once so pre-eminent, and so worthy of a place in our permanent list of American leaders in government and politics.

Mr. Seward was born in Orange County, New York, in May, 1801. He studied at Union College, Schenectady, where he graduated in 1820, having paid his way, toward the end of his course, by spending most of a school year teaching in the State of Georgia. At twenty-one he was a practising lawyer, living at Auburn, New York. Two years later

WILLIAM H. SEWARD
A portrait of the period when, at the age of thirty-seven, the Auburn lawyer was elected Governor of New York. He served in that office during the four years 1839-42. Previously, for forty years, without interruption the State Executives had been Democrats.

he was active in politics, opposing the so-called "Albany Regency" as certain Democratic leaders of the State were then—and for a good while afterwards—designated. He led the young men of New York in the support of John Quincy Adams for a second term in 1828, and himself declined the nomination for Congress. He went to the State Senate in 1830 on the high tide of the Anti-Masonic movement. In 1834 he was the Whig candidate for Governor, and was defeated by the famous Gov. William L. Marcy, having meantime traveled in Europe and written letters for the Albany *Evening Journal.* In 1838 he was elected Governor by a good majority over Marcy, who had served three terms in that capacity, and who was afterwards Secretary of State in the cabinets of Polk and Pierce.

Mr. Seward earned a high reputation for his efforts while Governor, in the fields of education and judicial reform, and in undertakings for the welfare of new immigrant populations. He was re-elected Governor in 1840, and after leaving office attained rank with the foremost lawyers of the country in the practice of his profession. He was a leading supporter of Henry Clay in 1844, and was soon thereafter elected to the United States Senate, where he became at once the foremost leader of the Whigs, supporting Taylor as against Southern opposition.

It was in a speech on the admission of California in 1850 that Seward, declaring that "the Constitution devotes the domain to union, to justice, to defense, to welfare, and to liberty," then proceeded to make a remark that forever afterwards held its association with his name. It is well to quote it because it undoubtedly had a bearing upon his future disappointments, as well as his triumphs. "But there is a higher law than the Constitution, which regulates our authority over the domain, and devotes it to the same noble purposes. The territory is a part, no inconsiderable part, of the common heritage of mankind, bestowed upon them by the Creator of the Universe. We are his stewards, and must so discharge our trusts as to secure in the highest attainable degree their happiness."

In the minds of the country, North and South, Mr. Seward had thus come to be regarded as a radical on the slavery question, although remaining the foremost member of the Whig party in New York. This reputation was maintained during the discussion of the repeal of the Missouri Compromise; and his speeches were widely read, particularly the speech at Rochester in 1858, which contrasted the Northern system of free labor and the

Southern system of slave labor, and which became a document cited constantly throughout the South, while widely influential in the North from the Atlantic to the Pacific.

In that Rochester speech he said: "It is the irrepressible conflict between opposing and enduring forces, and it means that the United States must and will, sooner or later, become either entirely a slave-holding nation, or entirely a free-labor nation." He had been reelected to the Senate in 1855 in spite of strong opposition. There were many New York Whigs, particularly members of the mercantile and banking class in New York City with large trading and financial interests in the South, who did not like Seward's anti-slavery radicalism.

But not less important was the opposition of those who belonged to the "Know-Nothing" or American party, which just then was at the height of its influence. Seward had opposed the Compromise of 1850, and had disapproved of the Whig platform of 1852, although he gave reluctant support to the candidate, Gen. Winfield Scott. In 1856 he worked hard for the Frémont ticket, having been one of the advanced Whigs who entered the new Republican party. He had not desired the nomination in 1856 for himself, though it would have been his if he had consented.

He had traveled widely in Europe and the Near East in 1859, and had returned to take a leading part in the Senate debates of the sessions that opened the first week of December and continued to June 25, 1860, while the political conventions were being held. It is an evidence of Seward's intellectual authority and political grasp that in spite of several elements of distinct opposition he held his unquestioned leadership in the State of New York, with the assured certainty that he could carry it as a presidential nominee against Douglas or any other Democrat.

But it was not certain that he could carry other States, where Republican success was necessary, and

THE "OLD HACK" TURNED OUT TO "GRASS"!

Horace Greeley received more credit (or blame) than anyone else for Seward's defeat in the Chicago convention. There had been a long period when the *Tribune's* editor and the New York Senator were the best of friends; but the political firm of Seward, Weed, and Greeley had been dissolved long before 1860. The cartoon is an example of the rudeness and bad taste that was occasionally exhibited in the heat of a political campaign.

JUNE 2, 1860.]   VANITY FAIR.

MARK ANTONY RAYMOND
CÆSAR SEWARD.

CASCA BLAIR.
BRUTUS GREELEY.

"ET TU, GREELEY?"

Another of the cartoons appearing immediately after the Chicago convention that charged Horace Greeley with bringing about Seward's defeat. Henry J. Raymond, of the New York *Times*, plays the rôle of Mark Anthony, and denounces "Brutus" Greeley, "Casca" Blair, and the other assassins of "Caesar" Seward.

where, in this period of drifts and transitions among parties and factions, the particular candidate meant much more than in a time of normal party cohesion. Many Whigs, Democrats, and Know-Nothings or Americans, were coming over to the Republican cause, carrying with them a certain inheritance of prejudice. Not a few of these new Republican voters had formerly thought of Seward as recklessly radical in his anti-slavery speeches. There were others, with their old American predilection

and their dislike of recent immigrants in politics, who had in times past opposed Seward as too friendly to the naturalized citizens.

There was a strong anti-Catholic feeling; and Seward, while Governor, and while working for the cause of common schools in the cities and among the immigrants, had informed a friendly Catholic bishop that he had no objection to the use of a part of the public school fund for the aid of Catholic parish schools under certain restrictions. No Republican of standing was holding these things against Seward in point of principle, but only as affecting his availability in certain States and communities.

Seward's defeat at Chicago, as Greeley remarked some time afterwards, turned upon one essential question — which candidate "could obtain more electoral votes than any of his competitors." And Greeley went on to say that this reason "rarely or never fails in a national convention. It nominated Harrison in '40; Polk in '44; Taylor in '48; Pierce in '52; Buchanan in '56, and Lincoln in '60. Those who compose national conventions are generally, at least, s h r e w d politicians. They want to secure a triumph if for no better reason than they hope thereby to gratify their own personal aspirations. So they consult and compare and balance popularities and weigh probabilities; and at least the majority center upon that candidate who could poll the most votes."

DAVID WILMOT

The temporary chairman of the Republican convention was prominent in the movement to nominate some other candidate than Seward. His name is remembered for the Wilmot Proviso, formulated when he was a Democratic member of Congress from Pennsylvania in 1846, which sought to limit funds for the prosecution of war with Mexico unless slavery were forever excluded from any territory acquired.

Mr. Halstead, commenting on Seward's defeat, stated that "The fact of the convention was the defeat of Seward rather than the nomination of Lincoln. It was the triumph of a presumption of availability over pre-eminence in intellect and unrivaled fame—a success of the ruder qualities of manhood and the more homely attributes of popularity, over the arts of a consummate politician, and the splendor of accomplished statesmanship."

We have many sources of information, some of them appearing more recently in memoirs and letters, showing what happened behind the scenes in the convention. David Wilmot, the foremost Republican of Pennsylvania, who served as temporary chairman of the Chicago convention, had played an important part in the defeat of Seward. His biographer, Mr. Going, declares: "It was an unwritten part, played behind the closed doors of caucuses, and very incompletely told even in the many contemporary reports and later reminiscences."

Much was expected to depend upon the State elections, which at that time were held a month or two earlier than the presidential election. Mr. Going, summing up the views held by Wilmot and his friends, declares:

THURLOW WEED
(1795-1882)

An influential journalist and politician. His early activities were at Rochester, N. Y., but in 1830 he founded the Albany *Evening Journal*, making it a Whig and later a Republican organ. He was a political partner of William H. Seward, whom he favored for President in 1860.

"It was absolutely necessary for the Republicans to carry at least three of the four States — Illinois, Indiana, Pennsylvania, New Jersey. The critical problem was to find the candidate who could do it. Seward was much the strongest in the convention, but in Indiana and in Pennsylvania t h e r e was a strong remnant of the old Native American or Know-Nothing party, adverse to Seward because of his former hostility to that party. Lane and Curtin, gubernatorial candidates from those States, said Seward's nomination would insure defeat. Illinois declared that Seward's nomination would kill off Senator Trumbull and give the legislature into the hands of the Democrats. New Jersey asserted that Seward's nomination would mean defeat in their State. Illinois wanted Lincoln; Indiana, according to Ray, had come over to Lincoln before the convention got to work, but Pennsylvania was for Cameron and New Jersey for Dayton."

We are told how the delegations from these four States came together in a caucus at noon on May 17th and appointed a committee consisting of three from each State, to meet in the rooms of Mr. Wilmot during the evening. The anti-Seward movement gained strength as it found its focus during this protracted night session of the committee in Wilmot's sitting room. Throughout the night there was interchange of views, resulting in the agreement that Cameron and Dayton would be withdrawn as candidates after one or two complimentary votes, and that their delegations would then go to Lincoln.

Judge McLean of Ohio was 75 years old, universally acceptable on personal grounds, but evidently handicapped by the burden of his years. He was a member of the United States Supreme Court. Mr. Bates of St. Louis, who had been favored by Greeley and many others, might have been chosen as the compromise candidate but for the vigorous efforts of the Illinois men, the staunch Lincoln support of the Indiana delegation, and the preferences of several individuals, one of them being Wilmot.

Not less interesting as a sidelight on the situation at Chicago is the story told in the life of David Dudley Field, by his brother, Henry M. Field. David Dudley Field was one of the leaders of the New York Bar, and perhaps the

HORACE GREELEY

From the age of fifteen until his death, forty-six years later, Greeley was a newspaper man. The New York *Tribune* was founded by him in 1841, when he was thirty years old, and as its editor he came to wield an influence unprecedented in American journalism.

GREELEY EXAMINES A FAMILIAR WEED

A pun at the expense of Greeley's fellow-editor and political opponent, Thurlow Weed of Albany.

most scholarly authority upon legal science and upon the codification of statutes in our entire history. It was David Dudley Field, with William Cullen Bryant, who had escorted Lincoln to the platform of Cooper Institute. At that time Henry M. Field was on the platform, and like his more prominent brother he was deeply impressed by Lincoln's speech. Mr. Field tells us that Thurlow Weed had dictated the names of the New York delegates to Chicago in the interest of Seward. David Dudley Field had gone to Chicago with Greeley (who acquired a delegate's seat in the convention by favor of Oregon), Mr. Field being simply a distinguished guest on the platform of the Wigwam. After the convention Henry J. Raymond, the eminent editor of the New York *Times,* attributed Seward's defeat —which Mr. Raymond regarded as a calamity —to his editorial rival Horace Greeley.

Greeley disclaimed the responsibility of having usurped the rôle of Thurlow Weed in playing the part of Warwick at the convention; but Raymond retorted that Greeley "awards to others the credit that belongs transcendently to himself," and proceeded with his accusations: "The great point aimed at was Mr. Seward's defeat; and in that Mr. Greeley labored harder, and did tenfold more, than the whole family of Blairs, together with all the gubernatorial candidates to whom he awards the honors of the effective campaign." Mr. Raymond further brought in the name of "Dudley Field who labored with equal energy in the common cause." Field had never been a Seward man, but had more recently left the Democratic party and become a Republican because, in his opinion, the Democratic party had surrendered to the slavery interests.

Mr. Field's legal experience had made him acquainted with the political methods prevailing at Albany, and he opposed Seward largely because of Thurlow Weed's activities, and of the relationship between the Albany politicians and certain commercial and franchise interests in New York City.

However much Mr. Greeley might, like Dudley Field, have been opposed to Thurlow Weed's dictation to the Chicago convention, he was working rather to defeat Seward than to nominate Lincoln. Even after the convention had concluded its work, Greeley, on May 21, 1860, declared: "I think that Judge Bates, to whom I never spoke nor wrote, would have been the wiser choice." David Dudley Field, however, while equally opposed to Seward's nomination, was definitely for Lincoln.

While the Four-State Committee was at work in David Wilmot's rooms, Mr. Field was holding consultations in his own room with Greeley and others, and his all-night efforts, coinciding with those that were under the influence of the Pennsylvania and Indiana men, succeeded, before the morning of nomination day, in making it reasonably certain that Lincoln, rather than Chase, Bates, or anyone else, was to be the second choice of several States having favorite sons to present: specifically, Cameron, Dayton and Collamer.

Lyman Trumbull of Illinois, who was serving in the Senate, and who had earlier turned away in Illinois from the Douglas Democrats and become a Republican and a warm supporter of Lincoln, was looking to the election of a new legislature for his return to the Senate for a second term. He was for Lincoln unselfishly, just as Lincoln was unselfishly favoring Trumbull's continuance in the Senate. But with an opposing presidential candidate other than Lincoln, Douglas was likely to sweep Illinois, and to carry with him a control of the legislature, and thus defeat Trumbull.

This had not a little to do with the tactics that packed the galleries of the Wigwam with Lincoln men, and intensified the atmosphere which, while defeating the powerful Seward organization, was favorable to Lincoln rather than to some other substitute for the New York statesman. In his valuable Life of Lyman Trumbull, Horace White remarks: "Seward was the logical candidate of the party, if, upon a comparison of views it were believed that he could be elected. One-third of the delegates of Illinois desired his nomination, and intended to vote for him after a few complimentary votes for Lincoln. There were some indispensable States, however, which many people believed Seward could not carry. In Pennsylvania, Indiana, New Jersey, Connecticut, and Rhode Island, he was counted too radical for the temper of the electors. Illinois was reckoned by Trumbull and other experienced politicians as doubtful if Seward should be the standard bearer."

As late as the 24th of April, Trumbull, writing from Washington to Lincoln, said that it was his impression that Seward would have the larger number of delegates and would be nominated, and that this was the prevailing belief at the Capital, even among those who did not favor Seward. "It was Trumbull's opinion," Mr. White says, "that McLean was the only man who could succeed in the convention as against Seward, and he could do so only as a compromise candidate beginning with a few votes, but being the second choice of a sufficient number to outvote Seward in the end."

Although the convention was so enthusias-

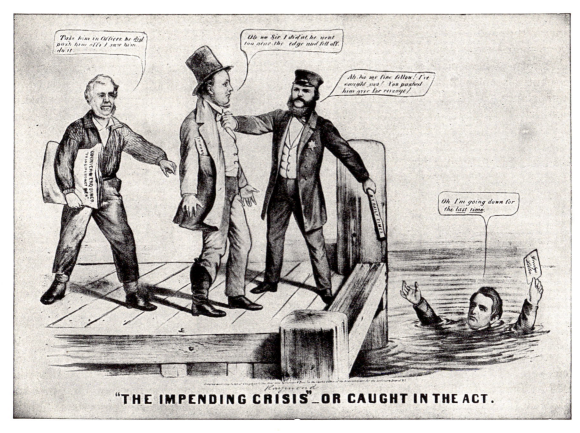

"THE IMPENDING CRISIS"—OR CAUGHT IN THE ACT.

James Watson Webb of the New York *Courier and Enquirer* supports Henry J. Raymond of the *Times* in accusing Horace Greeley of having caused Seward's defeat for the nomination at Chicago. This is a drawing by Louis Maurer, one of a notable series of lithographed posters published by Currier & Ives during the campaign of 1860.

tic, and the party acquiescence in the result so cheerful and unbroken on the whole, there was at first no slight sense of disappointment; and much bitterness was privately displayed on the part of the Seward following.

Mr. Bancroft, Seward's biographer, reviews the situation ably and accurately from the standpoint of his subject. He describes the perfect New York political machine with Weed as commander-in-chief, with Governor Morgan and Henry J. Raymond as Weed's lieutenants, and with William M. Evarts as the official spokesman. They had badges, banners, bands and music, and organized parades to divert and impress the people of Chicago.

"The early appearance of Horace Greeley at Chicago," says this writer, "was an evil omen to the followers of Seward. It startled the irrepressibles that he was staying at the Tremont House where the Bates and Lincoln men had their respective headquarters, and that he was making it his first aim to defeat Seward. His peculiar head, manners, and dress attracted attention wherever he went. The curious, hoping to learn something of his plans, swarmed about as he passed along the streets and through the hotel corridors. To western farmers and backwoods politicians he was an oracle. They were impressed when they heard him insist that Seward could not carry New York or the doubtful States, but that Bates could do so and, in addition, win over Missouri where there was to be an election in the summer. With ceaseless activity and self-assurance, he hurried from delegation to delegation to coax or warn the undecided."

Let my readers bear in mind that this convention was the most critical in the history of the United States with the sole exception of the Democratic gathering at Charleston, and

that these individuals—Horace Greeley, Thurlow Weed, and other personages on that Chicago stage—were playing with the destinies of
America. These pictures, therefore, of personalities are of primary rather than of casual
importance. Mr. Bancroft expresses the opinion that "but for the original anti-Seward influence, which Greeley's actions at Chicago
greatly emphasized,
there seems to be no
room to doubt that
the popular call for the
New York Senator's
nomination would
have been obeyed, in
the expectation that
the money and en-
thusiasm that this
would call forth would
carry a sufficient num-
ber of the doubtful
States to assure his
election."

Mr. Bancroft holds
that the Pennsylvania
influence turned the
scales against Seward:
"Know - Nothingism
was still a strong in-
fluence in Pennsyl-
vania politics. In no
State had the hostility
to foreigners been more bitter or of longer
duration. Thaddeus Stevens, who nearly
a generation before had saved the State
public-school system from destruction, was a
member of the convention and was one of the
most resolute of Seward's opponents." Stevens is quoted as having said repeatedly:
"Pennsylvania will never vote for the man
who favored the destruction of the common-
school system in New York to gain the favor
of Catholics and foreigners." Thaddeus
Stevens was a man of fanatical intensity, and
his opposition to Seward was probably more
bitter than that of Greeley.

Since this attack upon Seward by Pennsylvanians and other elements in the Chicago convention may cause curiosity in the minds of
present-day readers, I think it may be well to

DAVID DUDLEY FIELD
(1805-1894)

The distinguished New
York lawyer whose influ-
ence at Chicago was
thrown against Weed's dic-
tatorial championship of
Seward. He became a
noted advocate of reform
in the methods of legal
procedure.

digress for a moment and answer inquiries
once for all. When the New York Legislature
assembled in January, 1840, Seward, who was
then Governor, made recommendations in his
message dealing with the conditions that prevailed among many thousands of newly arrived immigrants. In proposing the establishment of separate schools for the children of
foreigners, with instruction to be given in their
own languages, and by teachers of their own
religious faith, Governor Seward was following the advice of the famous Dr. Eliphalet
Nott of Union College, Dr. Luckey, a leading Methodist clergyman, and many other
Protestants.

Mr. Alexander, in his "Political History of
the State of New York," adds the following
information: "The suggestion created an unexpected and bitter controversy. Influential
journals of both parties professed to see in it
only a desire to win Catholic favor, charging
that Bishop Hughes of New York City had inspired the recommendation. At that time, the
Governor had neither met nor been in communication with the Catholic prelate; but, in
the excitement, truth could not outrun mis-
statement, nor could the patriotism that made
Seward solicitous to extend school advantages
to the children of foreign parents, who were
growing up in ignorance, be understood by
zealous churchmen." To this clear statement
it may be well to add the remark that in those
days no such thing as compulsory education
had been thought of, and the public schools
had no provisions fit for the needs that Governor Seward was so generously considering.
His plan may not have been a feasible one, but
it did him credit rather than otherwise. Certainly Lincoln would not have been in sympathy with the bigotry that was in part responsible for Seward's defeat and his own success
at Chicago.

Just as New York Democrats had been represented at Charleston by two contrasting elements—a delegation of cultivated gentlemen,
and another of Tammany politicians—even so
at Chicago the Seward hosts contained the cultivated idealists like George William Curtis,
and a trainload or two of New York heelers
led by Tom Hyer, a prize-fighter and ward

politician. Local influences had much to do with the results. As the Douglas men had met with unyielding resistance in South Carolina, just so, in less degree, had the atmosphere of the new Western metropolis been unfavorable to the leader who was doubtless the private choice of a great majority of the delegates themselves, as well as of their constituents. The three Republican editors of New York State, Horace Greeley, Thurlow Weed and Henry J. Raymond, carried their differences to the open forum of public opinion, with Weed especially bitter and exasperated.

Mr. J. H. Barrett, in his useful work on "Abraham Lincoln and His Presidency," sums up in the following paragraph some of the factors in the defeat of Mr. Seward:

He had long been a public man, writing and speaking much, from the days of his epistolary controversy with the Governor of Virginia onward, and had placed himself among the foremost of those called radicals. Old prejudices thus engendered had been persistently nursed, and were not to be at once overcome. "Americans" complained that he was on too cordial terms with Archbishop Hughes, and alleged that he had made unallowable submissions to foreign and Roman Catholic influences. His course on other questions—Anti-Masonry and Anti-rentism in particular—as well as his ultra position in regard to slavery, had alienated from him a portion of his late party in his own State. The division into Seward Whigs and Fillmore Whigs, with the consequent prolonged altercations, had left antagonisms somewhat allayed, but not extinguished. There were objections, also, to certain New York political methods, and to what was deemed an unseemly lobbyism at Albany, assumed by some (however unjustly) to be in danger of finding shelter or toleration at Washington, should Mr. Seward become President.

Seward had left Washington, and had waited at his quiet home in Auburn for con-

SEWARD'S GRAND STARRING TOUR.

KING RICHARD III.—UP WITH MY WIGWAM! HERE WILL I LIE TO-NIGHT.

The New York Senator was greatly disappointed when he failed to receive the presidential nomination of his party; but as the weeks passed he accepted the situation gracefully and became the principal speaker in the Republican campaign. The cartoon shows him as a member of the Wide Awakes, an organization formed to promote the candidacy of Lincoln and remembered especially for its torchlight parades in costume.

vention news. No man could have accepted the results in a finer spirit than Seward, who made over at once, for Lincoln's benefit, the slogan that he had prepared to be used in his own prospective campaign, namely: "Let the watchword of the Republican party be 'Union and Liberty' and onward to victory"! His letter of thanks to Weed was equally worthy of a man of his patriotic spirit. He was able to say with sincerity that his candidacy was not a matter of his own seeking. To his friend Senator Sumner of Massachusetts he wrote in similar vein. He expressed a preference for rest and retirement, and wrote to Weed that he was "contented to quit with the political world when it proposes to quit with me, but I am not insensible to the claims of a million of friends, nor indifferent to the opinion of mankind."

He merely thought it well not to rush in at the beginning of the canvass, but to wait a little until it should be seen that he was wanted for the public interest. There could never have been any doubt of Mr. Lincoln's appreciation, and of Seward's important future in case of Lincoln's election. He was soon to tour the country, and especially the States of the West and Northwest, as the most eloquent and eagerly welcomed orator of all those engaged in prosecuting the Lincoln campaign.

At the Chicago convention, the tributes of individuals had followed rather than preceded the balloting. Thus it was when rising to make the nomination of Lincoln unanimous that Mr. Evarts found opportunity to eulogize the leader in whose behalf he was speaking. Mr. Andrew of Massachusetts in a brilliant speech accepting the results, called Seward "the brightest and most shining light of this generation, him who—by the unanimous election of the foes of our cause and our men—has for years been the determined standard-bearer of liberty." And there were other tributes to Seward, as the convention, without dissent, nominated Lincoln by acclamation.

The speaker on behalf of the Illinois delegation, acknowledging the generous action of the Seward leaders, was not less eloquent in his references to Governor Seward, who had upon many occasions "risen to the very height of moral sublimity in his conflicts with the enemies of free institutions." A man whose sheer strength as a party leader has lessened his availability for elective office, in view of the varying local exigencies of a federated republic like our own, is by no means disqualified for appointive office under a President who seeks to strengthen his administration by selecting his Cabinet from men of diverse background. Thus Mr. Seward was to head the cabinet as Secretary of State, Governor Chase of Ohio was to become the great finance minister, Mr. Cameron of Pennsylvania and Mr. Bates of Missouri were also to enter the cabinet, as was Caleb Smith of Indiana, Gideon Welles of Connecticut and one of the kinsmen of the tribe of Blairs.

I might conjecture, at the cost of many pages, and with the help of many previous conjecturers, upon what would have happened (1) if Seward had been nominated: (2) if, having been nominated, he had been defeated by Douglas; (3) if, having won at the polls, he had stood face to face with the situations resulting from the secession movement. He had been defeated at Chicago on the earnest plea that he could not be elected, and that one faction or other of the Democrats would win. In the case of his defeat would his nomination at Chicago have saved the country from immediate civil war, while postponing the slavery issue until another crisis had arisen?

If elected, Mr. Seward could not have compromised his principles in regard to slavery; but he might have been actuated by his non-resistance views to allow the Southern States to withdraw without precipitating civil war. The student of political history can never avoid reflecting upon possible alternatives, as he studies the decisions that have shaped the careers of men and nations through all recorded periods. We know that the issues of war and peace were involved in the decisions made by party conventions in 1860, and it is hard to think of Seward as a War President.

The Compromise That Made Lincoln Famous

The "rail-splitter" in campaign symbols—Illinois packs convention galleries—A candidate first-choice at home and second-choice else-where—Cordial support of rivals, who later entered Lincoln's Cabinet

WHEN THE CIRCUMSTANCES of politics have lifted a man to a post of high authority, the qualities that his neighbors had long recognized are brought to the attention of millions. Often, on the other hand, capacities that familiar associates have not known how to estimate are brought to light, when tested in some public crisis. The man might be of heroic mould, yet never find the opportunity to prove it. Opportunities sought but not gained may make all the difference between the immortal fame of a Lincoln and comparative oblivion.

In Lincoln's case, obviously, the opportunity lay in the chance of nomination by the Republican convention at Chicago in 1860. His career turns upon that convention as the pivotal event. He might indeed have lived to render useful public service for a long time to come, even if he had not defeated Seward and been chosen as the standard-bearer of a party that was hopeful of success in the campaign. One of his competitors at Chicago, Judge McLean, a member of the United States Supreme Court from Ohio, was already seventy-five years of age. Lincoln would not have reached that age until 1884, almost a quarter of a century later, and nine-

ABRAHAM LINCOLN IN 1860
A photograph by Brady, made in New York at the time of the Cooper Union address, less than three months before the nomination at Chicago. It is said that Lincoln himself once remarked that this portrait and that speech made him President.

teen years after his assassination. Lincoln himself had a great regard for Judge McLean, and had long admired Senator Crittenden of Kentucky. Both of these veterans were near the end of distinguished careers that were built upon foundations of struggle and effort in Lincoln's own Ohio-valley country.

If Lincoln had not been nominated for the Presidency, he might within a few years have been appointed to the United States Supreme Court by a President Chase or a President Bates or a President Seward, to succeed a jurist like McLean. Or, what is more probable, he might have gained a seat in the United States Senate, to succeed a Douglas, and to sit as a colleague of Trumbull. In either case it is reasonable to suppose that he would not have been lifted to solitary pre-eminence, among the statesmen of the Civil War period. His larger opportunity came, however; and he proved himself equal to it. It lies in human nature, where the people of a country possess in common some moral standards, and some training in the principles of democratic government, to set upon pinnacles those men who seem to them to personify whatsoever is just and righteous in public leadership.

With Lincoln thus established in the minds and hearts of his countrymen, it is not strange that research into the facts of his life was continuing, with greater zest than ever, more than fifty years after his assassination. In a later chapter I shall make some allusions to the nature of these efforts to cast new light upon biographical details. In the present chapter, I am recounting the methods and circumstances of his nomination. It is natural enough that biographers should show more interest in the personal and private aspects of a hero's life than in the conditions that had made it possible for them to discover him. They take politics, like weather, for granted. American politicians, however, can never forget the fact that the fate of statesmen under our system is largely determined by the outcome of political conventions. In those conventions the elements of chance and accident are often so important as to be beyond the control of the most skilful strategists.

Millions of intelligent women now realize that national politics is no longer merely a man's out-of-door game, reaching its climax of excitement every four years. The study of political methods acquires a serious and intelligent place. Women citizens will not neglect the new books upon Lincoln's domestic life; but they will be far more interested than ever before in his principles as a statesman and his tactics as a politician.

How he fared, then, in the Chicago convention is worth the summary and review that I am presenting, as we find him crossing the threshold of his illustrious period of national leadership. Entrance upon the great stage of action, involving the present and the future well-being of the American Republic, was to turn for Abraham Lincoln upon one competitive ordeal, namely, the balloting of the delegations in a party convention.

To this goal his efforts of thirty years had been the approach. He had studied party methods and presidential politics with unflagging diligence. He had formed mature convictions about public affairs, and had learned to express his views without rancor but with resistless logic. His life had been singularly free from personal controversy. Even in his long and sometimes intense party conflicts with Douglas, he had not been betrayed into quarrelsomeness or vindictive speech. Even if the country had discovered him somewhat suddenly, it was not the hazardous selection of an untried man that the convention made. There was discovery on the Illinois prairies of a man who was the equal of his rivals in intellectual and moral stature, and in legal and political training. Moreover, he was superior to all the others in the essential factor of availability.

However keen his disappointment, no rejected candidate sulked in his tent. Each one accepted the results of the convention with dignity and good will, although in one way or another the Chase men, like the supporters of Seward, could not hide the belief that their own candidate was a superior person. The praise of Lincoln in the flight of years has become so unqualified, and his name is spoken with such reverence by political idealists, that it is now difficult for the average citizen to keep in mind the fact that Senators Seward and Chase, like Senator Sumner of Massachusetts, were regarded as men breathing a loftier atmosphere than the favorite son of Illinois. It was to the credit of these world-famed, scholarly, and eloquent anti-slavery leaders that they quickly overcame their prejudices. They now re-read Lincoln's speeches carefully, and accepted him on his merits as a man of convictions, of ability, and of capacity for statesmanship. But they were not wrong in the view that convention strategy had been responsible for Lincoln's success.

A few months before the convention Lincoln had begun to think of himself, not indeed as a leading candidate, but as a possible compromise choice. He realized that if Seward's nomination were not achieved on the first ballot he would probably be defeated. Salmon P. Chase, although the man who stood second in prominence, would not be likely to win where Seward had lost. McLean was too old, but Bates of Missouri, by reason of strength in the border Slave States, seemed a likely compromise. Yet Lincoln realized that the selection of Chicago as the convention city might prove advantageous to a candidate supported by local sentiment. He was now in

HONEST ABE TAKING THEM ON THE HALF SHELL.

Here Douglas is pictured as a "soft-shell" Democrat and Breckinridge as a "hard-shell," referring to the distinctions then made at the North between the Democratic factions on the slavery question. This campaign poster, by Louis Maurer, portrays Lincoln in a genial mood, and he remarks: "These fellows have been planted so long in Washington that they are as fat as butter. I hardly know which to swallow first." Douglas had been in the Senate for thirteen years, and Breckinridge had not only served in the House but was then in his fourth year as Vice-President.

high favor at home. The Chicago *Tribune* had come out strongly for him early in February, and various local Illinois newspapers were urging his name well in advance of the State convention which had been held on May 9th and 10th at Decatur.

Herndon says: "His recent success had stimulated his self-confidence to unwonted proportions. He wrote to influential party workers everywhere. I know the idea prevails that Lincoln sat still in his chair in Springfield and that one of those unlooked-for tides in human affairs came along and cast the nomination into his lap; but any man who has had experience in such things knows that great political prizes are not obtained in that way. The truth is, Lincoln was as vigilant as he was ambitious, and there is no denying the fact

that he understood the situation perfectly from the start."

Norman B. Judd had managed to bring the convention to Chicago, and Lincoln wrote to Judd intimating that it would not hurt him to fail of the nomination, but it would hurt him if he should fail to have the support of the Illinois delegates. There were only a few days between the Illinois convention, meeting at Decatur, and the national gathering. As regards this State convention, Lincoln said he was "too much of a candidate to go, and not quite enough of a candidate to stay away." He finally went, and a demonstration was staged that played a great part in his victory at Chicago a few days later.

Richard J. Oglesby, a friend of Lincoln's who afterward became Governor, happened to discover that Lincoln in his youth had been employed to split rails on a farm in the Decatur vicinity. He found John Hanks, Lincoln's kinsman and fellow-worker of those early days, and together they brought two or three rails into the convention, carrying a banner upon which was inscribed: "ABRAHAM LINCOLN THE RAIL CANDIDATE FOR PRESIDENT IN 1860." The convention was in a mood for something of this kind, and its endorsement of Lincoln was wildly enthusiastic.

Dr. Barton recording this incident says: "Seward no longer had standing with the State delegates of Illinois. The effect upon the country was hardly less picturesque than that upon the Decatur convention. The name and fame of Abraham Lincoln were borne aloft on the rails which he had split while a laborer in the Prairie States. John Hanks became notable in Illinois political gatherings. He accompanied Oglesby on various expeditions. The bringing in of the rail was a feature in several ratification meetings; John C. Frémont rode a considerable distance toward the White House on the sobriquet of 'Pathfinder.' Abraham Lincoln was destined to go down to fame as 'Rail-splitter'."

At the opening of the campaign the cartoonists caught and made convenient use of this emblem. The whole country became familiar with it, as used in the lithographed campaign posters that took advantage of the purely accidental episode of the rails in the Illinois State convention. The enthusiasm of the Decatur body gave confidence to the Illinois delegates; and the convenience of access brought to Chicago not merely the official delegation, but practically all the Republican politicians of the State, in order to press upon the national convention the merits of their candidate. Lincoln and his Illinois supporters had been careful not to antagonize the friends of other candidates; but they were skilful in taking advantage of the anti-Seward sentiment in various delegations. This assiduous local effort, most of it spontaneous but wisely directed, contributed decisively to the final result.

The only opposing demonstrations were those organized on a lavish scale in the interest of Seward. But with all his qualities of loyalty and sincerity as a Republican, Thurlow Weed's methods as a political manipulator in New York State proved to be a positive detriment to Seward's candidacy. It is possible that if the convention had met in Ohio, at Columbus or Cleveland, Senator Chase would have been nominated. He had been disappointed, however, in the Ohio convention of March 3rd. It had declared him the first choice of Ohio Republicans by a vote of 385 to 69, but it had left the choice of delegates to district conventions and he had failed to secure the benefit of a rule requiring action as a unit.

Judge McLean of Ohio held to the presidential ambitions that he had cherished for decades. Senator Ben Wade, who was Chase's colleague at Washington, was ambitious in

"THE NIGGER" IN THE WOODPILE.

Published by Currier & Ives, 152 Nassau St N Y

An 1860 application of a phrase that later came into general use. Greeley assures Young America: "You can safely vote our ticket, for we have no connection with the Abolition party; but our platform is composed entirely of rails split by our candidate." Nevertheless, Young America is sure that his eyes do not deceive him. He sees the colored gentleman enclosed within the fence rails.

his own interest. Up to the opening of the convention at Chicago, Chase was not only hopeful, but fairly confident. On the first ballot, however, he and his friends realized that their cause was lost. He felt entitled to solid support from his own State; but of the Ohio votes Chase received only 34, while 8 were captured by Lincoln and 4 were cast for Judge McLean. On the second ballot Ohio gave Chase 29, Lincoln 14, and McLean 5. On the third, Chase held only 15, while 29 went to Lincoln and 2 to McLean.

In a private letter written a few days after Lincoln's nomination, Chase declared: "I suppose that nobody doubts that, had the Ohio delegation manifested the same disregard of personal preferences which was exhibited by the New York, Illinois, and Missouri delegations, and given to me, as the nominee of Ohio, the same earnest and genuine support which was given to Mr. Seward, Mr. Lincoln and Mr. Bates by those delegations respectively, my vote on the first ballot would have largely exceeded Mr. Lincoln's." Of course, without unanimity and aggressive effort on the part of the Ohio delegation, Mr. Chase had no chance.

There is no evidence that Lincoln had sanctioned the use of improper methods, although political life in 1860 was not free from the taint of bribery and corruption. Whether or not appointments to the Cabinet, and to other lucrative and coveted offices, were due to pledges made at the critical moment of the convention by Mr. Judd and the Lincoln managers, there is no reason to think that Lincoln had authorized the use of such means.

"THREE TO ONE YOU DON'T GET IT."

When the conventions of 1860 came to an end there were three candidates opposing Lincoln: Douglas, Breckinridge, and Bell. The cartoon is a rather subtle interpretation of the meaning of the pawnbroker's "three balls." Lincoln can hardly hope for an advance on his bundle of fence rails if the national Democracy, with President Buchanan as the White House watchdog, can stand him off.

Doubtless there is some evidence that the Pennsylvania delegation was assured that Mr. Cameron would be considered for a high position, and the same thing may have been true as regards Caleb Smith of Indiana and one or two others. There was no lack of adroit management, but it would be overstraining minor details to assert that Lincoln's nomination had been brought about by deliberate bargaining. The gradual development of his strength as a political leader in Illinois sufficiently accounts for his nomination, when the tide had turned against Seward.

Lincoln had known so well the temper of

southern Illinois and the border States that he had not antagonized certain conservative elements, as had Seward and Chase. Nevertheless, in his great contest with Douglas he had completely gained the support of the more radical anti-slavery sentiment of northern Illinois. He had known how to speak to Kentucky from the bank of the Ohio at Cincinnati, and he had taken precisely the right tone in addressing the people of Missouri when he looked across the muddy stream from Atchison, Kansas. He had gained friends and influence in Indiana to the eastward and in Iowa to the westward.

His recent appearance in New York and New England had gained for him the favorable acquaintance of many leading men who were not committed to Seward. Above all, the Cooper Union speech had paved the way for the decisive support of Horace Greeley, who was at that time the most influential personage in the political life of the United States. Thus it was that with the "field" against Seward, all the circumstances of time and place were skillfully utilized by the Lincoln men. The convention majority, which had either to accept Seward or agree upon an acceptable compromise leader, finally made the decision behind the scenes in the secret conferences and caucuses of the night before the first ballot was taken.

Lincoln was preferred not merely because he was the one man who could beat Seward in the convention, but because it was believed that he could in the election carry the necessary States which for one reason or another could not be carried by Seward. The process of natural selection had been going on for a long time. Many are called but few are chosen. In situations of such anxiety and danger as those of 1860, something more than ambition is necessary, in the physical, mental, and moral constitution of a simple citizen, to give him strength for the facing of the terrible risks and responsibilities of leadership. Events were to prove that above all the other able and outstanding men whose names were under discussion at the Chicago convention, Lincoln had the qualities of patience, firmness, judgment and courage requisite for the crisis.

In the course of time, many letters and documents have been brought to light that disclose the mental attitude of statesmen in the convention period of 1860. In the case of Seward as well as Chase, one discovers along with much that gives evidence of public spirit and devotion to the principles of the Republican party, the quality of self-appreciation, with something of vanity and egotism. Leaders of this type who have achieved influence and popularity on their proved merits, are sometimes a little spoiled by the flattery of their followers. That was true of Seward and Chase in the Republican group, as also of Douglas and Jefferson Davis, the Democratic leaders.

I do not believe that any one of these men, however, had allowed personal ambition or blinding vanity to dominate his motives or control his actions. All had risen to great positions, and had shown moral courage under severe tests. Their ambition was justified, and their self-esteem was not inordinate. My only object in referring to these traits, more clearly disclosed in later memoirs and discovered letters, is merely to set in contrast the characteristics of Abraham Lincoln. He had been trying a law case in Chicago in March or early April, and on returning to his home wrote the following letter to an Ohio Republican Congressman:

Springfield, Ill., April 6, 1860.

Hon. R. M. Corwine.

My dear Sir:

Reaching home yesterday after an absence of more than two weeks, I found your letter of the 24th of March. Remembering that when a not very great man begins to be mentioned for a very great position, his head is very likely to be a little turned, I concluded I am not the fittest person to answer the questions you ask. Making due allowance for this, I think Mr. Seward is the very best candidate we could have for the North of Illinois, and the very *worst* for the South of it. The estimate of Gov. Chase here is neither better nor worse than that of Seward, except that he is a newer man. They are regarded as being almost the same, seniority giving Seward the inside track. Mr. Bates, I think, would be the best man for the South of our State, and the worst for the North of it. If Judge McLean was fifteen, or even ten years younger, I think he would be stronger than either, in our state, taken as a whole, but his great age, and the recollection of the deaths of Harrison and Tay-

THE NATIONAL GAME. THREE "OUTS" AND ONE "RUN".
ABRAHAM WINNING THE BALL.

This is a Currier & Ives lithographed poster caricature, one designed to be purchased and displayed by Republicans during the campaign. It shows all the four candidates—Bell, Douglas, Breckinridge, and Lincoln—playing a game that was one of baseball's predecessors, probably "One Old Cat," or Town Ball. Lincoln's three opponents have all been put out on fouls. Lincoln alone scores a home run. Douglas attributes Lincoln's success to the fact that he had a rail to bat with (the rail being labeled "Equal Rights and Free Territory"). Bell's "Fusion" bat indicates the projected co-operation of the Douglas Democrats and the moderate Constitutional Union party. The term "National Game," as used in 1860, is to be interpreted in a political rather than a sports sense. Baseball had not yet attained such distinction as later caused it to be known as "the national game."

lor, have, so far, prevented his being much spoken of here.

I really believe we can carry the State for either of them, or for any one who may be nominated; but doubtless it would be easier to do it with some than with others.

I feel myself disqualified to speak of myself in this matter. I feel this letter will be of little value to you; but I can make it no better, under the circumstances. Let it be strictly confidential, not that there is any thing really objectionable in it, but because it might be misconstrued.

Yours very truly,

A. LINCOLN.

This letter, written only about five weeks before the Chicago convention, shows how little Lincoln was asserting himself above others, although he had become as definitely a candidate as any of the men whom he named. On May 1st, he wrote a letter to Senator Trumbull, then in Washington, marked "private," as follows:

Springfield, May 1, 1860.

Hon. L. Trumbull
Dear Sir:

In my last letter to you I believe I said I thought Mr. Seward would be weaker in Illinois than Mr. Bates. I write this to qualify the opinion so far as to say I think S. weaker than B. in our close Legislative districts; but probably not weaker taking the whole State over.

We now understand that Douglas will be nominated today by what is left of the Charleston convention.

All parties here dislike it—Republicans and Danites [anti-Douglas Democrats], that he should be nominated at all; and Doug. Dem's that he should not be nominated by an undivided convention.

Yours as ever,

A. LINCOLN.

On May 2nd he was able to write to Mr. Corwine as to his own prospects. This letter, like the two I have quoted above, appears in the volume of "uncollected letters" published in 1917. He proceeds to give his own estimate of the situation:

First I think the Illinois delegation will be unanimous for me at the start, and no other delegation will. A few individuals in other delegations would like to go for me at the start, but may be restrained by their colleagues. It is represented to me by men who ought to know, that the whole of Indiana might not be difficult to get. You know how it is in Ohio. I am certainly not the first choice there; and yet I have not heard that anyone makes any positive objection to me. It is just so everywhere as far as I can perceive. Everywhere, except here in Illinois and possibly Indiana, one or another is preferred to me, but there is no positive objection. This is the ground as it now appears.

This letter was written about a week before the enthusiastic Illinois convention that endorsed Lincoln. It shows a perfectly clear understanding of the situation at large. With all their resources and opportunities for obtaining accurate estimates, both Seward and Chase were at the same time writing letters that show how completely they failed to grasp the facts.

Published in the edition of Lincoln's complete works, there is a letter written to the Hon. Samuel Galloway of Ohio, on March 24th, in which Lincoln said:

EDWARD BATES

Judge Bates had presided over the Whig national convention in 1856, and was a leading candidate in the balloting for the presidential nomination at Chicago in 1860. He had been a member of Congress from Missouri more than thirty years earlier. Bates became Lincoln's Attorney-General, serving from March, 1861 to September, 1864.

If I have any chance, it consists mainly in the fact that the whole opposition would vote for me, if nominated. (I don't mean to include the pro-slavery opposition of the South, of course). My name is new in the field, and I suppose I am not the first choice of a very great many. Our policy, then, is to give no offense to others—leave them in a mood to come to us if they shall be compelled to give up their first love. This, too, is dealing justly with all, and leaving us in a mood to support heartily whoever shall be nominated. I believe I have once before told you that I especially wish to do no ungenerous thing toward Governor Chase, because he gave us his sympathy in 1858 when scarcely any other distinguished man did. Whatever you may do for me, consistently with these suggestions, will be appreciated and gratefully remembered.

Other letters written by Mr. Lincoln show that he was carefully and accurately observing the course of politics in every State, East and West, where Republicans were active. On May 12th, several days before the Chicago convention, in answer to an inquiring correspondent as to his tariff views, Lincoln wrote: "In the days of Henry Clay I was a Henry Clay tariff man, and my views have undergone no material change upon that subject. I now think the tariff question ought not to be agitated in the Chicago convention, but that all should be satisfied on that point with a presidential candidate whose antecedents give assurance that he would neither seek to force a tariff law by executive influence, nor yet to arrest a reasonable one by a veto or otherwise."

To sum it up, Lincoln was nominated by taking skillful advantage of the opportunities the convention afforded for a candidate against whom there was no marked antagonism, and who therefore might reap the reward that was to come to the man who was the second choice of the largest number. Seward, who headed the list as a first choice, failed because he was

SALMON PORTLAND CHASE   JOHN McLEAN   BENJAMIN FRANKLIN WADE

OHIO'S THREE CANDIDATES FOR THE REPUBLICAN PRESIDENTIAL NOMINATION IN 1860

Governor Chase was born in New Hampshire, and in 1860 was completing his fourth year as Governor of Ohio. He had previously served a six-year term in the Senate. Mr. Lincoln brought him into his cabinet as Secretary of the Treasury, and in 1864 appointed him Chief Justice of the United States in succession to Taney.

Judge McLean was born in New Jersey. He had been a member of Congress from Ohio, resigning to go to the Supreme Court of his State. He had also been Postmaster-General in the cabinets of Monroe and John Quincy Adams. Since 1829 he had been an Associate Justice of the Supreme Court, serving for the first seven years under Chief Justice Marshall. He was seventy-five years old at the time of the Chicago convention, and died early in the following year.

Senator Wade was born in Massachusetts. He had been a member of the upper house since 1851. Previously he had been prosecuting attorney for Ashtabula County, Ohio, and a judge of the circuit court.

not the second choice of the States that had other favorite sons to present. Chase was too positive a character, and too advanced a radical, to be acceptable for compromise purposes.

The Republican party had to derive its support in 1860 from coalition elements not yet thoroughly fused. As Mr. Barrett puts it, the new movement was made up of "the old Free-Soil party, of Anti-Slavery Whigs, of conservative Whigs, of Wilmot Proviso Democrats, Anti-Nebraska Democrats, Anti-Lecompton Democrats (results of three distinct and successive schisms), and of Anti-Slavery Americans. It had also recruits in fact and in expectancy from the conservative Americans and the old-line Whigs." Mr. Seward had been too long identified with certain factions to be acceptable to the others.

Lincoln's friends, therefore, were able to ·crystallize on behalf of their candidate the convention's demand for a nominee who would be nowhere on the defensive. Of three Republican newspapers at Chicago, the two leading ones were supporting Lincoln strongly, and the third, edited by a friend of Seward, was

for Lincoln as a second choice, and in the event of Seward's success was for "Seward and Lincoln" as the completed ticket. Local influences, therefore, were brought to bear upon the convention with great effect; and those who understand something of convention psychology will realize the importance to be attached to the fact that Mr. Judd had been able to bring the convention to Chicago.

At a certain stage in the midnight caucuses, behind closed doors, there had been some reason to think that Edward Bates rather than Lincoln might be chosen by the anti-Seward delegates from Pennsylvania and certain other States. If the convention had been held at St. Louis rather than Chicago, assuming that local efforts of a similar sort would have been made, it is reasonable to venture the guess that the Missouri candidate might have become the choice of the convention.

Mr. Bates had been born in Virginia in 1793, and had gone out to St. Louis as a young lawyer in 1814 at the age of twenty-one, where he rose to a position of great influence at the Bar and in public affairs. He had taken strong ground against the repeal of the Missouri Compromise in 1854, had presided over the Whig national convention in 1856, and had now become a Republican through the march of events. He was a man of solid merit, whose talents spoke for themselves, and who was not politically ambitious. He was soon to enter Lincoln's cabinet as Attorney General.

Remarkable as was Lincoln's rapid rise from relative obscurity before 1860 to well-advertised leadership of a new party that was now assuming control of Congress and promising to seize masterful supremacy in national affairs, it was not less remarkable that he had reached this high place without incurring resentment or ill-will on the part of any disappointed aspirant. In his own preliminary candidacy, he had said nothing in public or in private that could be brought to light as unfriendly or offensive to Seward, to Chase, to McLean, to Bates, to Ben Wade, or to any other man who was an active or receptive candidate. It was easy, therefore, for him to invite them into the cabinet; and it involved no

swallowing of pride, or efforts at appeasement, to bring about their cordial acceptance.

These rival candidates gave their best efforts to the support of the Lincoln ticket and the Chicago platform, in the campaign that followed. There was indeed resentment toward Horace Greeley on the part of Seward's New York friends, notably Thurlow Weed and Mr. Raymond of the *Times*. But they did not visit this feeling in the slightest measure upon Mr. Lincoln. In like manner Mr. Chase found it hard to forgive men of the Ohio delegation who had destroyed at Chicago the prestige of that full support by one's own State without which a candidate fails in a national convention. But Lincoln and his managers had been careful to avoid aggressive preliminary work in the home territory of other prominent candidates. Thus it was not necessary afterwards to bind up the wounds of offended competitors, or to promise rich spoils as an inducement to bring into the field the needed champions who might otherwise have been sulking in their tents.

THE POLITICAL RAIL SPLITTER
Lincoln, with the Negro-headed mallet, splits the Union in two while Horace Greeley and Senator Seward look on in dismay.

CHAPTER IX

Northern Democrats Nominate Douglas

The adjourned convention meets at Baltimore—The Charleston breach is not closed—The regulars adopt the Cincinnati platform of 1856, and nominate Douglas with acclaim and high expectations

IN THEORY THE CITIZEN is sovereign and votes as he will. In practise he is restricted to alternatives. The major parties present their candidates and the voter merely takes his choice. He may follow the banners of his own party. He may shift his allegiance and seek the enemy's camp. He may sulk in his tent and refuse to vote. Or he may throw away his ballot in more or less futile protest, by casting it for the candidate of a casual minor group or remnant. There are times of transition, when leaders in convention can by no means guarantee the support in full strength of the supposed normal membership of the party. Such a time, obviously, was the crucial year 1860.

It is fortunate when the leaders are discerning enough to write platforms and select nominees in full accord with the views and preferences of a fairly homogeneous party membership. In 1912 the Democratic convention was thus discerning and successful, while the Republican convention misjudged the temper of the voters. In 1928, on the other hand, the Republican convention made decisions notably responsive to the prevailing opinion of the rank and file, while Democratic leadership, in an acquiescent and harmonious convention, failed to heed the clear warning of voting masses that were essential to success.

In the four years between the contest of 1856 and that of 1860, shifts and changes were so rapid as to baffle all time-serving and cautious politicians, while greatly arousing the hopes and energies of those leaders for whom success was dependent upon re-alignments. The Pierce and Buchanan administrations were bringing the long period of Jeffersonian and Jacksonian Democratic ascendency to a climax, and to an approaching downfall. Wiser leadership might have given the party four more years of power, but an early break

was inevitable. The North with its free labor and its industrial growth, its fresh tidal waves of hard-working European immigrants, and hundreds of thousands of new quarter-section farms in the West, was beginning to feel that the perennial slavery issue in American politics was a nuisance. The Slave States correctly sensed this growth of anti-Slavery feeling in the North and West.

Abraham Lincoln, while never an extremist, and while always logical and legal-minded, had become, without any apologies, a true leader of this maturing Northern and Western sentiment. Stephen A. Douglas, through the

HARMONY AT THE CONVENTION

The Democratic convention that reassembled at Baltimore, on June 18th, was a continuation of the ineffective Charleston meeting which had adjourned late in April. It was a stormy six days' session, marked by bitterness and controversy that resulted in the withdrawal of Southern delegates, and the launching of rival tickets.

compromising period from the days of Van Buren to those of Buchanan, with his political genius and his astonishing gifts of popular leadership, was the unrivalled inspirer of Democratic dogma and shibboleth, and master of party policy. With his Squatter Sovereignty doctrine, he had been hailed as the man who had found a practical way to safeguard the expansion of the cherished institution of the South. But in the sharp Kansas test it had turned out—according to Slave-States' opinion—that the Douglas idea was not a principle, but rather a frail and treacherous expedient.

And so the Lower South, ceasing to find salvation through Douglas, was determined at all hazards to destroy this once adored political idol. Lincoln had always held Douglas as a clever politician but an unreliable statesman. Seward and many Eastern Republicans had suddenly begun to praise Douglas, because of his unexpected aid in the defeat of the Lecompton Constitution and his bitter quarrel with President Buchanan. But the very fact of this co-operation in the Senate between Douglas and Seward, as against the effort of the Southern men aided by the Buchanan Administration to admit Kansas as a pro-Slavery State, had made the South the more determined to reject Douglas as a presidential candidate.

It is barely possible that the South might have forgiven Douglas if he had been willing to run in 1860 on Jefferson Davis's platform. On the other hand, there were many who thought that the Douglas men of the North might have been willing to vote for Breckinridge or some other pro-Southern candidate if the platform had gone no farther than to have copied the resolutions adopted at Cincinnati in 1856. Upon this all Democrats had been in agreement, and upon it Buchanan had been elected. But, while the North regardless of party had shifted to firmer anti-Slavery ground, even so the South had become by far more aggressive. After the Kansas disappointment, the John Brown episode, and the Speakership fight, there was resistless advance to the new position that Slavery should have full recognition, and that there should be

genuine guaranties for its future safety. The South was for the Union, if there could be assurance of absolute equality of the rights of States and of their citizens everywhere, under the Constitution. But the South was now opposed to the Union, unless measures to prevent the extension of Slavery were to be positively rejected as national policy. With the Republicans under Lincoln's leadership regarding Douglas and his doctrines as temporizing and unprincipled, and with the Lower South, for opposite reasons, holding the same opinion as to the shifty and uncertain character of Douglas and his professed panacea, it seems plain to us in the retrospect that there was small chance for a Douglas victory at the polls. The Chicago platform was now before the country. It was essentially hostile to Slavery as a thing wrong in itself and foredoomed to extinction. Lincoln was also before the country, as a candidate in accord with the platform. Evidently Douglas was now in an ambiguous position—Laodicean and unavailable for 1860, standing on the abandoned field of 1856, "whence all but him had fled."

But what is clear after the smoke of battle has lifted cannot always be seen at the moment by men on the fighting line. The Democratic convention reassembled at Baltimore on the 18th of June. Forty-six days had elapsed since the adjournment at Charleston. Thirty days had gone by since the Republicans had nominated Lincoln at Chicago. But Democratic factions remained obdurate. They had taken small counsel of expediency, each faction really believing that the situation must compel the other to yield its ground. The Douglas camp was more defiant than ever. The South, with more tact and less declamation, remained as unyielding as a perfect syllogism in the face of Douglas sophistry. Jefferson Davis was like a school-master insisting upon the only correct answer to a simple problem in arithmetic.

After a stormy convention of six days, from which most of the Southern delegates had withdrawn, Douglas was nominated amid scenes of enthusiasm, in the apparent belief that he would sweep the country. The Douglas men supposed that the South would have a

THE MODERN PYRAMUS AND THISBE

Thisbe by John C. Breckinridge. *The Wall* by James Buchanan. *Pyramus* by Stephen A. Douglas.
Pyramus speaks: "O, wicked Wall, through whom I see no bliss!"—"A Midsummer-Night's Dream,"
Act V, Scene 1.

Vanity Fair cartoons by H. L. Stephens, in 1860, were usually based upon scenes from Shakespeare's plays. *Pyramus* and *Thisbe* are lovers separated by a wall through which they converse. The reference here is to the fact that President Buchanan finally supported Breckinridge in the campaign, rather than Douglas. Breckinridge, it will be remembered, had been elected Vice-President in 1856, on the ticket with Buchanan.

change of heart and support their ticket, rather than run the risk of having the Black Republicans win, with the consequence of Secession and probable war. In like manner they contended that the North would prefer Douglas as the best of all the candidates, in view of the dangerous alternatives.

There were about two hundred and fifty delegates in the convention as it assembled. Caleb Cushing of Massachusetts, who had been the presiding officer at Charleston, resumed his place at Baltimore, conspicuous in his old-fashioned Websterian coat of blue material with brass buttons—always smooth-tongued, plausible, and competent, while in sympathy with the Southern leaders and the anti-Douglas element.

The Seceders from the Charleston convention had followed their plan of coming quietly to Richmond, where they organized informally, and waited for signals from the larger body at Baltimore. The principal delegations at Richmond were those of South Carolina, Alabama, Florida, Louisiana, Mississippi, Georgia, and Texas. The strong and brilliant South Carolina delegation was headed by Hon. R. B. Rhett; and one of its members, Hon. Andrew E. Calhoun (son of John C. Calhoun) as chairman of the Committee on Organization, presented the name of Hon. John Erwin of Alabama as permanent president of the convention. Leading the Alabama delegation was the redoubtable orator, W. L. Yancey, and the influential A. B. Meek.

In his opening remarks Mr. Erwin dwelt upon the disinterested efforts of the Southern delegates to reach agreement at Charleston, and declared that their withdrawal had been approved by their constituents. He expressed it as his understanding that this Richmond body "shall not act definitely—that we shall make one more attempt at reconciliation. But," he added, "we must yield nothing, whether we remain here or whether we go elsewhere. Wherever we go, we must demand the full measure of our rights. The serpent of 'Squatter Sovereignty' must be strangled. (Vehement applause). What! Are we to be told that we are not to go into the Territories and enjoy equal rights, when that principle has been settled by the Supreme Court of our country?"

Upon motion of Mr. Hatch of Louisiana, the convention unanimously declared that: "As the delegations from all the States represented in this convention are assembled upon the basis of the platform recommended by a majority of the States at Charleston, we deem it unnecessary to take any further action upon that subject at the present time." This Rich-

LITTLE STEPHEN TRYING TO CLIMB INTO A
VERY HIGH CHAIR

A tempting bowl of federal patronage pap is on the table, awaiting the successful aspirant to the presidential high-chair. But when little Stephen Douglas tries to mount the chair, using the Negro and the Kansas stool, he meets with disaster.

mond group was entirely harmonious, and it was, plainly enough, awaiting the opportunity to accept an invitation from Baltimore and to make one more attempt to overcome the Douglas control of a reunited national convention.

It is necessary to keep in mind the fact that the Douglas men at Charleston had a clear majority of the delegates, but slightly less than a majority of the States—California and Oregon acting with the Lower South, with Massachusetts (under the lead of Cushing and Ben Butler) also anti-Douglas, and with New York, as usual, playing politics. The platform committee at Charleston, made up of one member from each State delegation, had reported a majority document that included the Jefferson Davis resolutions. A minority (pro-Douglas) report presented the Cincinnati platform of 1856. The Douglas delegations, having a larger aggregate membership, had promptly adopted the minority report.

This action had caused the break at Charleston, the Southern delegations led by Alabama withdrawing as duly set forth in our chapter on the Charleston convention. The full membership of the convention had been exactly equal to the membership of the Electoral College, or to the united membership of both houses of Congress. After the withdrawal of the Southern delegates, the original convention of 303 members was reduced to a voting strength of 252. The platform having been adopted, there arose the practical question, in balloting for a presidential nominee, whether the two-thirds rule should still be construed to mean 202 votes, or two-thirds of those actually remaining and voting, which would have required only 168.

Southern delegations remaining in the convention, especially those of Kentucky, Tennessee, and Virginia, with ten members non-seceding from Georgia, insisted strongly upon the view that in order to secure the support of the party as a whole the candidate must receive the support of 202 votes. Gen. Cushing, the presiding officer, upheld this construction of the two-thirds rule, and he was sustained by a vote of 141 to 112. As previously stated, a total of fifty-seven ballots resulted in giving Douglas 145½ on the first, 150 on the fourteenth, 152½ on the twenty-third, and, with practically no further variation, 151½ on the fifty-seventh, with Guthrie next, polling 65½. Under either construction of the two-thirds rule, Douglas had signally failed at Charleston, enough Southern men remaining in the convention to see that the substantial majority for the Illinois leader should never rise to the two-thirds level.

Mr. Halstead, writing at the time, gives the following account of the Baltimore situation as the convention was about to open on Monday morning, June 18th:

THE POLITICAL INVALID

STEPHEN A. DOUGLAS: "Do you think I'm a very sick man, Doctor!"
DR. JONATHAN: "Yes, Stephen; the Charleston air disagreed with you decidedly, and I'm afraid that of Baltimore won't be much better."

The Democratic politicians assembled in great force in Washington City the week before the convention was called to meet in Baltimore, and caucused the matter in the usual way.

On the Saturday before the meeting of the convention, the politicians concentrated in Baltimore, where a much greater crowd than that at Charleston came together. It was not, however, numerically so great, by many thousands, as that at Chicago. The weight of the outside pressure was for Mr. Douglas. The talk about the hotels was principally favorable to Mr. Douglas, whose friends were full of confidence and determination. It was evident that he could not be nominated without the division of the party, and placing two tickets in the field; yet his friends gave no symptoms of flinching from taking any responsibility. The hostile feeling between the factions of the Democracy was even more embittered than at the time of the adjournment at Charleston, and the more the points of difference were caucused, the more intense was the warfare.

The debate in the Senate, during the recess—the speeches of Douglas and Pugh on the one hand, and Benjamin and Davis on the other—had served to deepen and exasperate the controversy, and make it more personal in its nature, and therefore more incapable of compromise. The friends of Mr. Douglas, encouraged by the presence and support of Soulé of Louisiana, Forsyth of Texas, and other strong Southern men, assumed an arrogance of tone that precluded the hope of amicable adjustment of difficulties.

As at Charleston, every person and passion and prejudice was for or against Mr. Douglas. The opinion was almost universal that the friends of Mr. Douglas would be able to nominate him, and they were certainly resolved to give him the nomination at any hazard or sacrifice. There was no question, however, that the New York delegation had the fate of the Convention in its keeping; and while it was understood that the strength of Mr. Douglas in the delegation had been increased, during the recess, by the Fowler defalcation (the substitute for Mr. Fowler being reported to be a Douglas man), and by the appearance of regular delegates who were for Douglas, and whose alternates had been against him at Charleston, it was obvious that the action of the politicians of New York could not be counted upon in any direction with confidence.

Rumors were circulated before the meeting of the convention, that a negotiation had been carried on in Washington, by the New Yorkers with the South, the object of which was to sell out Douglas, the Southerners and the Administration offering them their whole strength for any man New York might name, provided that State would slaughter Douglas. On the other hand, it appeared that Dean Richmond, the principal manager of the New Yorkers, had been engaged in private consultations with Mr. Douglas and his fast friends, and had pledged himself, as solemnly as a politician could do, to stand by the cause of Douglas to the last.

The President of the Charleston convention, Hon. Caleb Cushing of Massachusetts, opened the Baltimore gathering with a clear statement of the business left unfinished at Charleston, and the Secretary read the final resolution that had been adopted as follows:

"Resolved, that when this convention adjourns today it adjourn to reassemble at Baltimore, Md., on Monday, the 18th day of June, and that it be respectfully recommended to the Democratic party of the several States to make provision for supplying all vacancies in their respective delegations to this convention when it shall reassemble."

As this resolution appears on its face, it would seem to us merely an obvious matter of routine. But its effect and its construction held the Baltimore convention through five days of embittered controversy, with the result of a sharp break at the end of the fifth day. Two rival conventions were sitting on the morning of the sixth day, with Gen. Cushing, the Massachusetts chairman, himself a solemn Seceder. He was promptly and unani-

DOUGLAS AND HIS EVIL SPIRIT
Throughout a long career, and particularly in the debates with Lincoln, Douglas had assumed positions on the slavery question which cost him support in one section or another. It is easy to believe that the slavery issue alone stood between him and the Presidency.

mously appointed chairman of the anti-Douglas Southern faction, sitting in the great Hall of the Maryland Institute.

There had been immediate disagreements in the main body over the question whether or not those delegations that were pausing tentatively at Richmond should be welcomed to their original places as members of the national convention. Finally a Committee on Credentials was appointed to deal with membership problems in detail. With Georgia, Florida, Alabama, Louisiana, Mississippi, Texas, and Arkansas absent from the convention, there were only twenty-six members of the Credentials Committee; and a majority was now in position to handle the difficult problem of membership as fully in the interests of Douglas as could be done with any semblance of justice. Majority and minority reports were made on the fourth day, the convention holding brief sessions while waiting for the settlement of membership contests. Meanwhile, rival mass meetings every evening in Monument Square were intensifying the bitterness of factions.

Judge Krum of Missouri at length presented the long-awaited majority report, and Mr. Stevens of Oregon that of the minority. Of the twenty-six members, the minority included nine, with the partial support of a tenth. The majority report favored new delegations from several Southern States, while the minority held with great ability to the logical view that the original Charleston delegates were entitled to resume their seats at their own pleasure. The points at issue as to seats in the convention were complicated and numerous; and the convention acted by separate vote upon each detail. With considerable variation the votes ran about 150, as a rule, for the majority report, and about 100 for the minority. Under great excitement not only in Baltimore but throughout the entire country—the proceedings having been telegraphed everywhere—the convention took final action in favor of the report of the majority, during the evening of the fifth day.

Then came the motion to proceed to the nomination of candidates for President and Vice-President, and this was the signal for the sensational action that had not been unexpected. Mr. Russell, head of the Virginia delegation, arose and declared that since the action of the convention had "become final, complete, and irrevocable," as regards credential questions, it had become his duty "by direction of a large majority of the delegation from Virginia, respectfully to inform this body that it is inconsistent with their convictions of duty to participate longer in its deliberations."

The galleries were tumultuous, and rather favorable than otherwise to the Virginia withdrawal. Mr. Moffatt then announced that eight out of the ten votes of North Carolina were retiring. "The rights of sovereign States and of gentlemen of the South," said Mr. Moffatt, "have been denied by a majority of this body. We cannot act as we conceive in view of this wrong." The Tennessee delegation, after consulting for some time, announced that nineteen of the twenty-four would retire and five would remain. Ten Kentucky delegates decided not to participate further, while nine remained. In the hour or two of informal discussion, there was here and there a Southern delegate who denounced bolting, and who held on doggedly to his former faith in Douglas. But the net result was to transfer a considerable number of Border State delegates from the national body to that of the Lower South seceders.

In the morning session of the sixth day, Mr. Cessna of Pennsylvania called for a vote upon his resolution to ballot for candidates for President and Vice-President. At this point Gen. Cushing begged the indulgence of the convention to say that he deemed it his duty to resign his seat as presiding officer, and to take his place with the Massachusetts delegates. Mr. Halstead says that the Northwesterners

THE GREAT MATCH AT BALTIMORE, BETWEEN THE "ILLINOIS BANTAM", AND THE "OLD COCK" OF THE WHITE HOUSE.

Cock-pit cartoons were much in vogue while cockfighting was a popular pastime. Douglas as the Illinois bantam has come out best in a fight with Buchanan, the old cock of the White House, and boasts that he can beat Breckinridge, the Kentucky chicken. President Buchanan's pre-convention attitude had been unfavorable to Douglas, who nevertheless received a presidential nomination at Baltimore. Later Buchanan endorsed Breckinridge, though he was not active in the campaign.

cheered him violently as he retired from the chair to show their joy in getting rid of him, while the Baltimore spectators in the gallery cheered him in approval. Governor David Todd of Ohio, one of the vice-presidents of the convention, took the chair. Ben Butler of Massachusetts hereupon announced the desire of the majority of the Massachusetts delegation to withdraw from the convention, and not many minutes later the suave Cushing, sitting modestly in the rear at the Maryland Institute Hall, was escorted up the aisle to take the chair of the Seceding Convention and to help give it the appearance of regularity.

As the first ballot was being taken in the main convention there was some brilliant debate, with the distinguished Pierre Soulé of Louisiana as the star orator. He predicted that the people of the South would not respond to the call made upon them by the Secessionists. His own State of Louisiana, he declared, was unwilling to risk her future and the future of the Union upon impracticable issues and theoretical abstractions.

The first ballot produced a total vote of 190½. Of this number, 173½ were for Douglas, 10 for Guthrie, 5 for Breckinridge. Although a second ballot was not necessary it was actually taken, with the result of 181½ for Douglas, 7½ for Breckinridge, 5½ for Guthrie. The nomination was made unanimous with a storm of cheers.

The convention with entire accord adopted the more reasonable construction of the two-thirds rule. Mr. Church of New York, Mr. Hoge of Virginia, and Mr. Clark of Missouri secured the acceptance of a motion as follows:

"Resolved unanimously, that Stephen A. Douglas of the State of Illinois, having now received two-thirds of all votes given in this convention, is hereby declared, in accordance with rules governing this body, and in accordance with the uniform customs and rules of former Democratic National Conventions, the regular nominee of the Democratic party of the United States to the office of President of the United States."

It was argued and sufficiently demonstrated that Gen. Cushing's construction of the two-thirds rule at Charleston, as accepted by the convention there, did not follow earlier convention practice. Distinguished individuals, among them Horatio Seymour of New York, Mr. Mason of Kentucky, and Mr. Dawson, chairman of the Pennsylvania delegation, who

had not been original Douglas men, joined in a series of warm tributes to the nominee. The convention seemed, for the time, to have so played upon the emotions of its entire membership as to have dispelled altogether the fear that Douglas might be crushed between the upper and the nether millstone.

Several things happened during an evening session, the first being the announcement of the names of the National Executive Committee, which was to carry on the Douglas campaign. A Tennessee delegate gave notice that the Southern men in the convention had agreed to nominate for Vice-President the Hon. Benjamin Fitzpatrick of Alabama. No other name was offered, and Mr. Fitzpatrick was chosen without opposition. Although the convention had refused to add anything to the Cincinnati platform of 1856, Governor Wickliffe of Louisiana for the Resolutions Committee offered one further plank by way of interpretation for the sake of its supposed influence upon Southern votes. This new resolution was adopted viva voce and was as follows:

"Resolved, That it is in accordance with the interpretation of the Cincinnati Platform, that during the existence of the Territorial Governments the measure of restriction, whatever it may be, imposed by the Federal Constitution on the power of the Territorial Legislature over the subject of the

THE CITY AND HARBOR OF BALTIMORE, FROM AN EARLY ENGRAVING
In 1860, Baltimore was the third largest city in the United States, New York being first and Philadelphia second. Our illustration, from a print made in London, is of a period just twenty years earlier.

domestic relations, as the same has been or shall hereafter be finally determined by the Supreme Court of the United States, should be respected by all good citizens and enforced with promptness and fidelity by every branch of the General Government."

Two days later Mr. Fitzpatrick declined the nomination for Vice-President, and the National Committee substituted the name of the Hon. Herschel V. Johnson of Georgia. Mr. Johnson, then in his forty-eighth year, was a well-known lawyer and politician, who had once been a United States Senator, and afterwards for four years Governor of his native State. (After the secession of Georgia in 1861 Mr. Johnson became a member of the Confederate Senate at Richmond. He lived until August, 1880).

Certain Southern men at Baltimore who spoke so bravely for Douglas, and certain Northern men at Baltimore—like Cushing, Butler, and Hallett, of the Massachusetts delegation—whose Southern sympathies won them so much applause from the anti-Douglas Seceders, were equally wrong in assuming to speak for their respective localities. Thus Governor Wickliffe of Louisiana had predicted a sweeping Douglas vote in his part of the South on the passage of his resolution. But on Election Day Louisiana gave only 7,625 votes for Douglas, with three times as many for Breckinridge, and almost three times as many for Bell. The proportion for Douglas in Alabama was still smaller, and his votes in Mississippi were a negligible 3,000.

Looking in the other direction, the Seceders' Convention at the Maryland Institute Hall had been persuaded by Messrs. Cushing and Butler to believe that Massachusetts Democrats would support the Southern ticket rather than vote for Douglas. But on Election Day Massachusetts cast 106,533 votes for Lincoln, 34,372 for Douglas, 22,331 for Bell and Everett, and only 5,939 for the Breckinridge ticket.

The clever but opinionated Caleb Cushing of Boston was presiding at the Maryland In-

HERSCHEL V. JOHNSON

If Douglas had been elected in 1860 this man might have been President of the United States during the political crisis that resulted in secession and war; for Douglas himself died in June of the following year, three months after the date of inauguration. Johnson was a native of Georgia, a graduate of the State University, and had been a member of the United States Senate, a judge of the Superior Court, and Governor. He endeavored to prevent Georgia from seceding, but after the decision was made he sided with the Confederacy.

stitute in an atmosphere of adulation that seems to have warped his judgment altogether in respect to the real feeling of Massachusetts voters. But this merely illustrates my remarks at the beginning of this chapter, to the effect that 1860 was a year of radical drifts and changes. Northern Democrats had ceased to follow slavishly the leadership of Southern statesmen. And the South had abandoned all pretense of affiliation with a non-sectional, homogeneous, national Democratic party. Douglas, meanwhile, had been so aspersed in the Senate that he declared that he had only sought vindication at Baltimore, and was ready to relinquish all ambition to be President, caring only for the principles and policies involved.

PROGRESSIVE DEMOCRACY—PROSPECT OF A SMASH UP.

Published by Currier & Ives, 152 Nassau St. N.Y.

As a result of the various Democratic conventions in 1860, there were two pairs of nominees representing that party. The Douglas-Johnson team in the cartoon pulls in one direction, while that of Breckinridge and Lane tries to draw the same Democratic wagon in the opposite direction. Meanwhile the advancing Republican locomotive, manned by Lincoln and Hamlin, provides the prospect of a smash-up. "A Squatter Sovereign," the Douglas teamster, conveys the impression that Tammany and Douglas had joined forces. Buchanan, still nominal head of the party, is the Breckinridge teamster; and he declares his willingness to have the organization split rather than allow Douglas to run away with it. This was one of the famous series of Currier & Ives posters.

CHAPTER X

Breckinridge the Southern Choice

A seceding convention at Baltimore launches the Breckinridge-Lane ticket—Full endorsement of Cotton-States delegations at Richmond—The Douglas men embittered, and the Solid South wrecks the party

LINCOLN AT HIS HOME in Springfield, Illinois, was following the proceedings at Baltimore with absorbed interest and keen political intelligence. He had expected Douglas to run; and a principal argument in his own favor at Chicago had been his demonstrated ability to meet his old rival at the polls in Illinois and the Northwest. Having gained the nomination, Lincoln was intent upon winning the election. He was aware that he had made his own path smoother and safer by helping to divide the Democrats. Although Douglas had secured a majority in the legislative

election of 1858 and thus retained his seat in the Senate, Lincoln had carried the State on popular vote.

Furthermore, with the winds of sentiment changing in Illinois, Lincoln had forced Douglas to take a tone more agreeable to Chicago, and therefore less agreeable to Charleston and New Orleans. Since Lincoln's nomination at Chicago, the South had spent a diligent month reading the Lincoln-Douglas debates. Printed in a cheap volume, the debates were accessible to every politician and literate voter. Southern men had now adopted the view that Lincoln

82

THE SPLIT-TAIL DEMOCRACY
The deed is done, their day is o'er,
Two possums fought at Baltimore;
Now let them scratch, now let them wail,
Old Abr'm has them "in a rail."

From the *Rail-Splitter*, Chicago, July 21, 1860.

was a dangerous and menacing radical, rather than a mere local nonentity selected by timid Northern politicians in conspiracy against the commanding leadership of Seward.

But while learning to view Lincoln's candidacy with dread because they discovered in him a man of fixed convictions and of undeviating purpose, they were still more strongly confirmed in their scornful rejection of Douglas as the leader of their own party.

On June 23rd, Lincoln was following the despatches in his Springfield, Chicago, and Louisville newspapers that kept him alive to the proceedings of four distinct Democratic bodies. Three of these were highly active, while the fourth, though significant and influential, was marking time. The first was the Senate at Washington, over which John C. Breckinridge of Kentucky was presiding in his capac-

ity as Vice-President of the United States. The second was the original party convention at Baltimore, dominated by Senator Douglas, with Governor Todd of Ohio now presiding. The third was the Seceders' Convention at Baltimore, with Gen. Cushing of Massachusetts presiding, but with men of Virginia and the Border Slave States in control. It was ready to adopt the majority platform that had been rejected at Charleston and that had included the famous Senate resolutions, presented by Jefferson Davis and approved with no party opposition except that of Douglas and Pugh.

The fourth body, dominated by South Carolina and Alabama, was still at Richmond, having adjourned to resume sessions on the 21st. Each of these four bodies played a major part in shaping the political history of 1860. Many of the delegates to the Richmond gathering of

Seceders had meanwhile gone to Baltimore, and several of them had entered the main convention—only to walk out again to join the new Secession movement at the Maryland Institute. But the South Carolina men, and some others, had preferred to remain at Richmond.

The Institute Hall was spacious, with seats for eight thousand spectators; and the galleries were packed as the Seceding delegates took their places in a mood of extraordinary satisfaction because of the atmosphere of harmony that prevailed. As temporary chairman, Mr. Russell of Virginia assured the delegates that they represented the majority of the people of the Democratic States and of the party. "They will look to you," he said, "to perform the functions of a National Democratic Convention, and you will be so recognized alike by the North and the South, the East and the West." Mr. Yancey and other members from the Lower South were on the floor, but men like Senator Bayard of Delaware, Mr. Ewing of Tennessee, Mr. Russell of Virginia, Mr. Stevens of Oregon, and delegates from the North, in association with members from Kentucky and the upper tier of Slave States, were in active management.

Ten States had no delegates at all, and these were Maine, New Hampshire, Rhode Island, Connecticut, Ohio, Indiana, Illinois, Michigan, Wisconsin and Minnesota. Cushing and Butler had led over the sixteen delegates of Massachusetts. One Vermonter had drifted in, and two casual New Yorkers. New Jersey was apparently absent, and South Carolina preferred to wait at Richmond. Pennsylvania was partly represented. By the time the evening session had convened the Lower South was strongly represented.

A good many Congressional leaders had by this time caught the trains from Washington and run up to Baltimore. Among these were extremist Southern Senators like Toombs of Georgia. Mr. Yancey, "who always wears a surface smile, twisted about in his seat with the unrest of intolerable felicity and glowed with satisfaction," to quote Mr. Halstead.

At the evening session, Mr. Cushing was escorted to his place as permanent president.

"He was instantly recognized by hundreds, and his familiar blue coat and brass buttons, his Websterian garments and Caesarian head, were hailed with extraordinary acclamation."

Not to amplify routine details, it will suffice to state that in this body there were no differences of opinion, and therefore the credentials committee reported a membership list that was instantly approved. In similar manner the majority platform brought up from Charleston was reported and adopted without dissent or discussion. This convention was doing business. Mere talking was sharply discouraged.

Nominations were in order, and it fell to the lot of the Hon. George B. Loring of Massachusetts to speak first. He complimented Southern statesmen who had come to his part of the North "fearlessly defending their principles—aye, and bringing the sectionalism of the North at their feet by their gallantry. We have admiration for this courage, and I trust to live by it and be governed by it." Mr. Loring then proceeded as follows: "Among all these men to whom we have been led to listen and admire and respect, there is one standing pre-eminently before this country—a young and gallant son of the South."

Whereupon he named John C. Breckinridge of Kentucky. The applause was enough to indicate the probable outcome. Mr. Ward of Alabama nominated a Virginia statesman, R. M. Hunter. Mr. Ewing of Tennessee nominated Daniel S. Dickinson of New York. An Oregon man presented Gen. Joseph Lane, a hero of the Mexican War, and now in the Senate from the new State of Oregon. The name of Jefferson Davis of Mississippi was offered but withdrawn, and Hunter's name was also taken out of the running.

A first ballot resulted in 81 votes for Breckinridge, and 24 for Dickinson. But the delegates from five States who had voted for Dickinson immediately announced a change of mind, and Breckinridge was chosen unanimously.

Mr. Green of North Carolina proposed Hon. Joseph Lane of Oregon for the Vice-Presidency, with the California delegation seconding the nomination. The delegations voted

THE POLITICAL GYMNASIUM.

Published by Currier & Ives, 152 Nassau St N.Y.

Sitting on the dumbbell which Edward Everett raises is his running-mate on the Constitutional Union ticket, John Bell. Horace Greeley, on the horizontal bar, is portrayed as trying to gain the nomination for Governor of New York. In the foreground is the editor of the *Courier and Enquirer,* James Watson Webb, boasting that he can beat any man in the party at turning political somersets. The boxers are the rival Democratic nominees, Douglas and Breckinridge. At the right is Senator Seward, crippled by tumbling from the nomination bar before he was fairly on. Safely poised on his fence rails is Lincoln, advising Greeley: "You must do as I did. Get somebody to give you a boost. I never could have got up here by my own efforts." The cartoon is by Louis Maurer.

unanimously for Lane on a roll call; and then the great audience in Institute Hall made a tumultuous and resistless demand for the thing they had most wanted, this being a speech by the incomparable Yancey of Alabama.

There was nothing of the appearance of the frenzied fanatic about this orator, whose name had become known in every hamlet of the United States as the most outspoken and irrepressible of the pro-slavery exponents and disunionists. Halstead's extended description of Yancey, writing at the moment of the Baltimore speech, presents an attractive personality, "frank and unassuming," "placid in appearance," "at perfect ease under all circumstances." "But you do not know him until you have heard him speak. His voice is clear as a bugle note, and at the same time singularly

blended with its music is a sharp, high, metallic ring, like that of a triangle of steel. . . . He speaks with great animation of gesture with his arms, meanwhile walking quietly up and down the platform."

Mr. Yancey believed that the Democracy and the Constitution—and through them the Union—were yet safe. "I am, however," he proceeded, "no worshipper at the shrine of the Union. I am no Union shrieker. I meet great questions fairly on their own merits. . . . I am neither for the Union nor against the Union—neither for disunion nor against disunion. I urge or oppose measures upon the ground of their constitutionality and wisdom or the reverse."

Speaking of Douglas Mr. Yancey said, "I will let Mr. Douglas rest where his friends

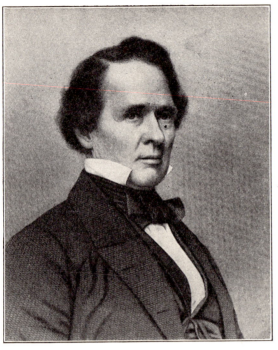

JOSEPH LANE
Nominated for the Vice-Presidency by the seceders' conventions at Baltimore and Richmond, on the ticket with Breckinridge. He was at the time serving as the first United States Senator from Oregon, having previously been Governor of the Territory and its Delegate in Congress. In the Mexican War, Lane had been commissioned a Colonel of Indiana volunteers and had risen to the rank of Major-General. His migrations had been typical of his period. He was born in North Carolina in 1801, had grown up in Kentucky and Indiana, and died in Oregon in 1881.

have placed him, contending, however, that they have buried him today beneath the grave of squatter sovereignty. The nomination that was made—I speak it prophetically—was made to be defeated and it is bound to be defeated."

Unfortunately, coming up from a State where audiences always hung spellbound upon his words for endless hours at a time, Mr. Yancey failed to sense the conditions at Baltimore. He greatly disturbed the managers of the convention by talking too long, and by ruining his previous reputation for tact. Having adopted a platform and nominated a ticket that was sure to carry the Lower South, there was anxiety to reassure the North. The last thing that the managers desired to hear was Yancey's disturbing creed of indifference to the future of the Union. They felt that with every sentence Yancey was frightening North-

ern votes away from the Breckinridge ticket.

"The people left the hall by hundreds; yet he spoke on as if unconscious that instead of captivating the multitudes he was boring them. Cushing became uneasy, nervous and fidgety. Yancey was speaking the people out of the hall and using up all the time with Alabama matters. It had been intimated that Burnett of Kentucky should respond to the nomination of John C. Breckinridge, but now there was no time for Burnett. . . . By talking so loud and long then and there, and putting himself and Alabama so prominently forward, he was identifying his name and the ultraism of Alabama, too intimately and conspicuously, with the movement represented in that hall."

There was only time for Gen. Cushing to accept the thanks tendered him by the convention, and to make a speech of one sentence as follows: "I do not intend to say anything more except to congratulate you upon the most felicitous termination of your labors both in the adoption of the platform and in the nomination of your candidates."

The convention that nominated Douglas had concluded its business at fifteen minutes before ten o'clock in the evening of June 23rd, and the rival convention that nominated Breckinridge—having been detained by Yancey's long speech—was adjourned *sine die* some forty-five minutes later.

The Douglas men had been blinded to the essential facts. The career of Douglas had been so conspicuously associated with the general pro-Southern Democratic program for almost a quarter-century that, until the shock of the Baltimore convention, they had not believed that gratitude for Douglas's past services was absolutely non-existent in the South. As Douglas, when the split came, began to see things in the true light, he urged his friends to withdraw his name. But this had become politically impossible.

With the South so relentless and bitter towards Douglas, however, the so-called "Dough-face" Democrats of the Northwest had found their spunk and spirit. A party split, like a family quarrel, cannot be vindictive on one side and remain meek and gentle on the other. In general, the Northern Demo-

BALTIMORE, A YEAR AFTER THE DEMOCRATIC CONVENTIONS OF 1860

A regiment of Boston light infantry, with artillery. swings into position in Monument Square, where in June, 1860, rival Democratic mass-meetings had been held during convention week. Baltimoreans had not realized that party strife was leading to Civil War.

crats stood strongly with Douglas, and New England repudiated the leadership of such Massachusetts "Dough-faces" as Cushing, Butler, Hallett, and Loring. Because their own man, Lane, was on the ticket, Oregon Democrats gave Breckinridge a slight preference over Douglas, while Lincoln carried the State into the Republican camp.

Illinois Democrats, however, gave Douglas 160,000 and Breckinridge only 2,400. Ohio, Indiana, Michigan, and Wisconsin were quite as emphatic as Illinois in their overwhelming repudiation of the Breckinridge ticket. The seven Northwestern States, Ohio, Indiana, Illinois, Michigan, Wisconsin, Iowa, and Minnesota—although every one of them was carried by Lincoln—gave Douglas such strong support as to justify fully his claims to party leadership. The aggregate vote for Douglas in these seven States was in round figures 660,000, while the Breckinridge ticket, with full opportunity for voters to give it endorsement, secured a total of only 29,500. Even

in the Lower South (except for Texas, which ran no Douglas electoral ticket) the preference for Breckinridge over Douglas was by no means as sweeping as was the relative support of Douglas by Northwestern Democrats. In the Border Slave States Douglas fared much better. In Missouri, indeed, he beat Breckinridge by almost two to one. In Kentucky Breckinridge beat Douglas by a two-to-one vote, but Bell carried the State handsomely.

With the break actually achieved, and two Democratic tickets in the field, it was inevitable that the bitterness engendered at Baltimore should not disappear in the activities of the campaign. Mr. Halstead observes that "the Northwestern delegates, on their return home, congratulated themselves upon the presumption that if they had ripped up the Democratic party they had shown the Republicans that they as Democrats were not dough-faces. The reflection that they were no more to be reproached as serfs of the South seemed sweet and ample consolation for all the struggles

RICHMOND PAUSES TO DEDICATE A STATUE
OF HENRY CLAY

On April 12, 1860, in the period when Southern States were
asserting the most extreme pro-slavery doctrine, the people
of Richmond dedicated a statue of Henry Clay. On the
same day, the people of New Orleans were similarly honoring the Kentucky statesman (see page 199), April 12th
being his birthday. Lincoln, earlier in this year 1860, had
written to Alexander H. Stephens that he had "hoped and
prayed that the gradual emancipation plan of Henry Clay
might lead to its [slavery's] extinction."

The Southerners have been ruling over niggers
so long they thought they could rule white men
just the same. The South should not go out
of the Union either. They would stay in and
sweat. The fugitive slaves might go to
Canada or to the devil and welcome, and their
masters after them. He never would trouble
his head about them any more. He did not
care whether the Fugitive Slave Law was enforced or not. He declared the South had
alienated her best friends forever, and must
now do the best she could for herself. He was
also disposed to disparage the Southern country, depreciate the resources of the South, and
magnify the evils that beset her."

The results were soon to show that Mr.
Halstead was justified in believing that this
conversation truly represented the feeling with
which the Northwestern delegates crossed the
Alleghanies as they returned homeward, and
indicated the extent and bearings of the political revolution which had shattered the long-
dominant party of Jefferson, Jackson, and
Van Buren.

It remains merely to add a Richmond post-
script to my extended story of the conventions
of 1860. The Baltimore conventions had
ended in the evening of June 23rd, and on the

and perils through which they
had passed, and the pangs they
had suffered in the dissolution of
the party."

Sharing a railroad seat with
one of these partisans of Douglas, Mr. Halstead found him
angry because the South showed
ingratitude after all the battles
the Northern Democrats had
fought for the benefit of the
Slave States. The Cincinnati
editor summed up this irate
Democrat's conversation in the
following terms: "He wanted the
South to be made to sweat under
an Abolition President. He was
glad Seward was not the Republican candidate, for he would be
too easy on the South. He hoped
Lincoln would make them sweat.

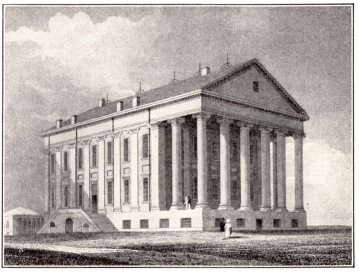

THE ORIGINAL STATE CAPITOL AT RICHMOND
Situated in a park on the highest ground in the city, the building has al-
ways been a landmark. It was completed in 1796, modeled after the famous
Maison Carrére, at Nimes in France, itself a relic of Roman architecture.
Our illustration is from an engraving made in 1831. Wings were added to
the building, at a later period.

A SCENE IN RICHMOND A YEAR AFTER THE CONVENTION OF 1860
An Alabama regiment marches through Capitol Square on its way to join the Army of the
Confederacy. Less than a year had intervened between political debate and armed strife.

24th the Southern delegates were passing through Washington on their return to Richmond and their various States, from Georgia and Florida all the way to Texas. On the 25th they were reinforced by Senators and Representatives leaving Washington, the long session having adjourned on that date. On the 26th, the South Carolina delegates, who still remained at Richmond, were joined by Yancey and Scott of Alabama, and by other party seceders from Virginia, Florida, Alabama, Mississippi, North Carolina, Georgia, Louisiana, and Texas, making a total group of about fifty. They met in an evening session on that date and adopted two resolutions. First, it was resolved, "That this convention approve of the platform of principles recommended by the majority report at the Charleston convention." Next, it was resolved, "That John C. Breckinridge of Kentucky, and Joseph Lane of Oregon, are, and they are hereby declared to be the choice, unanimously, of this convention, for President and Vice-President of the United States."

While this convention was small in membership, it was not obscure or neglected. It was assembled in what was then known as the Metropolitan Hall, and the Richmond *Enquirer* reported that "the galleries during the session were thronged, and while there was great enthusiasm, there was no one occasion in the slightest degree to disturb good order. All the proceedings were conducted with a calmness, dignity and decorum which we have never seen excelled." Thus ended the season of conventions, with four rival tickets extant.

"TAKING THE STUMP" OR STEPHEN IN SEARCH OF HIS MOTHER.

All four candidates for the Presidency in 1860 appear in this cartoon, and in addition there are President Buchanan and Governor Wise of Virginia. Most prominent is Senator Douglas, nominated by the Northern wing of the Democratic party, who proved to be the first presidential candidate to "take the stump," or carry on an active speaking campaign. He is here soliciting help from Bell, nominee of the Constitutional Union party, and from Governor Wise, explaining that in seeking a nomination he had fallen over a big lump of Breckinridge and had been lame ever since. President Buchanan is offering a stump to Breckinridge, nominee of the Southern Democrats and his own preference among the four candidates. Breckinridge replies that taking the stump will be of no use, for he feels that he has not got a leg to stand on. At the extreme right of the cartoon stands Lincoln, who made no speech at all in the campaign, declaring: "Go to it, ye cripples! Wooden legs are cheap, but stumping won't save you."

CHAPTER XI

What Manner of Men Are These?

The four candidates at their best—Lincoln increasingly approved as a
Republican type—Douglas a masterful leader, with a solid record—
Breckinridge an attractive figure and well-chosen candidate

EVEN BEFORE the contending tickets were officially proclaimed, the Lincoln biographers had taken the field in force. Miss Tarbell, author of one of the most important of the later lives of Lincoln reminds us that on May 19th, the day following the nomination at Chicago, five different biographies of the Illinois Rail-splitter were announced by the New York *Evening Post,* of which the best were those by W. D. Howells and David W. Bartlett. Mr. Halstead in the Cincinnati *Commercial,* two or three weeks later, made note of the report that fifty-two applications had been received by Mr. Lincoln from authors who wished to become his immediate campaign biographers. Many such volumes were written; few if any were authorized. Most of them did their best to create the distorted Lincoln traditions that have survived, in spite of the fuller knowledge and better-balanced estimates of writers who are primarily historians.

The analysis of character and motive, and the study of personality as such, are the principal pursuits of the serious novelist. The biographer whose methods are those of the novelist cares about historical situations only as they help to prove his thesis, whatever it may be, regarding the manner and the character of his hero as a private individual. Biographers of this class are indeed not unmindful of the more obvious facts of history; but they use these almost entirely as incidents that illustrate the dramatic career of the hero. The private lives of great men must always command the interest of readers; and sometimes the strictly personal biography of a political leader who is so placed by circumstances as to be identified with thrilling and fateful events, is written with intelligence and discernment and has value for its sidelights upon movements too general and profound to have been shaped by any individual.

Mr. Greeley, who had come to know Lincoln especially well, opened his well-known lecture with the following allusion to biographers of a certain kind: "There have been ten thousand attempts at the life of Abraham Lincoln, whereof that of Wilkes Booth was perhaps the most atrocious; yet it stands by no means alone. Orators have harangued, preachers have sermonized, editors have canted and descanted; forty or fifty full-fledged biographies have been inflicted upon a much-enduring public; yet the man, Abraham Lincoln, as I saw and thought I knew him, is not clearly depicted in any of these so far as I have seen. I do not say that most or all of these are

TOO MANY COOKS SPOIL THE BROTH
The divided opposition to Lincoln was largely responsible for his election. These three cooks—beginning at the left —are Breckinridge, Douglas, and Bell.

91

not better than my Lincoln—I only say they are not mine." Continuing, Mr. Greeley said that he sincerely hoped "to make the real Lincoln with his thoroughly human good and ill, his virtues and imperfections, more instructive and more helpful to ordinary humanity than his unnatural, celestial, apotheosized shadow ever was or could be." Mr. Greeley knew Lincoln in no such familiar and intimate way as did Lincoln's White House secretaries, Nicolay and Hay, who afterwards became his biographers. But the New York journalist knew Lincoln through his vast knowledge of public affairs, and through his acquaintance with a thousand other men, of all sections and all parties, active in the politics of several decades.

We find Greeley arriving at no disparaging conclusion; but his estimates are those of the political critic who has himself been a part of the movements that he describes, and he fixes Lincoln's superior place only after using the sifting processes of comparison and contrast. "Other men," he declares, "were helpful to the great renovation and nobly did their part in it; yet, looking back through the lifting mists of seven eventful, tragic, trying, glorious years, I clearly discern that the one providential leader, the indispensable hero of the great drama, faithfully reflecting, even in his hesitations and seeming vacillations, the sentiment of the masses—fitted by his very defects and shortcomings for the burden laid upon him, the good to be wrought out through him—was Abraham Lincoln."

It might be said, without attempt at paradox, that to understand Lincoln one must forget him long enough to read the biographies of a number of his contemporaries. At the time of his nomination Republicans were comparing him with the other candidates, and there was keen disappointment on the part of many Republicans who felt that Lincoln fell below even the irreducible minimum of personal qualifications and public experience requisite in the nominee of a great party.

The reader who studies the biographies of Lincoln exclusively is too likely to sweep away the mistaken and belittling estimates of Lincoln, so widely current in the summer of 1860,

with a kind of resentful scorn. The student would do well to read carefully the second volume of James Ford Rhodes's History of the United States, the fifth volume of James Schouler's History, and the corresponding volumes of the histories of Mr. McMaster and Professor Channing. They would find it instructive to read the biographies of Seward and Chase, and those of several other Republican leaders of the period, by no means ignoring the life of John McLean of the Supreme Court—who would have been nominated in place of Lincoln but for his burden of years, and who, with one other judge, Curtis of Massachusetts, had dissented from Chief Justice Taney's opinion in the Dred Scott case.

Especially, however, the reader would find it profitable to approach the study of the personal qualities and public character of Abraham Lincoln by means of a better acquaintance with the Democratic candidates, who were competitors in the presidential race of 1860. Differences within the Republican party had disappeared with commendable rapidity when the rank and file discovered that Seward, Chase, Sumner, Giddings, Bates, the Blairs, and all the other leaders were endorsing Lincoln with unqualified praise, and were carrying the party's banners with enthusiasm and without bickering. Lincoln himself declared that he was the humblest of all the Republican candidates. He was bearing himself without vanity, but with a simple dignity and a keen intelligence that fully reassured the Republican editors who proclaimed his merits in their influential newspapers all the way from Boston to the Pacific Coast. These included Medill at Chicago, Carl Schurz and others in the German press, Halstead at Cincinnati, Weed at Albany, McClure and Forney at Philadelphia, Greeley, Raymond, and Bryant in New York, Samuel Bowles at Springfield, Massachusetts, and many others—party journalism everywhere having reached the very height of its influence in that desperate campaign.

But having been nominated, Lincoln's concern was with the election, and with the relative strength of his opponent. He did not agree with the doctrines of Douglas, and did not always approve of his opponent's political

STORMING THE CASTLE
"OLD ABE" ON GUARD.
Published by Currier & Ives, 152 Nassau St N.Y.

Here are the four candidates for the Presidency of 1860. It is a pro-Lincoln cartoon, with Lincoln's rivals portrayed as trying to break into the White House. Douglas finds that his keys—"Regular Nomination," "Nebraska Bill," and "Non-Intervention"—will not open the White House door. Bell reports the approach of Watchman Lincoln. From a window in the White House, President Buchanan is endeavoring to help Breckinridge in, though he confesses that his strength is failing and Breckinridge in turn admits that he himself is too weak. Buchanan made only one speech in the campaign, expressing himself "in favor of Mr. Breckinridge because he sanctions and sustains the perfect equality of all the States."

methods. But the two men, in spite of long years of intense rivalry—personal and political—in the State of Illinois, had a high regard for each other's ability. And it is a remarkable fact that while each had every reason to know well the faults and failings of the other, they had never been enemies.

To the political student it is not quite satisfying to dismiss Douglas with the mere assertion that in his time he was the leader of the Democratic party and the most influential member of the United States Senate. They feel bound to inquire whether Douglas was merely a fluent debater and a spectacular but superficial politician, or whether he was in truth a statesman whose neglected reputation deserves to be re-established. The admirers

of Lincoln should remember that to undervalue his opponents, over whom he gained victories, is not to accord the highest honor to their hero. To cheapen and disparage Lord Beaconsfield is not to prove the matchless statesmanship of Mr. Gladstone.

In times like our own, when it is hard to find leisure for thinking as well as for reading, we are prone to identify statesmen of the last century by some one action. Douglas made the profound mistake of coupling the repeal of the Missouri Compromise of 1820 with his Kansas-Nebraska Bill of 1854, and his adherence to the non-intervention or squatter sovereignty theory as all-sufficing. It is a mark of his extraordinary influence and ability that he was able to carry such a measure through both Houses of Congress, only four years after the crowning work of Henry Clay, as supported by Douglas himself, who had in 1850 proclaimed the agreement of 1820 as sacred and unchangeable.

If Douglas had failed in this attempt at repeal, Kansas would automatically have entered the Union in due time as a Free State. With the Dred Scott Decision arousing new hopes in the South, the fight over the Lecompton Constitution became desperate and tragical. Douglas now found himself in heroic, almost single-handed combat with the Buchanan Administration, the Supreme Court, and the unrelenting and arrogant statesmanship of the slaveholding States. But for these extraordinary happenings of the six years before the campaign of 1860, the long previous record of Douglas would not have been relegated to oblivion.

I have written something of the earlier career of Douglas in a previous chapter; but now that in 1860 we find him a nominee for the Presidency, a few sentences of rapid allusion to his earlier career would seem to be in order. At the age of twenty, in 1833, he had arrived in Illinois after his youth in Vermont and western New York, with no money, but with ambition to become a lawyer. Mr. Clark Carr, who was well acquainted with both Douglas and Lincoln, summarizes the external facts regarding Douglas in a single paragraph: "Within ten years, after the friendless boy walked into that town [Winchester, in Scott County], he had been admitted to the bar, immediately becoming a successful lawyer; had been a member of the Illinois Legislature; had been Prosecuting Attorney; had been Register of the Land Office at Springfield; had been Secretary of State of Illinois; had been a Judge of the Supreme Court of Illinois, presiding upon the bench; and was on his way to Washington to take his seat in the Lower House of Congress, to which position he had been elected. When the Congressional term expired he was re-elected, and then re-elected again, each time by increased majorities. When about to enter upon his third term in the Lower House of Congress, he was elected to the United States Senate for six years. When that term in the Senate expired he was re-elected for another term, practically without opposition. Six years later he was confronted by Abraham Lincoln in the great debates; he was victorious, and was re-elected to a third term; upon this he served but little more than two years, when he died, at forty-eight years of age."

From the time that he had reached the constitutional age of thirty-five Douglas had been regarded as presidential timber, and his name had been presented for the office at three previous conventions before his nomination in 1860. At the age of thirty-five, he was slight and boyish-looking and had been only five years in Congress; so that his name was not seriously considered by Democrats outside of Illinois. But in 1852 he was a recognized power in the party, infinitely superior in ability and influence to Franklin Pierce; while in 1856 it was his very strength as the foremost statesman of his party that impelled him to withdraw gracefully in favor of the inoffensive and venerable Buchanan.

To understand Douglas it is necessary at once to study his personal characteristics, his amazing prescience, his independence of mind, and his commanding and authoritative position as the ablest debater and public speaker of his generation. His vindication of President Jackson in 1844 ranks as one of the great efforts in Congress. His speech in 1846 on the annexation of Texas and the Mexican War should be read in conjunction with Lincoln's speeches taking the opposite view. He was the staunchest advocate of the American claim to the entire Oregon country as bounded on the North by the parallel 54-40. He was the ablest and most intelligent critic of the Clayton-Bulwer Treaty; and his speech of 1853 was amply justified in its exact prediction of the embarrassments from which we obtained partial escape long afterwards by means of the second Hay-Pauncefote Treaty.

Douglas, rather than Clayton, should have been Secretary of State, with his views of our future interest at Panama and in Central America. He advocated the purchase of Cuba from Spain, and was an expansionist without apology, and with a more than Jeffersonian

THE POLITICAL ECLIPSE OF 1860 AS IT APPEARS NORTH.

Most of the poster caricatures of the campaign of 1860 were produced in New York. This one was published at Cincinnati. Bell, looking through his telescope, reports to Douglas that "the entire Northern limb seems to be eclipsed" by the shadow of Lincoln. Douglas thereupon remarks: "If that is the case, John, we had better fuse." The effort to defeat Lincoln did result in a fusion of electoral tickets in New York, Pennsylvania, Rhode Island, and New Jersey, in spite of which Lincoln carried all the Northern States.

belief in the future of the country. He was the foremost authority on railroad legislation. He was the exponent of the best methods by which to utilize land grants for the construction of western and trans-continental railway systems. He was an advocate of inland waterways. In short, he was a master of the problems of domestic and foreign policy.

Let our educational authorities say what they will about the processes of self-education by means of which Lincoln and Douglas—and many others only less eminent in that generation—had acquired their grasp of the problems of government; their knowledge of constitutional law and of political history, and, not

least, their admirable mastery of the English language, for accurate statement and for sentimental appeal, are remarkable.

As to his manners and appearance, Douglas was as unlike Mr. Lincoln as possible. Having taken up his residence in Chicago, and having gone at an early age to Washington, he had become urbane and polished in address, exceedingly careful in attire, always dignified, although perfectly at home with men of every class and rank.

A writer in the New York *Times,* probably Mr. Raymond himself, described Mr. Douglas in 1850, ten years before the presidential contest, in the following terms: "The Little Giant as he has been well styled is seen to advantage on the floor of the Senate. He is not above the middle height; but the easy and natural dignity of his manner stamps him at once as one born to command. His massive head rivets undivided attention. It is a head of the antique, with something of the infinite in its expression of power; a head difficult to describe, but better worth description than any other in the country. Mr. Douglas has a brow of unusual size covered with heavy masses of dark brown hair, now beginning to be sprinkled with silver. His forehead is high, open, and splendidly developed, based on dark, thick eye-brows of great width. His eyes large and deeply set, are of the darkest and most brilliant hue. The mouth is cleanly cut, finely arched, but with something of bitter, sad expression. The chin is square and vigorous, and is full of eddying dimples—the

JUDGE DOUGLAS AT THE WRONG DOOR

DOUGLAS: "Stand aside, Woman, and let me into the White House. I am going to live there the next four years."

GODDESS OF LIBERTY: "You can't come in, unless you are Abe-L."

Judge Douglas stood by the White House door,
    Asking for leave to come in.
The Goddess of Liberty barred the way,
    As an Angel resisting sin, sin, sin,
    As an Angel resisting sin.

From the *Rail-Splitter*, Chicago, September 3, 1860.

muscles and nerves showing great mobility, and every thought having some external reflection in the sensitive and expressive features. Add now a rich, dark complexion, clear and healthy; smoothly shaven cheeks and handsome throat; small white ears; eyes which shoot out electric fires; small white hands; small feet; a full chest and broad shoulders; and with these points doubly blended together, we have a picture of the Little Giant."

The Southern wing of the Democracy at Baltimore might have named Jefferson Davis of Mississippi, who was as clearly its accepted leader as was Douglas that of the North. Or the nomination might have gone to one of three influential Georgia statesmen, Robert Toombs, Howell Cobb, or Alexander H. Stephens. But the Lower South was more concerned about the platform than about the candidate; and it displayed sound political judgment in uniting without dissent upon the name of John C. Breckinridge of Kentucky. All the parties had sought candidates who would appear to be somewhat less sectional than their platforms, or their main voting strength. Mr. Bell was influential in the Border States, and Mr. Lincoln, whose home was not far from Kentucky on the one side and Missouri on the other, and whose birthplace was in Kentucky, was regarded as more acceptable to the upper tier of Slave States than Seward or Chase. In like manner, the Seceding Democrats preferred a candidate who would poll as many votes as possible in the Free States, as well as in the more northerly Slave States that were still strongly Unionist in their sentiments.

Kentucky at that time was a State of commanding political influence, and of many distinguished public men, several of whom were regarded as of presidential calibre, among them being Crittenden and Guthrie. As for Mr. Breckinridge, the reader must not forget that he was sitting at the moment of his nomination in the chair of the presiding office of the United States Senate. He had been chosen for the Vice-Presidency at Cincinnati in 1856, and had been elected with Mr. Buchanan. In the great debates over which he had been presiding during the period of more than six months preceding his nomination at Baltimore, his reputation had grown in contact with the issues and the men of that period. The Southern Senators were amply assured of his consistent adherence to the position they had taken at Charleston and later at Baltimore. But he was regarded as more available than others because Democrats North as well as South had already voted for him in 1856. He had not, like Davis, Toombs, and others, fought in the arena with Douglas and thus antagonized Northern Democrats.

Mr. Buchanan was nominated in 1856 because as Minister to England he had been out of the country and was not embroiled in recent controversies. Breckinridge, in like manner, was nominated in 1860 because he had been isolated by his position as Vice-President. In the White House, with his measureless responsibilities as President, Buchanan could not avoid making decisions; and he had favored the pro-Slavery view until he had become involved somewhat helplessly in movements beyond his control. Breckinridge, on the other hand, observing the peculiar traditions of the office of Vice-President, and having no part in the councils of the President and the Cabinet, had been sitting as a voiceless moderator over the proceedings of the Senate. He had antagonized nobody, while as an attractive and distinguished personality he had lost no prestige since his election in 1856. It was the purpose of the Southern Democrats, with the aid of conspicuous Northern leaders here and there, to carry the Breckinridge movement into all the States, running either separate electoral tickets or joining in fusion arrangements as conditions might indicate.

John Cabell Breckinridge was the youngest of the four nominees, John Bell of Tennessee being the oldest. Bell was born in 1797 near Nashville, Tennessee; Lincoln in 1809 in Kentucky; Douglas in 1813 in Vermont; and Breckinridge on the 21st of January, 1821, near Lexington, Kentucky. When elected Vice-President, therefore, in 1856, Breckinridge was only thirty-five years of age. He was of distinguished family, and had enjoyed early advantages of a kind not available for the other candidates. His grandfather had been

LITTLE STEPHEN A VERY BAD BOY

MRS. COLUMBIA: "Stephen, you have been a very bad boy for some years. I have tried every way to make you behave yourself, and there is nothing else for me to do but to take you under hand. You have got my whole family into a general quarrel."

DOUGLAS: "Booh-hoo! It wasn't me, mother. It was Bill Seward and Yancey."

MRS. COLUMBIA: "You can't get off that way. You must be whipped. So, now, take that! and that! and that!"

From the *Rail-Splitter*, Chicago, September 29, 1860.

elected United States Senator from Kentucky in 1801, and his father was a man of prominence, while two of his father's brothers had long been distinguished as educators and as Presbyterian clergymen. One of these uncles, Robert Jefferson Breckinridge, was for many years the foremost educational leader of Kentucky. Curiously enough, this uncle was the "keynote" speaker and temporary chairman of the National Republican Convention that four years later re-nominated Lincoln in 1864.

For more than a century it has been the privilege of the Breckinridge family to nurture strong and independent personality, and to supply prominent members to all the rival political organizations. John Cabell Breckinridge went from Centre College, Kentucky, to Princeton in the State of New Jersey, and returned to Kentucky to study in the Law Department of Translyvania University at Lexington. Like most Western and Southern men

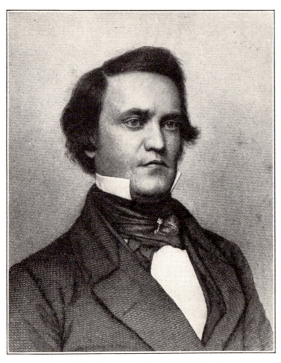

JOHN CABELL BRECKINRIDGE

The youngest of the four nominees for the Presidency in 1860, Breckinridge was a Kentucky lawyer who had been a Major in the Mexican War, a member of Congress, and when nominated by the Baltimore and Richmond seceders he was Vice-President of the United States. In the election he carried nine States of the far South, besides Delaware and Maryland. He became a Major-General in the Confederate Army, and from January to April, 1865, he was Secretary of War in the Cabinet of Jefferson Davis.

to stay in Congress until his election as the most youthful of our long line of Vice-Presidents. It is set down in all accounts of the great controversies that raged in the Senate from 1857 to 1861 that Breckinridge had presided with "conspicuous fairness and impartiality." Referring to his action in a certain parliamentary situation, Mr. Rhodes alludes to Breckinridge as having "more than once contributed his efforts in the direction of harmony."

Mr. Breckinridge, indeed, had not been tested as a masterful leader of men; but in his youthful way he somewhat resembled the veteran John Bell in exhibiting a character that combined honesty and sincerity with gallant bearing, poised judgment, and conciliatory temperament. With these characteristics of John C. Breckinridge, Lincoln was entirely familiar. He did not underestimate the personal qualifications or the political strength of any one of the three men who were his rivals for the Presidential office.

of that period, his preparation was not unduly prolonged. He was practising law at Frankfort, Kentucky, at the age of nineteen, and not long afterwards he decided to try his fortunes in the West.

He penetrated a little farther than the homes of Lincoln and Douglas, settling across the Mississippi at Burlington, Iowa. He remained there from 1841 to 1843, returning as a mature and experienced lawyer to practise at Lexington, which was to be his home until his death in 1875. As Major in a volunteer regiment he went to Mexico in 1847, but found the fighting ended. Two years later he was serving in the State Legislature, and at the age of thirty he found himself at Washington in the House of Representatives.

President Pierce designated him for the position of Minister to Spain, but he preferred

A QUARREL IN THE HOUSEHOLD

Douglas occupies the rôle of peacemaker between Breckinridge and Old Abe, the respective candidates of South and North.

THE GREAT EXHIBITION OF 1860.

The cartoon is meant to imply that Lincoln's campaign was conducted by Senator Seward of New York (who holds the Negro child) together with three New York newspaper editors. Lincoln's mouth is padlocked: he made no speeches during the campaign. Horace Greeley, of the *Tribune*, plays the hand-organ. Henry J. Raymond, of the *Times*, confesses that he has his "own little axe to grind." James Watson Webb, of the *Courier and Enquirer*, passes the tambourine and pleads for help for a family in reduced circumstances, very hard up, trying to "keep the little Nigger alive."

CHAPTER XII

Lincoln in the Half-Year's Contest

A puzzling political game—The Electoral College and the pivotal States—Lincoln spends six months in Springfield, avoiding fresh commitments while conferring with party leaders on campaign strategy

I T WAS PROBABLE that Lincoln would be elected, but it was by no means a conceded situation. As it turned out, his fanciful plurality was large. Yet, such are the strange paradoxes of our system of choosing Presidents, a shift of less than 4 per cent. in the popular vote of a single State would have defeated him. Locality preferences were more sharp and distinct than in these days of a wider distribution of political intelligence, and a more homogeneous party sentiment. No one of the four tickets was in an absolutely hopeless position. In the North and in the Border

States there were drifts and changes that obliterated the ancient landmarks. The sense of dangerous emergency was so widespread that nobody could confidently predict which bellwethers the frightened sheep would follow.

Douglas spoke not only throughout the North, but he pushed courageously into what had become for him the "enemy's country," addressing audiences as far South as New Orleans, in the greatest speaking campaign that has ever been made by any nominee in the history of the country, if we except those of Bryan. I shall describe the Douglas campaign in a following chapter. The other nominees did not make speaking tours, but they were active behind the scenes in directing the strategy of their respective campaigns; and the demonstrations—especially those for Lincoln—were as colorful and incessant as those of the Harrison campaign in 1840.

How did Lincoln expect to be elected? First, he counted upon the 114 electors that had been won by the Frémont ticket in 1856. Minnesota's admission added 4, and for a clear majority he had to seek 34 additional votes. The circumstances of his nomination at Chicago had distinct reference to this necessity. The delegation of his own State of Illinois with 11 electoral votes, that of Pennsylvania with 27, Indiana with 13, and New Jersey with 7, had gone to his support in the convention in the belief that he, rather than Seward or Chase, could win the necessary 34 from all or some of these States, with the further chance of carrying Oregon's 3 or California's 4.

Mr. Rhodes remarks: "Had Douglas been the candidate of the united Democracy on the Cincinnati platform, the contest would have been close and exciting and the result doubtful. Douglas himself boasted that had that been the case he would have beaten Lincoln in every State of the Union except Vermont and Massachusetts." This was asserted by Douglas in a speech at Baltimore in September.

Continuing, Mr. Rhodes says: "Had the Democrats been united on Breckinridge and the Southern platform, the only conceivably different result would have been larger Lincoln majorities in the Northern States. But with the actual state of affairs, after the two nominations at Baltimore, the success of the Republicans seemed to be assured. . . . As the contest went on, a glimmer of hope arose. While it was absolutely impossible for Douglas, Breckinridge, or Bell to obtain a majority of the electoral votes, it was within the bounds of possibility to defeat Lincoln by throwing the election into the House of Representatives. Then Breckinridge might be elected, or, the House failing to make a choice, Lane would become President by virtue of having been chosen Vice-President by the Senate."

This was by no means a purely fanciful surmise. Although Jackson in 1824 had gained a plurality in the Electoral College, he lacked a clear majority, and the choice was thrown into the House of Representatives under the Constitution. The Clay men, preferring John Quincy Adams to Jackson, defeated the man who had stood highest in the popular vote and in the Electoral College. If Lincoln had gained a plurality but not a majority in the Electoral College, the voting would have been by States in the House, and it was estimated that the delegations from fifteen States would support Lincoln, with at least twelve for Breckinridge, and with six doubtful, or for Douglas or Bell.

It is quite conceivable that neither Lincoln nor Breckinridge could have won enough from these six States to have been elected. It is hardly probable that either of the major groups would have turned to Douglas or Bell, although it is barely possible that Bell would have gained the Lincoln support in order to prevent the undesired result that must inevitably follow a deadlock in the House. For, under these circumstances, according to the Constitution, it would have devolved upon the Senate to choose the Vice-President. And in case Buchanan's successor had not been chosen by the House before noon on the 4th of March, 1861, the new Vice-President-elect would have been sworn in as President.

Mr. Breckinridge himself was still presiding over the Senate, which remained strongly Democratic and pro-slavery. Gen. Joseph Lane would certainly have been chosen Vice-President, as against the Hon. Hannibal Hamlin of Maine. Mr. Breckinridge, himself failing to gain the Presidency, would have had the extraordinary experience of holding the gavel at the session of the Senate which chose his running mate, Joseph Lane of Oregon, as Vice-President. And the accession of Mr. Lane to the White House would have meant practical victory for Jefferson Davis's platform and for pro-slavery policies. Such a result would at least have retarded the Secession movement, although it is idle to conjecture what might have been the further course of our political history. This, at least, is enough to show that the election results of 1860 were precarious.

LETTING THE CAT OUT OF THE BAG!!

Published by Currier & Ives.

This is from a well known Currier & Ives lithographed poster, by Louis Maurer. Senator Sumner of Massachusetts had recovered from the results of wounds inflicted by Brooks, the South Carolinian, in the Capitol at Washington in 1856. He had no part in the Chicago convention. Sumner's extreme position on the slavery question threatened to alienate elements of the Republican party that Lincoln wished to retain as supporters. In the parlance of a later day, there was "dynamite" in Sumner's leadership. Greeley and Raymond (at Lincoln's side in this cartoon), who were at odds on several points in the campaign, were agreed on this: Radicalism must be repressed until after election. Lincoln is made to remark to Sumner, who holds the bag: "Oh! This is too bad! I thought we had her safely bagged at Chicago. Now there will be the old scratch to pay unless I can drive her back again with my rail." But Sumner persists in his rule-or-ruin attitude. Hannibal Hamlin, on the ticket with Lincoln, counsels prudence and recalls his own success, as a seasoned politician, in the ironing-out of difficulties.

Lincoln himself was not too sanguine, although he had reason to be somewhat confident. Writing to a friend on July 4th he commented in the following vein:

We know not what a day may bring forth, but to-day it looks as if the Chicago ticket will be elected. I think the chances were more than equal that we could have beaten the Democracy united. Divided as it is, its chance appears indeed very slim. But great is Democracy in resources; and it may yet give its fortunes a turn. It is under great temptation to do something; but what can it do which was not thought of, and found impracticable, at Charleston and Baltimore? The signs now are that Douglas and Breckinridge will each have a ticket in every State. They are driven to this to keep up their bombastic claims of nationality, and to avoid the charge of sectionalism which they have so much lavished upon us.

It is an amusing fact, after all Douglas has said about nationality and sectionalism, that I had more votes from the Southern section at Chicago than he had at Baltimore! In fact, there was more of the Southern section represented at Chicago than in the Douglas rump concern at Baltimore!

Recent party custom has postponed the formal ceremonies of notification and acceptance for several weeks; and the nominees are then ready to present to the country elaborate discourses expounding doctrines from the standpoint of their respective parties. An example of this method was furnished by Mr. Hoover and Governor Smith after the conventions of 1928. A simpler fashion was observed in 1860. On the second day after Lincoln's nomination an eminent committee from the Chicago body—including its President, George Ashmun of Massachusetts, with Governor

Boutwell of that State, Mr. Evarts of New York, Judge Kelley of Pennsylvania, Mr. Cartter of Ohio, Mr. Blair of Missouri, Gideon Welles of Connecticut, Carl Schurz of Wisconsin, and several others—appeared in Springfield and was received in the comfortable parlor of the Lincoln home. We have an admirable description of the proceedings in Miss Tarbell's "Life of Lincoln." The following paragraphs are not imaginary but are based upon thorough and accurate reports:

As the committee filed into Mr. Lincoln's simple home there was a sore misgiving in more than one heart; and as Mr. Ashmun, their Chairman, presented to him the letter notifying him of his nomination, they eyed their candidate with critical keenness. They noted his great height; his huge hands and feet; his peculiar lankness of limb. His shoulders drooped as he stood, giving his form a look of irresolution. His smooth-shaven face seemed of bronze as he listened to their message and amazed

them by its ruggedness. The cheeks were sunken, the cheek-bones high, the nose large, the mouth unsymmetrical, the under lip protruding a little. Irregular seams and lines cut and creased the skin in every direction. The eyes, downcast as he listened, were sunken and somber. Shaded by its mass of dark hair, the face gave an impression of a sad, impenetrable man.

Mr. Ashmun finished his speech and Mr. Lincoln lifting his bent head began to reply. The men who watched him thrilled with surprise at the change which passed over him. His drooping form became erect and firm. The eyes beamed with fire and intelligence. Strong, dignified, and self-possessed, he seemed transformed by the simple act of self-expression.

His remarks were brief, merely a word of thanks for the honor done him, a hint that he felt the responsibility of his position, a promise to respond formally in writing, and the expression of a desire to take each one of the committee by hand; but his voice was calm and clear, his bearing frank and sure. His auditors saw in a flash that here was a man who was master of himself. For the first time they understood that he whom they had supposed to be little more than a loquacious and clever State politician, had force, insight, conscience—that their misgivings were vain.

HONEST OLD ABE ON THE STUMP

At Springfield, in 1858: "Nobody ever expected me to be President. In my poor, lean, lank face nobody has ever seen that any cabbages were sprouting out."

At Springfield, in 1860: "I appear here at this time only for the purpose of affording myself the best opportunity of seeing you and enabling you to see me."

During the entire campaign, from May to November, 1860, Lincoln remained in Springfield. He made no speeches, except one of less than three hundred words addressed to a great mass meeting held in August at the State Fair grounds in Springfield. To those who sought a statement of his views he declared that he had expressed himself fully, and he referred them to printed copies of speeches made before the nomination.

Mr. Leonard Volk of Chicago, a meritorious sculptor who had previously made a bust of Lincoln, arrived at Springfield on the day of Lincoln's nomination, to carry out plans for modeling a full-length statue. He went at once to the Lincoln home, and his account of what he saw and heard is one of the most authentic of those agreeable personal descriptions that have always been so acceptable to the lovers of anecdotes about the every-day, private Lincoln. Mr. Volk also gives us the following testimony that relates to political events that he himself witnessed:

On Saturday evening, the committee appointed by the Convention to notify Mr. Lincoln formally of his nomination, headed by Mr. Ashmun of Massachusetts, reached Springfield by special train, bearing a large number of people, two or three hundred of whom carried rails on their shoulders, marching in military style from the train to the old State House Hall of Representatives, where they stacked them like muskets. The evening was beautiful and clear and the entire population was astir. The bells pealed, flags waved, and cannon thundered forth the triumphant nomination of Springfield's favorite and distinguished citizen. The bonfires blazed brightly and especially in front of that prim-looking white house on Eighth Street. The com-

CANDIDATES AND PLATFORMS: A CINCINNATI POSTER CARICATURE OF 1860

Lincoln's platform is solid and substantial. Douglas stands on the crumbling Cincinnati platform of 1856 while he straddles the Mason and Dixon's Line. For the South he waves a "Dred Scott Decision" flag; for the North, one marked "Unfriendly Legislation." Bell, candidate of the Constitutional Union party, has no platform on which to stand.

mittee and the vast crowd following it passed in at the front door, and made their exit through the kitchen door in the rear, Mr. Lincoln giving them all a hearty shake of the hand as they passed him in the parlor.

Four days later, Lincoln's brief letter of acceptance was transmitted and made public. Since it contains only three sentences of less than one hundred and fifty words altogether, we may well quote it without abridgment:

Springfield, Illinois, May 23, 1860.
Hon. George Ashmun,
President of the Republican National Convention.

Sir: I accept the nomination tendered me by the convention over which you presided and of which I am formally appraised in the letter of yourself and others acting as a committee of the convention for that purpose.

The declaration of principles and sentiments which accompanies your letter meets my approval; and it shall be my care not to violate or disregard it in any part.

Imploring the assistance of Divine Providence, and with due regard to the views and feelings of all who were represented in the convention—to the rights of all the States and Territories and people of the nation; to the inviolability of the Constitution; and the perpetual union, harmony, and prosperity of all—I am most happy to co-operate for the practical success of the principles declared by the convention.

Your obliged friend and fellow citizen,
A. LINCOLN.

With the camaraderie of friendly acquaintance in Congress regardless of party, there were Republican congressmen who surrounded Douglas with disparaging interrogatories about the obscure Lincoln. But Douglas encouraged no such belittling of his prospective opponent, declaring that "There won't be a tar-barrel left in Illinois to-night." He knew that the plain people of the West would rejoice in the nomination of a plain fellow-citizen. The sneers at Lincoln's deficiencies prevailed in Democratic circles both North and South; but the Republican press, strongly supported by all the eminent Republican leaders, began to idealize Lincoln, their descriptions fitting, as it were, the future Saint-Gaudens statues rather than those of George Grey Barnard.

"Among the common people," says Miss Tarbell, "the jeer that Lincoln was but a rail-splitter was a spur to enthusiasm. Too many of the solid men of the North had swung an axe, too many of them had passed from log hut to mansion, not to blaze with sympathetic indignation when the party was taunted with nominating a backwoodsman. The rail be-came their emblem and their rallying cry, and the story of the rail fence Lincoln had built became a feature of every campaign speech and every country store discussion. In a week after his nomination, two rails declared to have been split by Lincoln were on exhibition in New York, and certain zealous Pennsylvanians had sent to Macon, Illinois, asking to buy the whole fence and have it shipped East. It was the rail which decorated campaign medals, inspired campaign songs, appeared in campaign cartoons. There was something more than a desire to stand by the candidate in the enthusiasm. At bottom it was a vindication of the American way of making a man."

In a previous chapter on Seward's defeat at Chicago, I have remarked upon the prompt and loyal support he gave to the Lincoln ticket. In view of many subsequent criticisms of Seward on the ground of his assumptions of superiority over his chief when serving in the Cabinet,

AN ANTI-REPUBLICAN DEMONSTRATION IN NEW YORK CITY, TWO WEEKS
BEFORE ELECTION

The effort to defeat Lincoln in 1860 resulted in a uniting of the opposition in New York. In support of this fusion, the combined forces of Douglas, Breckinridge, and Bell paraded through the streets of the city on the evening of October 23d. The *New York Illustrated News,* from which we reproduce our sketch, described the occasion as follows: "The Democrats of all grades and the opponents of the Republicans in all guises congregated in our city to outdo all the political demonstrations of the season—and they have done it. The Wide Awake processions were grand in their way, and seemed vast and brilliant enough to leave no possibility of being outdone. But they have been most decidedly surpassed in this overwhelmingly huge display which called forth into active combination all the elements opposed to the election of Lincoln."

A PROCESSION OF "WIDE-AWAKES" IN NEW YORK, IN SUPPORT
OF THE LINCOLN CANDIDACY

A feature of the campaign of 1860 was the parade of Republican enthusiasm in various cities of the North. The men carried coal-oil torches and colored lanterns, and were dressed in costume. These "Wide-Awakes" had originated at Hartford, Connecticut, and it is said that their cambric capes and glazed caps were at first merely improvised to protect their clothing from the rain; but the uniform soon became popular. In this illustration, from *Harper's Weekly,* the reader will note the *Tribune* and *Times* buildings, in old Newspaper Row. City Hall Park is at the right of the picture. Both these newspapers, many years afterward, moved farther uptown.

it is worth while to note somewhat further the services he rendered during the campaign, when his active disapproval or even his retirement in silence might have dealt a fatal blow to the Republican cause. So disappointed were his immediate neighbors that there was no pen to write an approving word for the *Daily Advertiser,* which was the Seward organ in his home city of Auburn. But Seward himself, on the very day of the nomination wrote and published the following paragraph:

"No truer exposition of the Republican creed could be given than the platform adopted by the convention contains. No truer or firmer defenders of the Republican faith could have been found in the Union than the distinguished and esteemed citizens on whom the honors of

the nomination have fallen. Their election, we trust by a decisive majority, will restore the government of the U. S. to its Constitutional and ancient course. Let the watchword of the Republican party be Union and Liberty, and onward to victory."

The leading Republicans of the period were a notably able group, alike in the East and in the West, and none of them shirked campaign effort. Sumner and other Massachusetts men were at their best, and so were Seward and the Republican editors and statesmen of New York. Seward made a five-weeks' western tour, speaking incessantly. Chase, Wade, and many Ohio leaders were heard in different States. Thaddeus Stevens and many Pennsylvanians worked indefatigably to carry what was, next to New York, the most essential State. Edward Bates, with the Blairs and their associates, performed the miracle of procuring more than half as many votes for Lincoln as were cast for Breckinridge in the Slave State of Missouri. The newer States were, in the nature of things, swinging strongly into the Republican line.

Certain Southern leaders, praising slave labor, made unfortunate remarks about the industrial workers and small farmers of the North; and these were spread everywhere by the Republican newspapers and campaign speakers, in order to win the labor and farmer votes for Lincoln. Young men were organized into marching clubs, known as "Wide-Awakes" which adopted a form of cape made of glazed material, and they paraded at night carrying torch-lights. This costume had been improvised at Hartford because of an unexpected downpour of rain; but it had caught somebody's fancy and was adopted as a campaign device throughout the country, with the result of crystallizing the support of thousands of young voters. The Wide-Awakes were drilled in marching, and their parades had something of a military character.

Lincoln himself consistently abstained, throughout the campaign, from fresh committals upon controverted issues. He had accepted the party platform; and his previous speeches, including the one delivered at Cooper Union, in the city of New York, were circulated in pamphlet form throughout the country. He watched every situation, and was constantly alert until the election day, November 6th.

That the Republicans would have a *plurality* in the Electoral College was doubted by few intelligent citizens. But that Lincoln would have a *majority* was a matter of anxious doubt until the votes were counted. The results gave Lincoln and Hamlin 180 electoral votes, Breckinridge and Lane 72, Bell and Everett 39, and Douglas and Johnson only 12. Thus Lincoln had 57 more electoral votes than his three opponents combined. The popular vote was distributed quite differently and stood as as follows: Lincoln 1,866,452, Douglas 1,376,957, Breckinridge 849,781, Bell 588,879. As against Lincoln's 1,866,452, the combined vote of his opponents was 2,815,617, almost a million in excess.

It should be explained that the popular votes assigned to Douglas in New York, Pennsylvania, New Jersey, and Rhode Island were cast for fusion electoral tickets, thus consolidating the entire opposition against Lincoln. New York gave 362,466 for the Lincoln electors and 312,510 for what is set down as a Douglas electoral ticket.

If Lincoln had not secured the 35 Electors of New York State, he would have been defeated. He would have had only 145, and the combined opposition would have had 158; and so the election would actually have been thrown into the House of Representatives. A change of 25,000 votes in a total of nearly 700,000 in the State of New York would have

NEWS FROM THE STATES

MISS PENNSYLVANIA: "Now, Friend Bennett, don't thee think it's most time for thee to change thee garment for a better one?"

JAMES GORDON BENNETT: "'Deed, lassies, it's a bonnie braw coatie, and this auld Buchanan thing is gettin' unco ragged. Weel, weel; I dinna keen—"

The State elections in Pennsylvania and Indiana, held in October, were carried by the Republicans. The cartoon suggests that it was time for the editor of the New York *Herald* to "get on the bandwagon." He had been a faithful supporter of President Buchanan.

defeated Lincoln in the Electoral College, with the further prospect of his defeat in the House, and the placing of a pro-slavery Democrat, Joseph Lane of Oregon, in the White House on March 4, 1861.

Fully anticipating this situation, all of the anti-Lincoln parties were in a combination to defeat the Lincoln ticket in the Empire State. They were all voting for an electoral ticket nominally headed by Douglas, with the advance agreement that, if this was successful, seven electors were to vote for Breckinridge, ten for Bell, and the remaining eighteen for Douglas. It is only when these facts are explained —and they have been quite too generally overlooked—that one can appreciate the significance of the loyal support tendered by Senator Seward. Prodigious efforts made by Seward, Weed, and their wing of the New York Republican party—laying aside past differences with Greeley, David Dudley Field, and the other wing—resulted in the New York victory to which alone Lincoln's election was due.

It should be remembered that throughout the stirring period of almost six months between his nomination and election day, Mr. Lincoln had remained at his home, in what was then the small prairie city of Springfield, Illinois. The enthusiasm of his supporters throughout the entire North was increasing from week to week. Eminent party leaders and humble friends and supporters came to Springfield from time to time, and Lincoln was assigned a room in the State House, which was in the heart of the town not far from his

THE COMING MAN'S PRESIDENTIAL CAREER
Motto: Don't give up the ship!
From *Harper's Weekly,* August 25, 1860.

home and his law office, where from morning till night he was accessible to his callers without formality. He was constantly studying the progress of the puzzling and complicated struggle among the rival party organizations.

There were Southern visitors among the Springfield arrivals who assured him that he stood better, even with the extremists of the South, than did Douglas. He was making note of the threats of Secession in the South, and trying to distinguish between those that were sincere and others that were political bluff, intended to strengthen the vote for Breckinridge. Upon the whole he did not believe that Secession would follow his election.

All factions, of course, were ready to preserve the so-called "glorious Union," *if* only they could control the Government and dictate permanent lines of policy. How serious was this *"if,"* nobody could state with authority. Mr. Rhett of South Carolina and Mr. Yancey of Alabama, with many others less conspicuous, were giving the "if" a definite meaning. *If* Lincoln were elected, they were stating with boldness and precision throughout the campaign, there would certainly be Secession in the Lower South, to be followed probably by Secession of the Border Slave States.

Lincoln did not believe that his election would drive the Border States to Secession, and was not ready to think that South Carolina, with only one or two other States perhaps following, would be so rash as to secede on her own account. He was exceedingly careful to avoid creating further antagonism by assertive utterances of any kind. All sorts of people were trying to draw him out in correspondence, and he arranged a brief form letter of reply which was sent out with the signature of his secretary, John G. Nicolay. This stated that Mr. Lincoln had received many letters asking him to express his views on certain political points, but that he had also received still more letters advising him not to widen the areas of campaign controversy by re-statement of any kind.

These advisers had besought him to write nothing whatever upon any point of political doctrine. "They say his positions were well known when he was nominated, and that he must not now embarrass the canvass by undertaking to shift or modify them." This was a wise position to take. His Cooper Union speech was extensively circulated from New York in pamphlet form, and his speeches in the debates with Douglas delivered two years before, were made available everywhere.

No one could have given us more trustworthy information about Mr. Lincoln's activities during the summer and autumn of 1860 than Mr. Nicolay, who was with him constantly as his private secretary, and who in later years became his biographer. Mr. Nicolay says: "He employed no literary bureau, wrote no public letters, made no set or impromptu speeches, except that once or twice during great political meetings at Springfield he uttered a few words of greeting and thanks to passing street processions. All these devices of propagandism he left to the leaders and committees of his adherents in their several States. Even the strictly confidential letters in which he indicated his advice on points in the progress of the campaign did not exceed a dozen in number; and when politicians came to interview him at Springfield, he received them in the privacy of his own home, and gen-

CAMPAIGN DOCUMENTS.

We invite the attention of friends of the Republican cause to the following list of documents:
Please pay particular attention to the remarks on Postage on these documents, as prepayment is required.

I. THE IRREPRESSIBLE CONFLICT: Gov. Seward's Rochester Speech of 1858; with Charles O'Conor's Union-Meeting Speech, December 19, 1859.

II. THE DEMOCRATIC LEADERS FOR DISUNION: Speech of Henry Wilson of Massachusetts, in the Senate, January 25, 1860.

III. THE ADMISSION OF KANSAS: Gov. Seward's great Speech, in Senate, February 29, 1860.

IV. NATIONAL POLITICS: Speech of Abraham Lincoln, of Illinois, at the Cooper Institute, New-York, February 27, 1860; James R. Doolittle's Vindication of Wisconsin.

V. LAND FOR THE LANDLESS: The Hon. Galusha A. Grow's Speech, in the House, February 29, 1860.

VI. THE LIFE OF ABRAHAM LINCOLN: By an Illinois Republican, who knows well the man and his history. A large compact pamphlet of 32 double-column pages, for general circulation as a campaign document. Price 4 cents a copy, 40 cents per dozen, $2 50 per hundred, $20 per thousand. If required by mail, one cent additional must be sent to prepay postage. Cash orders are solicited, and will be filled in the order of their reception.

VII. PROTECTION OF HOME LABOR AND HOME PRODUCTIONS NECESSARY TO THE PROSPERITY OF THE AMERICAN FARMER: By Henry Carey Baird. 16 large octavo pages.

The above are printed on fair type and good paper, each forming a large octavo tract of 16 pages, except No. 6, which is double size and price. They are sold in quantities of One Thousand, or over, for ONE CENT per copy, and the Thousand may be made up from the list above given, as the buyer may desire. In smaller quantities, $1 25 per hundred; 25 cents per dozen; singly, 4 cents. By mail, postage prepaid, 5 cents per copy, 30 cents per dozen, $1 60 per 100, $13 50 per 1,000.

IN GERMAN.

I. Seward's late Speech on the Admission of Kansas.
II. Land for the Landless: The Hon. Galusha A. Grow's Speech.
III. National Politics: Abraham Lincoln's Speech.
IV. The Irrepressible Conflict: Gov. Seward's Rochester Speech.
V. State Rights and Supreme Court: The Hon. James R. Doolittle's Speech.
VI. The Democratic Leaders for Disunion: The Hon. Henry Wilson's Speech.
VII. The Barbarism of Slavery: The Hon. Owen Lovejoy's Speech.

Price of all these German Speeches, 5 cents a single copy; $2 50 per 100; $15 per 1,000. By mail, postage prepaid, 6 cents each, 60 cents per dozen, 25 for $1, 100 for $2 75, 1,000 for $17 50.

Will not our Republican friends aid us to "circulate the documents?" Now is the time when thousands of minds can be reached and influenced.

Address   **THE TRIBUNE,**
Tribune Buildings, New-York.

The New York *Tribune*, under the editorship of Horace Greeley, played a leading part in the campaign to elect Lincoln. Reproduced above is an advertisement of speeches by Lincoln and other Republican leaders, and a biography of the candidate. They could be obtained either in English or German. If bought in quantities these pamphlets cost from one to two cents each. They were widely distributed.

erally their presence created little or no public notice."

Perhaps Mr. Lincoln wrote more letters during the campaign that Mr. Nicolay was concerned with. A very considerable number have come to light that did not appear in the collection of addresses and letters of which Mr. Nicolay himself was one of the editors some thirty years after Lincoln's death. In that collection, however, we find the following typical letter to a young girl, dated October 19, 1860.

Miss Grace Bedell.

My dear little Miss: Your very agreeable letter of the 15th is received. I regret the necessity of saying I have no daughter. I have three sons—one seventeen, one nine, and one seven years of age. They, with their mother, constitute my whole family. As to the whiskers, having never worn any, do you not think people would call it a piece of silly affectation if I were to begin it now? Your very sincere well wisher

A. LINCOLN.

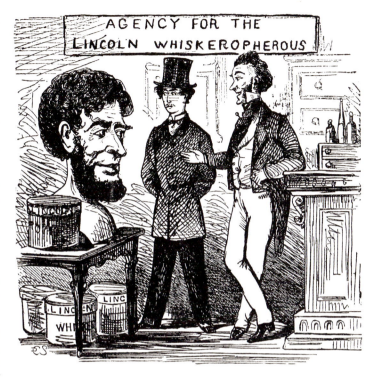

MR. LINCOLN SETS A STYLE

DRUGGIST: "Try one of those pots, sir, and in three weeks you will be as hairy and handsome as he is."

Up to the time of his election Lincoln was smooth-faced. But before his inauguration day he had allowed his beard to grow, in the prevailing fashion.

Since we are concerned in these volumes with many caricatures of Mr. Lincoln, without whiskers through the 1860 campaign, but with whiskers at inauguration time and always thereafter, it may be well to quote again from the accurate reminiscences of Mr. Volk, the sculptor. The day after the notification ceremonies in May, Mr. Volk had returned to Chicago, "with the moulds of his hands, three photographic negatives of him, the identical black alpaca campaign suit of 1858, and a pair of Lynn newly-made pegged boots." Continuing, Mr. Volk says: "The clothes were all burned up in the great Chicago fire [referring to the conflagration of 1871.] The casts of the face and hands I saved by taking them with me to Rome, and they have crossed the sea four times. [They have served the purposes of many sculptors and painters since that time, including Mr. Volk's distinguished son, Douglas Volk.] The last time I saw Mr. Lincoln was in January, 1861, at his house in Spring-field. His little parlor was full of friends and politicians. He introduced me to them all, and remarked to me aside that since he had sat to me for his bust he had lost forty pounds in weight. This was easily perceptible, for the lines of his jaws were very sharply defined *through the short beard which he was allowing to grow.*"

The country was indeed at the end of one era and entering upon another. The smooth-faced gentlemen in broadcloth suits who had ruled the country from 1820 to 1860, and whose chief resource was conventional oratory, were now to give place to a generation of bearded men of action. With the incoming of Lincoln, the men of words, North and South, were preparing to fight and were changing their methods, manners, and appearance. Even the boys of the Wide-Awake companies, soon to be formed into companies and regiments of soldiers, were letting their beards grow. And so Lincoln took a small girl's advice.

CHAPTER XIII

Douglas in the Campaign, and After

*At first confident of success, Douglas takes emphatic ground against
disunion—He vindicates his party regularity—His extended speaking
tour—Dies in 1861 as a warm Lincoln champion*

Mr. Lincoln had been chosen as a compromise candidate to represent a great party movement, rather than as a personal leader of pre-eminence. The position of Mr. Douglas was exactly the reverse of that of his old neighbor. His candidacy was altogether that of an unrivalled chieftain. He was the embodiment of certain doctrines and

SCANDALOUS GOSSIP AT WASHINGTON

Miss J. B. is speaking to Nancy of Alabama (the one being President Buchanan, the other William L. Yancey, who had led the Southern extremists in withdrawing from the Charleston convention): "Yes, my dear, and they do say Steve Douglas is going to sell out to Old Abe, and Old Abe is to give him ever so much money and quicksilver, besides the whole town of Chicago. But I wouldn't mention it for anything." Throughout the campaign there were efforts at combination among the four candidates, which did result in fusion electoral tickets against Lincoln in New York and several other States.

policies, and the undisputed head of the Democracy of the North. Of all the four presidential nominees, he alone had been nominated on personal rather than representative and party grounds. The South had many leaders, and it did not require active speaking or managerial efforts on the part of its candidate, Mr. Breckinridge. The Bell-Everett ticket had been launched by highly respectable, conservative elements, that included a number of men of similar experience, and also of presidential caliber. For Mr. Douglas, the plan of a campaign of much travel and of constant platform argument was quite as logical as was the opposite plan for Mr. Lincoln—that of staying quietly at home.

Senator Douglas had remained at Washington for a few days following the Baltimore convention and the adjournment of Congress. Leaders of the convention had waited upon him promptly as a notifying committee, and had received his verbal acceptance. His written letter soon followed, and was dated Friday, June 29th, four days after the adjournment of Congress and six days after the Baltimore convention had completed its work.

This letter was a skillful document. It began with endorsement of the platform, as "a faithful embodiment of the time-honored principles of the Democratic party as the same were proclaimed and understood by all parties in the presidential contests of 1848, 1852, and 1856." Regarding the legitimacy of his nomination, he declared: "Upon looking into the proceedings of the Convention, also I find that the nomination was made with great unanimity in the presence and with the concurrence of more than two-thirds of the whole number of delegates, and in accordance with the long-established usages of the party." He expounded somewhat further his past and present record of strict party regularity.

Continuing, he argued the danger of federal interference in the domestic affairs of the people of the Territories. "If the power and the duty of federal interference is to be conceded, two hostile sectional parties must be the inevitable result—the one inflaming the passions and ambitions of the North, the other of the South, and each struggling to use the federal power and authority for the aggrandizement of its own section at the expense of the equal rights of the other." Referring to the controversies of a previous period he remarked: "It required all the wisdom, power, and influence of a Clay, a Webster, and a Cass, supported by the conservative and patriotic men of the Whig and Democratic parties of that day, to devise and carry out a line of policy which would restore peace to the country and stability to the Union. The essential living principle of that policy as applied in the legislation of 1850, was, and now is, nonintervention by Congress with slavery in the Territories." The letter ended with a demand for the preservation of the federal Union, maintenance of the Constitution, and full deference to the judicial authority.

Mr. Douglas proceeded to New York to speak at a ratification meeting, and was undoubtedly in a hopeful and buoyant mood. At that time, according to his biographer, while conceding South Carolina and possibly Mississippi to Breckinridge, and the Border Slave States to Bell, he expressed the firm conviction that he would carry the rest of the Southern States and enough Free States to be elected by the people. Supporters had assured him that he would carry Maine, New Hampshire, Rhode Island, and Connecticut. If the election should go to the House of Representatives he thought that the choice must lie between himself, Lincoln, and Bell, with Breckinridge excluded. Mr. Johnson says that Douglas "enjoined his friends everywhere to treat the Bell

STEPHEN ARNOLD DOUGLAS
The Little Giant was vigorous enough in 1860 to carry out a speaking tour that lasted until Election Day; but in June of the following year he died. This campaign for the Presidency was the climax of a public career that had extended over a quarter of a century. Our portrait is from a steel engraving which did not have wide circulation, and it will thus be unfamiliar to most readers.

and Everett men in a friendly way and to cultivate good relations with them, 'for they are Union men.' But, he added, 'we can have no partnership with the Bolters.' 'Now organize and rally in Illinois and the Northwest. The chances in our favor are immense in the East'."

The New York *Times* followed the Douglas movement with more complete and favorable reports than other newspapers, although it was not a Democratic organ. It recorded his tour of New England—where he was treated as a distinguished guest regardless of party. Entering the State of New York, his numerous appearances began to take the form of stump speeches. Gradually, Mr. Johnson tells us, "the true nature of this pilgrimage was apparent to everybody. It was the first time in our history that a presidential candidate had taken the stump in his own behalf."

Perhaps as the weeks went on he realized that Lincoln would be elected, but was planning ahead for the reorganization of the

Democratic party under his own leadership, and in vindication of his supporters at Charleston and Baltimore. The fusion tickets in New York, Pennsylvania, and New Jersey were, of course, not to his liking; but they were a practical scheme, and in his substantial interest.

At Norfolk, Virginia, late in August, a Breckinridge supporter put to him two prepared questions. The first was as follows: "If Abraham Lincoln be elected President of the United States, will the Southern States be justified in seceding from the Union?" Douglas, though taken by surprise, was ready with his answer, which was as follows: "To this I emphatically answer, No. The election of a man to the Presidency by the American people, in conformity with the Constitution of the United States, would not justify any attempt at dissolving this glorious confederacy."

The second question was phrased as follows: "If they secede from the Union upon the inauguration of Abraham Lincoln, before an overt act against their Constitutional rights, will you advise or vindicate resistance to the decision?" The answer Mr. Douglas gave to this question was more extended. "I answer emphatically," he said, "that it is the duty of the President of the United States and all others in authority under him, to enforce the laws of the United States passed by Congress and as the courts expound them; and I, as in duty bound by my oath of fidelity to the Constitution, would do all in my power to aid the Government of the United States in maintaining the supremacy of the laws against all resistance to them, come from whatever quarter it might."

Even if he regarded the political opinions of a President-elect as "hostile to the Constitution and safety of the Union," Mr. Douglas held that his inauguration would not be such a grievance as would justify revolution or secession. He added sentences of sharp and defiant attack upon the disunionists.

At Raleigh, North Carolina, he was still more emphatic in his denunciations. Mr. Douglas was at home in North Carolina, because in the spring of 1847 he had married Miss Martha Martin, daughter of Col. Robert Martin of Rockingham county, a prosperous North Carolina farmer, with a few slaves in that State and with a much larger number on the cotton plantation that he owned in Mississippi. Through the intimacy of his relationships with his father-in-law, who was a man of the finest Southern type, and through the inheritance by Mrs. Douglas, soon after her marriage, of her father's possessions, Douglas had been drawn into a personal knowledge of Southern life and the plantation system at its best, such as few Northern statesmen had ever possessed in equal measure. He had been unwilling to be a custodian—much less an owner—of a slave property, and Colonel Martin had provided in his will for future emancipation. Douglas reminded the North Carolinians of the blending in the great West of pioneer families from both sections; and his pleas for the preservation of the Union were expressed with fine sentiment on behalf of his own boys.

He had refused to accept a plan of fusion for the electoral ticket in North Carolina, and spoke against fusion with Breckinridge elsewhere. It was the local politicians rather than Douglas himself who brought about the fusion schemes in New York, Pennsylvania, Rhode Island, and New Jersey. He was, of course, shrewdly utilizing all opportunities to strengthen the Bell movement against Breckinridge in the South and Lincoln in the North. His speech at Richmond, Virginia, brought him enormous ovations; and he proceeded northward, speaking at Baltimore, at important centers in Pennsylvania, and then westward at Cincinnati, Indianapolis, Chicago, and points in Iowa.

It was while he was in Iowa that he received the news of the success of the Republicans in the October State elections of Pennsylvania and Indiana. It is reported that he turned at once to his secretary, and said, "Mr. Lincoln is the next President. We must try to save the Union. I will go South." His further movements are thus described in Mr. Allen Johnson's authoritative biography:

"He at once made appointments to speak in Tennessee, Alabama, and Georgia, as soon as he should have met his Western engagements. His friends marveled at his powers of endurance. For weeks he had been speaking from

A REPUBLICAN CAMPAIGN PAPER MAKES LIGHT OF THE DOUGLAS RECEPTION
AT CHICAGO IN OCTOBER, 1860

From the *Rail-Splitter,* Chicago

Chicago Republicans are represented as minimizing the Little Giant's reception in his home city just
before he started upon his final speaking tour in the South. The *Rail-Splitter* explains that Douglas
is shown "expounding the great principle of making Democratic voters sovereigns of the Negroes."
Senator Seward had spoken for Lincoln in Chicago and the demonstration had been enormous.

hotel balconies, from the platforms of railroad
coaches, and in halls, to monster mass meetings. Not infrequently he spoke twice and
thrice a day for days together."

After carrying on this incessant type of
campaigning in Iowa, Wisconsin, and Michigan, he reached St. Louis, on October 19th,
where he disavowed personal interest in the
Presidency, and declared: "I am here to make
an appeal to you in behalf of the Union and
the peace of the country." It is to be noted
that the second Mrs. Douglas accompanied her
husband throughout these travels; and with no
one else in the party except his wife and his
secretary, Mr. Douglas pressed on to Memphis
and the farther South.

There was something heroic about this
Southern tour on the part of a candidate who
had now ceased to believe that he would be

elected himself, and who realized that the
threats against his life were not all idle.

Early in 1853 the first Mrs. Douglas died,
leaving two small sons. The blow was a heavy
one, compared with which the recent defeat
in the Democratic Convention of 1852 was
merely a trifling political incident. Senator
Douglas was married again in 1856 to Miss
Adele Cutts, a Washington social leader of
beauty and charm, and of the highest qualities
of character—a grand-niece of Dolly Madison,
and a member of an old Maryland family. In
the period intervening between this second
marriage and the exciting events of 1860,
Adele Cutts Douglas was perhaps the most
brilliant and popular of all the hostesses in
official life at Washington, supporting her husband's political ambitions with the utmost tact
and with rare intelligence. It was her com-

panionship which sustained him through his unprecedented speaking tour, East and West, North and South, during the campaign.

He was in the office of the Mobile *Register,* a paper that had continued to support him, when the news of Lincoln's election was received. Although the paper had not been secessionist, the editor prepared an alarmist article calling for a State convention to decide upon the course that Alabama would take; and he published it the following morning, against

MRS. STEPHEN A. DOUGLAS

Rose Adèle Cutts, great-niece of Dolly Madison and a belle of Washington society, became the bride of Senator Douglas in 1856, nearly four years after the death of his first wife. All the friends of Douglas agreed that this marriage, like the first, was a most happy one. As a place of entertainment the Douglas home at Washington outshone the White House in 1858. The second Mrs. Douglas was a Roman Catholic, and the two sons of the first marriage were brought up in that faith. Douglas himself was not a member of any church. Mrs. Douglas entered actively into her husband's campaign for the Presidency, accompanying him in his tour of the South. In 1866, five years after the Senator's death, she was married to General Robert Williams, U. S. A., and became the mother of six children. It is interesting to note that when Mrs. Lincoln went to Washington in March, 1861, Mrs. Douglas became at once a close friend and social counselor.

Mr. Douglas's urgent advice, after hearing the article read aloud in a sanctum conference. Instead of ending his efforts in the South after this election news, Douglas spoke at New Orleans and again at Vicksburg before returning North, urging the Southern business men to accept accomplished facts.

He reminded the South that Mr. Lincoln would be a minority President, and would have to submit his appointments to a Democratic Senate. In short, he held that the election of Mr. Lincoln could only serve as a pretext for those who proposed to break up the Union and form a Southern Confederacy. Mr. Johnson's summary of the result from the Douglas standpoint is well justified by the facts. He notes Douglas's apparently overwhelming defeat, his electoral ticket having carried only the single State of Missouri, with three out of seven of the New Jersey electors.

Yet, as the popular vote in several States was ascertained, defeat wore the guise of a great personal triumph. Leader of a forlorn hope, he had yet received the suffrages of 1,376,957 citizens, only 489,495 less votes than Lincoln had polled. Of these, 163,525 came from the South, while Lincoln received only 26,430, all from the Border Slave States. As compared with the votes of Breckinridge and Bell at the South, Douglas's vote was insignificant; but at the North, he ran far ahead of the combined vote of both. It goes without saying that had Douglas secured the full Democratic vote in the Free States he would have pressed Lincoln hard in many quarters. From the national standpoint, the most significant aspect of the popular vote was the failure of Breckinridge to secure a majority in the Slave States. Union sentiment was still stronger than the Secessionists had boasted. The next most significant fact in the history of the election was this: Abraham Lincoln had been elected to the Presidency by the vote of a section which had given over a million votes to his rival, the leader of a faction of a disorganized party.

Even in a contest with only two parties in the field, presidential election statistics are susceptible of a great variety of analytical interpretations. This fact was well illustrated by the radically different conclusions reached by political experts in their study of the election of 1928 in which Mr. Hoover carried several Southern States that had long been solidly Democratic. The object of the Douglas men, south of Pennsylvania and the Ohio River,

DIVIDING THE NATIONAL MAP

Lincoln and Douglas struggle for possession of the western and northern regions, while Breckinridge seizes the entire South. Bell, on the high chair, appears to be attempting to restore the damage with a pot of glue. This is one of the series of Cincinnati poster caricatures.

was to prevent Breckinridge from carrying all the Slave States. In a State like Kentucky, this could be done by voting for the Union man who could poll the most votes; and that happened to be John Bell of the Constitutional Union party.

Taking Kentucky as an illustration, Bell received 66,058 as against 53,143 for Breckinridge, 25,651 for Douglas, and 1,364 for Lincoln. If the Bell ticket had not been in the field, and the contest had been between Douglas and Breckinridge, it is reasonably certain that Douglas would have had the twelve electors of Kentucky. The Breckinridge vote remaining exactly the same (53,143), it is also obvious that if one in five of the Bell supporters had voted for Douglas, Breckinridge would have been in the lead and would have carried the State. It is reasonable to infer, therefore, that no small part of the Douglas influence

against the candidate of the Southern Democrats was expressed in the practical form of votes given to the Bell-Everett ticket, as the only way to defeat Breckinridge.

A slight diversion of Douglas voters to the Bell ticket in Louisiana would have given that State to the Bell-Everett electors. If Douglas had run a little more strongly in Tennessee he would still have been in a hopeless minority. but would have thrown the State to Breckinridge by diverting strength from Bell. Although Bell carried Virginia, his vote of 74,681 was so nearly balanced by Breckinridge's vote of 74,323, that the transfer of a few Bell votes to Douglas, who received 16,290, would have put Virginia in the Breckinridge column. North Carolina gave 48,539 to Breckinridge, and 44,990 to Bell, with only 2,701 to Douglas. A Bell-Douglas fusion in that State, pressed with energy, might have been successful. In Missouri, which was carried by Douglas with a vote of 58,801, Bell received 58,372, Breckinridge 31,317, and Lincoln 17,028.

The shifting of a mere handful of votes, therefore, would have given the Missouri electors to Bell. In that case Douglas would have had no electoral votes whatsoever—except for his 3 in New Jersey as against Lincoln's 4, resulting from some mixed and confused voting for particular names on electoral tickets. Thus it becomes evident that with no loss of his popular vote, beyond an insignificant fraction of one per cent, Douglas might have been defeated in every State and had no electoral votes at all. Yet his immense popular vote would have contributed decisively to the election of Lincoln, and would have deserved credit for the country's escape from the dangers of an election thrown into the House of Representatives.

When the student of history and politics becomes immersed in the complex situations of 1860, reading contemporary newspapers, speeches in all the conventions, debates in Congress and campaign utterances on the stump, with much correspondence and documentary material that has come to light in recent years, the impression of Douglas as an aggressive leader, ambitious, courageous, and resourceful, is vivid, and by no means disappointing. Standing alone in the Democratic Senate, except for the support of Mr. Pugh of Ohio, he had not quailed before the attacks of the men who had deprived him of his chairmanship of the Committee on Territories. Professor Dodd reminds us that "in view of the almost certain success of the Republicans, Davis visited Douglas in the early summer of 1860, at the instance of Bell and Breckinridge, to suggest a withdrawal of all candidates and the nomination of a united, conservative ticket, with the sole purpose of defeating Lincoln." Continuing Mr. Dodd observes: "Doubtless Buchanan, forgetting for the time the bitter campaign so long waged against Douglas, supported this scheme of Davis and Breckinridge. It was, in fact, a confession that the party organization had erred in its fight against the 'Little Giant.' He received the overture kindly, but refused to accept the suggestion to withdraw from the canvass on the ground that his followers would certainly vote for Lincoln and Hamlin. This was a proper estimate of the Northern Democracy. Douglas was the only man in the country who could have defeated the Republicans."

Mr. Dodd's conclusions are as follows: "Davis must have seen this, but the Southern Democracy could not. No amount of persuasion could have induced the Lower South to vote at this late day for Douglas. Squatter Sovereignty had become as distasteful to them as the outspoken program of the Abolitionists; and their leader, Davis, entertained an in-

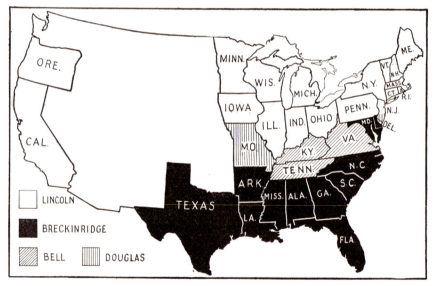

HOW THE STATES VOTED IN 1860

Sectional lines are clear. All the Free States of the North and far West were carried by Lincoln. All the States of the far South went for Breckinridge, and in addition he won in Maryland and Delaware. The Constitutional Union ticket of Bell and Everett prevailed in the three States of Virginia, Kentucky, and Tennessee. Douglas was successful in Missouri, and received part of the electoral vote of New Jersey.

DARING LEAP MADE BY THE CELEBRATED ACROBAT, LITTLE GIANT

Douglas was first and foremost among the Democrats of the North who rallied to Lincoln's support in the supreme effort to save the Union. When Sumter was fired upon, in April, 1861, the great Democratic leader and lifelong political opponent of Lincoln publicly pledged his aid to the Administration. Two months later he died.

eradicable dislike for Douglas which blinded him to all the man's good traits. 'If our little grog-drinking, electioneering demagogue can destroy our hopes, it must be that we have been doomed to destruction,' he (Davis) wrote to Pierce in June."

Less than a year after his nomination at Baltimore, Stephen Arnold Douglas had passed away. If we were devoting these pages to the details of his career, several chapters would be necessary to recount the part that he played in the events that quickly followed each other in the months after his defeat at the polls. He returned to Washington for the opening of Congress in December, and went West to make two speeches in Illinois some five months later. He had no doubts as to the colossal character of the civil war that was threaten-

ing; and sought in every way to avert the appeal to arms. He urged upon the Southern leaders the important fact that when the new Congress should assemble, after Lincoln's inauguration, there would be only twenty Republicans in the Senate of sixty-six members, and less than a clear majority of Lincoln supporters in the newly elected House of Representatives. He urged that Lincoln was honest. patient, conciliatory by nature, and not fanatical in his sectional views. Granting the worst that could be said from the Southern standpoint about Lincoln, Douglas held that there was nothing to be gained for the South by Secession.

On the other hand, Douglas was urging upon the North the view that it would be better to yield temporarily to the Secessionists rather than to take boldly assertive views of the duty of the federal government to hold Southern forts and to keep up the pretense of normal activities in custom-houses and other federal places. He held that if a wise course were pursued at Washington, the more northerly slave States could be kept from following the lower South into Secession, with the probability that after two or three years of negotiation the six or seven States extending from South Carolina to Texas could be brought back into the Union.

As the crisis developed, however, with startling rapidity during the last two months of the Buchanan Administration, Douglas recognized the war as a fact. It had been precipitated by Southern action. Whereupon he entered the Lincoln camp, with that quality of whole-heartedness that he had always shown alike in public and private affairs. He was the first and foremost of that host of Northern citizens—several millions of them altogether—known as "War Democrats." As a life-long personal and political acquaintance, Senator Douglas met the new President at inauguration time as a friend, supporter, and adviser. In Katherine Helm's volume entitled "Mary, Wife of Lincoln," we read of the intimacy of Senator and Mrs. Douglas in affairs at the White House. "Mrs. Douglas, who combined wit and beauty with sweet, gentle manners, was one of the belles of the White House," and she "was frequently asked to receive with Mrs. Lincoln."

The last journey of Senator Douglas to meet his fellow-citizens of Illinois was in acceptance of an invitation to address the State Legislature; and this speech was followed by one at Chicago which packed the Wigwam where Lincoln had been nominated in the previous year. He had risen above the level of partisanship and of personal ambition. He had always been actuated by a devotion to the Union as a whole, that marked the men of the new Western States. To these men, most of whom had been born in older States, the country in its entire sweep meant much more than the newly created commonwealths in which they now happened to reside. The test of war revealed the full measure of this Western devotion to the idea of undivided nationality.

It seems impossible to imagine speeches of greater ardor in their patriotism, or of more convincing power in their exposition of the fallacies and evils of all kinds that lurked in the doctrine of Secession, than these last efforts of Mr. Douglas. He was by nature and by circumstances an expansionist, and he hated the thought of a disintegration of the great American nation that he had helped to build up. A high authority, who had earlier been a political opponent declared of his speech before the Legislature: "I do not think that it is possible for a human being to produce a more prodigious effect with spoken words."

Mr. Cullom, afterwards a United States Senator, at that time the Speaker of the Illinois House, testified: "Never in all my experience have I been so impressed by a speaker." The speech was delivered on April 25th, and printed in the New York *Tribune* of May 1st. It stirred Illinois to the depths, and inspired the spirit of resistance. It was worth many regiments. "The shortest way to peace," said Douglas, "is the most stupendous and unanimous preparation for war." He continued: "I have struggled almost against hope to avert the calamities of war and to effect a reunion and reconciliation with our brethren in the South. I yet hope it may be done, but I am not able to point out how it may be."

In Chicago, where he had always been the idol of the somewhat noisy Democratic masses, he now received the homage of all parties. Chicago was his home city; he had been proud of its growth and had made and lost fortunes in the ups and downs of its expansion. Immediately following the great Chicago speech, he was seized by an illness that proved fatal on June 3rd. From his dying bed he sent a cheering message to President Lincoln. There is authority for the statement that if he had lived Lincoln would have given him a high position in the Administration.

The remarkable fact stands in the story of the career of this great political leader, so long Lincoln's rival and opponent in Illinois, that he ended his life as Lincoln's private and personal friend, and above all as Lincoln's unqualified political supporter.

CHAPTER XIV

Mr. Buchanan Entertains, in a Trying Season

*The President favors Breckinridge—He receives the first official
visitors from Japan—The Prince of Wales tours the country, and
witnesses the election—General Scott offers strange advice*

JAMES BUCHANAN was an incessant correspondent, and we are fortunate in having access to his letters written upon many subjects over a long period of activity in American politics. On June 13, 1860, five days before the Democratic convention reassembled at Baltimore, President Buchanan wrote as follows to one of his influential political friends: "I have hardly time now to say my prayers. Should they succeed at Baltimore in rejecting the regular delegates from the seceding States and admitting those who are *'bogus,'* then Douglas will or may be nominated. In that event the unity and strength of the Democratic party is annihilated and Lincoln elected. This is not the worst. The Democratic party will be divided and sectionalized and that, too, on the slavery issue. Everything looks bad not only for the party but for the country. The information from New York is not very encouraging."

Although President Buchanan was so strongly opposed to the nomination of Douglas, and in avowed sympathy with the Southern delegations that had put the Breckinridge ticket in the field, he was fully conversant with the intricate possibilities of a contest in which four tickets were competing. He was ready to encourage even Douglas support, in States where it might help to defeat Lincoln. As a master of Pennsylvania politics, he was always concerned about Democratic success in his own State; and as the campaign advanced he became increasingly doubtful. Gen. Henry D. Foster was running for Governor against the Republican candidate, Andrew G. Curtin. Foster had the united support of the three opposing parties. Pennsylvania's State election occurred early in October, a month before the presidential election. Mr. Buchanan, on September 5th, wrote a letter marked "private and confidential" as follows:

"Somebody sent me the enclosed slips. If General Foster has 'made a very able and powerful speech fully endorsing the position of Judge Douglas on the Territorial question,' I do not think he will be elected Governor of Pennsylvania. I draw this inference from letters which I have received from the interior of the State from good Democrats when speaking of Judge Douglas and Squatter Sovereignty. Notwithstanding I heartily desire his election, because it may be the means of defeating Lincoln."

Mr. Buchanan was justified in his prediction. Andrew G. Curtin carried the State over General Foster by 32,164 majority. This result was regarded as indicating almost certain success for the Lincoln electors in November as against the fusion ticket, although the Republicans continued to be extremely anxious until

OUR GREAT ICEBERG MELTING AWAY
Mr. Buchanan was in his last half-year as
President, and the Lincoln sun was rising.

JAMES BUCHANAN
President of the United States, 1857-1861

Buchanan came into the presidential office after a notable career in preparation. A Pennsylvania lawyer, he served a term in the House of Representatives at Washington, became Minister to Russia, was for twelve years a member of the Senate, and was President Polk's Secretary of State during the Mexican War. Under President Pierce, in 1853-56, he consented to become Minister to Great Britain in order to deal with several important diplomatic problems. He lived for seven years after his term expired, and died at his home, "Wheatlands," in his seventy-eighth year.

the votes were cast and counted. With Buchanan's influence so strongly in favor of Breckinridge, it was estimated, in analyzing the popular vote for Pennsylvania fusion electors, that about 100,000 were cast by the Breckinridge men, something less than 79,000 by the Douglas voters, and approximately 13,000 by the supporters of Bell and Everett.

In New York, on the other hand, it was considered that Bell and Breckinridge had each about 50,000 of the fusion voters and Douglas well above 200,000, the Lincoln vote being nearly 354,000. In New Jersey, estimates gave Douglas and Breckinridge equal strength, each having about 30,000 votes, Bell having less than 3,000, and Lincoln more than 58,000.

It was agreed on all hands that the Pennsylvania vote was greatly influenced in favor

of the Republicans by the strong local sentiment in favor of high protective tariffs, the Republicans making skillful use of tariff arguments in this campaign. In New York, on the other hand—particularly in New York City—the leading business interests were mercantile, in contrast with the manufacturing interests of Pennsylvania. The great merchants of New York were doing credit business in the South on an extended scale at this time, and they were persuaded to believe that Lincoln's election would mean war as well as Secession. Their contributions to defeat Lincoln were enormous.

There were of course many Lincoln supporters among New York business men, although the vote of the city was strongly Democratic. As I have already remarked, it would not be claiming too much to hold that Seward's leadership throughout the State at large was sufficient to account for the margin of voting strength that saved the Lincoln electoral ticket from defeat. This alone prevented the serious deadlock and dangerous possibilities that must have resulted from a transfer of the final choice to the House of Representatives.

Even when the most stupendous crisis stares peoples and governments in the face, they only half-way believe that the impending tragedy is inevitable. They buy and sell, sow and reap, cling to all that is normal in private occupations, and make more preparation for the continuity of ordinary affairs of a public nature than for horrible cataclysms. President Buchanan himself was complacent throughout everything. He made one political speech during the campaign, this being from the portico of the White House on July 9th. In the opening part of this calmly flowing discourse, he made the best argument for the two-thirds rule in Democratic conventions that I have ever heard or read.

As things were, a mere majority nominee might be chosen by the delegates from States which would choose few Democratic Electors. The two-thirds requirement, on the other hand, would make it probable that "under this rule no candidate could ever be nominated without embracing within the two-thirds the votes of a decided majority of the Democratic States." "If," said Mr. Buchanan, "the con-

THE POWER OF THE RAIL

Old Buck sat in his chair of state,
  His face was pale and wan;
The darkest passions of rage and hate
  In his sunken eyeballs shone.

Oh! Very uneasy, the Old Man said,
  Is the head that wears a crown—
The man who serves the slave-power now,
  Must certainly go down.

The Covode dogs are on my track,
  I hear their loud-mouthed wail;
The treacherous chair begins to crack.
  Upheaved by Lincoln's rail.

A smile played on old Abram's lips,
  He sprang that rail upon
And backward went poor old J. B.,
  Down to Oblivion.

From the *Rail-Splitter*, (Chicago), September 3, 1860

As a Republican campaign paper, the *Rail-Splitter* was disposed to avail itself of the unpopularity that attended the last six months of the Buchanan administration. The allusion in the third stanza to "the Covode dogs" has to do with an investigation of Buchanan, undertaken in the summer of 1860 by a Congressional committee headed by Hon. John Covode of Pennsylvania. It was unsparingly condemned by the Democrats as a partisan and unconstitutional proceeding. The House was then controlled by the Republicans.

vention which nominated Mr. Douglas was not a regular Democratic convention, it must be confessed that Breckinridge is in the same condition in that respect." It was plain, therefore, that every Democrat was at liberty to vote as he thought proper "without running counter to any regulation of the party."

Having prefaced his speech in this way, Mr. Buchanan gave the reasons why he preferred Breckinridge to Douglas, and proceeded as follows: "To return to the point from which I have digressed, I am in favor of Mr. Breckinridge because he sanctions and sustains the perfect equality of all the States within their common Territories, and the opinion of the Supreme Court of the United States establish-

ing this equality. The sovereign States of this Union are one vast partnership. The Territories were acquired by the common blood and common treasure of them all. Each State and each citizen of each State has the same right in the Territories as any other State, and the citizens of any other State, possess." Going back to the platform of 1856, Mr. Buchanan held firmly to the view that Territories could exclude slavery when they adopted constitutions and set up statehood, but not before.

Like all of Mr. Buchanan's utterances, this speech was exceedingly well phrased, but it lacked the penetrating logic of Lincoln's speeches, and it presented what now are seen as obvious fallacies. His great anxiety seemed

GARIBALDI AND THE NEW ITALIAN BOOT
A cartoon from *Punch* (London)

Great Britain showed little interest in the critical presidential campaign in the United States. If the American States were drifting toward disunion, a movement with just the opposite purpose and effect was nearer at hand. The Italian patriot, Giuseppe Garibaldi, was carrying on a war which resulted in the enthronement of Victor Emmanuel as the first King of united Italy.

to be for the restoration of unity in the Democratic party. He spoke of the "numerous, powerful, pious, and respectable Methodist Church," which had now become divided on sectional lines, and declared that this division was a severe shock to the Union. "A similar division of the great Democratic party, should it continue, would rend asunder one of the most powerful links which bind the Union together."

But our amiable President, with his unequalled opportunities for knowing what perils were in store, was willing to give the weight of his testimony—speaking not merely to the crowds on the White House lawn, but to the whole country—in favor of the view that the country was safe. This he held especially true because the Democratic party would surely "close up its ranks and become more powerful even from defeat . . . It will never die whilst the Constitution and the Union survive. It will live to protect and defend both. It has its roots in the very vitals of the Constitution, and, like one of the ancient cedars of Lebanon, it will flourish to afford shelter and protection to that sacred instrument and to shield it against every storm of faction."

ENGLISH VOLUNTEERS IN THE ITALIAN REVOLUTION—A SKETCH BY THOMAS NAST
Nast had begun to draw for the *New York Illustrated News* in 1860, and had gone to England to make sketches of the championship prizefight between Heeney and Sayres. From London he went to Italy; and his enterprise brought him an assignment to the staff of Garibaldi. Our pictorial weeklies were giving almost as much attention to the advance of Victor Emmanuel as to Secession.

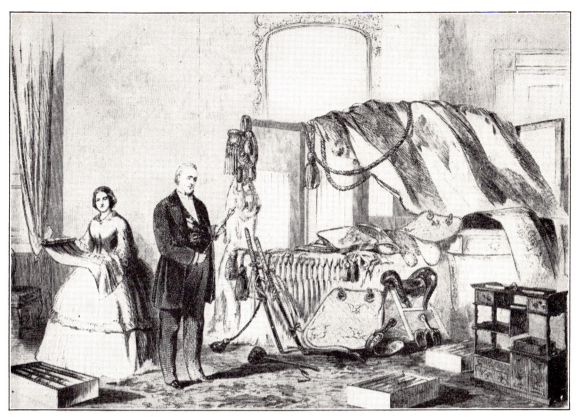

PRESIDENT BUCHANAN AND HIS NIECE, HARRIET LANE,
INSPECT GIFTS FROM JAPAN

During the critical campaign months of 1860, President Buchanan was called upon to entertain two
groups of distinguished foreign visitors: one, the Prince of Wales and his staff; the other, the first
mission that had ever come from Japan. The Japanese were here to ratify a treaty on May 23rd, the
result of the visit to their country in 1854 by Captain Matthew C. Perry (a brother of Oliver
Hazard Perry), which had marked the opening of Japan to foreign commerce and residence.

This unbreakable Democratic party, as President Buchanan saw it, while the campaign was already raging just fourteen days after the rival tickets had been launched at Baltimore, was to be trusted implicitly to save the country against any harm that might be threatened in case of Republican victory under Abraham Lincoln's leadership. Mr. Buchanan summed it up in the following paragraph:

"I entertain no such fearful apprehensions. The present issue is transitory and will speedily pass away. In the nature of things it cannot continue. There is but one possible contingency which can endanger the Union and against this all Democrats, whether squatter sovereigns or popular sovereigns will present a united resistance. Should the time ever arrive when Northern agitation and fanaticism shall proceed so far as to render the domestic firesides of the South insecure, then, and not till then, will the Union be in danger. A united Northern Democracy will present a wall of fire against such a catastrophe."

The adjournment of Congress on June 25th, two days after the final convention proceedings at Baltimore, had made Mr. Buchanan feel like a schoolboy on the advent of the long summer vacation. His own affairs had absorbed much of his attention. The House of Representatives had investigated certain scandalous charges having to do with patronage and contracts. Not merely members of the Cabinet, but the President himself had been subjected to such inquiry. Mr. Buchanan had been greatly affronted, and justly indignant. For almost half a century he had been

QUEEN VICTORIA AND THE PRINCE CONSORT
The granddaughter of King George III ascended the British
throne in 1837, when she was eighteen years old. Three
years later she married her cousin, Prince Albert of Saxe-
Coburg-Gotha. The Prince of Wales who visited America
in 1860 (later Edward VII) was their second child, born
in 1841. Two years after that visit the Prince Consort died,
and Queen Victoria reigned alone for nearly forty years,
until her death in 1901.

a politician, and had dealt with politicians of
higher and lower degree; but he had also been
a statesman and a diplomatist of high standing
and of a personal honesty that the new Republican members in the House of Representatives
ought never to have questioned. Mr. Buchanan had been deeply stirred, and had held his
ground with unyielding firmness and true
presidential dignity.

On June 22nd he had sent a long and eloquent message to the House of Representatives
protesting against the so-called Covode Investigation, as an attack upon the Executive
branch of the government. On the same date he
had sent to the Senate a similarly elaborate
document discussing the public land system,
and explaining his reasons for vetoing the
Homestead bill. Never, perhaps, had a Presi-

dent been more relieved at the thought of a
clear five months of empty legislative halls on
Capitol Hill.

He had time now to await with agreeable
expectations the answer to a certain letter that
he had written on June 4th. This letter had
indicated beyond a doubt his belief that our
family quarrels were not so devastating in
their effect upon our social manners that we
could not safely invite company to cross our
threshold. The letter was as follows:

Washington City, June 4, 1860.
To Her Majesty Queen Victoria:
I have learned from the public journals that the
Prince of Wales is about to visit Your Majesty's
North American dominions. Should it be the intention of His Royal Highness to extend his visit to the
United States, I need not say how happy I shall be
to give him a cordial welcome to Washington.
You may be well assured that everywhere in this
country he will be greeted by the American people
in such a manner as cannot fail to prove gratifying
to Your Majesty. In this they will manifest their
deep sense of your domestic virtues, as well as the
conviction of your merits as a wise, patriotic, and
constitutional sovereign.
Your Majesty's most obedient servant,
JAMES BUCHANAN.

The answer that President Buchanan received was in the most cordial terms:

Buckingham Palace, June 22, 1860.
My Good Friend:
I have been much gratified at the feelings which
prompted you to write to me inviting the Prince of
Wales to come to Washington. He intends to return from Canada through the United States, and
it will give him great pleasure to have an opportunity of testifying to you in person that those feelings
are duly reciprocated by him. He will thus be able
at the same time to mark the respect which he enter-
tains for the Chief Magistrate of a great and
friendly state and kindred nation.
The Prince will drop all royal state on leaving
my dominions, and travel under the name of Lord
Renfrew, as he has done when travelling on the
continent of Europe.
The Prince Consort wishes to be kindly remembered to you.
I remain ever your good friend,
VICTORIA RA.

It is no part of our task in these chapters
to describe the American visit of the Prince
of Wales, who was entertained at the White
House and elsewhere. Mr. Buchanan's per-

sonal relations with the royal family had
been agreeable while he was Minister at
London in the preceding Administration;
and his niece, Miss Harriet Lane, was
well qualified for the duties of official
hospitality at Washington.

At New York and elsewhere, there
were many people more concerned about
what they would wear at balls and dinners given in honor of the Prince of
Wales than about the fate of the country.
These same people, a few months later,
made themselves unhappy because Abraham Lincoln wore black gloves instead
of white, at an opera performance in New
York on his inaugural journey to Washington; and even after the storm of civil
war had burst upon us they were not
ready to sacrifice the habit of criticising
Mrs. Lincoln's costumes.

Meanwhile, the distinguished young
heir to the British throne with his attending
group of governmental agents and courtiers,
was keenly interested in the progress of an
election in which it was plain to them all that
the fate of America was at stake. A. K.
McClure of Philadelphia, whose political
reminiscences are of more than slight historical value, and who was in charge of the

A DANCE WITH COUSIN COLUMBIA

LORD PUNCH (to the Prince of Wales): "Now, my boy! There's
your pretty Cousin Columbia. You don't get such a partner
every day."

From *Punch*, London, October 20, 1860.

Lincoln campaign headquarters in his own
city, describes a scene witnessed by the
Prince of Wales on election night:

"The Prince of Wales was then on a visit
to this country, and had just arrived at the
Continental Hotel in Philadelphia. My headquarters as chairman of the Lincoln Committee were at the Girard House immediately opposite, and I saw the handsome young Prince,
then a picture of manly vigor and beauty,
stand on the Chestnut Street balcony for an
hour, surrounded by his suite of nobles, watching what he regarded as the dying agonies of
the Republic. The main streets of the city
were crowded with shouting, wrangling, and
rioting partisans, and the Prince obviously
congratulated himself that he had just happened in this country in time to see its angry
dissolution. He witnessed the riotous enthusiasm of the Republicans, and the much
more riotous madness of the defeated party,
until he wearied of it, and he was astounded
the next morning to discover that the city was
as quiet and serene as an average Philadelphia
Sunday."

Apart from the single speech from which
we have quoted, President Buchanan was not
personally engaged in party discussions during the campaign. He was anxious that **his**

PRINCE OF WALESIANA

The Prince of Wales had spent two months in Canada before entering the United States. He came by way of
Detroit, on September 21st and left from Portland, Maine,
on October 20th. Everywhere he was cordially received and
entertained. From the 3rd until the 7th of October he
was the guest of President Buchanan. The cartoon is
from *Vanity Fair*.

QUEEN VICTORIA'S SON AT WASHINGTON

MRS. BUCHANAN, the Step-Mother of her country: "Bless me! Now, ain't he so like his blessed Ma?"

From *Vanity Fair,* New York.

Public opinion changed rapidly, both North and South, after the John Brown raid. Thus President Buchanan was placed in a position which cost him in turn the confidence and good-will first of one section and then of the other, leaving him in after years with few people impartial enough in their reminiscences or in their later contributions to history to do him even scant justice.

On the 29th of October, a week before the election, the venerable head of the United States Army, Gen. Winfield Scott, sent a strange communication to President Buchanan from his military headquarters in New York. First, he notified the President that in the event of Mr. Lincoln's election there would doubtless be secession of one or more Southern States. This would be accompanied by an immediate seizure on the part of the Secessionists of Southern forts that General Scott enumerated. Certain of these, in his opinion, ought at once to be reinforced, in order to protect the interests of the United States. His

own State should endorse his views; and the large vote for Breckinridge in Pennsylvania— in contrast with the small Breckinridge vote of the neighboring States of New York and Ohio—may fairly be attributed to the great hold of the President upon the Democracy of his own Commonwealth. He had evidently lost confidence after the State election had been carried by the Republicans, and he was concerned over the intensity of sectional antagonism displayed on both sides.

Mr. Buchanan's alliance with the Southern wing of the party seems to the casual student of that period to have been an unnatural and unsuitable attitude for a Northern statesman. But he had been Secretary of State in the Administration of President Polk, and closely identified with policies that the Southern leaders had favored. He had been high in the councils of the Pierce Administration; and President Pierce himself, with many other New England Democrats, was, in 1860, an anti-Douglas man and a supporter of Breckinridge.

THE PRINCE REACHES HOME

H. R. H. JUNIOR (to H. R. H. SENIOR): "Now, Sir-ree, I'll tell you all about my travels."

From *Punch,* November 20, 1860.

(Note the English conception of American manners of the day, as acquired by the Prince during his sojourn.)

purpose was not so much that of preparation for civil war as to provide temporary remedies against situations that might incite to conflict. But there were only five companies, with a total of four hundred men, anywhere available for the transfers that General Scott advocated. The entire army of the United States consisted of about 16,000 men, nearly all of whom were on Western frontiers protecting settlers against Indians.

General Scott had a peculiar fondness for large political and historical problems, and his garrulity often took the form of philosophical reasoning. In this communication to President Buchanan, at what might have been regarded as a critical juncture, General Scott advised that the right of secession had better be conceded for the sake of argument. His own contribution to the subject consisted of the urgent advice that the territory of the United States should be left without "gaps." He proposed to protect what he called "interior" positions. He contemplated the possibility of the division of the United States into several confederacies, probably four, as a

VANITY FAIR.

RICHELIEU,
ADAPTED TO THE TIMES

RICHELIEU (*his first appearance in the character.*)   WINFIELD SCOTT
KING LOUIS (*his farewell engagement.*)   JAS. BUCHANAN

RICHELIEU—*Remember my grand maxims! First employ all methods to conciliate.*
LOUIS—*Failing these?*
RICHELIEU—*All means to crush!*

General Scott, as head of the United States Army, had recommended to President Buchanan in October, 1860, a course of procedure in the event of secession following the election of Abraham Lincoln. The document was not made public until General Scott himself gave it out, in the middle of January, 1861.

smaller evil than civil and sectional wars. He drew the boundaries of such new Unions, and suggested as the capitals for three of them Albany, New York; Columbia, South Carolina, and either Alton or Quincy, Illinois. His fourth capital might have been San Francisco or Sacramento.

The practical point of General Scott's proposal was that the President should immediately announce the movement of troops to Fortress Monroe, Virginia, the two forts in Charleston harbor, one below Mobile, one below Savannah, two in Pensacola harbor, and two below New Orleans on the Mississippi. It would of course have taken a considerable time to transport the handfuls of men available from Boston and elsewhere to these Southern coast fortifications. But this point was of no consequence. The only matter to be considered was the effect upon public opinion in the South

—and hardly less throughout the North—of the announcement that such movements had been ordered by way of precaution against threatened Secession.

It is hard to estimate in sum total what would have happened if Buchanan had acted upon Scott's advice. South Carolina would have taken immediate steps to seize Forts Moultrie and Sumter, and Secession would have been precipitated everywhere in the Lower South, with the sympathy of every Slave State from Delaware to Texas. For Mr. Buchanan to have issued such an order would have been wholly inconsistent with his views. No Southern State could secede without certain formal steps, none of which had yet been taken. For South Carolinians or citizens of any State to have held a convention, for the discussion of any phase of the State's position and relationships, would have been entirely lawful. President Buchanan had no official grounds for assuming that any State was proposing to withdraw from the Union.

If South Carolina some weeks later had not led the way, there is the smallest reason to believe that any other State would have taken the initiative. General Scott's proposals in this communication of October 29th to the President, which he repeated with some further detail in a communication to the Secretary of War on the following day, had no military value or justification. The fact that the memorandum was submitted to the Administration on the very eve of an exciting election, when for all purposes of military precaution it would have sufficed to await the results of that contest, is sufficient to show that General Scott's motive was political.

To anticipate somewhat, it may be well to add that General Scott himself made this document public in the middle of January after the secession movement was well advanced, and some six weeks before Mr. Buchanan turned his office over to Mr. Lincoln. In the ensuing controversy between the superannuated General and the former President, the statesman had no trouble in vindicating himself against the fantastic absurdities of the old soldier.

I am not recalling this circumstance relating to Scott and Buchanan for any reason except to help the reader better to understand the difficulties of a situation in 1860 that had not yet resulted in any definite conclusions. On the turn of the year, action began to follow discussion. It soon became easy to analyze the uncertainties of 1860 in the light of subsequent events. General Scott, remaining on the scene and holding his place for some time to come as General in command of the Army of the United States, lives in history as a loyal patriot and a hero of the Union cause.

Mr. Buchanan, passing into retirement at his home in Pennsylvania, celebrated his seventieth birthday on April 23rd. He had never been a Secessionist, and the entire South had turned against him. If he had been in the Senate from Pennsylvania, rather than in the White House, he would doubtless have become one of President Lincoln's strongest supporters. With his great experience, especially in foreign affairs, he would have made a more valuable member of the Foreign Relations Committee than Charles Sumner or any of the Republican members of that body.

"SPEAK! CAESAR IS TURNED TO HEAR!"

President Buchanan addresses Soothsayer Forney (who was Clerk of the House, but had been Buchanan's campaign manager in 1856), who thereupon warns him: "Beware the Ides of March!"

Douglas, who had turned "Lincoln man," died too soon to have built up a new reputation as, quite probably, Lincoln's Secretary of War. And so it follows that it has never been easy for historical scholars—much less, therefore, for the ordinary citizen—to reach a firm conclusion as to the place Douglas should properly hold in the annals of statesmanship.

While Buchanan was President of the United States, Breckinridge was Vice-President and was the presiding officer of the Senate. Breckinridge had not attained the first rank as a leader, for he was still one of the younger men in public life. But he was a chivalrous and attractive figure,

KING JAMES AND THE GHOST OF GAFFER FORNEY
The cartoons on these two facing pages relate to the inquiry into charges made against President Buchanan early in 1860, in the House of Representatives. It was alleged that the Administration had brought pressure to bear for the passage of the Lecompton bill. A committee of five members investigated, and in their report they divided upon party lines: three Republicans sustaining the charges, and two Democrats exonerating the President. No further action was taken. John W. Forney, who appears in both cartoons, was an influential journalist of Philadelphia and Washington and at the time he was Clerk of the House.

eloquent but not fanatical or extreme, an excellent type of the great school of Kentucky lawyers and publicists. He was young enough to make a new record and to achieve lasting fame in the Southern armies and in the government of the Confederacy. As a hero of the Southern cause and a favorite scion of a great family in his own State, his career was not broken or hopelessly obscured by the cataclysm of the Civil War.

President Buchanan, however, was removed from the scenes of stirring activity at a time when the Republicans of the North were calling him a conspirator and a traitor. He was accused of having connived at the transfer of Government war material to places in the South for the express purpose of enabling his so-called "fellow-conspirators" in the Cotton States to seize it at their convenience. Those who were not so blinded by impatient partisanship as to call him a traitor, stigmatized him as weak and vacillating. He was accounted upon the whole a contemptible figure in the

long line of American Presidents and foremost statesmen.

Mr. Buchanan had not done anything to precipitate the Secession movement, but on the contrary had done his best to restrain it. Having no illusions as to the terrible nature of the threatening conflict at arms, his one object was to avert war. He occupied himself in the quiet of his home in the composition of a volume entitled "Mr. Buchanan's Administration on the Eve of the Rebellion." It is far more valuable and trustworthy as a statement of the facts, as Mr. Buchanan knew them intimately and, especially, of his actions and motives, than most of the subsequent disquisitions upon that period by historians, whether Northern or Southern.

With that consideration which was the unfailing quality of one of the most courteous public men of his period, Mr. Buchanan did not publish his book until after the conclusion of the war. He survived until June 1, 1868, near the beginning of his seventy-eighth year.

He then explained that "the publication was delayed to avoid the possible imputation, unjust as this would have been, that any portion of it was intended to embarrass Mr. Lincoln's Administration in the vigorous prosecution of pending hostilities." That he was always conciliatory in mood, preferring to support the McClellan ticket in 1864, and wishing that Lincoln after his second victory at the polls might offer generous inducements to the South that would end the war, is merely to say that he could not be otherwise than consistent with his own mental and moral constitution.

Mr. Buchanan by nature was a diplomatist and a compromiser. As Secretary of State in the Polk Administration, he had done his share to avert a war with England by accepting a compromise of our Oregon claims. If we were undertaking to eulogize or vindicate Mr. Buchanan we might hold that his continuing influence at the British Court was of some assistance to President Lincoln in the most threatening external incident of the war period. On October 6, 1860, Mr. Buchanan had written a most agreeable and well-phrased letter to Queen Victoria in praise of the Prince of Wales.

"The visit of the Prince to the tomb of Washington," said Mr. Buchanan, "and the simple but solemn ceremonies at this consecrated spot, will become a historical event, and cannot fail to exert a happy influence on the kindred people of the two countries." One paragraph in the letter was as follows: "The Prince left us for Richmond this morning with the Duke of Newcastle and the other members of his wisely selected suite. I should gladly have prolonged his visit had this been possible consistently with previous engagements. In our domestic circle he won all hearts. His free and ingenuous intercourse with myself evinced both a kind heart and good understanding. I shall ever cherish the warmest wishes for his welfare."

The answer of Queen Victoria was dated November 19th. The Prince had remained in the United States another month, having seen something of the Southern States and having witnessed the election at Philadelphia, as we have reported in a previous paragraph. His homeward voyage had been retarded, and the Queen explained that she had purposely delayed answering the President's letter until she could "couple it with the announcement of the Prince of Wales's safe return to his home." The following paragraphs from Victoria's letter are of more than ordinary historical significance:

He [the Prince] cannot sufficiently praise the great cordiality with which he has been everywhere greeted in your country, and the friendly manner in which you have received him; and whilst as a mother I am grateful for the kindness shown him, I feel impelled to express, at the same time, how deeply I have been touched by the many demonstrations of affection, personally, toward myself, which his presence has called forth.

I fully reciprocate towards your nation the feelings thus made apparent, and look upon them as forming an important link to cement two nations of kindred origin and character, whose mutual esteem and friendship must always have so material an influence upon their respective development and prosperity.

The interesting and touching scene at the grave of General Washington to which you allude may be fitly taken as the type of our present feeling, and I trust of our future relations.

It was in November, 1861, just a year after the Queen had written the letter quoted above, that an American naval officer overhauled a British passenger vessel and forcibly seized the Confederate Commissioners to Great Britain and France. A war with England was prevented only by the wise diplomacy of President Lincoln himself, aided, as against the infuriated and war-seeking John Bull, by the personal intervention of Queen Victoria and the Prince Consort. The sentiment of this letter of the Queen's had been heartfelt and genuine. Mr. Buchanan as Minister to England had been a friend of both of these high personages, and as President he had extended American hospitality to the heir-apparent of the British throne. It may be true that gentle and diplomatic personages like Mr. Buchanan are for the piping times of peace rather than for the bold adventures of war; but if peace had not been maintained in 1861 with the government of Great Britain, the United States would have been in the worst predicament of the country's entire history.

"UNCLE SAM" MAKING NEW ARRANGEMENTS.

Uncle Sam takes down his "Help Wanted" sign, informing the three defeated candidates that he has concluded to "let Old Abe Lincoln have the place." President Buchanan is seen through the window, packing up to leave. The cartoonist has made excellent portraits of Bell, Breckinridge, and Douglas, as well as of Lincoln and Buchanan; but this smooth-faced and well-appareled Uncle Sam is a different sort of person from the tall, full-bearded and sharp-featured gentleman who has now become the standard type. The cartoon is one of the best of the Currier & Ives lithographed posters.

CHAPTER XV

South Carolina Takes Steps

Lincoln's election crystallizes sentiment at Charleston—A conscientious and sincere community—The Rhetts as crusaders—President Buchanan takes firm ground and rebuilds his Cabinet

HUMANLY SPEAKING, nothing was more certain than the Secession of South Carolina in the event of Lincoln's success at the polls. If Douglas had been elected, South Carolina's action would hardly have been retarded. Efforts made by Jefferson Davis and other Southern men to induce Douglas and Breckinridge to withdraw during the campaign in favor of a compromise candidate were hopeless from the beginning. Douglas had replied that his withdrawal would only result in throwing his Northern support to Lincoln. Even if the Constitutional Union ticket had overcome impossible obstacles and won the day, there is no evidence to indicate that the Secession of South Carolina would have been averted; for, if the election of the Bell-Everett ticket could have appeased the South, nothing would have been simpler than to have withdrawn the Breckinridge-Lane ticket before election in favor of Mr. Bell of Tennessee. This would probably have had in-

fluence enough to have elected Bell by a plurality over Lincoln, and probably by a clear
majority over both Lincoln and Douglas.

If a very little more success had attended
the combined opposition to Lincoln in the State
of New York, the election would have been
thrown into the House of Representatives. In
that case South Carolina would have awaited
the result, knowing that General Lane—who
was Breckinridge's running mate—would
without question be chosen Vice-President by
the Senate. The South would have endeavored
to persuade the House to elect Breckinridge,
but above all to prevent its electing Lincoln.
Only the three highest in electoral standing
could be considered, and the only other resort
would have been to compromise on Bell. But
since the South vastly preferred Lane to Bell,
the strategy of Southern leaders would have
been directed towards maintaining a parliamentary deadlock until noon of March 4th, in
which case Lane would have been sworn in as
President, and Secession would have been
postponed, perhaps indefinitely, but almost certainly until after another presidential election.

A SOUTH CAROLINA SHIP OF WAR
A Northern paper fails to be impressed with rumors that South
Carolina was planning to seize control of the harbor of Charleston,
and it ridicules the Secessionist demand for Sumter and Moultrie.

These conjectures may seem rather dull,
but they affect the essence of our governmental
system as it operates at a moment of extreme
crisis. It is bad machinery; and it is hardly
creditable to our intelligence and our energy
that we do not reform it.

The North saw no reason why the South
should secede on account of the election of
Lincoln, and thought that the threats were
merely sectional and partisan bluff for campaign purposes. Most of the best leaders of
the South did not desire Secession, doubted
its wisdom, dreaded its consequences. But
they became the victims of the doctrines they
had inculcated. There were lesser leaders—
locally influential, failing to understand national and world conditions, making politics a
passionate and absorbing pursuit, blinded by
feelings to the point where all the facts were
seen in distortion—to whom it seemed absolutely necessary that words should be trans-
lated into action. These men had inflamed the
popular mind. Even as matters stood, the demand for immediate Secession had not yet
swept like a cyclone across the entire South.

But the impulse to action, given certain conditions, affects the minds of
men in the mass more powerfully
than the counsels of negation or of
caution and delay.

One might write a book upon the
temperament and the psychology of
South Carolina in 1860. The author
of the book would read the files of
the Charleston *Mercury*, which was
at that time the most influential
organ of opinion in the United
States. He would turn back to the
speeches of John C. Calhoun, not
neglecting those of many other men
less famous but hardly less masterful
in the shaping of local sentiment.
South Carolina had been so educated
as never to understand that a nation
is a growth and not a governmental
mechanism. They were still talking
in South Carolina about the Virginia and Kentucky resolutions of
1798. They entertained a theory to
the effect that the United States was

a partnership of certain sovereign entities, and that this voluntary partnership must conduct itself to the satisfaction of each partner, because otherwise a given partner might exercise the choice of refusing to agree to a particular action of the firm, and might withdraw altogether from the partnership.

That these views were correct, they undertook to prove to themselves and to others by legal and metaphysical disquisitions. Unfortunately, South Carolina was dealing with words and ignoring facts. In the family of nations the United States of America was an entity like France or Brazil. Alabama or Iowa had no more the character of a sovereign State in the sense of international law than had one of the State divisions of Mexico or one of the counties of England. Looking at things from the standpoint of a political scientist rather than a metaphysician, an American State had less excuse for claiming the partnership theory than had Scotland in Great Britain, and much less than Ireland in the United

AN ENGLISH COMMENT ON LINCOLN'S ELECTION
From *Punch*, London, December 1, 1860

Accompanying text in *Punch* is as follows: "In consequence of the election of Abraham Lincoln as President of the United States, it is announced that South Carolina, in an ecstasy of slave-owners' rage, has ordered a solemn day of humiliation, on which all the slaves in the State are to be flogged, and all the copies of the Scriptures burned. Moreover, she calls a convention and declares that she is going to separate from the Union, and be an independent State, and have representatives at the courts of Europe."

THE BEGINNING OF SLAVERY'S END

Thus far shall Slavery go, no farther;
  That tide must ebb from this time forth.
So many righteous Yankees are there,
  Who Good and Truth hold something worth,
That they outnumber the immoral
  Throughout the States, on that old quarrel
  That stands between the South and North.

The great Republic is not rotten
  So much as half; the rest is sound.
Most of her sons have not forgotten
  Her own foundation; holy ground!
The better party is the stronger,
And by the worse will now no longer
  Bear to be bullied, ruled, and bound.

Enough of frantic stump-haranguing,
  Invectives of a rabid Press,
Tarring and feathering, flogging, hanging,
  To stop free mouths; the mad excess
Of human-fleshmongers tyrannic
Who rant and revel in Satanic
  Enthusiasm of wickedness!

Come, South, accept the situation;
  The change will grow by safe degrees.
If any talk of separation,
  Hang all such traitors if you please.
Break up the Union? Brothers, never!
No; the United States for ever,
  Pure Freedom's home beyond the seas!

**A POEM FROM "PUNCH" AFTER LINCOLN'S
ELECTION**

Kingdom. Texas might have had a little claim to ask release in view of the circumstances of its annexation. But the Secession doctrine anywhere west of the Alleghanies involved nothing but the substitution of legal fictions for obvious facts.

We had now thirty-three States instead of the original thirteen. With Texas an exception, all the new States had been carved out of territory of the United States. They had been given their powers under their State constitutions purely by virtue of national grants. Under legal fiction, they had created a federal Union as their agent for certain common purposes which were to be strictly construed. But laying aside the legal fiction, they were merely convenient subdivisions of national territory authorized to govern themselves locally on a plan of distributed functions, which they proceeded further to carry out by creating counties, townships, and municipalities.

Seemingly endless discussion had at last been adjourned for a more drastic test. Theories of nullification and secession, even in South Carolina, would in due time have become merely interesting chapters in the history of political thought, if there had been nothing involved except the conflict of abstract views. Students of Jackson and Calhoun would always have been reminded of those theories, just as students of metaphysics and theology are obliged to study the tiresome verbiage of early pan-ecumenical councils. In these observations I am not meaning to treat too slightingly the creeds and the doctrines of our fellow-citizens of South Carolina. I am merely reminding the reader that they were kept alive until 1860 because they had become associated in the minds of well-educated people with issues of a practical nature.

I have remarked in an earlier chapter that secession ideas had been floating up and down the Atlantic seaboard for a long time. Many Federalist leaders of New England had upheld secessionism because they hated the second war with England and found Jefferson's embargo ruinous to their shipping business. For a number of years previous to 1860 there were Abolitionist leaders who proclaimed their belief in secession because they would not have Free States associated in an unholy league with States that supported the abomination of slavery. Men always and everywhere have tried to make their beliefs tally with their interests.

South Carolinians held the more firmly to their doctrines because they were high-minded and conscientious. Speculators in slaves and cotton lands in Mississippi and Alabama were hurling coarse defiance at the North, and talking wildly of southward annexations and the aggrandizement of their slave empire, with wealth and prosperity beyond the dreams of avarice. They were not bothered about scruples or doctrines, but were floating rather madly on the high tides of a tremendous boom. The bank panic of 1857, from which the North was only painfully emerging, had hardly touched the Cotton States.

South Carolina had felt keenly the injustice of the tariff of 1832. Free Trade as a doctrine is merely a device to suit the temporary needs of an exporting industrial State, or of an importing and exporting agricultural State. But South Carolina, for reasons exactly opposite those that were leading England to the abolition of the Corn Laws, had demanded Free Trade as a high principle of economic policy, and a matter of essential justice. Hence Nullification; which did not yield to Jackson's fiat, but rather to Clay's prompt revision of the tariff.

So conscientious were the South Carolinians that they could not and would not believe in slavery merely for the fattening of their pocket-books. In an earlier period they, like the Virginians, had fully admitted the evils of slavery, and had joined in the reproaches that the Revolutionary leaders heaped upon Great Britain for its reckless conduct as a slave-trading nation, and its crime of having fastened slavery upon our colonies for its own enrichment. But gradually South Carolina had risen to an acceptance of responsibility for the maintenance of an institution that it had not originally established. Africa was a vast continent of warring savages, where cannibalism prevailed and where the most cruel forms of enslavement were practised universally. The one bright picture of the Negro race in the whole world was to be found in our Southern States, where four millions of these people of inferior heredity had been redeemed from the savagery of the dark continent.

The North had become interested in foreign missionary work; and the American Colonization Society was sending a few free Negroes to Liberia. But the South argued, and with probable truth, that all the missionary work of all the American and European societies for the spread of Christianity in heathen countries, was not for a moment to be compared—in volume or in influence—with the Christianizing and civilizing work that the Southern planters and slave-owners were carrying on among the helpless black people who had been brought within the sheltering arms of that domestic institution, the existence of which had so infuriated the fanatical Abolitionists of the North.

Those Abolitionists had not only preached the doctrine of insurrection, fomenting it by the distribution of incendiary tracts and news-

DEPLORABLE RESULT OF LINCOLN'S ELECTION

James Gordon Bennett's New York *Herald* was extremely pessimistic after the votes were counted in November, 1860. Its readers at that time might have looked for some such results as these depicted by *Vanity Fair's* artist: Mr. Bennett shutting up shop preparatory to a return to Scotland, cows grazing in Fulton Street, widespread desolation, and Horace Greeley fiddling over the ruins.

papers throughout the South, but they had contemplated a series of slave insurrections of which the John Brown raid was the precursor. They had succeeded in several States of the North in absolutely nullifying the Constitutional provision for the return of fugitive slaves. Reasonable men in the South admitted that slavery had its dangers and abuses. They deplored the breaking up of slave families. Certain phases of the domestic traffic, such as had converted Virginia into a breeding ground for the supply of the unlimited and desperate demand of the new cotton regions, were viewed with grave concern. South Carolina knew that the status of slavery—looking to the future—would be modified, even with slavery at its best. But they asked to be let alone in the working out of problems that they understood and that were peculiarly their own.

The experiences that came later during the war went far to justify the South Carolina view. White men of the Confederacy, middle-aged, and young, were rapidly drawn into the vortex of a conflict that, for the South, required universal enrollment for military service. The plantations with their women and children were protected by the loyalty and fidelity of the affectionate colored people who were bound to service, but most of whom were so identified with the labors, the recreations, and the fortunes of the plantations to which they belonged that freedom for them was merely a puzzling and anxious word. Later, when the time came, they could accept it emotionally; but to learn how to use it was a slow and painful process which may approximate completion one hundred years after Lincoln's proclamation of 1863.

Being conscientious, the South Carolinians had to believe that they were legally and morally justified. Being prosperous and practical, they had also to be convinced that Seces-

HOISTING THE PALMETTO FLAG ON THE
LIBERTY POLE AT CHARLESTON
This was on November 17, 1860, a month before the State
withdrew from the Union.

In this conjecture they were undoubtedly right. A number of States that preferred not to secede were so opposed to coercion that even the attempt to protect federal property and to hold coastal forts actually threw them into the arms of the Secessionists. They believed in South Carolina; and the belief was shared across the Lower South that the Republican party had become aggressively Abolitionist, and that in preventing the extension of slavery through the new Territories a girdling movement would begin slowly, but inevitably, to strangle slavery in the States where its legal existence had not been denied.

In short, arguments had failed, and the persuasions of those who urged further patience and compromise fell on deaf ears. With Lincoln's election, it was a matter of days or of weeks, rather than of months, for bold action in South Carolina.

Mr. Buchanan had four months more in the White House, but he had no army that he could use beyond four or five hundred men in eight or nine scattered companies. Congress was giving him no support or help, because no two members of Congress seemed to think alike. And no powerful congressional leader of the North, unless it were the discredited Douglas, had the quality of decisive courage for emergencies.

In one spot there was no hesitation, and that was in the editorial offices of the Charleston *Mercury.* Mr. Rhodes says: "The crowds that thronged the streets of Charleston on the morning of November 7th were of one mind. From their point of view they had an undoubted grievance; consequently their complaint was just. With one accord they invoked Secession as the remedy. When the resignations of the Judge and the District Attorney of the United States Court were announced the excitement grew. At noon the palmetto and lone star flag was stretched across the street from an upper window of the Charleston *Mercury* office, and was hailed with cheers and expressions of passionate attachment." The Charleston *Courier,* with a little more caution, while holding the same views, warned against "symptoms of ill-advised demonstrations." But the sentiment of Charleston was

sion would be a good thing for them. They had consulted constantly with people in other States, and believed that if Lincoln should be elected and if they acted firmly and decisively, they would not stand alone, but would carry with them Georgia, Florida, Alabama, Mississippi, Louisiana, and Texas.

With ample federal contacts at Washington, these South Carolinians knew the exact military and naval equipment of the United States Government. Furthermore, they believed that the purposes of the North were far less clear and definite than those of the South. They earnestly hoped that if Secession came it would be peaceable, and that intimate relations would at once be established between the governments of the North and the South. They believed that the remaining Slave States, Virginia, Maryland, North Carolina, Kentucky, Missouri, Arkansas, and the new Territory of New Mexico (which of its own accord had now established slavery), would never permit Northern armies to cross their territory to attack the seceded States of the Lower South.

THE FIRST STATE RIGHTS FLAGS UNFURLED BY THE SECESSIONISTS
AT COLUMBIA, THE CAPITAL OF SOUTH CAROLINA

THE SECESSION MOVEMENT

(An editorial from the "New York Illustrated News" accompanying the sketch reproduced above.)

As we had every reason to expect, the people of the South indignantly avow the shock which the election of Lincoln to the Presidency has given them. South Carolina, Georgia, Alabama, and Florida have already made declarations of a very decisive character. They do not mean to stay in the Union, as they are now advised; and if the spirit which at present rules the temper of the South prevail long, there can be no question as to the result—the South or a great part of it will form an independent confederacy. It is claimed that they have a distinct right to this if they can effect it peaceably. Several of these States have already assumed an air of independence, and South Carolina has "lifted the Palmetto flag." Our sketch of a scene at Columbia is a fair indication of the disposition of the South in its march from the Union. But although they do hoist the "States right flags," their "Palmettos" and their "lone stars," we have confidence in calmer thoughts over-taking them, and guiding to meeter action than the disruption of our glorious confederacy.

While we have no disposition to accept as validly based any of the alarm which the movement at the South is calculated to generate, we cannot overlook the fact that immense mischief may too soon ensue to the commercial interests of the whole country. The South is unquestionably in a fever of indignation; be the cause well founded or not. The North looks complacently on; be the calmness deep felt or not. That we have reached a crisis in our country's history, there is no need of assurance from any political sage. The financial disquiet which is at work, and which has already seriously disturbed the "funded arrangements" of our great commercial marts, attests the fact too plainly. By forbearance at the North the irritation at the South may soon be induced to reason itself into a belief that nothing is designed by the new government likely to interfere with the vested interests of the South or the peculiar institution which it is bound to protect in all its forms.

not that of ignorant or unruly mobs. It was decidedly more serious and genuine than the sentiment of Boston in pre-Revolutionary days, when the tea was thrown overboard. Mr. Rhodes reminds us that the South Carolina leaders were constantly making this particular comparison.

Governor Gist had called the Legislature in extra session, some weeks earlier, in order that presidential electors might be appointed who would act simultaneously with those of the other States on November 6th. Readers will remember that South Carolina was the one State in which electors were chosen by the Legislature and not by popular vote. The Legislature had not adjourned the session, waiting to see whether the dreaded election of Lincoln was to become a terrifying fact. This was a new Legislature, chosen in October, with particular reference to foreseen emergencies, and it was

THE PARTING

"A certain man had two sons; and the younger of them said to his father, 'Give me the portion of goods that falleth to me.'"—A New York cartoon relating to the South Carolina secession movement.

an unusually representative body. The question for immediate decision was whether or not to call a convention. The proposal to act only after reaching an understanding with Georgia, to be followed by a convention of the Southern States, was defeated. Strong pressure on the part of newspapers and citizens resulted in action on Saturday, November 10th.

It is highly significant that every member of both Houses of the Legislature voted for the bill providing that the people of South Carolina should hold a convention on December 17th, to consider the relations of the State "with the Northern States and the Government of the United States." Senator Chestnut on the same day resigned from the United States Senate, and the Legislature took steps to put South Carolina on a military footing. The State at large as represented at Columbia, the capital city, was even more enthusiastic for these bold steps than was the State's chief city and seaport, Charleston; and the Charleston men were praised for not thinking too much of their commercial relations with the North which might suffer some inconvenience.

Charleston was, in fact, wild with enthusiasm, and the city was brilliant with fireworks and illuminations when on Monday, two days after the action by the Legislature, a great ratification meeting was held. Senator Hammond's resignation had followed that of his colleague. Mr. Rhodes advises those who are in doubt as to the sincerity and the clearheadedness of these decisions in South Carolina to read carefully the speeches that were made, the editorials that were published in the press, and the discourses of accomplished and high-minded clergymen who dealt with the subject from the pulpit. On November 17th Charleston raised a great liberty pole, and hoisted the palmetto flag, dedicating it with religious services. But the bands also played the "Marsellaise," and the people did not hide the fact that the steps they were taking, while in their own opinion legal, would be regarded as revolutionary.

CHAPTER XVI

Secession vs. Coercion — The Dilemma

*South Carolina decides upon separation in advance of other States—
Buchanan is hesitant, but Northern opinion is even less decisive—
"No right to secede"—"No authority to coerce"*

THE MOST UNCOMPROMISING spokesmen of the Secession movement were Robert Barnwell Rhett, owner of the Charleston *Mercury*, and his son Robert Barnwell Rhett, Jr., editor of the paper. The responsibility for leadership in the withdrawal of the South from the Union is ascribed so commonly to Jefferson Davis that the not less equal influence of several others is too little recognized. The elder Rhett was born in Beaufort, South Carolina, on December 24, 1800, and was therefore about to celebrate his sixtieth birthday when the convention in which he was a leader unanimously adopted the Secession Ordinance on December 20th. He and Yancey of Alabama were the most conspicuous of the pro-slavery Southern leaders of 1860, apart from the men whose activities were then centered at Washington, where Senators Toombs, Davis, and Slidell, with Cobb, Mason, and several others, were in the limelight.

Mr. Rhett at the age of thirty-seven had dropped his family name, Smith, and adopted an ancestral one which was doubtless more distinctive. As a young man he was scholarly, and a talented speaker and writer. He became a lawyer and a member of the State Legislature, and in 1832 he was the Attorney-General of South Carolina who, as a devoted follower of Calhoun, was taking a foremost part in the repudiation of the new tariff law. Thus in 1860 he had spent thirty years in unwavering advocacy of the doctrines of States Rights, Nullification, and Secession. He was elected to Congress in 1838, serving through five successive terms and was a prominent member during Lincoln's term. Following his ten years in the House he sat for a year or two in the United States Senate. As owner and conductor of the Charleston *Mercury*, he made it the medium through which a coterie of brilliant writers influenced the entire South.

MRS. CAROLINA ASSERTS HER RIGHT TO "LARRUP" HER NIGGER

From *Punch,* London, January 10, 1861

That *Punch* looked upon the secession of South Carolina as temporary may be inferred from an additional descriptive title which it used under this cartoon: "Divorce à Vinculo." Such a divorce is legal and binding, but it carries the right to marry again.

In a period when political editors in all parts of the country exercised a more commanding control over public opinion and party action than at any other time before or after, the *Mercury* was almost unrivalled. Mr. Rhett's long service in Congress had given him a personal acquaintance with men from all parts of the country, and had made him intimate with leaders in the other Cotton States. During the campaign of 1860 he and his son, now a young man of thirty-two, were writing and receiving many letters, following their marked interest in the strategy of the nominating con-

139

ROBERT BARNWELL RHETT, Jr.   ROBERT BARNWELL RHETT

As Attorney-General of South Carolina during the nullification fight with Jackson in 1852, the senior Rhett's extreme State's Rights attitude had attracted the attention of the country. He was a member of Congress in 1837-49 and in 1850 was chosen to fill out Calhoun's unexpired term as U. S. Senator. He resigned in 1852 because South Carolina had refused to secede from the Union at that time. He was regarded as one of the most radical members of the South Carolina Secession Convention of 1860 and wrote the address to the people that accompanied the Ordinance of Secession. During the Civil War he served as a member of the Confederate Congress. He had acquired a controlling interest in the Charleston *Mercury* and in the ante-bellum agitation his son, Robert Barnwell Rhett, Jr., was installed as editor of that exponent of secession. The son was also a member of the South Carolina Legislature. He was a brilliant writer and logician.

ventions. Particularly after the State elections and in anticipation of a Lincoln victory, they were asking opinions on what course South Carolina should pursue.

There was disappointment over the reply of Jefferson Davis, written just after Lincoln's election. Davis had thought South Carolina ought not to withdraw without assurances from the entire southernmost tier of States. "If a convention of the States was assembled," said Mr. Davis, "the proposition to secede from the Union, independently of support from neighboring States, would probably fail." The letter urges the need of securing the co-operation of Georgia, in order to bring Alabama and Mississippi into geographical connection with South Carolina. "If the Secession of South Carolina," continued Mr. Davis, "should be followed by an attempt to coerce her back into the Union, that act of usurpation, folly, and wickedness would enlist every true Southern man for her defense. If it were attempted to

blockade her ports and destroy her trade, a like result would be produced, and the commercial world would probably be added to her allies."

Mr. Davis's letter as a whole throws an important light upon the sentiment that was prevailing in the South upon the news of Lincoln's election. The belief was expressed that the Cotton States would, in due time, be found acting together, whether South Carolina led off immediately or waited for a time. "United, they will have ample power for their own protection, and their exports will make for them allies of all commercial and manufacturing powers. . . . . My opinion is, therefore, as it has been, in favor of seeking to bring those States into co-operation before asking for a popular decision upon a new policy and relation to the nations of the earth." Mr. Rhett had expected a more enthusiastic response, and thought ill of Mr. Davis.

On November 24th, Mr. Rhett (senior) wrote the following "private and confidential" letter to President Buchanan:

Charleston, November 24, 1860.
My dear Sir:

You know that for many years I have been a personal and political friend of yours. I have truly sympathized with you in the difficulties which have surrounded your Administration of a Government tottering amidst the contending sections of the Union. Pardon me, therefore, if I now take the liberty to say a very few words to you on the condition of things in this State.

South Carolina, I have not a doubt, will go out of the Union—and it is in your power to make this event peaceful or bloody. *If you send any more troops into Charleston Bay it will be bloody.* Now, in giving you this information and opinion, I trust you will not suppose that I intend to *direct* your judgment as to your course of duty, but simply to *inform* it. If you have any hopes of reconstructing the Union, after South Carolina shall have seceded, they will, in my judgment, be utterly defeated by

PRESIDENT BUCHANAN'S DILEMMA
He inquires of the small boy: "Is it North or South I'm going?"

The reader of *Vanity Fair*, from which this cartoon is reproduced, readily acquires the feeling that the periodical itself was in doubt, and that it too did not know where it was going, in the critical days between Lincoln's election and his inauguration.

any demonstration of coercion in the Bay of Charleston.

Believe me, Dear Sir.
               Yours most sincerely,
James Buchanan   R. B. RHETT.
   President of the United States.

Mr. Rhodes, who shows us so clearly and impartially the attitude of the South and the reasons for it, was himself too close to the sectional prejudices of the war period to forgive President Buchanan for failing to take certain vigorous military steps. Yet upon Mr. Rhodes's own showing of facts, such steps would not have been expedient, even if they had been possible. That so wise an historian should, in 1895, have been swayed by the almost universal prejudice against James Buchanan that had survived from the bitter days of the interregnum between November 6, 1860, and March 4, 1861, is to be regretted, although it can readily enough be understood.

Since nobody of any consequence knew what to do in the month of November, 1860, it seems rather unfair for us of later generations to scold Buchanan for not having nipped rebellion in the bud. Mr. Rhodes is not felicitous in making the trite comparison with Jackson, the admired leader of Buchanan's younger days. Senator Alexander H. Stephens, of Georgia, soon to become Vice-President of the Confederacy, had, in November, made a powerful speech in his own State against Secession, and was at that very time engaged in an earnest correspondence with his former intimate and devoted friend, Abraham Lincoln. Stephens did his best to prevent Secession, but he knew, like every other Southern man, that if the government at Washington made any show of preparing to coerce South Carolina, nothing could prevent the spread of the Secession movement across the entire belt of Cotton States.

Mr. Buchanan had not made the situation; still less could he unmake it. Mr. Rhodes thinks that Buchanan might have been co-operating with General Scott in "secretly" planning for military measures against the impending Southern movement; and he goes so far as to surmise that the entire North—Republicans, Douglas Democrats, and even Breckinridge men—would have joined in sup-

porting a Jacksonian attitude on Buchanan's part. But here Mr. Rhodes is manifestly inconsistent. Buchanan could either have planned secretly to resist rebellion, or he could have blustered like a Jackson in manifestoes of defiance. Since no actual military resources worth a moment's notice were at Buchanan's disposal, the "secret" proceedings would have had no effect whatever, while stern and bold denunciations would have united the South in instant measures of defense, and would have had no considerable support in the North.

Mr. Rhett knew very well that South Carolina's gesture of defiance in 1832 was child's play compared with the profound sectional movement of 1860. It is easy to say that Mr. Buchanan was feeble and vacillating. In justice, however, it should be added that he was not nearly as undecided and as vacillating as was the public opinion of the United States, without the support of which, obviously, he could have taken no radical steps. The later course of events cured most people, North and South, of their indecision. If James Buchanan had been destined to remain in the office of President, one may be inclined to think that he would have stood firmly for the defense of the United States of America, its integrity, and its possessions.

Congress reassembled on December 3rd, and Mr. Buchanan's annual message claimed immediate attention. The document began with observations on the danger of further agitation in the North of the slavery question. He held that the people of the North were not responsible, and had "no more right to interfere than with similar institutions in Russia or in Brazil." He appealed for forbearance, declaring that otherwise it was "beyond the power of any President, no matter what may be his own political proclivities, to restore peace and harmony among the States." In well-phrased sentences the message held that the election of a particular citizen (referring to Lincoln) afforded no cause whatever for Secession. He saw no prospect at all of any action, whether by the newly elected President or by Congress, "impairing in the slightest degree the rights of the South to their property and slaves."

CLOUDY TIMES

1st. Pedestrian—"Bill—can you find your way through this state of things?
2nd Pedestrian—"Nary find."
1st P.—"Going South or North, D'ye know?"
2nd P.—"Nary know."
1st P.—"You don't see me?"
2nd P.—"No—nor any other man."

From *Vanity Fair*, November 17, 1860

WONDERFUL SURGICAL OPERATION

PERFORMED BY DOCTOR LINCOLN ON THE POLITICAL CHANG AND ENG

Here again the cartoonist was inspired by a freak on exhibition at Barnum's Museum in New York, the original Siamese twins. His political twins were James Gordon Bennett of the New York *Herald* and President Buchanan, who had been held together by a mysterious bond which the Covode investigating committee of the House of Representatives had tried to uncover in the summer of 1860. Dr. Lincoln announces his readiness to perform the needed operation that would sever the twain. In the background are reminders of the Pryor-Potter episode, in which two Congressmen—one from Virginia and the other from Wisconsin—had lately figured. The Virginian having sent a challenge to a duel, the Wisconsin man, as the challenged party, had availed himself of his right to a choice of weapons and had named bowie-knives! Needless to say, that duel never came off.

Even in the differences over slavery in the Territories, nothing had happened, in Mr. Buchanan's view, that gave the South just ground for apprehensions or for threats. He admitted that the Southern States had a right to demand, as an act of justice, that the States of the North should observe their Constitutional duty as regards fugitive slaves. As for the principle of Secession, Mr. Buchanan emphatically denied its validity, and declared it "fully inconsistent with the history, as well as the character, of the Federal Constitution." The powers and the duties of the Federal Government are set forth by Mr. Buchanan with dignity and with firmness. The message makes clear distinction between revolution against an established government, and voluntary Secession claimed as an inherent right.

The message then takes up the power of the President to execute the laws. It is shown that in the case of South Carolina, events over

This medal is presented by Vanity Fair to James Buchanan, President of the United States, as a testimonial of respect for his MANLY and PATRIOTIC stand in defence of the rights of the Union.

The reader will not fail to recognize *Vanity Fair's* sarcasm in suggesting the presentation of this medal to President Buchanan after the secession of South Carolina. When the same State had asserted its right of Nullification in 1832, Andrew Jackson issued a forceful proclamation asserting that he would enforce the laws of the Union.

which the President could have exercised no control had rendered him helpless. "All the Federal officers within its limits, through whose agency alone these laws can be carried into execution, have already resigned. We no longer have a District Judge, a District Attorney, or a Marshal in South Carolina. In fact the whole machinery of the Federal Government, necessary for the distribution of remedial justice among the people, has been demolished, and it would be difficult, if not impossible, to replace it." Mr. Buchanan made it clear that without further legislation the President could not "overcome a united opposition in a single State, not to speak of other States which may place themselves in a similar attitude."

As regards the property of the United States in South Carolina, Mr. Buchanan said that the officer in command of the forts had received orders to act strictly on the defensive in case of any attempt "to expel the United States from its property by force." The President next showed that apart from executing the laws, "the Executive has no authority to decide what shall be the relations between the Federal Government and South Carolina." He elaborates this point, showing that a mere executive officer had no power to recognize dissolution of the thirty-three States, the situation bearing no resemblance to the recognition of a foreign *de facto* government. And he declared it his duty to submit to Congress the whole question in all its bearings.

Then comes Mr. Buchanan's famous discussion of the right of Congress to coerce a State into submission. He had come to the conclusion that no such power had been delegated to Congress or to any other department of the Federal Government. It has always been said that Mr. Buchanan had asserted that the South had no right to secede, and that the United States had no right to oppose Secession. This does not perfectly disclose his position. He had already shown that Secession was a matter of revolution—always and everywhere an inherent social possibility. It was too obvious for statement that if the extra-constitutional right of revolution could be asserted by the South, there must exist the equal extra-con-

DOGBERRY'S LAST CHARGE.

Dogberry	-	-	-	-	-	J B——n.
Seacoal	-	-	-	-	-	A L——n.
Verges	—A good old man—but who will be Talking		-		-	J G. B——tt

DOGBERRY.—*Come hither, neighbor Seacoal. Well, for your favor, sir, why, give God thanks, and make no boast of it ; and for your writing and reading, let that appear when there is no need of such vanity. You are thought here to be the most senseless and fit man for the constable of the watch ; therefore bear you the lantern this is your charge ! you shall comprehend all vagrom men ! you are to bid any man stand, in the prince's name.*

SEACOAL.—*How if he will not stand ?*

DOGBERRY.—*Why then, take no note of him, but let him go.*—SHAKESPEARE.

Dogberry and Verges, the two ignorant constables in Shakespeare's "Much Ado About Nothing," are represented in the cartoon by President Buchanan and his supporter, James Gordon Bennett of the New York *Herald*. Buchanan charges Lincoln, his successor, in these words: "You shall comprehend all vagrom men! You are to bid any man stand, in the prince's name!" And when Lincoln asks "How if he will not stand?" there is the further injunction: "Why then, take no note of him, but let him go." The cartoon was inspired by Buchanan's last annual message to Congress, dated December 3, 1860.

stitutional right of resisting that revolution on the part of the States of the North. Mr. Buchanan's meaning simply was that "war would not only present the most effectual means of destroying the Union, but would banish all hope of its peaceable reconstruction."

He foretold clearly and accurately the perils and losses of civil war, declaring that if the Union "cannot live in the affections of the people it must one day perish. Congress," he added, "possesses many means of preserving it by conciliation; but the sword was not placed in their hands to preserve it by force." Passing from his sincere and eloquent appeal against resort to arms, Mr. Buchanan recommended a Constitutional Convention for the purpose of adopting an "explanatory amendment" on the subject of slavery. Such an amendment might: (1) give express recognition of the right of property in the States where it now exists or may hereafter exist; (2) the duty of protecting this right in the common Territories until they decide the question for themselves when admitted as States; (3) a like recognition of the right of the slave-owner to recover his property, this confirming in whole or in part the Dred Scott Decision.

The remainder of a very long message is devoted to the intelligent discussion and review of many public questions that had required treatment during Mr. Buchanan's administration, together with others still pending and of immediate concern. These passages are of value if the reader is intent upon studying the career of Mr. Buchanan and is trying to form his own estimate of the qualities and capacities of that statesman. But they do not relate to the topics of our present narration.

It was only a few months after the presentation of this message to Congress that Mr. Buchanan was at work with full mental concentration, and with a great supply of documents, letters, and requisite material, upon the volume to which we have already referred, entitled "Mr. Buchanan's Administration on the Eve of the Rebellion." In this volume he declares that the Cotton States throughout the presidential campaign had been clearly in earnest in their talk about Secession in case of the election of Lincoln; while the Republicans had

been quite incredulous. He also shows that "immediately after Mr. Lincoln's election much was said and written by Republicans in the North calculated to delude the Cotton States into the belief that they might leave the Union without serious opposition."

He cites the New York *Tribune*, and quotes from a resolution of the New York Historical Society, adopted on November 9th, strongly opposing all coercive measures against the South. He shows that a tendency was widespread in the North to invoke the Declaration of Independence in favor of the view that the South might secede if it so desired. Also he observes that "the people of the Cotton States, unfortunately for themselves, were also infatuated with the belief, until the very last moment, that in case they should secede they would be sustained by a large portion, if not the whole Democratic party of the North." He adds further that, "in this delusion they were also greatly encouraged by sympathy and support from influential and widely circulated anti-Republican journals in the North, and especially in the city of New York." Mr. Buchanan concludes Chapter IV with the following paragraph, expressive of his own position:

"It was in vain, therefore, that the late President warned them, as he often said, against this delusion. It was in vain he assured them that the first cannon fired against either Fort Moultrie or Fort Sumter would arouse the indignant spirit of the North— would heal all political divisions amongst the Northern people, and would unite them as one man in support of a war rendered inevitable by such an act of rebellion."

Referring to the position in which he had been placed, Mr. Buchanan defends himself as follows:

"No public man was ever placed in a more trying and responsible position. Indeed, it was impossible for him to act with honest independence without giving offense both to the anti-Slavery and Secession parties, because both had been clearly in the wrong. In view of his position, and after mature reflection, he adopted a system of policy to which ever afterward, during the brief remnant of his term, he inflexibly adhered. This he announced and explained in the annual message of the 3rd December, 1860, and in the special message thereafter of the 8th January, 1861."

The Cabinet at that time was headed by the venerable Lewis Cass of Michigan, Secretary of State, who had been once a nominee for the Presidency and for a long time a United States Senator. Howell Cobb of Georgia was Secretary of the Treasury. He had seen long service in Congress, had been a Speaker of the House and a Governor of Georgia, and was destined within a few months to become the presiding officer of the Confederate Congress. The Secretary of War was John B. Floyd of Virginia who left the Cabinet in December, soon after the President had transmitted his message to Congress, later becoming a General in the Confederate Army. The Secretary of the Navy was Isaac Toucey of Connecticut, who had been long in public life as a member of Congress, Governor of his State, Attorney-General toward the end of the Polk Administration, and a Senator for four years previous to his

SAMBO AGONISTES.

DEY DONT "BUDGE"

The cartoonist of *Vanity Fair* here turns to Milton instead of to Shakespeare, as was his custom. The drama "Samson Agonistes" was based upon the Biblical story of Samson, whose prodigious strength enabled him to lean against the pillars of the house of the Philistines and bring down the roof upon the heads of his captors.

accepting a place in the Buchanan Cabinet. The Secretary of the Interior was Jacob Thompson, who had served in Congress for a long time from Mississippi, who became Governor of that State during the Confederacy, and was afterwards an agent of the Richmond government in Canada.

Joseph Holt of Kentucky was a lawyer of exceptional ability, who was transferred by Mr. Buchanan from the office of Postmaster-General to head the War Department after John B. Floyd's retirement early in December.

Jeremiah S. Black was a Pennsylvania lawyer of eminence and exceptional force as a public man, and Mr. Buchanan made him Secretary of State after the resignation of General Cass on December 12th. Three new men of immense vigor, and of decidedly greater courage in the assertion of Union rights and principles than such Republican leaders as Greeley and Seward, were Edwin M. Stanton, who became Attorney-General; General John A. Dix of New York, who was made Secretary of the Treasury; and Horatio King of Maine, who was promoted from the position of first assist-ant in the Post Office Department to that of Postmaster-General.

Stanton afterward became Lincoln's Secre-tary of War, while no men were more alert and vigorous in upholding the Union cause than Dix and King. Thus in December, at the very moment of the unanimous adoption by the con-vention of South Carolina of its Secession Ordinance, the Buchanan Cabinet had been made over into a vigorous and aggressive body, intent upon the preservation of the Union.

President Buchanan had now distinctly sep-arated himself from the Southern radicals, and they had no further hope of favor at his hands. "The leaders of this latter party in Congress," says Mr. Buchanan, "and especially Mr. Jefferson Davis, objected to the message because of its earnest argument against Se-cession, and the determination expressed to collect the revenue in the ports of South Caro-lina by means of a naval force, and to defend the public property. From this moment they alienated themselves from the President. Soon thereafter, when he refused to withdraw Major Anderson from Fort Sumter on the de-mand of the self-styled South Carolina Com-missioners, the separation became complete. For more than two months before the close of the session all friendly intercourse between them and the President, whether of a political or social character, had ceased."

Meanwhile, Mr. Buchanan charges, Con-gress refused, during the entire session, to take any decisive measures. It took no steps to furnish either President Buchanan or Presi-dent Lincoln with a military force to repel any attack which might be made by the Cotton States. "It neither did the one thing nor the other. It neither presented the olive branch nor the sword. All history proves that inac-tion in such an emergency is the worst possible policy, and can never stay the tide of revolu-tion. On the contrary, it affords the strong-est encouragement to rebellion."

"HELLO, BILL! THERE GOES THE CRISIS!"

Helper's book had given a new vogue to the word "crisis." It was now applied to whatever was related to the slavery question. The motive of this particular New York car-toon was to create prejudice against Republicans in the presidential campaign. The over-dressed Negro seemed more racially typical to rough whites in New York than did the more unfortunate slaves of the South.

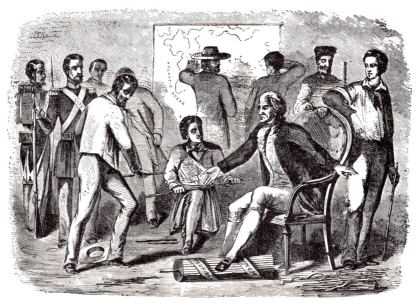

THE OLD MAN AND HIS SONS

The sons had quarreled. The father had exercised his authority, and used other means to reconcile them, all to no purpose. He called his sons before him and asked that a bundle of sticks be brought. Then he commanded each to try if with all his strength he could break the bundle. They failed. After this the father ordered the bundle to be untied, and gave a single stick to each son, bidding him to try to break it. This each did with ease. Thereupon the father addressed them: "Oh, my sons, behold the power of unity. When once your ties of brotherly affection are dissolved, you become exposed to every injurious hand that assaults you."

CHAPTER XVII

Three Months of Futile Talk in Congress

Senator Crittenden holds the floor with a compromise plan—To revise the Constitution and guarantee slavery below a fixed line—Virginia calls a Peace Convention at Washington

THERE ENSUED about thirteen weeks of dreary and futile debate in Congress, most men doubtless really desiring to arrive at a compromise, and to preserve the Union without resort to civil war. To this session belongs the story of the efforts of the so-called Committee of Thirteen of the Senate, and that of the Committee of Thirty-three of the House. There occurred the unavailing visit of the Commissioners of South Carolina to Washington. A Peace Congress with delegates from all parts of the country falls into the record of these strivings to avoid war. Conciliatory steps taken by Northern legislatures, to offset revolutionary movements in Southern legislatures, have their place also

in the account of the opening weeks of 1861.

As the South grew more warlike, the North grew more anxious and timid. In this chapter we shall briefly recount some of the circumstances and conditions of this trying season. In the next chapter the events in Charleston harbor must have our attention as constituting the immediate cause of the great struggle. Thereupon we must follow the movements of particular States as they hold their conventions and withdraw from the Union, at the same time planning for the formation of their Confederate government.

In the Senate, the usual motion for printing the President's message precipitated a violent debate. Senator Clingman of North Carolina

149

declared that Lincoln had been elected because he was known to be a dangerous man.
"He declares that it is the purpose of the North
to make war upon my section until its social
system has been destroyed, and for that he
was taken up and elected. That declaration
of war is dangerous because it has been endorsed by a majority of the votes of the Free
States in the late election." Mr. Clingman
pointed to the fact that a Republican President
must gradually be followed by complete control of Congress and the government.

"The guiding principle of the party that was
thus to come into full power," said Mr. Clingman, "was hostility to the Southern States. I
am free to say, as I have said on the stump this
summer repeatedly, that if that election were
not resisted, either now or at some day not far
distant, the Abolitionists would succeed in
abolishing slavery all over the South."

Senator Lane of Oregon, who had been defeated for the Vice-Presidency, said of Mr.
Lincoln: "He is an 'irrepressible-conflict'
man; he holds that the Slave States and Free
States cannot live together. I apprehend the
result will be that they will not live together."
Senator Hale of New Hampshire answered de-
fiantly on behalf of the North. Senator Brown
of Mississippi declared that war was inevitable
if the South was allowed neither peace in the
Union nor "the poor boon of seeking it out
of the Union."

Senator Iverson of Georgia admitted that
the Personal Liberty bills of the North were
opposed not because "in their practical operation they ever do any harm;" it was the
existence of anti-slavery public sentiment in
the Northern States that was objectionable,
and it was this that "moves us to look for security and protection in Secession and a Southern Confederacy." Senator Wigfall of Texas
declared: "We simply say that a man who is
distasteful to us has been elected, and we
choose to consider that as a sufficient ground
for leaving the Union, and we intend to leave
the Union." Senator Saulsbury of Delaware
pronounced the debate unnecessary and unfortunate, and closed it with the promise that
his State would do nothing to lead to a break-
up of the Union.

Senator Powell of Kentucky presented a
resolution providing that the President's message, in such parts of it as were related to the
slavery and sectional issues, be referred to a
special committee of thirteen members. This
led to another debate, a little less acrimonious
but far from reassuring. The Southern
spokesmen were of two kinds, the difference
owing to temperament and mental training.

The bold and blunt leaders were eager for
Secession, and had already dismissed all
thoughts of compromise. The better trained
and more accomplished debaters, like Jefferson Davis of Mississippi, continued to profess
their great love for the Union, and their extreme reluctance even to admit the thought of
separation. They pleaded for fraternity, and
spoke with grief and sorrow of the wrongs of
the South and the unprovoked hostility of the
North. Senator Douglas and his friend Senator Pugh of Ohio were anxious to help forward some policy of reconciliation.

Senator Mason of Virginia said that he
would vote for the resolution, but thought it
was too late for Congress to accomplish any-

THE RIGHT BAIT TO USE

Uncle Sam tries both the flag and the cannon—patriotic
appeal and force—in his effort to get the secession fish
into the Union basket. This is an excellent example of
the envelope caricature, which gained wide popularity in
the period of Secession and War.

thing. He believed that there was already "a war of sentiment and opinion, by one form of society against another form of society." Senator Iverson of Georgia considered that the question was already settled. "I know the efforts that are now being made to stay the hand of the Southern people and to cool down the patriotism which is burning within the Southern heart, but it will be ineffectual."

Senator Pugh of Ohio did not believe that one in a hundred of the men who voted for Lincoln thought anything about the subject of slavery in the States. They were opposed to the introduction of slavery into the Territories. Some of them as partisans wanted the spoils of office, and others as protectionists wanted high tariff on iron. As Republicans they hated the Democratic party, but they had no thought of interfering with the institutions of the South. Senator Douglas said that nine-tenths of the complaints regarding non-execution of the Fugitive Slave Law in the North were unfounded.

Senator Wade of Ohio, Mr. Pugh's Republican colleague, reminded the Senate that no Republican as yet had ever held a federal executive office, and that Southern Senators were merely indulging in unwarrantable prejudices. He defended Mr. Lincoln's right to the office that he had been chosen to fill, and saw no ground for humiliating compromises.

I am citing this debate as indicating the spirit of the times, and the seeming hopelessness of allaying the fears of the Union-loving Southern element, or quenching the Secessionist ardor of the more aggressive leaders of the

BROTHER JONATHAN AILING—MUST HIS ARM BE CUT OFF?

DOCTOR: "Poor fellow! His Constitution is so run down that I fear he cannot survive without an amputation."

NURSE COLUMBIA: "Oh! Don't give up, Doctor. Good nursing will do anything —everything—if you will only give him the opportunity."

Vanity Fair's comment upon the secession movement in South Carolina.

South. There now followed a constructive proposal. It was brought forward by the venerable and greatly respected Senator Crittenden of Kentucky, who had, for many years past, been held in Mr. Lincoln's affectionate regard. The Crittenden resolutions are one of the chief landmarks in the progress of events that preceded Secession and war.

It was proposed by Mr. Crittenden that Congress should submit to the States, for ratification by conventions of at least three-fourths of them, an amendment to the Constitution consisting of six articles. The first recognized slavery south of latitude 36 degrees 30 minutes (the old Missouri Compromise line)

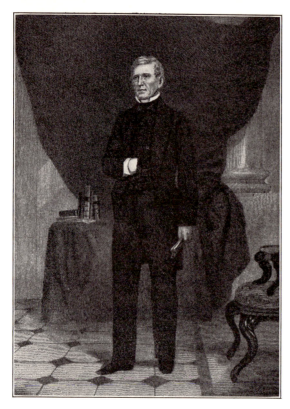

JOHN J. CRITTENDEN (1787-1863)

A brilliant Kentuckian who at thirty was a veteran of the War of 1812 and a United States Senator, Crittenden had an unusual career in its alternations, never holding any one office for a long period, but receiving repeated marks of public favor. He left the Senate in 1819, betaking himself to the practice of the law, served as U. S. District Attorney for several years, and in 1835 was again chosen Senator. President Harrison appointed him Attorney General, but he did not remain in Tyler's cabinet, returning to the Senate for another term. Having been Governor of Kentucky and Fillmore's Attorney General, he became a Senator for the fourth time in 1855. In 1860 he proposed the famous Crittenden Compromise, consisting of constitutional amendments intended to define the right of property in slaves; but this measure, designed to avert civil war, was defeated in committee. Its author's sincerity and devotion to the Union remained unquestioned. After retirement from the Senate he served one term in the House and upheld the Lincoln administration, helping to keep Kentucky in the Union.

provision for compensation in any case. Article 4 protected the right of transporting slaves from one Slave State to another. Article 5 provided that the owner of a fugitive slave should be entitled to compensation in case the recovery of the slave was prevented by mobs or similar illegal intimidation.

The final article provided that the preceding five should not be subject to future amendment, and that Congress should never be given authority to abolish or interfere with slavery in any of the States where it existed under State laws. Besides this proposed amendment to the Constitution, Senator Crittenden's motion provided further resolutions expressing the sentiment of Congress regarding the duty of Northern States to repeal laws which conflicted with the Fugitive Slave Acts of Congress, and at the same time called for complete suppression of the African slave trade.

At that time the Free States and the Slave States were of similar aggregate area, the Free States having 832,000 square miles, and the Slave States 890,000. The extension of the proposed parallel of latitude provided for Kansas, Nebraska, Minnesota, Washington, and Utah as Free Territories, and for what was then New Mexico and the Indian Territory as an extension of the Slave areas. Under the census of 1860, the total population of Free States, and Territories as proposed, was 19,000,000. The population of Slave States and proposed Territories was 12,000,000.

If the Crittenden plan could then have been placed directly before the voters, it would probably have been acceptable to a majority of the people of the United States. Mr. Breckinridge, who was at that time Vice-President and presiding officer of the Senate, and who became a member of the Senate from Kentucky on the fourth of March, declared publicly in July, some six months later, that he "happened personally to know the fact that the leading statesmen of the Lower Southern States were willing to accept the terms of settlement which were proposed by the venerable Senator from Kentucky, my predecessor."

It was Mr. Breckinridge himself who had appointed the members of the Committee of Thirteen which had before it the Crittenden

so long as the territorial status existed, new States having the right to decide the question for themselves when admitted into the Union. Article 2 denied the right of Congress to abolish slavery in places of Federal jurisdiction within the limits of Slave States. Article 3 denied to Congress the right to abolish slavery in the District of Columbia so long as it existed in the adjoining States of Virginia and Maryland, or in either of them, with further

A CURE FOR REPUBLICAN LOCK-JAW

The Crittenden Compromise is being forced down the throat of the Republican. After the election, Senator John J. Crittenden, a Kentucky Whig, had offered a constructive proposal designed to avert the impending crisis. It took the form of a constitutional amendment with six distinct provisions, as described in this chapter. Two days before Lincoln's inauguration the Crittenden Compromise was defeated in the Senate by vote of 20 to 19. This cartoon was drawn and published by Benjamin Day, whose process for mechanical stippling, or shading, is still used by photo-engravers.

resolutions, as well as other proposals relating to the question at issue. Mr. Powell, having proposed the committee, was made chairman. The other members were Senators Hunter, Crittenden, Seward, Toombs, Douglas, Collamer, Davis, Wade, Bigler, Rice, Doolittle, and Grimes. An analysis of the committee shows five Southern Democrats (three of them from the Border Slave States and two from the Cotton States), three Northern Democrats, and five Republicans. Mr. Breckinridge had named a committee above criticism, properly distributed, every member a man of character, ability and intelligence, and thoroughly representative of his own section or party.

As at certain stages in the French Revolution, the precise dates have significance in respect to each other. Thus it was on December 20th that the South Carolina convention had taken action. As Mr. Rhodes puts it, the convention "had unanimously adopted the Ordinance of Secession, an action which kindled enthusiasm in the Cotton States and awakened some demonstrations of approval in North Carolina and Virginia. It was believed that unless a composition could be effected, Georgia, Florida, Alabama, and Mississippi would certainly secede, and that Louisiana and Texas would probably follow their example. The stake which the North had to play for was these six Cotton States. If they were not won, might not the game be shifted to a contest where the Border Slave States would be at hazard?"

The telegraph lines, of course, were working freely from South Carolina, the convention having adjourned from Columbia, the capital of the State, on account of an epidemic of smallpox, to reassemble on the 20th at the city of Charleston. While the country was reading about this startling event, it was informed from Washington of the first meeting, on the following day, December 21st, of the Senate's Committee of Thirteen. Undoubtedly there was great reliance upon the capacity of these leaders to find some way to meet the crisis. There seemed to be momentary resumption, among these Senators, of the friendly personal relations that had previously existed.

Thus, there had long been the warmest social and family relationships between Senator Seward and Mr. and Mrs. Jefferson Davis. Mr. Douglas was notably a man of genial spirit, on excellent terms with his colleagues. Of the Republican five, two were from the East and three from the West. Collamer of Vermont was a man of sound sense; and Seward, of course, was the pre-eminent man of the party. Senator Wade of Ohio was accounted more partisan and aggressive, but Senator Grimes of Iowa and Senator Doolittle of Wisconsin were by no means narrow partisans. The two Kentucky Senators, Crittenden and Powell, with Hunter of Virginia, were the Democrats from the Border Slave States, while Toombs of Georgia and Davis of Mississippi were from the Lower South. The Northern Democrats were Bigler of Pennsylvania, Douglas of Illinois, and Rice of Minnesota.

Mr. Davis expressed the view that it would not be worth while to adopt any report unless at least three of the five Republican members favored it, and at least five of the eight Democrats. This was a sensible opinion and was accepted. There was a tendency for the six Democrats from the Upper Slave States and from the North to unite upon principles that were alike unacceptable to the Cotton States and to the Republicans. Thus on the first Crittenden resolution there were six yeas and seven nays. As regards the other articles of the Crittenden amendment, the five Republicans were unanimously opposed and the eight

Democrats—counting Crittenden, a Bell-Everett Whig, as among them—were ready to support them all.

The important item of the Crittenden document was that which provided for the extension of the territorial line to the Pacific. Although the two Southern Senators, Davis and Toombs, opposed this re-establishment of the Missouri Compromise, there is some evidence that they would have accepted it if all the Republicans had been willing to consent. There is much ground for the opinion that if the Committee of Thirteen had reported favorably upon this first article of the Crittenden Amendment, the Senate would have adopted it by more than a two-thirds majority. Such action in the Senate would perhaps have checked the Secession movement, but even this is questionable. Thurlow Weed's paper, the Albany *Evening Journal,* and the two Seward Republican papers of New York City supported the Crittenden compromise as a whole.

On December 31st, the Committee simply reported that it had not been able to agree on any general plan of adjustment. Thereafter the Senate itself took up the consideration of these Crittenden resolutions, with various other proposals. Mr. Douglas eloquently deplored disunion and asserted Federal rights, but believed civil war a hopeless remedy and compromise the only alternative. Mr. Crittenden, finding that his resolutions did not obtain a requisite two-thirds majority in the Senate, proposed a plan for a direct appeal to the people by referendum. Mr. Toombs of Georgia declared that "such efforts would be useless because the Union was already dissolved by the action of South Carolina, with the other Southern States certain to follow in the near future."

While the Senate was talking compromise, Mr. Toombs declared: "Those brave men are coolly and calmly voting what you call Revolution—ay, sir, doing better than that—arming to defend it." His war talk was in a tone which made it seem that he was afraid that the South might be allowed to withdraw peaceably. But the Crittenden resolutions were deferred while the Senate chose to debate the Pacific Railroad bill, which Crittenden re-

COMING 'ROUND.

LINCOLN: "I say, Yancey, if you'll let me have these stables in peace for
the next four years, I'll give you some of the best stalls and see that your nag is
well taken care of."

William L. Yancey (1814-63) was one of the most prominent secession advocates. He resisted every
suggestion of compromise on slavery, and it was he who introduced the secession ordinance in the
Alabama legislature in January, 1861. Lincoln, after the election, was merely asking the South to
let him conduct the government "in peace." As to slavery, his position had been stated again and
again. Thus he wrote to Lyman Trumbull in December, 1860: "It is but repetition for me to say
I am for an honest enforcement of the Constitution—fugitive slave clause included."

garded as "very solemn trifling before this
people, that the Senate should sit here legis-
lating upon the making of roads for future
generations, and for a nation, when that nation
is trembling upon a point between life and
death; yet the Senate preferred to act upon
a railroad, rather than to act on these measures
calculated to give permanence to the Union
itself."

Thus the hopeless discussion went on from
week to week intermittently, while the South
steadily pursued its policy of Secession with a
view to a new Confederacy. On the 28th of
January, Senator Iverson of Georgia withdrew in a statement quoting the Ordinance of
Secession that had been adopted by his State

on the 19th. He declared that the first gun
fired would cause the withdrawal of all slave-
holding States and forever destroy all hope of
reconstruction.

Thus far I have not spoken of the action
taken in the House of Representatives. At
once upon the reading of the President's message the following resolution was adopted:

"Resolved, that so much of the President's
message as relates to the present perilous condition of the country be referred to a special
committee of one from each State."

It was passed by a vote of 145 to 38, several men from the South opposing it on the
ground that Secession conventions had already
been called in their particular States, and they

THE RISING OF THE AFRITE.

In its original publication of this cartoon *Vanity Fair* gives the following explanation: A good old story always bears a new application. In "Arabian Nights" the fishermen netted a bottle of brass from which, when it was opened, there flew a tremendous Afrite whose nostrils were as trumpets and whose eyes were like lamps. He had been sealed up by Solomon. Years ago the wisdom of America sealed up a terrible Afrite, the devil of dissension and anarchy, and threw it into the ocean of the future. The fishers in troubled waters—the Yanceys, Toombs, and Keitts of our day—have found the bottle, and have opened it. What tremendous fiend is it that bursts madly out! Furious and devilish, he threatens ruin—death. The fishermen of the old story, however, had the wit to conjure the Afrite back into the bottle. Have we the wisdom to do it?

believed there was no further possibility of compromise. There were criticisms of the selections made by the Speaker of the House for this committee, Mr. Vallandigham of Ohio remarking that there was not a single representative of the Democratic party on the committee from the sixteen Free States of the Union. This was not a reasonable complaint.

On December 31st the Congressmen from South Carolina withdrew, because their State was no longer in the Union. In due time this Committee of Thirty-three reported a joint resolution to amend the Constitution to admit New Mexico as a State, and to revise the Fugitive Slave Law. Meanwhile, the Southern States were seceding and delegations were withdrawing from Congress, leaving a situation which made further compromise actions without influence or value.

With the Republicans now in control, the House adopted the following resolution: "Resolved that neither the Federal Government nor the people or the governments of the non-slaveholding States have the right to legislate upon or interfere with slavery in any of the slaveholding States in the Union." This of course touched upon no issue that was pending, and was so obviously without pertinence that it aroused no interest anywhere.

Pending appropriation bills naturally involved a discussion as to how the army and the navy might be employed in face of the situation, rebellion being already a glaring fact. John Sherman of Ohio, who had been defeated for the Speakership after a long contest, but was prominent on the Republican side, disagreed with such proposals as those of Mr. Crittenden, and saw little chance of compromise. "I know," he said, "that the movements in the Cotton States have gone so far that we cannot arrest them." He hoped that the Border States would be less precipitate. He did not think that the army should be used

WHO TOOK THE STARS FROM THE SACRED FLAG?

Topsy, a familiar character in "Uncle Tom's Cabin," is upbraided by Miss Ophelia (or Miss Columbia) and admits that she is "mighty wicked"! Miss Ophelia threatens to hand the miscreant over to "Uncle Abe, the new overseer."

to coerce a State, but that the government ought to be maintained and defended in the exercise of its just powers.

As the session advanced, six States had gone out of the Union, and it was plain enough that no policy could or would be adopted until the new President was inaugurated and the old Congress had expired by limitation on the 4th of March. Mr. Kellogg was the Illinois member of the Committee of Thirty-three, and was known to be in correspondence with Mr. Lincoln. He proposed amendments to the Constitution somewhat like those of Senator Crittenden, but his motion was rejected by an overwhelming majority. The Virginia Congressmen proposed an elaborate compromise project which also was voted down. Then came a report from the Committee of Thirty-three, devoted mostly to an appeal to Northern States not to interfere with the recovery of fugitive slaves; and this series of resolutions was passed by a vote of 136 to 53.

The Committee further reported in favor of an amendment to the Constitution, designed to protect permanently the individual States in their right to maintain their own domestic institutions. This was passed by 133 to 65; but events moved so swiftly toward the revolutionary conditions of actual war that the amendment never made its round of the State Legislatures. Since it merely proposed to protect a Southern right that had never been threatened, its only interest lay in the evidence it furnished of the utter futility of compromise proposals.

Mr. Buchanan, in his autobiography, deplored the failure of the Crittenden amendment. "It will be recollected," he wrote, "that Mr. Crittenden's amendment was submitted before any of our forts had been seized, before any of the Cotton States except South Carolina had seceded, and before any of the conventions which had been called in the remaining six of those States had assembled."

He adds: "Not one of all the Republicans in the Senate at any period or in any form, voted in its favor, doubtless for the reason that it tolerated slavery within New Mexico in opposition to the Chicago platform."

Mr. Douglas and Mr. Breckinridge had afterwards testified that every member from the South would have accepted the Crittenden proposals if the Republicans could have been induced to concur. President Buchanan, on the 8th of January, had sent a special message to Congress, begging for some action that would cause delay. "Time," he said, "is a great conservative power. Let us pause at this momentous point and afford the people, both North and South, an opportunity for reflection. Would that South Carolina had been convinced of this truth before her precipitate action! I, therefore, appeal through you, to the people of the country, to declare in their might that the Union must and shall be preserved by all Constitutional means."

In this special message the President strongly supported the Crittenden compromise. Mr. Buchanan reminds us that a direct vote on Mr. Crittenden's proposal to submit the question to the people could not be obtained until the day before the final adjournment of Congress, when it was defeated by a Senate vote of 20 to 19. The majority comprised the New England Senators and eleven other Republicans, most of them Western, including Mr. Lincoln's friend, Senator Trumbull of Illinois. Mr. Buchanan regards it as worth while to set down the fact that for some reason Sena-

tors Seward of New York, Cameron of Pennsylvania, Collamer of Vermont, Hale of New Hampshire, and Simmons of Rhode Island, though present in the Senate, refrained altogether from voting on the question.

The famous Peace Convention originated in a vote of the Legislature of Virginia on January 19, 1861, recognizing the imminence of a permanent dissolution of the Union, pronouncing it a dire calamity, and inviting the States, whether slaveholding or non-slaveholding, to appoint Commissioners to meet on the 4th of February, 1861, at the city of Washington. These Virginia resolutions favored, in general, the Crittenden compromise, and expressed the belief that "it would be accepted as a satisfactory adjustment by the people of this Commonwealth."

There was hope that North Carolina and Tennessee would remain in the Union and do their best to win back the seceding States. President Buchanan approved of the initiative of Virginia. Later historians have perhaps passed over the assembling of the Peace Convention with

JOHN TYLER, WHO PRESIDED OVER THE PEACE CONFERENCE

After fifteen years of retirement at his estate on the James River, the former President headed Virginia's representatives at the peace conference which met in Washington during February, 1861, and presided over its deliberations. He was then seventy years old. When Secession was a fact, Tyler accepted election to the Confederate Congress. He died at Richmond in January, 1862.

too little regard for its dignity, and for the hopes that the country entertained of its success. One hundred and thirty-three Commissioners appeared, and they represented twenty-one of the thirty-three States. The Border States were most active in the promotion of this movement. When the convention opened, the six States of South Carolina, Alabama, Mississippi, Georgia, Louisiana, and Florida had not only completed the process of formal secession, but were on the point

AN IMAGINARY MEETING OF THE FIVE LIVING PRESIDENTS

VAN BUREN: "I think I should preside at this meeting, for I laid the foundation of this treason by splitting the Democratic party on the Buffalo platform."

PIERCE: "I think I deserve especial consideration, for I put Jeff Davis in my cabinet as Secretary of War, after he had been rejected by the people of Mississippi for his disunion sentiments."

BUCHANAN: "I should have precedence, for with Floyd and the rest of my cabinet I brought about the present rebellion."

TYLER: "I deserve the first place, for I am identified with the traitors as openly working for the disruption of the Union."

FILLMORE: "As positive councils are now only available, and as I am not in that line, I'll leave."

Among the proposals for saving the Union by compromise and conference was a suggested meeting of the four former Presidents with Mr. Buchanan. These five appear in this *Vanity Fair* cartoon. President Buchanan sits at the reader's left; Mr. Van Buren sits in front with Mr. Pierce opposite; Mr. Fillmore, differing strongly, has his hand on the door to depart. Mr. Tyler stands at the right.

of adopting—at Montgomery, Alabama—the provisional constitution for the Confederate States that was promulgated February 8th.

The members of this Peace gathering were men of conspicuous influence and standing in their respective States. William P. Fessenden headed a strong delegation from Maine. Amos Tuck was the New Hampshire chairman. Hiland Hall was the first named of the five from Vermont. John Z. Goodrich of Massachusetts was accompanied by six associates, one of whom was George S. Boutwell. Samuel Ames was the first named of the Rhode Island group, and Roger S. Baldwin with five associates represented Connecticut. There were eleven members in the New York delegation headed by David Dudley Field and including such prominent men as James S. Wadsworth, Erastus Corning, William E. Dodge, and John A. King.

From New Jersey came a group of nine with Charles S. Olden named first, and Frederick T. Frelinghuysen and Robert F. Stockton among the others. James Pollock was the chairman of the Pennsylvania delegation which included David Wilmot among the remaining six. Delaware's delegation was headed by George B. Rodney, who was well supported, while Maryland's included John F. Dent, Reverdy Johnson, William T. Goldsborough, and several others. At the head of the Virginia delegation was the venerable ex-President, John Tyler, with William C. Rives and three others. North Carolina sent George Davis, D. M. Barringer, J. M. Moorhead, and two or three others. Tennessee sent twelve men including Samuel Milligan, Josiah M. Anderson, and Robert L. Caruthers.

In the Kentucky delegation was included the distinguished James Guthrie, with James B. Clay, Joshua F. Bell, and others. Missouri sent John D. Coalter, and four associates. Heading the Ohio delegation was Salmon P. Chase, who was to enter the Lincoln Cabinet exactly one month later, with Gen. Thomas Ewing, William S. Groesbeck, and several others. From Indiana came Caleb B. Smith (also soon to enter the Lincoln Cabinet), Godlove S. Orth, and three other colleagues. From Illinois came Lincoln's old partner Stephen T.

Logan, John M. Palmer, and other capable men. Iowa was represented by her two Senators, James Harlan and James W. Grimes, with two or three others. From Kansas came Thomas Ewing, Jr., with M. F. Conway and others. The absent States were South Carolina, Georgia, Florida, Alabama, Mississippi, Louisiana, Texas, Arkansas. California and Oregon also absent, were far distant, and Michigan and Minnesota were not represented.

The delegations brought various resolutions from their State legislatures, all of which form an interesting part of the record for those who may care to study in detail the political and constitutional history of the fateful months between Lincoln's election and his inauguration. To a committee of one from each State was referred all these proposals, and on the 15th of February the committee made its report to the convention. This report proposed amendments to the Constitution, the most important of which was the extension of the Missouri Compromise line of 36 degrees 30 minutes. The other clauses were similar to the Crittenden proposals, as these had been more or less modified in Congressional discussion.

Voting by States on the proposal to fix the specified geographical line, resulted in approval by a vote of nine to eight. Delegates from New York, Indiana, and Kansas were evenly divided, and therefore these were recorded as not voting.

The next section provided that no new territory should be acquired by the United States without securing ratification, by virtue of a majority vote of Senators from both sections. This was carried by eleven States against eight. Another section provided for the protection of slavery within the Slave States as against future adverse action by Congress, and was carried by twelve to seven. Additional sections, harmonious with those I have specified, were approved one after another.

Debate upon the report of the convention had continued from the 15th of February to the 26th, when the adoption of the report in its parts and its entirety was agreed upon, and with a brief preamble addressed to the Congress of the United States, the convention adjourned on February 27th.

CHAPTER XVIII

The Cotton States in Flight

*Mississippi, Florida, Alabama, Georgia and Louisiana secede in
January—North Carolina decides to await Virginia's action, but Texas
declares independence in February—Europe takes notice*

ISTORIANS HITHERTO have blazed certain paths through the wilderness of material relating to the period of four months between the election of Lincoln in November, 1860, and his inauguration on the 4th of March, 1861; but most of it remains to be accurately explored. Later research proceeds with less of prejudice and timidity, and we shall have much revision of judgments upon the course of events, together with changed estimates of the character and motive of political leaders.

Without a previous growth of misunderstanding, prejudice, and bitterness, war between nations or between sections of a single state or federation would be almost unthinkable. War is not a reasonable or logical affair. It grows out of distrust and suspicion which lead to fear, and then to animosity and passion that destroy judgment. The war fury is the most fatal of all epidemic maladies, because it perverts moral sentiment; makes a religion of hatred and intolerance; sweeps away common sense before resistless tides of homicidal insanity. A situation that brings communities to the extreme madness of war engenders miasmas that linger on to poison opinion and affect conduct for decades after the violence of conflict has spent itself. For at least two generations, history is likely to be written by men continuing to use the pre-war arguments. Post-war biography finds its chief motive in the making or unmaking of heroes.

It takes a long time—sometimes more than a century—to find descendants of a war-maddened generation who are able to abandon obsolete arguments as to "rights" and "wrongs." A fine sense of mental freedom at length comes with the knowledge that it is morally permissible to restudy historical situations in a new light, without dogmatism or prejudice. The self-righteous position that

ascribes blame, insisting that war guilt pertains exclusively to one side of a conflict, is always unscientific; and after the lapse of a few generations it is seen to be absurd.

The American Civil War was the greatest tragedy of our modern era. It ought to have been averted. But conditions were ripe for it, and centuries of history lay behind it, to provide the philosophic basis. There were a few men, North and South, more insane than their fellow-citizens, who seemed to welcome blood-

THE AMERICAN TWINS—NORTH AND SOUTH
A cartoon from *Punch,* London

A poem with nine stanzas accompanied this drawing in
Punch, the first of which is as follows:

United States, if our good will
Could but command a way,
You would remain united still,
For ever and a day.
Does England want to see you split,
United States—the deuce a bit.

WHAT THE TYRANTS OF THE OLD WORLD THINK OF SECESSION
"Oh! Ain't we sorry!" The cartoon is from *Harper's Weekly,* December 1, 1860. From left to right in the front row, one recognizes portraits of Queen Victoria of England, Louis Napoleon of France, King William of Prussia, and Emperor Alexander of Russia.

shed, either as a relief to their feelings or as a means to a public end. But the vast majority of Americans, South, North and West, dreaded the thought of war, hoped for the maintenance of the Union, and simply drifted into a political deadlock, from which a few local deeds of imprudence led on to a colossal and devastating struggle. Open-minded study is rewarded by the discovery that valuable material continues to accumulate, and that it justifies renunciation of the partisan or sectional attitude. The candid student is impelled to forgive mistakes, and to come to the rescue of reputations. But apart from the desire to make amends for past intolerance and disparagement, there is satisfaction in seeking for one's self the truth of history.

One finds in examining private records and public utterances that great confusion of mind existed almost everywhere in the country during the critical year that preceded the war. Political passions had been aroused in the campaign, the intensity of which had often been underestimated, even in definite neighborhoods. Doubtless a great majority, however, would have accepted compromise, in spite of this hardening of partisan attitude. But leadership was not powerful enough to bring together the men in all parties who were willing to agree to differ. The two sections might have continued to make their distinct economic history, while holding together in a political union to be more strictly limited by the terms of a revised Constitution.

But there was no voice of authority compelling enough to bring the compromisers together. Buchanan, in the presidential office, was governed by this motive. It is true that he lacked the attributes of dominant personality. Most of the interpreters of that period seem to have convinced themselves that he alone might have averted the crisis if he had been a second Jackson. He devoted a volume of autobiography—a work always too much neglected by posterity—to setting forth, conclusively, the reasons why he could not have saved the situation. I do not believe that any other American in Buchanan's place—the facts being as they were—could have assumed a successful dictatorship at that time.

Not the least thing to be kept in mind, is the tyranny of fixed dates. An elastic government like that of Great Britain is not hampered by so many arbitrary beginnings and endings. Thus the Thirty-sixth Congress had no power to act after noon of March 4, 1861. It was not until Wednesday, February 27th, that the Peace Convention had finally adjourned, having adopted its resolutions as described in the previous chapter. Its report had to be made and submitted to Congress. It was near the end of the week before this report could be debated in the Senate.

The venerable Kentuckian, Senator Crittenden, reached the climax of his long and patriotic career in urging the acceptance of the resolutions of the Peace Convention. Southern Senators opposing the resolutions argued that the Kentucky Senator should have stood firmly by his own original proposals. It was declared upon the highest authority, which stood unquestioned in the Senate, that if the Crittenden Compromise had been accepted early in the session, no State would have seceded except South Carolina.

The debate continued through Saturday, with little disposition to adopt the convention's report. It went too far to suit the northern Senators, and not far enough for the South. Trumbull of Illinois, undoubtedly speaking for President-elect Lincoln declared that the Constitution as it stood was sufficient and required no amendment.

LINCOLN AND THE NEGRO QUESTION—A GERMAN CARTOON
NEGRO: "May I be so bold—"
LINCOLN: "Step nearer, my friend."
SOUTHERN STATESMAN: "Then I beg to be excused." (He secedes from the Union.)

From *Kladderadatsch*, Berlin, by the famous Wilhelm Scholz.

The Senate met for its final debate on the state of the country at seven o'clock Sunday evening, March 3rd. The galleries were crowded and the fate of the country had seemed, in the minds of most men, to turn upon votes that must be taken before the Senate adjourned. Mr. Crittenden continued his pleas for acceptance of compromise—setting the Union above all things else—and it was in this session that Mr. Trumbull demanded a return of the seceding States to their allegiance, and told Senator Crittenden that if he had called upon the Government to enforce its authority there would have been a different state of things in the country. He concluded as follows: "This, in my judgment, is the way to preserve the Union; *and I do not expect civil war to follow from it.* You have only to put the Government in a position to make itself respected, and it will command respect."

A vote being taken, the Senate rejected the latest Crittenden resolution by a vote of 14 ayes and 25 noes. This brought to naught the work of the Peace Convention, and ended all efforts at compromise in the Thirty-sixth Congress.

The House had adopted a resolution which, in the closing hours, the Senate accepted, referring to the States a Constitutional amendment in the following words: "Article 13. No amendment shall be made to the Constitution which will authorize or give to Congress the power to abolish, or interfere, within any State, with the domestic institutions thereof, including that of persons held to labor or service by the laws of said State."

At an earlier period this might have been regarded as significant, but it was ignored and quite forgotten long before it could make its round of the State legislatures.

In England a change of government having constitutional character is made by a simple vote of the House of Commons, with the concurrence of the upper chamber. More than once critical situations in the United Kingdom or the British Empire have been met by prompt Parliamentary proceedings. But under our rules, cumbrous machinery must be set in motion, and a succession of fixed dates for the beginnings and endings of terms causes delays that may at times render the system ineffective when it is invoked to meet the dangers of impending revolution.

In view of the fact of Lincoln's election, there is no good reason to accept the opinion expressed by Senators Douglas, Pugh, and others, that favorable action on the Crittenden Compromise in December or January would have kept six other southern States from following the example of South Carolina. The Crittenden plan would have required acceptance by three-quarters of the legislatures, and the South would hardly have relied upon favorable action in the northern States.

Many of the southern leaders, when it was altogether too late, made themselves believe that they would have welcomed the compromises that Seward himself, with other Republican leaders, and several legislatures—that of New York for example—were advocating after secession had been accomplished in the Cotton Belt. But with the fixed Constitutional date approaching, the new Administration loomed ominously on the horizon, and the South firmly believed that the Republican party, evidently now acquiescing in the leadership of its new western chieftain, would hold to the Chicago platform. It was right in thinking that the sun of March 3rd had set upon the last possible hope of compromise.

The new leader of the North did not believe that any good thing could come from a surrender on the territorial question. He thought the Crittenden plan was merely to invite the expansion and perpetuity of a southern Slave Empire. In another chapter we may consider Lincoln's quiet but masterful assertion of authority during this waiting period of confusion and bewilderment.

Meanwhile the whole world was looking on at the unopposed process of national dismemberment. The Queen herself made note of it in her address to Parliament. Whether or not a State had the right to withdraw from the Union was purely a matter of differing Constitutional theories. The prevailing view in the South was that there could be no justified withdrawal except under circumstances of the most extreme gravity. Every one admitted that the Union had been built upon plans that contemplated permanence. Relationships were so interwoven that to break up the working partnership was no simple or easy thing. But the South held that the Right of Secession was infinitely more clear than was the Right of Coercion. Even the Abolition leaders denied the right to oppose Secession by force.

How far the two sections were willing to go to uphold their respective opinions on this point was not yet fully known to any man North or South. I have little taste for Constitutional metaphysics. In the long run political societies are governed in their actions by historic forces more impelling than the dialectics of debaters on the meaning of certain written instruments. As many thousand words could be written to show that coercion was revolutionary, as could be written to demonstrate the revolutionary character of the secession of southern States and their regrouping to form the new Confederacy. The course of events had made the Union permanent in the northern mind, and had transformed a partnership of States into a nation. A different set of conditions had kept alive in the southern mind

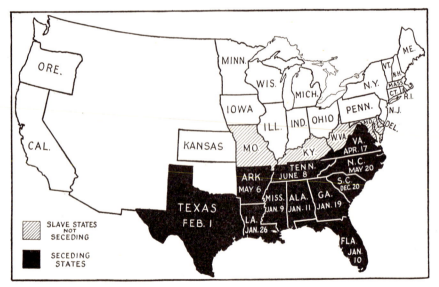

THE ELEVEN SOUTHERN STATES WHICH SECEDED FROM THE UNION
Seven States fronting on the South Atlantic and the Gulf of Mexico withdrew in the first wave of Secession, during the Presidency of Buchanan. That movement began with South Carolina, on December 20, 1860, and ended with the withdrawal of Texas on February 1, 1861. The second stage of the Secession movement came after the firing on Fort Sumter, in the Presidency of Lincoln. It carried out of the Union four border States lying north of the original seven. The last to leave was Tennessee, on June 8, 1861. That part of Virginia lying west of the Alleghanies refused to join the Confederacy. It formed a separate government immediately, and was admitted as a State in June, 1863.

THE "SECESSION MOVEMENT".

South Carolina leads in this mad dash for the "Secession humbug," followed by Florida, Alabama, Mississippi, and Louisiana. Georgia avoids the precipice but takes a road ending in the same place. Since this cartoon does not show Texas, the seventh State to go out, the reader who is interested in precise dates will know that it was published in the last days of January, 1861.

the conception of sovereign States whose destiny had not been merged beyond recall in the supreme destiny of an indivisible republic.

It is now conceded that the secession movement was developed publicly, as an open and undisguised assertion of State rights. It is quite necessary to abandon the mistaken view that Secession was accomplished through a treasonable conspiracy. Southern Senators and Members of Congress remained at Washington in many instances for some days after their own States had seceded. When they withdrew, they made addresses, for the most part dignified, and in many cases eloquent with the expression of sincere regret. No one lifted a finger to detain them, or to limit their freedom of word and action, as they bade farewell to their northern colleagues, and departed southward to help organize their individual States for defense, and to assist in bringing those States together in a new Confederacy. A Mexican President in Buchanan's place

would have assumed a dictatorship, and shot the leaders of the rebellion as they lingered at Washington. Hardly anything is more curious in the history of legislative bodies than the part taken by southern Senators and Representatives in debating and voting upon army and navy bills, and other federal measures at Washington, even after the secession movement had become a concrete fact.

South Carolina, as we have seen in an earlier chapter, had seceded with enthusiasm and virtual unanimity by a decision that took effect December 20, 1860. The South Carolina Senators had considered the election of Lincoln as equivalent to a break-up of the Union, and had not resumed their seats at the opening of the session on the first Monday in December. Mr. Rhett in the South Carolina convention had said: "The election of Lincoln and Hamlin was the last straw on the back of the camel." He declared that the secession of South Carolina was not, however, the event of a day, but a matter that had been gathering head for thirty years.

In correspondence with Mr. Rhett just after Lincoln's election, Mr. Davis had not been eager to commit his own State of Mississippi. I have quoted from his letter on page 140. He explained that his State, lacking a seaport, could not secede unless accompanied by contiguous States. He thought it desirable to wait, in order to connect South Carolina with Georgia and Alabama, and then with Mississippi in concerted action.

But South Carolina was impatient, and Mr. Rhett and his friends had received much encouragement from other States, even though Mr. Davis had expressed caution. On January 10th, soon after South Carolina had set up her independent government, Mr. Davis spoke at length in the Senate, in defence of the view that there was nothing in the Constitution which conferred upon the Federal Government the power to coerce a State. "This Union," he declared, "is dear to me as a Union of fraternal States. It would lose its value if I had to regard it as a Union held together by physical force. I would be happy to know that every State now felt that fraternity which made this Union possible; and if that evidence could go out, if evidence satisfactory to the people of the South could be given, that that feeling existed in the hearts of the northern people, you might burn your statute books and we would cling to the Union still. But it is because of their conviction that hostility and not fraternity now exists in the hearts of the people, that they are looking to their reserved rights and to their independent powers for their own protection."

Before South Carolina had taken the final step, but after the convention had been called which was quite sure to declare for secession, the South Carolina members in the House of Representatives had gone in a group to President Buchanan, to urge that nothing should be done to provoke hostilities in the Charleston Harbor. It was the ardent desire of South Carolina that there should be diplomatic negotiations between commissioners from that State and the Washington government, to the end that withdrawal might be a matter of

peaceable agreement, with all details regarding forts and other forms of Federal property settled by negotiation. There will be occasion to discuss in a subsequent chapter the beginning of those hostile activities at Charleston which were destined, in a short time, to convert the secession movement into a war between two groups of States.

On December 20th, the day of the adoption of the Secession Ordinance in South Carolina, an election was held in Mississippi, to choose members of a State convention to assemble on January 7th. There was much difference of opinion even in Mississippi on details of procedure; but virtually no difference as to the right and duty of the South to resist coercion. Many citizens were opposed to separate State secession, desiring to wait for simultaneous and general southern action. The convention consisted of ninety-nine members, and its deliberations were brief. Organizing on January 7th, it adopted an Ordinance of Secession on the 9th, and declared Mississippi to be a "free, sovereign, and independent State." It was further agreed that "the people of the State of Mississippi hereby consent to form a Federal Union with such of the States as have seceded, or may secede from the Union of the United States of America." There were 84 affirmative votes, and 15 negative, but the action of the majority was afterwards made unanimous.

Florida had been only fifteen years a State in the Union, and it had less reason for attachment on sentimental or economic grounds than most of the other southern States. It had been almost as ready for secession as South Carolina. Delegates to a State Convention met at Tallahassee on January 5th. One-third of the 67 members were by preference "Co-operationists," but on January 10th the Secession Ordinance was passed by a vote of 62 to 7. The steps taken by Florida to maintain her asserted position of independence belong to a subsequent narration.

Alabama's withdrawal was achieved by the vote of a State Convention at Montgomery on January 11th, one day later than the secession of Florida, and two days after Mississippi had passed her ordinance. The history of the movement in Alabama is of exceptional inter-

STRONG'S DIME CARICATURES.—No. 2.

Sic 'em, Buck! sic 'em! I wish poor old Hickory was alive. He'd bring 'em back in no time.

If we can only get them separated from the flock, we can pick their bones at our leisure.

LITTLE BO-PEEP AND HER FOOLISH SHEEP.

"Little Bo-peep, she lost her sheep,   Let 'em alone, and they'll all come home,
And didn't know where to find 'em;   With their tails hanging down behind 'em."

Miss Columbia observes her sheep as they leave the pack, one by one, and regrets that her old watchdog, "Hickory" (Andrew Jackson), is no longer alive. Her new watchdog, "Old Buck" (President Buchanan), refuses to bring back the wandering sheep. Off in the distance are the wolves of Europe, waiting their opportunity to pick the bones of the sheep that have strayed.

est. Mr. Yancey of that State had been hardly less conspicuous than Mr. Rhett of South Carolina as an advocate of the creation of a Southern Confederacy. He had no love whatever for the Union, and was obsessed by his dreams of a Slave Empire encircling the Gulf of Mexico and the Caribbean.

Mobile and southern Alabama had become completely convinced by the Yancey views of southern aggrandizement; and it is a mistake to suppose that such ambitions were fantastic on their face. As we have already noted in previous chapters, the South was rolling in wealth and prosperity, while the North was painfully recovering from the panic of 1857 that had been as destructive of property values as if hurricanes, floods and conflagrations had swept westward from New York to the new

boom towns of the prairies. With its cotton exports and its direct trade with the West Indies and South America, as well as with Europe, Mobile resented northern tariff policy as intensely as did Charleston.

Northern Alabama was differently situated, and would greatly have preferred to remain in the Union. But the northern counties were, at that time, less developed in population and wealth than the southern. The State was, of course, bound to secede, but in the upper counties there was general preference for the plan of awaiting simultaneous action after a convention of southern States. Assembling at Montgomery on the 7th of January, the convention found itself unanimous in adopting the following resolution: "That the State of Alabama will not submit to the administration

GOVERNOR WISE AS CAPTAIN BOBADIL

Bobadil is a character in Ben Johnson's play, "Every Man in His Humor"—a military braggart with a scheme for curing all the ills of Europe. He succeeded in creating the impression among his followers that he was heroic in the extreme. *Vanity Fair* thus looked upon the Governor of Virginia at the time when he proposed the peace conference which sought ineffectually to formulate a plan for preserving the Union. After his State seceded, in April, 1861, Governor Wise became a General in the Confederate Army.

Georgia is to be considered next, as we list the withdrawals of the southern States from their places in the Union. The Georgia Legislature, on the 7th of December, had avowed the right of any State to secede upon its own judgment, and (with evident reference to South Carolina) it was declared that "Georgia will give to the seceding southern State the aid, encouragement and assistance of her entire people." It was declared that "the interests and destiny of the slaveholding States of this Union are, and must remain, common." This legislative action was modified a week later; but it stood as expressing the Georgia view that the South must act as a whole.

The convention that had been chosen to meet at Milledgeville on the 16th of January was seemingly far from unanimous. The test came on a motion to secede, and to appoint a committee to draft an ordinance, which was sustained by 165 favorable votes, with 130 opposing. On the 19th, however, the

of Lincoln and Hamlin as President and Vice-President of the United States, upon the principles referred to in the foregoing preamble." The preamble had stated southern grievances in the strongest possible terms; and the acceptance of this statement by the entire convention showed how fully Alabama was impressed with the idea that the Republican victory could not be acquiesced in by the South.

The Ordinance of Secession was adopted on the 10th by a vote of 61 to 39. Those voting in the negative thought that the ordinance should be submitted to a vote of the people of the State, and also that secession should not take effect until the 4th of March. Although northern Alabama was not altogether happy, the State as a whole accepted the plan of immediate secession without further dispute and with evident enthusiasm.

"HARK FROM THE *TOOMBS* A DOLEFUL CRY"
From the *New York Illustrated News*

The senior Senator from Georgia, Robert Toombs, was in the forefront of the movement which resulted in the secession of Georgia on January 19, 1861. For a short time he was Secretary of State in the cabinet of Jefferson Davis, but he resigned in July to become a Brigadier-General in the Confederate Army.

STRONG'S DIME CARICATURES.—No. 1.

"*These Secession Ducks give me a great deal of trouble. They emptied the dish before they went, and there's no telling what will happen to 'em now they've left my wing. If that hungry hawk pounces on them, they will have no one but themselves to blame!*"

DOMESTIC TROUBLES.

The seven Secession ducks, having left the nest, are threatened by the Anarchy hawk. Meanwhile, in addition to worrying about them, the mothering Union hen complains that the troublesome ducks had emptied the Treasury dish before they went.

ordinance was adopted by a vote of 208 to 89. It was feared that the nature of the division of opinion in the convention might be misunderstood; and a resolution was accordingly adopted that was actually signed by every member of the convention. It was made plain that differences had only to do with ways to proceed, and not with essential principles. Thus the Georgia convention acted unanimously in the end.

The documentary history of the Secession movement, if printed in full, would require a volume for each State. Our space permits only the briefest summary. The great State of Louisiana was next to assert independence. On the 26th of January, at Baton Rouge, a convention declared "that the Union now subsisting between Louisiana and other States, under the name of 'The United States of America,' is hereby dissolved." There followed

in the next paragraph of the ordinance a sentence that discloses the curious legalistic view that blinded so many able men of that period to the simple facts of history. The sentence reads as follows: "We do further declare and ordain that the State of Louisiana hereby resumes all rights and powers heretofore delegated to the Government of the United States of America; that her citizens are absolved from all allegiance to said Government; and that she is in full possession and exercise of all those rights of sovereignty which appertain to a free and independent State." Louisiana, as a State, had been formed out of the immense territory which became a full national possession in 1803 by purchase from the government of France. Her status in the Union was precisely that of Iowa and other States carved out of the Federal domain. Whatever rights of secession the original

SAM HOUSTON (1793-1863)

The former member of Congress and Governor of Tennessee, Sam Houston, had a picturesque record before he
achieved fame as the liberator of Texas from Mexican rule
in 1836, through the victory over Santa Anna at San
Jacinto. He had been adopted into the Cherokee tribe
and had been sent to Texas by President Jackson to
negotiate Indian treaties. Remaining there he became
commander-in-chief and President of the new Republic.
After Texas was admitted as a State of the Union,
Houston was one of its first Senators, serving from 1845
until 1859 and opposing the Kansas-Nebraska bill.
Having been elected Governor of Texas in 1859, he opposed the Secession movement; and when the State finally
went out he refused to take the oath of allegiance to the
Confederacy and the convention deposed him from office.
He died at Huntsville, Tex., in 1863.

southward pro-slavery outlook, as they contemplated the future. Governor Moore issued
his call for a legislative session early in November, declaring "that the election of Abraham Lincoln to the office of President of the
United States, by a sectional and aggressive
anti-slavery party, whose hostility to the people and the institutions of the South has been
evinced by repeated and long-continued vio-
lations of Constitutional obligations and
fraternal amity, now consummated by this
last insult and outrage perpetrated at and
through the ballot-box" justified resistance
to any extent. The legislature met on December 10th and provided for a State convention,
which body met at Baton Rouge on January
23rd, with the result of the adoption of the
Secession Ordinance on the 26th by a vote of
113 to 17. Immediately after the secession
of South Carolina, there had been great demonstrations in New Orleans; and that city was
already informally an uncontested center of
the Secession movement. In Louisiana, as
elsewhere, it was the leaders, rather than the

"THE NOBLEST ROMAN OF THEM ALL"

A cartoon from *Vanity Fair*

Governor Houston attempts, without avail, to quiet the
Secessionists in the State of Texas.

States might have retained, it was absurd, on
its face, for Louisiana to claim that she had
"delegated" rights and powers to the Government of the United States which she was
now resuming as a lawful action of unques-
tionable right in the nature of her partnership
agreement. Her action was as clearly revolutionary as would have been the secession
from Louisiana of a group of counties or
parishes.

But the people of Louisiana, like those of
South Carolina and Alabama, had the strong

BRAVING THE STORM!!!

"I REGARD THE CONSTITUTION OF MY COUNTRY, AND I AM DETERMINED TO STAND BY IT."—*Extract from Gen. Houston's Letter of Nov. 14*

From *Vanity Fair,* December 15, 1860.

mass of the people, who determined the policy of the State. The feeling against the North was universal, while the demand for immediate secession was made effective by the skillful management of the secession leaders.

Among older men participating in the Secession movement at New Orleans, there were those who remembered well the debate in Congress on the Bill authorizing the formation of a State government, and the admission of Louisiana. Exactly fifty years had elapsed since that discussion at Washington in 1811, by members of the Eleventh Congress. Hon. Josiah Quincy of Massachusetts led the opposition, and he emphasized and reiterated his views in the following words: "If this Bill passes it is my deliberate opinion that it is virtually a dissolution of this Union; that it will free the States from their moral obligation; and as it will be the right of all, so it will be the duty of some, definitely to prepare for a separation, amicably, if they can, violently, if they

must." I am quoting this expression as no merely curious coincidence. New England having lost the motive, had abandoned the theory. Louisiana, impelled by supposed self-interest in 1861, asserted the theory.

The Secession movement in North Carolina met with vigorous resistance. The Bell-Everett ticket had secured almost as many votes in the "Tar-heel State" as the Breckinridge ticket. Even the voters who had supported Breckinridge were, to a great extent, Constitutional Unionists. North Carolina had never been in sympathy with the Charleston doctrines of Calhoun and Rhett. But as a Slave State it accepted the view that the South had grievances, and that the southern States should co-operate vigorously in trying to secure southern rights against the menace of northern Abolitionism. The legislature was in session at the time South Carolina was taking action in December, and showed a strong disposition to urge the neighboring State to delay

Secession and enter into conferences for an "honorable adjustment of the present difficulties," to the end that "a Constitutional Union may be preserved." A Convention bill passed the legislature on the 24th of January, but this bill—unlike that of any other southern State—provided not merely for choosing members of a convention, but for a direct vote on the question whether or not a convention should be held.

On the 28th of January the North Carolina voters decided against a convention, 47,323 voting in the negative, with 46,672 voting affirmatively. The vote for members of a possible convention resulted in a two to one majority of Anti-secessionists. Thus North Carolina remained in the Union until the actual issue of Civil War compelled the people of that State to decide whether or not they would respond to Lincoln's call for their quota of federal troops with which to carry the war into South Carolina and other centers of active rebellion.

A like situation was compelling Virginia to make a choice, with the result that Virginia adopted her Ordinance of Secession on April 17th. The North Carolinians, wedged between South Carolina and Virginia, could no longer hold aloof; and they adopted their Ordinance of Secession on May 20th. Arkansas had taken similar action on May 6th. The secession of Tennessee was postponed until June 8th.

The Governor of Texas was General Sam Houston. He was attached to the Union by sentiment, and also by firm conviction as to the disadvantages and losses that would accrue to Texas as a result of Secession. He was a national figure of great popularity. His name had been prominent in presidential conventions. He was one of the foremost leaders of the Constitutional Union party. He had a bold imagination, and a record of heroism. Of all the States in the Union, Texas was the only one that could make any historical pretensions to a past experience of independence and sov-

ereignty. Texas had retained control over her own public lands, and could secede with a better show of right, and fewer practical complications, than any other State. Governor Houston thought of the destiny of Texas as related rather to northern Mexico and the Pacific Coast than to the Atlantic seaboard.

There was much support for Houston's position, and he refused to call a session of the legislature, explaining to the people the dangers of precipitate action. He held as strongly as any one to southern views, but did not regard Secession as a remedy. A group of individuals on their own responsibility issued a call for a convention, and delegates were elected. Also, a member of the legislature invited that body to meet in extra session. These acts were revolutionary; and to avoid conflict, Governor Houston changed his attitude and issued a legal call for the session, which met at Austin on January 22nd.

The legislature gave its sanction to the informal election of delegates to a State convention, and Governor Houston reluctantly approved of this step. On February 5th this convention, which had not been chosen by more than half of the 122 counties of the State, adopted an Ordinance of Secession by a vote of 166 to 7. The legislature required that the ordinance should be submitted to the people, and February 23rd was fixed as the referendum date. Without waiting for the popular verdict, the convention, on February 11th, elected seven delegates to represent Texas in the Confederate Congress then in session at Montgomery, Alabama.

The popular vote resulted in a three-to-one majority for Secession, although only 36,000 votes were cast. It is to be noted that Texas went out of the Union by a State-wide popular vote of only 34,794 affirmative supporters of the Ordinance. The result was announced in the convention on the 4th of March, as Buchanan was retiring from office and Lincoln taking up the reins of authority.

THE COAT OF ARMS OF THE INDEPENDENT STATE OF SOUTH CAROLINA
At the left is the Latin inscription: "Prepared in Spirit
and Wealth." At the right: "While I breathe I hope."

CHAPTER XIX

The Confederacy Organizes

*Asserting the principles of '76—Delegates at Montgomery adopt a
Constitution—Jefferson Davis chosen President—Rhett, Yancey and
Toombs find the Moderates in control—The Cabinet takes office*

THE LAUNCHING of a new government, claiming sovereign rights, and demanding an equal place in the family of nations, is no light or casual enterprise. The great example held up to aspiring men in all the continents was that of the successful struggle of the American colonies to make good their Declaration of 1776. The Spanish-speaking colonists had been inspired by the achievements of George Washington and his compatriots, and the Latin-American republics had accordingly set out upon their careers of much vicissitude but ultimate success. From beginnings on the Atlantic seaboard, the United States had expanded to the Pacific. With new States winning admission, the centers of political influence were moving westward. Ever since the Mexican War and the annexation of Texas and the Southwest, the assertiveness of sectional differences had been increasing. Southern opinion had wholly changed since Jefferson's time, and the belief was now growing everywhere below the Potomac and Ohio, and especially in the Gulf States, that slavery could be maintained as a permanent system, so reformed and refined as to be advantageous to both races.

When success crowns political upheavals,

173

it is usually in consequence of the courage and persistence of a few leaders who have ideals and far-reaching aims. As a merely popular affair, the American Revolution muddled along. With four million people living in the Colonies, it is within bounds to say that a fraction of one per cent.—let us say twenty thousand individuals at the most—constituted that general and local leadership which supported Washington and carried the movement to its fruition.

The circumstances of that earlier Revolutionary success were constantly in the minds of the leaders of the new Southern rebellion. They felt themselves coming under a sort of imperialistic tyranny, about to be asserted by a centralized government at

THE PALMETTO FLAG OF SOUTH CAROLINA
A Southern envelope cartoon.

Washington, that could be compared with the policies of the British government under George III. While still loyal to the Crown, our colonies had helped to win Canada from the French and thus to transfer the northern half of the American continent to the expanding British Empire. Their services in this conquest of the North had, in the minds of our Revolutionary leaders, fully compensated Great Britain for the subsequent loss of her oldest trans-Atlantic settlements.

Pursuing the analogy, many leaders in the Secession movement of the slaveholding States felt that they had taken even more than their proportionate part in the transactions that had given to the United States California and Oregon, the upper Mississippi Valley, and the great western plains and mountain regions. In view of these facts, they thought that they should be allowed to withdraw in peace, to set up a new republic that would never seek expansion north of the Ohio River or the old Missouri Compromise line, and that would give pledges to maintain amicable political relations and advantageous commercial intercourse.

I am far from asserting that great numbers of southern leaders had identical visions of the future as they joined hands in the Secession movement. The separationists of the southern tier of States were far more ardent than those of the border. A great majority of the colonists of 1776 were seeking a redress of grievances rather than independence. Patriotism of that period was of all shades, from the conservative loyalists to the radical following of Sam Adams and Patrick Henry. Quite the same thing was true of the southern people in the opening weeks of 1861. A majority, doubtless, regarded themselves as devoted to the Union, and supposed that their leaders were merely taking steps intended to make the Union safe for southern institutions. The more ambitious southern leaders knew that Secession had to become a fully realized achievement before the Confederate government could begin to play what they conceived to be its destined part in the affairs of a still immature western hemisphere.

THE FRUIT OF THE PALMETTO TREE-SON
A Northern envelope cartoon.

Agents from South Carolina were active in the other Slave States, but Washington was the real focus of Secession activities. Caucuses of southern Senators were frequently held, and their plans and agreements were communicated to Governors and leaders at the State capitals. A caucus of Saturday night, January 5th, adopted these resolutions:

"*Resolved,* that we recommend to our respective States immediate Secession.

"*Resolved,* that we recommend the holding of a general Convention of the said States to be holden in the city of Montgomery, Alabama, at some period not later than the 15th of February, 1861."

It was the general opinion of the caucus that Senators and Representatives should linger on

DELEGATES FROM THE SECEDING STATES MEET TO FORM THE CONFEDERACY
Hon. Howell Cobb, former Governor of Georgia and recently Secretary of the Treasury in President
Buchanan's Cabinet, is seen presiding. The Convention is assembled in the Senate chamber of the
State Capitol at Montgomery, Alabama.

in Washington, in order to do what they could to prevent unfriendly legislation previous to the 4th of March. The report at that time listed, as attending the caucus, Senators Fitzpatrick and C. C. Clay, Jr., of Alabama; Johnson and Sebastian of Arkansas; Robert Toombs and Alfred Iverson of Georgia; Judah P. Benjamin and John Slidell of Louisiana; Jefferson Davis and Albert G. Brown of Mississippi; John Hemphill and Louis T. Wigfall of Texas, and David L. Yulee and S. R. Mallory of Florida. As we have already noted, the Ordinances of Secession in five of these States were adopted within less than a month, soon to be followed by Texas, and somewhat later by Arkansas.

Although individual States followed one another in asserting that they had *resumed* their sovereignty and independence, this form of words was to be taken as one of the legalistic fictions that have often puzzled European students of American history and politics. Even South Carolina had not withdrawn with any plans looking to an independent place among the nations, although for several weeks there existed nominally the "Republic of South

Carolina," with its own Palmetto flag. The announced separate sovereignties were immediately preliminary to the establishment of the southern Confederacy. Even before one or two of the States had completed their formalities of Secession they had appointed delegates to sit in the new Confederate Congress.

The plan of keeping their foremost statesmen sitting in Congress at Washington, under their oaths of office to maintain and support the United States of America, while the rival Congress of seceded States was in session at Montgomery, was not creditable to the southern States. It was without dignity, and without a shadow of justification. These very leaders at Washington were quite as responsible as any of the southern Governors for the hundreds of seizures of federal property that had already taken place in all of the seceded States. Their position was untenable and could not have been maintained without loss of self-respect. In a short time this was realized, and upon information of the adoption of Ordinances by their States, the delegations at Washington soon made their announcements and withdrew as members of Congress.

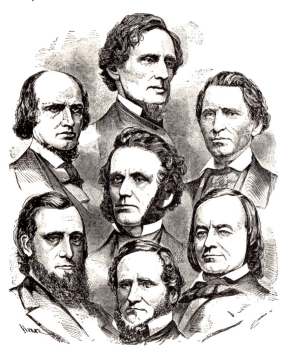

THE MISSISSIPPI DELEGATION IN CONGRESS
WHEN THE STATE SECEDED

From top to bottom in the middle row are: Senator
Jefferson Davis, Senator Albert G. Brown, and Representa-
tive William Barksdale. The two men at the left are
Reuben Davis (above) and Lucius Q. C. Lamar. At the
right are Otho R. Singleton and (below) John J. McRae.
Many years afterward Mr. Lamar was a member of the
Cleveland Cabinet, and a Justice of the Supreme Court.

In the State House at Montgomery, on
February 4, 1861, the Confederate Congress
held its first session, electing Howell Cobb of
Georgia as chairman. Mr. Cobb was an eminent southern leader, and he had been Secretary of the Treasury in the Buchanan Administration until December 10, 1860, less than
two months before he was presiding over the
Confederate Congress. Delegations from
South Carolina, Georgia, Alabama, Mississippi, Louisiana, and Florida were present,
those from Texas arriving a few days later.
Mr. Cobb, taking the chair, expressed the hope
that the other Slave States would join the new
Confederacy, and that "the most peaceful and
friendly relations, both political and commercial," might be maintained with the North and
with the world at large.

Business proceeded rapidly, the States at
first voting as equal units. On February 8th
the Constitution of the United States was pro-
visionally adopted, with certain alterations to

meet the situation of the Confederacy. Since
all these actions were temporary, no plan was
adopted for ratifying the Constitution. On
February 9th, all members of the Congress
took the oath of allegiance to the Constitution.
On that same day the States voted in secret
session for a President and Vice-President of
the Confederacy.

Each of the six States present, acting as a
unit, voted for Jefferson Davis of Mississippi
as President, and for Alexander H. Stephens
of Georgia as Vice-President. Committees of
the Congress on Foreign Affairs, Finance,
Military and Naval Affairs, the Judiciary,
Postal Affairs, Commerce, and some other
subjects were at once provided for, and it was
agreed to adopt all the laws of the United
States that were in force on the 1st of November, 1860, in so far as they could be consistently adapted to the needs of the Confederacy. The name "Confederate States of North
America," was adopted, and a committee was

THE GEORGIA DELEGATION IN CONGRESS
WHEN THE STATE SECEDED

The two Senators, Robert Toombs and Alfred Iverson, are
in the middle of the second row from the top. In the row
above them, from left to right, are: John W. H.
Underwood, Peter E. Love, and Lucius J. Gartrell. Across
the bottom are: Thomas Hardeman, Jr., John J. Jones,
and Joshua Hill. At the left of the middle row is Martin
J. Crawford; at the right, James Jackson.

THE CITY OF MONTGOMERY, ALABAMA, WHERE THE CONFEDERACY WAS FORMED
Representatives from the six States of South Carolina, Mississippi, Florida, Alabama, Georgia, and
Louisiana assembled here on February 4, 1861, and established the "Confederate States of North
America."   At the head of the street, in the distance, is the State Capitol.

appointed to report a Constitution for a permanent government.

Mr. Stephens, who was present in the Congress as one of the members of Georgia's distinguished delegation, took the oath of office as Vice-President. He had been one of Lincoln's closest friends during the single term of the Illinois statesman's service in Congress some fourteen years earlier. He had been opposed to Secession, and had vainly argued against it in the Georgia Convention. But he had accepted the verdict of his State without further question when the great majority overruled him. Less than a month before Georgia seceded, Abraham Lincoln had written his last letter to Mr. Stephens, and at this point we may well quote a few sentences from that frank and extended communication:

I fully appreciate the present peril the country is in, and the weight of responsibility on me. Do the people of the South really entertain fears that a Republican Administration would, directly or indirectly, interfere with the slaves, or with them about the slaves? If they do, I wish to assure you, as once a friend, and still, I hope, not an enemy, that there is no cause for such fears. The South would be in no more danger in this respect than it was in the days of Washington. I suppose, however, this does not meet the case. You think slavery is right and ought to be extended, while we think it is wrong and ought to be restricted. That I suppose is the rub. It certainly is the only substantial difference between us.

But this, in the eyes of the South, had come to be a substantial difference that removed the two sections as far apart as anything that could divide intelligent men. The southern point of view had changed since the days of Washington and Jefferson. In his brief remarks accepting the new office, Mr. Stephens expressed his high estimate of the confidence shown in him by the Confederate Congress. To understand how far Mr. Stephens himself had gone in accepting the new southern doctrines, we may quote briefly from a speech delivered by him at Savannah a few weeks after he had been made Vice-President. Reviewing the historic position of slavery, and citing Jefferson especially, Mr. Stephens said:

The prevailing ideas entertained by him and most of the leading statesmen at the time of the formation of the old Constitution were that the enslavement of the African was in violation of the laws of nature; that it was wrong in *principle*, socially, morally, and politically. . . . Our new government is founded upon exactly the opposite idea; its foundations are laid, its cornerstone rests upon the great truth, that the Negro is not equal to the white man; that slavery—subordination to the superior race—is his natural and normal condition. This, our new government, is the first in the history of the world based upon this great physical, philosophical, and moral truth.

Alexander H. Stephens was one of the most reasonable and upright men of his time. He had not been identified with the so-called "fire-eaters," and "nigger-drivers," or the blustering planters who were victims of the speculative craze in the newer cotton districts, many of whom had gone thither from the North. If the sane, moderate, and sensitive Stephens had become committed to the idea of slavery as the "cornerstone" of the new empire, it is not so difficult to understand how a drifting and uncertain political situation in the South had begun to crystallize. Nothing was needed to complete the process but the clash of arms. The war mania sweeps everything before it.

Jefferson Davis had become the foremost leader on the southern side at Washington, even as Seward of New York was pre-eminent as the spokesman of the North. The two men were radically different in character and temperament, but they were intimate friends, this being due chiefly to the great affection Mr.

MRS. JEFFERSON DAVIS

Mrs. Davis (born Varina Howell) was a woman of great personal charm and had many friends in the North. She wrote a two-volume memoir of her husband, whom she outlived by sixteen years. Her later years were chiefly passed in New York City. She died in 1906.

Seward felt for Mr. and Mrs. Davis, at whose home he was a constant visitor. Davis was a man of lofty sincerity, who spoke always as a statesman and never as a politician. Seward, with great talents, assumed a cynical pose in private that was not in keeping with his position before the country as a man of convictions. As a West Pointer, Davis had made a fine record in the Army, but had been drawn early into civil office. He had turned soldier again to take a brilliant part in the campaign against Mexico. Since that time he had served at Washington, where he and his family were especially happy in their associations.

With delicate health, Senator Davis had spent summer vacations in the North; and he and Mrs. Davis had many friends in New England and New York. He had been seriously ill for some months, and it was with difficulty he made his farewell speech in the Senate on January 21st, announcing the news of the secession of his State. His remarks were eloquent, but without menace or bombast. He rehearsed elaborately his familiar argument as to the right of Secession. With kindly personal words of good will toward all his fellow members, he concluded his career in the Senate of the United States.

The Davis family remained for another week in Washington, settling their private affairs, and bidding intimate farewells to many friends, Republicans and Democrats alike, and including President Buchanan and the members of the Cabinet. In view of the bitterness that was soon to make the name "Jeff Davis" a hissing and a by-word throughout the North, it is somewhat difficult to recover a true understanding of personal relations and political conditions in Washington during the last weeks of the Buchanan Administration.

Mr. and Mrs. Davis, with their young children, left Washington and made their way to their country home in Mississippi, with the prospect of retirement from legislative and political activities. Mr. Davis had been asked to take charge of the military organization of his State, and his election to the Presidency was not of his seeking. Extremists in South Carolina and other States, readers of the *Mercury* as their political guide, had expected presidential honors to be conferred upon their spokesman, the elder Robert Barnwell Rhett. The Georgians had considered the magnificent Robert Toombs as the most suitable figure for the headship of the Confederacy, and South Carolina and other States had at first acquiesced in this choice. There were others who were considered, especially Stephens and perhaps Yancey. Rhett, however, was too radical in many of his views, even for the delegation from his own State; Toombs was too aggressive and explosive; Stephens was not of the executive type; Yancey was orator and propagandist, not acceptable to Border States. Davis was found by common consent to be the most suitable man, and in the end there was the appearance of entire unanimity in his election.

The Charleston *Mercury* published a dispatch from Montgomery noting the arrival of the chosen leader, and proceeding as follows: "President Davis's trip from Jackson, Mississippi, to Montgomery was one continuous ovation. He made no less than twenty-five speeches upon the route, returning thanks for complimentary greetings from crowds of ladies and gentlemen. There were military demonstrations, salutes of cannon, etc., at the various depots." ... Addressing the welcoming throngs on his arrival Saturday night, the 16th, according to the *Mercury,* "he briefly reviewed the present position of the South. The time for compromise, he said, had passed, and our only hope was in a determined maintenance of our position and to make all who oppose smell southern powder and feel southern steel. If coercion should be persisted in, he had no doubt as to the result. We would maintain our right to self-government, at all hazards.

JEFFERSON DAVIS, OF MISSISSIPPI
The West Point graduate, cotton planter, former member of the House of Representatives and the Senate, and Secretary of War in the Pierce cabinet, who was chosen President of the Confederate States of North America on February 9, 1861.

We ask nothing, want nothing, and will have no complications. If other States should desire to join our Confederation, they can freely come on our terms. Our separation from the old Union is complete. No COMPROMISE; NO RECONSTRUCTION CAN BE NOW ENTERTAINED." (These words were capitalized, as above, in the *Mercury.*)

Speaking to another multitude as he arrived at his hotel, he said: "Fellow citizens and brethren of the Confederate States of America—for now we are brethren, not in name merely, but in fact—men of one flesh, one bone, one interest, one purpose, and of identity of domestic institutions. We have henceforth, I trust, a prospect of living together in peace with our institutions the subject of protection and not of defamation."

Referring to the tone of his addresses, at many places on his way to Montgomery, Mr. Dodd says: "He spoke to large gatherings at every stop of the train, and sought as he tells us in his 'Rise and Fall of the Confederate Government,' to disillusion the minds of those who thought there would be no war. The newspapers of the day, both northern and southern, make him fulminate against the North on every occasion. Davis undoubtedly uttered threats, at Opelika, Alabama, in case the South should be invaded. On the other hand, it was entirely unlike him to have indulged in the empty braggadocio attributed to him in the New York journals."

It was William L. Yancey who ardently welcomed him and introduced him, when he addressed the crowd from the portico of the Exchange Hotel, and it was Mr. Rhett who conveyed the hearty greetings of the Confederate Congress on the following day. These were the two uncompromising doctrinaires who had done most to convert partisanship into Secession, with the disasters of war as a sequel of embittered sectional politics.

Men must not be blamed too much if their private feelings and their public utterances are not always consistent. Mr. Rhett, the arch-secessionist, did not really like or trust Davis. He thought Davis was quite too ready to continue negotiations for reunion, looking to the Border States to mediate between the extremists of the Cotton States and the peace-at-any-price sentiment now prevailing in the Northeast. Yancey doubtless would have preferred Toombs for President, but to all outward appearances these leaders were harmonious

and were enthusiastic supporters of Davis.

A certain relief comes with the ending of suspense. President Davis and his associates had crossed their Rubicon. Already they had made a chapter of history that could never be blotted out. They had taken solemn oaths of allegiance to a new government that they had formed. With this step they felt their connection with the old Union as a thing of the past. Their courage rose to meet the hazards of the new situation. They proceeded to take count of their assets. They now hoped ardently for the permanent success of their experiment.

Mr. Davis read his inaugural address standing in front of the State Capitol at Montgomery on February 18th. He made a plea for the right of the southern States to withdraw, and declared: "The impartial and enlightened verdict of mankind will vindicate the rectitude of our conduct; and He who knows the hearts of men will judge of the sincerity with which we have labored to preserve the government of our fathers in its spirit." "If we may not hope to avoid war," he proceeded, "we may at least expect that posterity will acquit us of having needlessly engaged in it."

Referring to the South as "an agricultural people, whose chief interest is the export of commodities required in every manufacturing country," he reasoned that "our true policy is peace and the freest trade which our necessities will permit." Because their interests were not those of rivals, he thought that there should be mutual trading advantages between the South and what he termed "the northeastern States of the American Union." "If, however, passion or lust of dominion should cloud the judgment or inflame the ambition of those States, we must prepare to meet the emergency and maintain by the final arbitrament of the sword the position which we have assumed among the nations of the earth. We have entered upon the career of independence, and it must be inflexibly pursued."

Further on in the address he declared that "a reunion with the States

SECESSIONISTS LEAVING THE UNION

This envelope caricature is from a collection owned by Dr. Hughes Dayton, of Ardsley-on-Hudson, N. Y., loaned to the author. The envelopes were gathered by Dr. Dayton's father, who was attached to the War Department, and most of them possess the added interest and value of having been addressed either to President Lincoln or to the Secretary of War, Mr. Stanton.

IN A POSITION TO BE RECOGNIZED
"The celebrated Sepoy Juggler and Acrobat, Jeff Davis, in
his dangerous globe feat."

The globe in this case is the Confederacy, and the rope is Cotton. Mr.
Davis, with his familiar motto "Let Us Alone," was expected to roll the
globe to a position of security.

from which we have separated is neither practicable nor desirable," except upon terms for which "your Constitution makes adequate provision." He asserted that there would be no serious check upon the production of the South's great export crops, even if they were involved in war. If the export of cotton were interfered with, there would remain to the South "the well known resources for retaliation upon the commerce of an enemy." In a peroration making the usual appeal of American statesmen to "the God of our fathers," Mr. Davis declared that "it is joyous in the midst of perilous times, to look around upon a people united in heart, where one purpose of high resolve animates and actuates the whole; where the sacrifices to be made are not weighed in the balance against honor and right and liberty and equality."

I have, in these brief quotations, barely suggested the sustained eloquence of Mr. Davis's address, its tone of calm and untroubled assurance, and the air of intellectual and moral superiority with which he was surveying the plight of an unhappy and a baffled North. Two days later, however, he wrote in a less buoyant tone to Mrs. Davis, who was lingering with the family on the Mississippi plantation. The letter reveals the anxiety with which Mr. Davis was burdened, when he found himself facing the world as the ruling head of a yet unrecognized claimant for a safe place in the roster of civilized nations. Mrs. Davis has given us this letter as follows:

JEFFERSON DAVIS SPEAKING FROM THE BALCONY
OF HIS HOTEL

He had just arrived at Montgomery, on the night of February 16th, from
his home in Mississippi. A week earlier he had been elected Provisional
President of the Confederate States of America, and two days later
he was formally inaugurated.

MONTGOMERY, ALABAMA, February 20, 1861.
I have been so crowded and pressed that the first
wish to write to you has been thus long deferred.

I was inaugurated on Monday, having reached
here on Saturday night. The audience was large
and brilliant. Upon my weary heart was showered
smiles, plaudits and flowers; but, beyond them, I
saw troubles and thorns innumerable.

We are without machinery, without means, and
threatened by a powerful opposition; but I do not
despond, and will not shrink from the task imposed
upon me.

All along the route, except when in Tennessee,
the people at every station manifested good will and
approbation, by bonfires at night, firing by day;
shouts and salutations in both.

I thought it would have gratified you to have witnessed it and have been a memory to our children.

Referring to this temporary capital of the
Confederacy he added: "This is a gay and
handsome town of some eight thousand inhabitants, and will not be an unpleasant residence.

As soon as an hour is my own, I
will look for a house and write to
you more fully."

Mr. Davis lost no time in organizing a working government.
Both Davis and Stephens had been
chosen with a view to reconciling
the conservatives, and reassuring
Virginia, Tennessee, and other
Slave States still in the Union. In
the selection of his Cabinet Mr.
Davis further recognized moderate
sentiment and came short of satisfying the extremists. According
to Mr. Dodd, "he still more alienated those who had borne the brunt
of the long agitation by filling the
high positions in the new government with men who had at one time
or another publicly opposed Secession, some of whom had been
competitors with himself for the
chief positions, while others were
the open personal enemies of Rhett
and Yancey."

Continuing, Mr. Dodd lists the
members of the first Davis Cabinet
and characterizes them as follows:
"Robert Toombs, disappointed at
the sudden turn of things on February 8th, which defeated him for the Presidency, was placed in charge of the State Department; C. G. Memminger, a life-long opponent of the South Carolina revolutionists,
took the Treasury portfolio; L. Pope Walker,
from the Union section of Alabama, was
made Secretary of War; Mallory, strongly
opposed in his own State—Florida, took the
Navy; Benjamin, of decided Whig proclivities, became Attorney-General; and Reagan of
Texas, another conservative, was given the
Post-Office Department."

Underlying this policy was political wisdom
that becomes apparent as one considers the circumstances. The extremists did not need the
recognition of high office to hold them in loyal
support of their own cause. To put responsibility upon the elements that had been less
ardent for Secession was to strengthen rather
than to weaken the new government in its hold

upon the people of the Slave States at large.

Steps were at once taken to secure such military advantages as were available, but it was the accepted policy of Mr. Davis and his official advisers to preserve the *status quo* until after the inauguration of Mr. Lincoln on March 4th. Influences were at work to keep the Buchanan Administration from taking any steps on its part that might precipitate hostilities. Mr. Davis while still at Washington had been in constant correspondence with Governor Pickens of South Carolina. He had urged the avoidance of attempts to disturb the small garrison in Charleston Harbor under command of Major Anderson.

Mr. Lincoln was already on his leisurely journey from Springfield, Illinois, to Washington, having taken his departure on February 11th; and Mr. Davis at Montgomery was noting, day by day, the reports of the Lincoln speeches *en route,* just as Mr. Lincoln in turn was reading the Davis inaugural, while carrying the package of first-draft, privately printed copies of his own address in his personal handbag. Congress was in session at Washington, and unable to reach any conclusions. The Buchanan Administration had been reorganized and had become belatedly pro-Union. But its remaining days were few, and it was marking time, thankful that February had only twenty-eight days and hoping that the final issue of war or peace could be safely postponed, so that the Republican Administration might be held responsible.

Meanwhile, Europe looked on with gloating

THE GREAT SHOW AT MONTGOMERY

DOORKEEPER STEPHENS: "Very sorry, Mr. Palmetto, that all the front seats are taken; but we have a nice back seat reserved for you."

South Carolina—represented by the portly gentleman with a feather in his hat—had led in the movement for secession and was the first State to withdraw from the Union. But Mr. Rhett, who expected to be chosen for President, was considered too radical to please the Border States; and a "front seat" was not given to South Carolina.

eyes at the dismemberment of the formidable American Republic. England and France especially were inclined to the opinion that they had nothing to lose and much perchance to gain from the cleavage between South and North. They were prepared to receive southern commissioners or ambassadors, and to recognize the southern Confederacy as a going concern. Within the group of States that had thus coalesced, for better or for worse, there was a remarkable measure of agreement. The Confederate Congress in its earlier actions was showing itself capable of rapid decisions, and was avoiding the appearance to the world of divided councils.

If only the North could be persuaded to settle details in a reasonable spirit, the South was prepared on its part to assume its share of the national debt, and to account fairly for the various federal properties that had been taken in charge by the seceding States. A new government had appeared on the horizon, with a contiguous domain, some millions of inhabitants, fully organized State and local institutions, and a distinct economic character and position. It gave promise of united policies at home and successful commercial arrangements with the world at large. Its leaders were statesmen of experience, quite equal in accomplishments to those of any other contemporary government. It was able to command the services of military men whose exploits are studied and admired to this day, and who are listed as among the foremost strategists of all time.

The boldness with which seven States had completely suppressed all opposition to their Ordinances of Secession; had adopted a Constitution under which they became a united people; and had made their new central government an established fact—fully accepted throughout the States of South Carolina, Georgia, Florida, Alabama, Mississippi, Louisiana, and Texas—was without parallel in the history of the world. Thus far the launching of the Confederacy had been an unexampled success.

THE STATE CAPITOL AT MONTGOMERY

In which the Provisional Congress of the Confederacy assembled in February, 1861. On the steps of the portico Jefferson Davis took the oath of office. The building is considered to be one of the finest examples of classical Georgian architecture in America.

WRETCHED CONDITION OF THE OLD PARTY AT THE WHITE HOUSE

From the *New York Illustrated News*

The Northerner reminds President Buchanan of the Constitution which he had sworn to preserve, protect, and defend. The Southerner begins to display arms.

CHAPTER XX

Loyalists Now Surround Buchanan

Confusion and alarm in the North—The Administration more firm than Republican leaders—Southern men leave the Cabinet—Union men fill vacancies—Seizures of Federal property

WITH JAMES BUCHANAN still in the White House, seven States which had cast their electoral vote for him in 1856 had now left the Union. He had said in his message to Congress, while South Carolina was taking steps to withdraw, that he found no warrant in the Constitution for coercive action against a seceding State. But neither had he found that a State had any right to withdraw, or that the President could officially recognize the fact of Secession, or treat with agents from the South seeking the adjustment of mutual claims and obligations. It is true that Buchanan, as a Democrat of long public record and the foremost Cabinet personage in the brilliant administration of President Polk, had always been regarded as a sympathizer with southern views. But there can be no doubt of his devoted loyalty to the Union, or of his purpose to do his duty as President.

Congress was in session, and was constantly debating the crisis to the last moment of the Buchanan Administration, without doing anything to clear the way. The Peace Convention was at work, with many distinguished members from all parts of the country, and it did not adjourn until five days before the harassed President retired from office. It had failed to meet the expectations of any party or section. General Scott, as head of the Army, had made confidential suggestions to Mr. Buchanan, but we now know them to have been the weird vaporings of a fine old soldier who imagined himself also a statesman. The legislature of New York was in session and was demanding

DIGNITY AND IMPUDENCE

General Scott, head of the armed forces of the United States, is the personification of dignity in this cartoon from the *New York Illustrated News*. The artist explains that his drawing is "slightly altered from Landseer," the famous English painter of animals. Impudence, in the cartoon, is expressed by Senator Toombs of Georgia.

abstention from coercive measures, while advising a plan of gradual emancipation with full payment for the slaves. The leading business men of eastern cities were carrying huge petitions to Washington in favor of compromise.

Senator Seward, regarded as the supreme leader of the Republican party and the most formidable enemy of the southern cause, was openly declaring for compromise and peace. Thurlow Weed, Albany editor and astute manager of Republican politics in New York, was advocating his own compromise plan, which was more favorable to the South than were the concessions that most of the southern leaders themselves had previously declared to be acceptable. Horace Greeley, most influential and most widely read journalist of the anti-slavery movement, was now advocating—almost every day, in his lucid editorial style—the simple justice of allowing the seceded States to go in peace. Commerce and politics joined hands in New York City to support Tammany Hall's pro-Southern attitude. These influences were exerting themselves to make decisive action of any kind impossible, yet everybody was ready to blame President Buchanan as responsible for the bad political weather. Historians, even those of recent date, have usually agreed in

pronouncing him weak and vacillating, although they do not offer to show how he could have saved the country by some act of single-handed heroism. He could merely have precipitated a war, with no means to carry it on, and with no thanks from Mr. Lincoln who was waiting to extend an olive-branch.

While others were talking and writing, the Administration was trying its best to deal with practical questions now confronting every one of the federal departments. The State Department was affected through the changed circumstances of individual foreigners, as well as of external commerce in the southern ports. The Secretary of the Treasury, the Secretary of War, the Secretary of the Navy, the Secretary of the Interior, the Attorney-General, the Postmaster-General, all had to contend with extremely puzzling situations. They could not abjectly surrender their responsibilities, and abandon the federal properties that they were sworn to protect and administer, yet they found themselves helpless in the face of a revolution that had lodged authority in other hands.

There were custom houses and federal employees at the seaports, and internal revenue

THE SPUNKY COLT, MISS SOUTH CAROLINA

Mr. "Rarey" Buchanan does not see why he cannot put on the "coercion" strap. When he tries to pat the colt she bites; when he tries to apply the strap she kicks. He really does not see what is to be done with her—supposes she will have her own way. To which remark Miss Carolina does not say "neigh"!—From *Frank Leslie's Illustrated Newspaper*.

The Rarey whose name is coupled with that of President Buchanan, in the cartoon above, had perfected a system of horse-breaking now almost forgotten. Straps were so adjusted as to punish the animal when it plunged or reared.

PRESIDENT BUCHANAN AND HIS ORIGINAL CABINET

With the exception of one member, who had been appointed to fill a vacancy caused by death, these advisers served with the President from the day of his inauguration in March, 1857, until Secession disrupted the cabinet in December, 1860. From the left to right in the group are: Jacob Thompson of Mississippi, Secretary of the Interior; Lewis Cass of Michigan, Secretary of State; John B. Floyd of Virginia, Secretary of War; President Buchanan; Howell Cobb of Georgia, Secretary of the Treasury; Isaac Toucey of Connecticut, Secretary of the Navy; Joseph Holt of Kentucky, Postmaster-General, and Jeremiah Black of Pennsylvania, Attorney-General. Mr. Holt had succeeded Aaron Brown, deceased, in March, 1859.

officers everywhere. There were forts and arsenals, with military supplies and properties. There were naval stations and places and properties belonging, not to the individual States, but to the United States of America, under direction of the Secretary of the Navy. The federal judiciary had its judges and its marshals with offices and appointments. There were public lands belonging to the United States before Florida, Alabama, Mississippi, Louisiana, and Arkansas had been admitted to the Union, and those lands had never been made over to the States but remained as the property of all the people of the United States of America. Thousands of former soldiers and widows of soldiers, of the Mexican War and earlier wars, were pensioners of the federal government in the southern States, and were served at local offices by federal agents.

The postal service embraced thousands of offices, with postmasters who were sworn to loyalty as employees of the federal government.

Speaking in general, the federal establishments were seized by each of the seceding States simultaneously with the adoption of their Ordinances. In hundreds of instances local mobs or voluntary militia organizations had made seizures in advance of the formal decisions of their State governments. This was the less difficult because there was little or no resistance. With few exceptions the federal officials themselves, in the seceding States, were participants in the movement; were repudiating and defying orders from Washington; were actively promoting the confiscation of federal property.

Abundant instances in point are readily available to anyone who cares to study the de-

JOHN A. DIX, OF NEW YORK
He became Secretary of the Treasury on January 9, 1861, and served for the remaining eight weeks of the administration of President Buchanan. In later years he was Minister to France and Governor of New York.

tails in one or another of the seven seceding States. It is a useful maxim that "the greater includes the less." The overshadowing fact was that of Secession. Expulsion of federal authority and appropriation of federal agencies and properties could but have accompanied the main decision. Nevertheless, at the first, and for some time following, the Administration at Washington was in many practical ways intent upon the losing game of asserting various federal claims in the South, as if such rights of authority and jurisdiction could exist apart from the obligations of allegiance.

Such distinctions were, of course, neither sound in logic nor of everyday practical value. There was only one real question worth considering. If South Carolina had the right to secede, it had the plainest kind of right to control the defenses in its own harbor of Charleston. If the government at Washington had become that of a foreign power, it could demand compensation for its property under seizure by the Confederacy, but it could not expect, under international law, to make good its claim to any kind of jurisdiction over

its former establishments and agencies. The South was freely admitting that there were matters for financial adjustment between the two governments, including these various property confiscations, and also the allocation to the Confederacy of a part of the public debt of the United States. Any effort to continue federal services within the seceded States was, of course, a practical denial of the right of Secession. Attempts to hold forts or to collect revenues could not be made with persistence, without provoking war as the inevitable consequence. To enter upon a war merely over the question of holding or abandoning a fort or a naval station would have been to sacrifice wisdom and statesmanship to gratify irritated pride.

The Buchanan Cabinet as originally formed would have been reluctant to assert claims of federal authority over arsenals and other establishments after States had seceded. But the Cabinet had been reorganized after the election of Lincoln; and while it was not fully harmonious, it was strongly opposed to Secession. It was, in fact, more pronounced in its assertion of Union principles and policies than were the leading Republicans themselves at that time. In the original Cabinet of March, 1857, Lewis Cass of Michigan was Secretary of State, Howell Cobb of Georgia was Secretary of the Treasury, John B. Floyd of Virginia was Secretary of War, Isaac Toucey of Connecticut was Secretary of the Navy, Jeremiah S. Black of Pennsylvania was Attorney-General, Jacob Thompson of Mississippi was Secretary of the Interior, and Aaron V. Brown of Tennessee was Postmaster-General.

Messrs. Cobb, Floyd, and Thompson were strong Secessionists, at least after Lincoln's election; and within the week following President Buchanan's message of December 3, 1860, Cobb resigned. He was soon to become a figure as prominent in the Confederacy as he had been in the government at Washington. The next change in the Cabinet circle came for precisely opposite reasons. Cobb had retired because President Buchanan had denied the right of Secession. His resignation occurred on December 8th, and four days later General Cass, Secretary of State, resigned because he felt that the President was not acting vigorously to protect the forts which were national property in Charleston Harbor. Cass had previously acquiesced in the non-coercion doctrines that the President had enunciated on advice of the Attorney-General; yet now he demanded steps that would have been regarded throughout the entire South as the actual beginning of a war against Secession.

We are told, on authority of a Cabinet member who was present, that Mr. Buchanan after hearing General Cass's plea for reinforcement of the military works in Charleston

HOWELL COBB
Secretary of the Treasury

JOHN B. FLOYD
Secretary of War

Two Secessionist members of President Buchanan's cabinet who resigned in December, 1860. The portraits are from original photographs by Brady, in a collection owned by the author.

Harbor, replied in the following words: "I have considered this question. I am very sorry to differ from the Secretary of State; I have made up my mind. The interests of the country do not demand a reinforcement of the forces in Charleston. I cannot do it . . . and I take the responsibility upon myself."

Having served for two years as Postmaster-General, Aaron V. Brown, a former Governor of Tennessee, had died in office. Whereupon Joseph Holt of Kentucky, a strong Union man though coming from a Slave State, had been made Postmaster-General in March, 1859. Mr. Holt, through several days of anxious arguing, endeavored to persuade General Cass to change his mind, but without avail. As it happened, the withdrawal of Cass did not weaken the Cabinet in its growing disposition to support the Union with courage and vigor.

The Attorney-General, Jeremiah S. Black, was now shifted to the State Department, and his place was filled by the selection of Edwin M. Stanton, also of Pennsylvania, who was afterwards to serve as War Secretary under Lincoln. Mr. Buchanan began to lean heavily upon these two fellow-citizens of the Keystone

State. Black had previously expounded the doctrine that "offensive" coercion was not justified; but a month later he prepared for the President a memorandum asserting the right of "defensive" coercion, in resistance to attacks upon federal property. Mr. Stanton, the new Attorney-General, who took office on December 20, 1860, was a Democrat of strong Union sentiments.

Mr. Buchanan had thought it well to follow Democratic precedents by choosing another Secretary of the Treasury from a Slave State after Mr. Cobb had gone back to Georgia, and he selected Philip F. Thomas of Maryland, whose southern sympathies went so far as to make him a believer in the right of Secession, though he may not have been active in promoting the movement. However that might have been, he was not at home in a Cabinet that had quite lost its passivity, and that had begun to use such a disagreeable word as "treason." Mr. Thomas was not equal to the embarrassment of the situation, and served in the Cabinet and at the Treasury Department for less than a month. Referring to the retirement of Mr. Thomas, Mr. Buchanan himself after-

MAJOR ROBERT ANDERSON

The withdrawal of South Carolina from the Union focussed attention upon the forts in Charleston Harbor, and Major Anderson—even before the Sumter episode of April, 1861—became the military idol of the North.

From the front page of the *New York Illustrated News* for January 12, 1861.

South Carolina, and the purpose of the President to enforce the collection of the customs at the port of Charleston."

There followed a notable accession to the Cabinet in the person of John A. Dix of New York. As a mere boy Dix had been an officer in the War of 1812. He had afterwards become a lawyer, but had long been an office-holder and a Democratic politician. He had held a series of positions at Albany, and in 1845 had temporarily filled a vacancy in the United States Senate. Democrats in New York State had long been divided into distinct factions, the more radical element being known as "Barn-burners," while the Conservatives were "Hunkers." The Barn-burners had co-operated with the Free-Soilers in 1854, and, speaking generally, they were radicals and reformers. As an anti-slavery Democrat, Dix had been a candidate for Governor in 1848. President Pierce had thought so highly of him as to make him a tentative offer of the post of Secretary of State; but in view of the party factions in New York the offer had been withdrawn and the more prominent Marcy had been appointed as a man with a Hunker record. Instead of going into the Pierce Cabinet, therefore, Dix became an official in 1853 of the Treasury Department, in charge of the Sub-Treasury in New York City. He did not stay long in this post, but he had impressed himself upon the bankers and business men of the metropolis. President Buchanan had made

wards wrote: "The reason he assigned was a difference of opinion from the President and a majority of the Cabinet in regard to the measures which had been adopted against

MAJOR ANDERSON EVACUATES FORT MOULTRIE, ON CHRISTMAS NIGHT

South Carolina had seceded five days earlier. Major Anderson believed that by concentrating his forces at Fort Sumter he might hold the harbor of Charleston against the State authorities. He therefore abandoned Fort Moultrie after spiking the guns and burning the gun carriages.

RAISING THE STARS AND STRIPES OVER FORT SUMTER
The flag had been brought from Fort Moultrie. It was hoisted by Major
Anderson at noon on December 27, 1860, while the chaplain invoked a blessing.

him Postmaster at New York City, and he was holding that office when New York financial interests secured his advancement to the Cabinet as Secretary of the Treasury.

On the previous day, January 8th, Jacob Thompson had resigned as Secretary of the Interior. For some time his position had been ambiguous, to put it inoffensively. While serving in a high federal office, Thompson had been eagerly promoting the Secession movement, and had actually gone as a commissioner from his own State of Mississippi to the legislature of North Carolina, with the purpose of persuading that State not to delay its withdrawal from the Union. The expedition of the *Star of the West* to relieve Major Anderson at Charleston had just been undertaken. Thompson upbraided President Buchanan with having broken faith in not consulting him about the expedition. Since this incident was a turning point of some consequence in the history of that critical period, it seems to me desirable to print Mr. Thompson's letter and a portion of Mr. Buchanan's reply.

Washington, D. C., Jany. 8th, 1861.
To His Excellency James Buchanan,
    President, U. S.

Sir: It is with extreme regret I have just learned that additional troops have been ordered to Charleston. This subject has been frequently discussed in Cabinet Council; and when on Monday night, 31st of December ult., the orders for reinforcements to Fort Sumter were countermanded, I distinctly understood from you that no order of the kind would be made without being previously considered and decided in Cabinet. It is true that on Wednesday, Jany. 2nd, this subject was again discussed in Cabinet, but certainly no conclusion was reached, and the War Department was not justified in ordering reinforcements without something [more] than was then said.

I learn, however, this morning, for the first time, that the steamer *Star of the West* sailed from New York on last Saturday night with Two Hundred and fifty men under Lieut. Bartlett bound for Fort Sumter.

Under these circumstances I feel myself bound

SOUTH CAROLINA VOLUNTEERS RECEIVE
VISITORS

The wife and daughter of Governor Pickens pay a visit
to the Rhett Guard on the parade ground at Fort
Moultrie, in Charleston Harbor, after its evacuation by
federal forces. The sketch by *Leslie's* artist affords not
only an idea of military ardor in South Carolina in February, 1861, but also an authenic glimpse of feminine
raiment of the day.

to resign my commission as one of your constitutional advisers into your hands.

With high respect, your obt. svt.

J. THOMPSON.

On the following day, January 9th, the
President replied as follows:

Sir:

I have received and accepted your resignation on
yesterday of the office of Secretary of the Interior.

On Monday evening, 31 December, 1860, I sus-
pended the orders which had been issued by the
War and Navy Departments, to send the *Brooklyn*
with reinforcements to Fort Sumter. Of this I informed you on the same evening. I stated to you
my reason for this suspension which you knew from
its nature would be speedily removed. In consequence of your request, however, I promised that
these orders should not be renewed "without being
previously considered and decided in Cabinet."

This promise was faithfully observed on my part.
In order to carry it into effect I called a special
Cabinet meeting on Wednesday, 2 January, 1861,
in which the question of sending reinforcements to
Fort Sumter was amply discussed both by yourself
and others. The decided majority of opinions was
against you. At this moment the answer of the
South Carolina "Commissioners" to my communica-

tion to them of the 31st December was received
and read. It produced much indignation among the
members of the Cabinet. After a further brief conversation I employed the following language: "It is
now all over, and reinforcements must be sent."
Judge Black said at the moment of my decision
that after this letter the Cabinet would be unanimous, and I heard no dissenting voice. Indeed, the
spirit and tone of the letter left no doubt on my
mind that Fort Sumter would be immediately attacked, and hence the necessity of sending reinforcements thither without delay.

. . . . You are certainly mistaken in alleging that
"no conclusion was reached." In this your recollection is entirely different from that of your four
oldest colleagues in the Cabinet. Indeed, my language was so unmistakable that the Secretaries of
War and the Navy proceeded to act upon it without
any further intercourse with myself than what you
heard, or might have heard, me say. You had been
so emphatic in opposing these reinforcements that
I thought you would resign in consequence of my
decision. I deeply regret that you have been mistaken in point of fact, though I firmly believe, hon-
estly mistaken. Still, it is certain you have not the
less been mistaken.   Yours very respectfully,

JAMES BUCHANAN.

POOR PICKENS IN SOUTH CAROLINA

The *New York Illustrated News* explains that Governor
Pickens of South Carolina had failed to supply a photograph, the cartoonist drawing upon his imagination.

Secretary Thompson had previously served in Congress and was a man of repute in his own State. His resignation coincided with the meeting of the Mississippi convention; and the reply of President Buchanan was on the very date of the adoption by Mississippi of the Ordinance of Secession. Mr. Thompson returned to his home and soon became Governor of Mississippi and afterwards a General.

Thus the decision about Fort Sumter had given at least nominal occasion for the withdrawal from the Cabinet of two Southern men, Thomas and Thompson. A more prominent and active Southern member—namely, John B. Floyd of Virginia, Secretary of War —had withdrawn some days earlier, having served until January 1st. Joseph Holt of Kentucky, the Postmaster-General, had been transferred to the War Department to succeed Floyd. Horatio King of Maine, a man of the most intense Unionist sentiments and activities, had been promoted from his office as First Assistant Postmaster-General to the headship of the Department. The Interior Department

was carried on by subordinate officials, and Jacob Thompson had no successor in the Buchanan Cabinet. Isaac Toucey of Connecticut, Secretary of the Navy, was the only man who retained his place throughout the four years of the Administration.

No one could now justly complain that the Cabinet was lacking in men of high intelligence and of experience in public life. Certainly it had become a Cabinet of patriotic spirit, and of vigor enough to do anything reasonably possible to uphold the rights and the honor of the Union. Black had been Chief Justice of the Supreme Court of Pennsylvania, and deserves to rank with the exceptionally able lawyers who have so frequently filled the first place in the Cabinet. Stanton, Dix, Holt, and King were in each case above the average of "Cabinet timber" in ability and in fitness for their positions. It is not easy to see why, if praise should be accorded to these five capable Cabinet officers, it should be altogether withheld from the President who was solely responsible for appointing them.

THE STATE OF AFFAIRS AT WASHINGTON

Member after member of President Buchanan's cabinet resigns, or is allowed to withdraw. The Public Chest is empty. The President does nothing but wring his hands and bemoan himself.

From *Harper's Weekly*, January 12, 1861.

OLD MOTHER BUCHANAN IN DESPAIR

A cartoon from *Harper's Weekly,* after President Buchanan's retirement, which places upon him the blame for disunion and war.

CHAPTER XXI

"Defensive Coercion"—A New Policy

Business paralyzed as more States secede—Buchanan's special message urges duty of forcible defense—"In the midst of a great revolution"—Incidents at Charleston and New Orleans

IT WAS ON THE MOMENTOUS DATE of January 8th, with three States about to announce their decision to follow the example of South Carolina, that President Buchanan sent a special message to Congress. He declared that the hope of peace had been diminished by every hour of delay; further alarms had intensified the bad conditions that he had described in his message at the opening of Congress. "Trade was paralyzed, manufactures were stopped, the best public securities suddenly sunk in the market, every species of property depreciated more or less,, and thousands of poor men who depended upon their daily labor for their daily bread were turned out of employment." As evidence that conditions had not been improving he cited the fact that "the Treasury notes authorized by the act of 17 December last were advertised according to the law, and no responsible bidder offered to take any considerable sum at

par at a lower rate of interest than twelve per cent."

"From these facts," he continued, "it appears that in a government organized like ours, domestic strife, or even a well-grounded fear of of civil hostilities, is more destructive to our public and private interests than the most formidable foreign war." Mr. Buchanan went on to argue that since no State had a right to secede, and since the President had no authority to acknowledge the independence of such State, he was left with "no alternative as the Chief Executive officer, under the Constitution of the United States, but to collect the public revenues, and to protect the public property so far as this might be practicable, under existing laws."

Avowing this to be his continuing purpose, the President declared, "My province is to execute, and not to make, the laws. It belongs to Congress exclusively to repeal, to modify,

194

SOUTH CAROLINA'S "ULTIMATUM."

A Currier & Ives poster cartoon which expresses the desire of President Buchanan to postpone the crisis until Mr. Lincoln could assume responsibility. Governor Pickens of South Carolina, at the muzzle of the gun, voices the desire of his State to possess the forts which controlled its principal harbor. The faces in this cartoon are intended to be accurate portraits rather than caricatures.

or to change their provisions to meet exigencies as they may occur. I possess no dispensing power. I certainly have no right to make aggressive war upon any State, and I am perfectly satisfied that the Constitution has wisely withheld that power, even from Congress. *But the right and the duty to use military force defensively, against those who resist the federal officers in the execution of their legal functions and against those who assail the property of the federal government is clear and undeniable.*" The foregoing sentence was italicized, as we may believe, in the original document as well as in subsequent official printing.

Having asserted the right to resist by force, Mr. Buchanan proceeded to show that the situation was now beyond the Executive control. "The fact cannot be disguised that we are in the midst of a great revolution. In all its various bearings, therefore, I commend the question to Congress, as the only human tribunal, under Providence, possessing the power to meet the existing emergency. To them exclusively belongs the power to declare war, or to authorize the employment of military force in all cases contemplated by the Constitution; and they alone possess the power to remove grievances which might lead to war and to secure peace and union to this distracted country. On them, and on them alone, rests the responsibility."

It may be said, indeed, that, while Mr. Buchanan correctly stated the responsibilities of Congress, he was holding the one position to which the country might look—not, indeed, for the unlawful assumption of power as a military dictator, but for moral leadership, and for a ringing call to the people to forget differences, lay doubts aside, and save the Union. The answer is that if Mr. Buchanan had been a man of that quality, he would not have been nominated and elected in 1856.

Further on in this message of January 8th he declared: "At the beginning of these unhappy troubles I determined that no act of mine should increase the excitement in either section of the country. If the political conflict were to end in a civil war, it was my determined purpose not to commence it, nor even to furnish an excuse for it by any act of this Government. My opinion remains unchanged, that justice as well as sound policy requires us still to seek a peaceful solution of the questions at issue between the North and the South. Entertaining this conviction I refrained even from sending reinforcements to Major Anderson, who commanded the forts in Charleston Harbor, until an absolute necessity for doing so should make itself apparent, lest it might unjustly be regarded as a menace of military coercion, and thus furnish, if not a provocation, at least a pretext for an outbreak on the part of South Carolina."

The President in this message of January 8th informed Congress of what he regarded as the justifiable act of Major Anderson in removing his small garrison from Fort Moultrie to Fort Sumter. He had been assured by South Carolina leaders that no attack upon Major Anderson was intended; but after the President's refusal to meet the views of Messrs. R. W. Barnwell, J. H. Adams, and James L. Orr, the Commissioners from South Carolina who came to Washington, Major Anderson had become convinced that an attack was imminent, and so he had removed his command from a fort that he could not have held for more than a day or two, to another which could be defended for a considerable time. Along with this message, Mr. Buchanan sent to Congress his correspondence with these commissioners.

This was almost two months before the date for the inauguration of President Lincoln; but rumors were already rife, based upon many reckless boasts and threats, that Confederate sympathizers in Virginia and Maryland would come to Washington in armed masses and prevent Lincoln's assumption of office. Noting these rumors, Mr. Buchanan, at the end of his message, remarks: "It is said that serious apprehensions are, to some extent, entertained, in which I do not share, that the peace of this District may be disturbed before the 4th of March next. In any event, it will be my duty to preserve it, and this duty shall be performed."

WHO COMMENCED THE WAR ?

Those who would throw the guilt of the war upon the shoulders of Mr. Lincoln, are requested to read the following catalogue of " remarkable events," published in a *Southern* Almanac, all of which occurred during the Presidency of Mr. Buchanan:

Dec. 27, 1860.—Capture of Fort Moultrie and Castle Pickney by South Carolina troops. Capt. Coste surrenders the revenue cutter Aiken.

Jan. 3, 1861.—Capture of Fort Palaski by the Savannah troops.

Jan. 3.—The arsenal of Mount Vernon, Alabama, with 20,000 stand of arms, seized by the Alabama troops.

Jan. 4.—Fort Morgan, in Mobile Bay, taken by the Alabama troops.

Jan. 9.—The steamship Star of the West fired into and driven off by the South Carolina batteries on Morris Island. Failure of an attempt to reinforce Fort Sumter.

Jan. 10.—Forts Jackson, St. Phillip and Pike, near New Orleans, captured by the Louisiana troops.

Jan. 14.—Capture of Pensacola Navy Yard, and Forts Barrancas and McRae. Major Chase shortly afterwards takes command, and the siege of Fort Pickens commences.

Jan. 13.—Surrender of Baton Rouge Arsenal to Louisiana troops.

Jan. 31.—New Orleans Mint and Custom House taken.

Feb. 4.—Seizure of Little Rock arsenal by Arkansas troops.

Feb. 4.—Surrender of the revenue cutter Cass to the Alabama authorities.

Feb. 8.—Provisional Constitution adopted.

Feb. 9.—Jefferson Davis, of Mississippi, and Alexander Stephens, of Georgia, elected President and Vice-President.

Feb. 16.—Gen. Twiggs transfers public property in Texas to the State authorities. Col. Waite, U. S. A., surrenders San Antonia to Col. Ben. McCulloch and his Texan rangers.

March 2.—The revenue cutter Dodge seized by the Texan authorities.

In view of the foregoing, a friendly paper in a foreign country—*The Montreal Witness*—very pertinently remarks as follows.

"Now all these were warlike and treasonable acts, and *all were committed before Mr. Lincoln entered office*. It is simply ridiculous to say that he commenced the war. On the 12th of April Fort Sumter was bombarded, on the 13th it was surrendered, and on the 14th it was evacuated. It was not till the last named date that President Lincoln issued his first call for volunteers to put down the Rebellion in the United States.

A SOUTHERN CHRONOLOGY OF EVENTS WHILE BUCHANAN WAS STILL IN OFFICE

The summary above is reproduced by photo-engraving from an editorial in a Northern newspaper in 1861. It includes comments by the Montreal *Witness* upon a brief chronology that had been reproduced in a Southern almanac. Since all these actions were fully justified in the Southern mind, there was no attempt to conceal or ignore them.

Some five weeks later, namely on February 13th, which was the second Wednesday of the month, Congress assembled in joint session, to open and count the electoral votes. The ceremony was as undisturbed, in spite of some anxieties and apprehensions to the contrary, as on any similar occasion in the entire history of the country. It was Vice-President Breckinridge who announced the election of Abraham Lincoln as President of the United States.

An incident in the brief career of John A. Dix as Secretary of the Treasury has so identified his name with one quotable sentence as to keep it in familiar memory. It was the words he used, rather than the circumstances which called them out, that have been remembered. *"If anyone attempts to haul down the American flag, shoot him on the spot!"* This sentence, detached from its context, and without much knowledge of the exact situation that occasioned its utterance, went everywhere throughout the North as one of those positive, clarion notes that millions of people, who were tired of suspense, inaction, and hard times, were waiting to hear.

As a matter of cold historical truth, this message of General Dix, in its bearing upon the circumstances that led to its dispatch, served merely to illustrate the futility of the Administration's belated efforts.

The sentence occurred in a telegram from Secretary Dix to a Treasury agent at New Orleans. It bore date of January 29th, the State of Louisiana having officially seceded on January 26th and having assumed control of everything under the temporary title of the "Republic of Louisiana." On January 29th, on instructions from Washington, the revenue cutter *McClelland* was ordered to leave New Orleans at once and proceed to New York. The captain of the cutter instantly refused to obey the order. The special Treasury agent telegraphed for further instructions, and Secretary Dix ordered the arrest of Captain Breshwood. "If Captain Breshwood, after arrest, undertakes to interfere with the command of the cutter, tell Lieutenant Caldwell to consider him as a mutineer, and treat him accordingly. If anyone attempts to haul down the American flag, shoot him on the spot!"

A GOOD BOY

COLUMBIA: "Never mind, Bobby Anderson, if your father doesn't like what you have done, I do."

The New York cartoon, from *Vanity Fair*, of January 12, 1861, decorates President Buchanan with the Palmetto flag of the independent State of South Carolina.

This was indeed a thrilling dispatch, but it had no influence upon the course of events in Louisiana, because it was never received. The Republic of Louisiana was in full possession of the revenue cutter, and also of the telegraph offices and post-offices. It was not inclined to oblige the Treasury Department at Washington by the delivery of saucy instructions to federal agents, or to officers who had now entered the service of the seceded State.

Two weeks earlier the United States revenue cutter *Lewis Cass* had been seized at Algiers, opposite New Orleans, by a military company acting on its own authority. This vessel was well armed and a large quantity of ammunition was also taken. Similarly, the army barracks and marine hospital had been taken under the authority of the State of Louisiana, and no resistance worth mentioning had been made by the Government at Washington. The United States Mint at New Orleans, as well as the Custom House and the Sub-Treasury, with sums of money in all of them, were appropriated in the name of Louisiana.

The Collector of the Port at New Orleans, obeying the new authorities, refused to allow the importing merchants at St. Louis, Cincinnati, and other points northward, to receive their foreign goods by the usual steamboat services, unless they first paid import duties to the sovereign State of Louisiana. The sums of money seized in the Mint and Sub-Treasury, and those collected as customs duties from up-river importers, were duly transferred to the treasury of the new Confederate Government at Montgomery.

I have recited these incidents in order to give the reader an understanding of the Secession movement in its immediate methods and effects, and of the futility of most of the efforts at Washington to deal with mere details while the larger fact of Secession had already disposed of minor questions.

The most unfortunate of all the members of Mr. Buchanan's Administration, in his record as a public man, was John B. Floyd. He was the son of a former Governor of Virginia, and had himself served as Governor of that State for the three years ending January 1, 1853. From the beginning of President Buchanan's term until December 29, 1860, he was Secretary of War. In his letter of resignation he charged the President with having been guilty of "a violation of solemn pledges and plighted faith" in authorizing Major Anderson to transfer his garrison from Fort Moultrie to Fort Sumter. On December 27th, having learned of this transfer, Secretary Floyd had urged upon the President, as the "one remedy now left us by which to vindicate our honor and prevent civil war," that he should be permitted in his capacity as head of the War Department to order Major

"If any one attempts to haul down the American Flag, shoot him on the spot."
JOHN A. DIX.

An order issued by John A. Dix, Secretary of the Treasury under President Buchanan, became a rallying cry throughout the North. It appeared upon countless thousands of envelopes circulating in the mails, from one of which our illustration is reproduced.

Anderson to withdraw the garrison altogether, and leave Charleston Harbor wholly abandoned to the seceded State of South Carolina.

It is an undisputed fact, however, that the President had requested Floyd's resignation on December 3rd, for reasons totally unrelated to any of these conditions in the South. Certain State bonds in the total amount of $870,000, held in trust by the Government, for different Indian tribes, had been from time to time purloined from the Interior Department; and there had been substituted for these bonds, bills of corresponding amount drawn by a certain firm on Secretary Floyd and endorsed by him. For his part in these transactions, Mr. Floyd was afterwards indicted by the Grand Jury of the District of Columbia for conspiracy in attempting to defraud the Government. The case was not prosecuted, however, and it was dismissed on March 20th.

However guiltless he may have been of any serious crime, his part in this bond business does not seem to have been correct or commendable. A committee of Congress with members from all parties, after full investigation, made a unanimous report and found Floyd's conduct not consistent with "purity of private motives and faithfulness to public trusts." I am inclined to accept the later opinion that Mr. Floyd had not been guilty of any intentional misdeeds, and had not profited by transactions meant by him to relieve certain embarrassed contractors who were furnishing army supplies and services in the far West.

Much more generally remembered against Floyd are the charges that he used his position as Secretary of War to transfer more than 100,000 muskets and rifles to southern arsenals early in 1860. The prominence given to this matter is important chiefly for the light it throws upon the suspicions that were gathering strength to the effect that the South was all along quietly preparing for war, with the Buchanan Administration doing more to help than to hinder. The best evidence seems to show that Floyd had been a States-Rights Virginian of strong Southern sympathies, but not a believer in Secession until after the election of Lincoln. Mr. Rhodes analyzes these transactions with conclusive thoroughness. He emphasizes Floyd's incapacity and the inconsistency of his conduct. "I am aware," says Mr. Rhodes, "that it is a work of supererogation to defend Floyd from treachery which he and his friends boasted that he had committed."

A MEMORIAL TO HENRY CLAY IN NEW ORLEANS

Less than a year before Louisiana seceded from the Union, the people of New Orleans had dedicated with impressive ceremonies this statue of the Whig leader who had always believed in the idea of the gradual emancipation of slaves. Clay had himself been a Kentucky slaveholder.

The activities of the southern men in the Administration contributed only slightly to the military equipment of the Confederacy. But they did unquestionably contribute greatly to the alarm that was spreading among the friends of the Union. The reaction made itself felt in the reorganization of the Buchanan Cabinet, and in the President's own gradual change of tone.

Memoirs of more than one member of the Buchanan Cabinet add greatly to our understanding of this anxious period. One of the most useful volumes is a collection of the correspondence and papers of Horatio King, under the general title, "Turning on the Light." Mr. King was a native of Maine, who had been occupied with politics and Democratic journalism until in 1839 he had taken a subordinate position in the Post-Office Department. He became the leading postal expert, and under Postmaster-General Holt he was First Assistant. Upon Holt's transfer to the War Department, King was made Postmaster-General. He was widely acquainted, an inces-

THE CUSTOM-HOUSE AT NEW ORLEANS

Louisiana authorities took possession of this building, with other federal property in New Orleans, in January, 1861. At that time it was one of the largest and most expensive public buildings in the United States.

sant correspondent, a personal and political intimate of Postmaster Dix of New York and Postmaster Capen of Boston, and an extremely bitter opponent of the Secessionist influences that were pressing themselves upon the President's attention. At the same time he was a devoted adherent of Buchanan and a firm believer in the President's patriotism and sincerity. His memories are illuminating.

Nothing was quite so obnoxious to Mr. King as the conduct of a Washington newspaper, the *Constitution*. This paper had assumed to be the especial organ of the Buchanan Administration, and it derived its support mainly from Government advertising. It was fawning upon Buchanan and the Administration and yet, after Lincoln's election in November, it had become almost as pronounced an organ of Secessionism as the Charleston *Mercury* itself. It was filled, day by day, with letters, reports, and statements supporting Secession, and its own editorial utterances were growingly offensive to Union men.

Mr. King took it upon himself in letters and conversations to inform the President that he should disavow the *Constitution,* inasmuch as the public at large regarded him as making that paper his organ. In due time Buchanan followed this advice, and the withdrawal of

Government advertising would seem to have resulted in the suspension of the newspaper.

We have already indicated, in the case of Louisiana, the general policy of the Confederate States in exercising what they claimed to be the rights of sovereignty and of eminent domain in taking possession of federal establishments. Regarding the forts in Charleston Harbor, it had been announced by the Charleston newspapers and by public speakers that they belonged essentially to South Carolina and would be taken whenever needed.

Anderson had acted in view of what he believed to be the clear prospect of a bombardment. But the Charleston newspapers at once turned the tables and construed Major Anderson's move as an attack upon South Carolina, in violation of faith. There ensued at once the seizure of the important federal arsenal at Charleston, and the occupation of the other harbor defenses, Castle Pinkney, Fort Moultrie, and Sullivan's Island. It is almost superfluous to say that the Custom House, the Post-Office, and all other federal establishments in Charleston and throughout the State were appropriated; lighthouses were taken in charge; the Palmetto flag was floated over what had been federal institutions; volunteer troops were rapidly massed, and new fortifications begun.

In Georgia there were similar activities, with the Federal arsenal at Augusta promptly seized, and Forts Pulaski and Jackson at Savannah occupied in the name of the State.

In Alabama the arsenal at Mobile was taken under State control with its supplies of military material, and Fort Morgan commanding Mobile harbor was occupied by a garrison of State troops.

It was the 9th of January when the *Star of the West,* carrying 250 soldiers, and supplies of food and other materials for Major Ander-

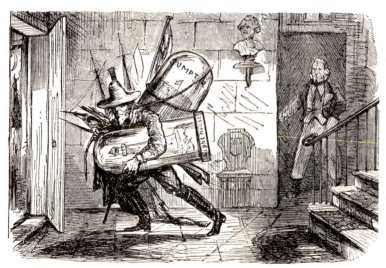

A NORTHERN SIDELIGHT ON THE SECESSION MOVEMENT
UNCLE SAM: "Hello there, you rascal! where are you going with my property?"
JEFF DAVIS: "Oh, dear Uncle! All I want is to be let alone."

From *Harper's Weekly.*

THE "STAR OF THE WEST" IS PREVENTED FROM CARRYING
SUPPLIES TO FORT SUMTER

A South Carolina battery discovered the vessel entering Charleston Harbor on the night of January
10, 1861, and opened fire. The *Star of the West*, unarmed, thereupon withdrew.

son, arrived outside the Charleston Harbor, having left New York secretly on January 5th. Friends at Washington and New York had, however, telegraphed notice to South Carolina, and the vessel was met in the harbor by shots from Confederate batteries, and accordingly returned to New York without having accomplished anything. On January 14th, the South Carolina legislature had adopted a resolution to the effect that "any attempt by the federal government to reinforce Fort Sumter will be regarded as an act of open hostility and a declaration of war."

Thus a very dangerous situation was created, and the suspense continued until after the beginning of a new Administration at Washington. At Pensacola, Florida, Fort Pickens was held by a small federal garrison, but the Navy Yard and Fort Barrancas were surrendered, and—apart from the less accessible Fort Pickens—all federal property in Florida was immediately absorbed by the State itself.

The federal commander of the Department of Texas, Brigadier General Twiggs, late in February made over to the seceded State a comparatively extensive inventory of military equipment; and a considerable part of the small regular army of the United States came under a new flag, with easy acquiescence.

For the purposes of this narration, little could be gained by a recital of the day-by-day activities of the Buchanan Administration through the month of February. A message to Congress on Fort Sumter, with a collection of letters and documents had been transmitted. On February 21st, a message to the Senate, with accompanying papers, explained the deadlock in negotiations with Great Britain over the disputed boundary line between Vancouver's Island and the American Continent. While we were losing so large a part of our national domain in the South, we were intent upon sacrificing nothing to Great Britain on the Northwest boundary line.

Washington's Birthday, February 22nd, was celebrated with equal enthusiasm in the Union

States of the North and in the seceded States of the South. A violent dispute arose in Washington over the question whether federal troops should be allowed to march in the holiday parade, along with volunteers of the District. President Buchanan somewhat apologetically (in a letter to ex-President Tyler, who was presiding over the Peace Convention) justified the participation of at least a company or two of regular troops. The incident was given importance at the moment, and it is recalled now because it illustrates the nervous strain that was wearing out the common-sense and self-control of almost everyone in the Administration, in Congress, in the Peace Convention, and in the entire aggregation of governmental and political personages at Washington.

On March 1st President Buchanan sent a message to the House of Representatives in reply to a resolution asking him to answer the question why so large a number of troops had been assembled at the capital. Apart from

some marines who were regularly at the Navy Yard, the President replied that the total number of troops amounted to 653 men. He explained that there had been reports of a secret organization hostile to the Government. He admitted that he had brought troops to the city as a precautionary measure. "At the present moment," he said, "when all is quiet, it is difficult to realize the state of alarm which prevailed when the troops were first ordered to this city." He added that he should not have forgiven himself if he had refused to take these steps and evil consequences had followed. He referred to the safety of public property and of Government archives, and among other objects that governed his action he mentioned, "the security of the inauguration of the President-elect."

A memorandum written by Mr. Buchanan, dated Monday, March 4, 1861, informs us that the Cabinet met in the President's room at the Capitol, "to assist me in examining the bills which might be presented to me for ap-

SURRENDER OF GENERAL TWIGGS TO THE TROOPS OF TEXAS, AT SAN ANTONIO

David Emmanuel Twiggs was in command of federal troops in the Department of Texas, probably the largest unit of the armed forces of the United States. He was a veteran of the War of 1812 and the War with Mexico, a native of Georgia and in sympathy with the South. He surrendered his forces to the Texas authorities on February 16, 1861, two weeks after the State had seceded from the Union. For his action he was dismissed from the Army. He was commissioned a Major General in the Confederate Army, but was too old for active service and died in the following year.

OUR NATIONAL BIRD AS IT APPEARED WHEN HANDED TO JAMES BUCHANAN. MARCH. 4. 1857

THE IDENTICAL BIRD AS IT APPEARED .A .D. 1861.
I was murdered i'the Capitol
Shakespere

This lithographed poster, appearing at the moment of Buchanan's retirement, shows the American Eagle as shorn of its feathers and its claws, with nothing to stand upon but Anarchy and Secession.

proval between the hours of ten and twelve of that day, when my own term and that of Congress would expire."

When Secretary Holt arrived, continues Mr. Buchanan's record, "he informed us that on that morning he had received extraordinary dispatches from Major Anderson, saying that, without a force of some twenty or thirty thousand men to capture the batteries which had been erected, he could not maintain himself at Fort Sumter and he (Mr. Holt) intended at once to communicate these dispatches to President Lincoln." Mr. Buchanan notes the surprise with which this information was received, in view of "repeated letters of the Major stating that he felt secure, and finally a letter after the affair of the *Star of the West,* stating that he did not desire reinforcements."

The Administration of President Buchanan in its last phase had antagonized and embittered the South without having succeeded in gaining the confidence of the North. While its manners and its utterances in respect of various details were highly provocative, it was endeavoring to be pleasant and persuasive to the very end in its treatment of the main issue. Its excuses were sincere and not to be gainsaid, and its explanations were too plausible and too well reasoned to be thrust aside. But the most undeniable groundwork of verified historical data can never make failure a thing that appeals to the popular mind. Charleston Harbor was still the critical point in a situation that had undoubtedly gone from bad to worse. If the maintenance of the Union were to be considered as the essential aim of White House statesmanship in the quadrennium ending March 4, 1861, the purpose had failed. If Peace had been the object, no firm foundations for it had been laid. The skies were ominous, and Mr. Buchanan's peace gave no more reassurances, to a country almost paralyzed with anxiety, than a painful lull before the visible approach of a terrific storm.

THE SAINT-GAUDENS STATUE OF ABRAHAM LINCOLN

It was proper that Chicago should have named a beautiful park on Lake Michigan in honor of Lincoln, and that the most generally accepted statue of Lincoln should have been erected there. This work by Augustus Saint-Gaudens is characterized by another eminent sculptor, Lorado Taft, as follows: "His noble statue of Lincoln was unveiled in 1887 in Lincoln Park, Chicago, and was at once accepted as the country's ideal." A replica of this statue was, in the year 1920, given a prominent place near Westminster Abbey and the British Houses of Parliament,

CHAPTER XXII

Lincoln Takes Command of His Party

*The overlapping period of four months—Four points of resolute policy
—The man who knows his own mind—Seward for the Cabinet—
Thurlow Weed and Governor Chase visit Springfield*

UNDOUBTEDLY THE SUCCESS of the Lincoln electoral ticket had precipitated the Secessionist movement. Southern threats and warnings of the pre-election months had been made good. The Buchanan Administration was now dealing with situations for which the Republican victory was responsible. In other countries the party endorsed at the polls would have had to step at once to the front and meet the crisis that had inevitably followed its success.

Our system is unique in its overlapping mechanism. In ordinary times, and especially when the same party remains in power, the anomaly is less striking. But in times of great hazard, when the public verdict condemns the party in power and ordains a radical change, it seems a baffling thing—too serious to be merely exasperating—to have the rejected ruler continue as head of the government. For a full four months after the people had spoken decisively at the polls, Mr. Buchanan was lingering on in an office which called every day for a stronger man. Under our system, it was the old Congress, rather than the new, that had assembled at Washington one month after election. And this obsolescent Congress had to decide questions of revenue and expenditure for a fiscal year that did not even begin until eight months after the election of the new Congress, and four months after the installation of the new President.

Many Union men were impatiently counting the days, while they declared their belief that things would be wholly different with Lincoln in the White House. They felt that something vital would happen at once with the Republican administration installed at Washington. A mature study of the facts, however, will perhaps strengthen the belief that there was little either lost or gained in any direction, as a consequence of the overlapping system that

CONSULTING THE ORACLE

LINCOLN: "And what next?"

COLUMBIA: "First be sure you are right; then go ahead!"

From *Harper's Weekly.*

was designed by our forefathers to save us from jolts of sharp and abrupt transition. Lincoln's election in itself had caused profound changes. To have installed him in office early in January rather than in March might in some way have changed the course of history; but there is little evidence to support argument on the affirmative side of the question.

Individuals and communities were spending this four-months' period wrestling with doubts and hopes, as it were, in their respective "valleys of decision." Millions of people were wavering and hesitating. A number of northern legislatures were repealing, or proposing to repeal, the Personal Liberty laws that their States had (only recently) adopted in virtual nullification of the Fugitive Slave Law. The ordinary citizen could change his views, or shift his party allegiance, without much dread of consequences. Those in public position, however, had to count the cost if they were breaking old political ties.

The election of Lincoln had been followed, within a few weeks, by the secession of the seven States, and by the retirement from Washington of fourteen Southern Senators and a large number of Representatives. It had brought about the reorganization of the Buchanan Cabinet. It had led to the testing of public opinion in the proceedings of the Peace Convention. It had been the occasion of thousands of public speeches in all parts of the country. It had resulted in kaleidoscopic changes of position on the part of influential newspapers. While it intensified disunion sentiment in the South, it produced a rapid realignment of party elements in every State of the North. The election itself, therefore, had created an active ferment the operation of which would, perhaps, not have been much affected by a shortening of the four-months period from November to March, while the Republicans were preparing to face their full responsibilities.

It was the Republican party, and not the individual leadership of Abraham Lincoln that had won a plurality in the Electoral College. The victory had been gained in four-cornered contests, locally waged in certain "pivotal" States, as I have explained in previous chapters. But the results of victory had now to be exhibited not lo-

cally but on the national stage. The party which had fought its way to power under varying conditions of leadership in different States must now consolidate and unify its forces. The local chieftains had to subordinate themselves to a supreme party authority. Should leadership devolve upon a "junta" or an individual? If a single person, should the leader be Abraham Lincoln of Illinois, William H. Seward of New York, or Salmon P. Chase of Ohio?

It was the accepted opinion that Mr. Buchanan, weakened in body and broken in spirit, was dominated by his Cabinet, under the leadership of the Secretary of State, Hon. Jeremiah S. Black of Pennsylvania. It soon became known that Senator Seward would hold this foremost place in President Lincoln's Cabinet, and there was a prevalent feeling that Mr. Seward would shape the party policies, Mr. Lincoln readily submitting to guidance.

But at the end of the four-months' period Abraham Lincoln was fully recognized as something more than a President-elect who had found men upon whom to lean. He had named Seward and Chase for Cabinet posts, and he was glad to have such able and renowned advisers. They, meanwhile, had already found that he would himself dominate his official family. During these weeks of quiet thinking and planning—weeks of comparatively few words on his part, but weeks of many decisions showing independent judgment and clear foresight — Lincoln had achieved the triumph of unquestioned leadership among the ranking personages of his party. He had not merely shown himself a master of men, but he had forced upon the wavering leaders of the Republican party the outlines of a national policy which he proposed to uphold and which they duly accepted.

THE COMET OF 1861
An envelope cartoon

BADGERING HIM

JAMES GORDON BENNETT: "Bow! Wow! Come out, Mr. Lincoln!"

Mr. Bennett was editor of the New York *Herald* and a supporter of President Buchanan. Mr. Lincoln, as President-elect, was in constant consultation with party leaders throughout the country, but he was not making speeches, and the *Herald* had been trying vainly to draw him out.

First, he would concede nothing to the demands for a re-establishment of the Missouri Compromise line. Second, he would not dally with the views advocated by Horace Greeley, and widely endorsed in New York City and the East, that secession should be accepted as an accomplished fact and not resisted. Third, while avoiding hasty steps and defiant language, and while seeking to reassure the South, he would uphold federal rights and authority. Fourth, if war were unavoidable, he would seek to have the Confederates make the first attack, in order to give to the world the impression that the United States was act-ing defensively to establish its control within its full and unimpaired domain.

In times of danger, leadership falls as a rule to the man who knows his own mind, and who has the courage to act. Seward as orator, parliamentarian, and brilliant exponent of the growing anti-slavery movement of the North, had made himself the foremost Republican in the Senate. But it was one thing to be verbal champion of a new national party that had never been in power, and it was quite a different thing to forego the habits of mind of the life-long debater, advocate, and critic, and suddenly acquire the habits of the man who must make practical decisions and carry them out. Seward had no such capacity for independent decision and action; and yet he was a man of great intellectual parts, and his virtues outweighed his failings.

On December 8, 1860, a month after the election, Mr. Lincoln wrote the following letter to Senator Seward, who had just then gone to Washington at the opening of the session of Congress:

My Dear Sir:
With your permission I shall at the proper time nominate you to the Senate for confirmation as Secretary of State for the United States. Please let me hear from you at your own earliest convenience.
Your friend and obedient servant,
A. LINCOLN.

Enclosed to Mr. Seward at the same time was a longer letter marked "private and confidential." In this letter occur the following sentences:

Rumors have got into the newspapers to the effect that the Department named above would be tendered you as a compliment, and with the expectation that you would decline it. I beg you to be assured that I have said nothing to justify these rumors. On the contrary, it has been my purpose, from the day of the nomination at Chicago, to assign you, by your leave, this place in the Administration. I have delayed so long to communicate that purpose in deference to what appeared to me a proper caution in the case. Nothing has been developed to change my view in the premises; and I now offer you the place in the hope that you will accept it, and with the belief that your position in the public eye, your integrity, ability, learning, and great experience, all combine to render it an appointment pre-eminently fit to be made.

Having issued this invitation to the New York statesman, Mr. Lincoln did not wait for a reply before putting himself on record in regard to the most crucial points of public policy. Hon. William Kellogg, then serving in Congress as a member from Illinois, was one of the Committee of Thirty-three that had been appointed by the House of Representatives to seek some means of conciliating the South. As a Republican from Mr. Lincoln's own State, he sought guidance. On December 11th a message was sent to him from

Springfield that must always stand as one of the most far-reaching utterances of any American statesman. We shall therefore quote it in the next paragraph in order that the reader may understand how the President-elect was taking a decisive part behind the scenes in the discussion at Washington. Various official bodies were concerning themselves with the one overshadowing issue. The House of Representatives was concentrating its efforts upon the problem of Secession, as were the Senate and the Cabinet. Southern agents were extremely active in Washington, seeking to open negotiations. The Army, under its venerable head General Scott, was endeavoring to reverse the Floyd policies of the War Department and especially to protect the District of Columbia.

The Lincoln message to Congressman Kellogg was as follows:

"Entertain no proposition for a compromise in regard to the extension of slavery. The instant you do they have us under again: all our labor is lost, and sooner or later must be done over. Douglas is sure to be again trying to bring in his 'Popular Sovereignty.' Have none of it. The tug has to come, and better now than later. You know I think the fugitive-slave clause of the Constitution ought to be enforced—to put it in its mildest form, ought not to be resisted."

The nerves of the anxious Kellogg were not strong enough to resist the pressure that came not alone from the Border States but from all directions for compromise; but his rejection of Lincoln's advice, while it proved unfortunate for himself, has no importance for our purpose. The matter of importance was the message itself; which was not confidential and private, but was passed on and had its influence with men of greater courage than Kellogg.

Mr. Lincoln was in close correspondence with his trustworthy friend, Elihu B. Washburne, who like Kellogg was a Congressman from Illinois, and on the 13th he wrote to Washburne as follows:

"Prevent as far as possible any of our friends from demoralizing themselves and their cause by entertaining propositions for

THE INSIDE TRACK

THURLOW WEED (to President-elect Lincoln): "Trust to my friend Seward
—trust to US. We'll compromise this little difficulty for you. But trust to US.
Gentlemen from the country are often egregiously swindled by unprincipled
sharpers. (Impressively) Trust to US."

Horace Greeley, of the New York *Tribune*, is listening behind the door. He was
at this time exceedingly unfriendly to Thurlow Weed, of the Albany *Evening
Journal*, who is seizing Mr. Lincoln by the arm while Senator Seward stands
in unctuous attitude on the other side of the President-elect.

compromise of any sort on slavery extension.
There is no possible compromise but what puts
us under again, and all our work to do over
again. Whether it be a Missouri line or Eli
Thayer's popular sovereignty, it is all the same.
Let either be done, and immediately filibuster-
ing and extending slavery recommences. On
that point hold firm as a chain of steel."

Meanwhile, Mr. Seward, having received
the invitation of the President-elect, waited
until December 16th to reply. He then stated
that his political friend and adviser, Thurlow
Weed of Albany, had found it "not inconven-
ient to go West," and proceeded: "I have had

some conversation with him [Weed] concerning the condition and the prospect of public
affairs, and he will be able to inform you of
my present unsettled view of the subject upon
which you so kindly wrote me a few days ago.
I shall remain at home until his return, and
shall then in further conference with him have
the advantage of a knowledge of the effects
of public events certain to occur this week."

Mr. Weed made his trip to Springfield. It
would be worth a volume of mere conjecture
on the part of later political writers to have
had an authentic record of the extended conversations between Lincoln and Weed. The

Albany editor, adroit, experienced, managerial, had doubtless expected to achieve a substantial triumph. He considered Mr. Seward's acceptance as essential to the Lincoln Administration; and he was expecting to drive a good bargain. It was not that he had any unworthy proposals to make, for he was sincere in his belief that he and Seward could formulate concessions that would save the Union, while not in the long run contributing anything to the extension or perpetuation of the slave system.

Weed now talked to Lincoln about "patriotism" as something higher than "partisanship" although he had always been an intense partisan. He was strongly under the influence of the business elements of the East, and it was natural enough that he should have thought himself capable of telling the President-elect how to save the Union. It was fortunate for Lincoln's position as President-elect that Thurlow Weed, of all the men who might have visited Springfield to argue for compromise, had made this pilgrimage. On Lincoln's west-

ern ground Weed found that the atmosphere was strikingly different from that of Albany and Auburn, where the political winds that prevailed were blowing from New York City and Boston. He was treated with entire courtesy and frankness by Mr. Lincoln, as he has shown us in his autobiography.

For three days Thurlow Weed lingered at Springfield. He was a welcome visitor who brought great stores of information, not only of past politics and affairs, but of Eastern public opinion and of current Southern activities. As usually happens in such cases, each of these two strong personalities quickly appreciated the character, ability, and good faith of the other, and a genuine and lasting friendship resulted.

Lincoln was not content to send Weed back to Seward with nothing more precise to report than conversations that had occupied many hours during the three days, touching upon a hundred matters of statesmanship, of practical politics, and of possible appointments to office, all rendered entertaining and palatable by the

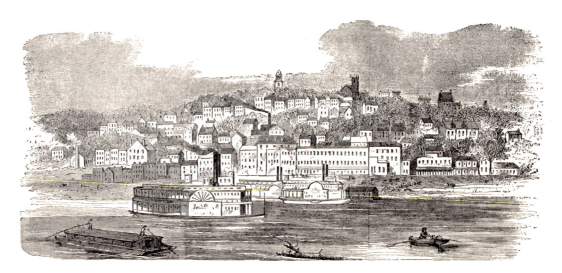

VICKSBURG, WHERE MISSISSIPPI AUTHORITIES ERECTED A
BATTERY TO CONTROL THE RIVER

Mississippi had left the Union on January 9, 1861, the second State to go out. Almost immediately it began to exercise control over the great inland waterway of the Mississippi. All vessels proceeding down the river were required to land at Vicksburg, though Governor Pettus announced that peaceful commerce would not be interrupted or annoyed. "This," he declared, "will materially aid in preserving peace between the Northwestern and Southern States, if it can be preserved." Our river scene and the news dispatches from Vicksburg were in a copy of *Harper's Weekly* that was in Lincoln's hands on the train as he was making his eastward pilgrimage to be inaugurated, as well as in the hands of Senator Seward and other statesmen at Washington. Lincoln was the more interested because he remembered seeing Vicksburg when he went down the Mississippi on a flatboat more than thirty years earlier.

exchange of innumerable anecdotes and witticisms. A brief written memorandum was placed in Weed's hands to be given to Seward for the benefit of the Republican members of the Senate Committee of Thirteen. Mr. Bancroft, in his "Life of Seward," 1899, identified for us a sheet in Lincoln's handwriting, discovered among the Seward manuscripts, which is undoubtedly the original memorandum that Nicolay and Hay had not found for inclusion in Lincoln's "Complete Works." The concessions that Lincoln was willing to make, as written in his own hand, are in three terse paragraphs as follows:

"Resolved, that the fugitive slave clause of the Constitution ought to be enforced by a law of Congress with efficient provisions for that object, not obliging private persons to assist in its execution, but punishing all who resist it, and with the usual safeguards to liberty, securing free men against being surrendered as slaves—

"That all State laws, if there be such, really or apparently, in conflict with such law of Congress ought to be repealed; and no opposition to the execution of such law of Congress ought to be made—

"That the federal Union must be preserved."

Mr. Seward soon afterwards wrote as follows to the President-elect: "This evening the Republican members of the committee, with Judge Trumbull and Mr. Fessenden, met at my house to consider your written suggestion and determine whether it shall be altered. While we think the ground has been already covered we find that, in the form you give it, it would divide our friends, not only in the committee, but in Congress, a portion being unwilling to give up their old opinion that the duty of executing the Constitutional provisions concerning fugitives from service, belongs to the States and not at all to Congress."

A few days after the departure of Mr. Weed from Springfield and his arrival at Washington, Mr. Seward wrote the President-elect (December 28th) cordially accepting the offer of the position of Secretary of State. Mr. Lincoln in response wrote expressing his appreciation, and saying that he had received

THURLOW WEED, OF NEW YORK
Senator Seward's special emissary to President-elect Lincoln.

much evidence that the appointment had been received with general favor. He also declared that with the shaping of the rest of the Cabinet he should encounter far greater difficulties.

In his autobiography Mr. Weed gives us an extended account of Mr. Lincoln's conversations on this subject. Weed thought there was some danger of choosing too many men who had formerly been Democrats; but Lincoln had the better of the argument (in the end carrying his own views), and the visitor soon came to perceive that while Mr. Lincoln would listen and confer with candor and open-mindedness, he would make his own choices. The New York editor surmised that it might be well to appoint a man or two from slave-holding States, mentioning North Carolina and Tennessee.

Lincoln minimized the advantages that would result, but said that he would be quite willing to invite John A. Gilmer (a North Carolina Congressman) to enter the Cabinet if his views were likely to be in accord with those of the new Administration. A letter dated December 15th was written, and given to Mr. Weed to carry personally to Mr. Gilmer at Washington. In that letter Lincoln declared that he could not shift the ground upon which he had previously stood, as disclosed in his speeches and in the Republican platform. "It would make me appear," said Mr. Lincoln, "as if I repented for the crime of having been elected, and was anxious to apologize and beg forgiveness. To so represent me would be the principal use made of any letter that I might now thrust upon the public. My old record cannot be so used; and that is precisely the reason that some new declaration is so much sought."

Among other things in this letter to Gilmer, Lincoln said: "I have no thought of recommending the abolition of slavery in the District of Columbia, nor the slave trade among the Slave States even on the conditions indicated; and if I were to make such recommendation it is quite clear Congress would not follow it."

On another point he said: "As to the use of patronage in the Slave States where there are few or no Republicans, I do not expect to inquire for the politics of the appointee or whether he does or does not own slaves. I intend in that matter to accommodate the people in the several localities, if they themselves will allow me to accommodate them. In one word, I never have been, am not now, and probably never shall be in a mood of harassing the people either North or South."

To Mr. Gilmer, as to other men North and South, Lincoln declared that he was inflexible on the territorial question, and thought slavery wrong and a thing not to be extended, but rather to be restricted. He wrote also on the question greatly agitated in the South, of State laws that were supposed to be interfering with the Constitutional duty of permitting the capture and return of fugitive slaves. Lincoln said he had never read or seen such a State law, and if they were in conflict with the Constitution he would be glad of their repeal. "But I could hardly be justified," he added, "as a citizen of Illinois, or as President of the United States, to recommend the repeal of a statute of Vermont or South Carolina." Mr. Gilmer consulted with his friends who were Union men in the Slave States lying north of

the Cotton Belt, and decided that it would not be best for him to go into the Lincoln Cabinet.

Mr. Weed had agreed that Edward Bates of Missouri would make an excellent Cabinet member, probably Attorney-General; and on December 18th Mr. Lincoln wrote to Mr. Bates suggesting that an editorial note might appear in the *Missouri Democrat* of St. Louis in language that he proceeded to suggest as follows: "We have the permission of both Mr. Lincoln and Mr. Bates to say that the latter will be offered and will accept a place in the new Cabinet, subject, of course, to the action of the Senate. It is not yet definitely settled which Department will be assigned to Mr. Bates."

Writing three days later to Mr. Washburne, who had reported to Lincoln an interview with General Scott, the President-elect said: "Please present my respects to the General and tell him confidentially I shall be obliged to him to be as well prepared as he can to either hold or retake the forts, as the case may require, at and after the inauguration."

On December 21st Lincoln wrote to his friend Lyman Trumbull, the Illinois Senator (this letter, with others to Lyman Trumbull, appearing in the "Uncollected Letters" brought together in 1917 by Mr. Tracy):

My Dear Sir:
Thurlow Weed was with me nearly all day yesterday and left last night with three short resolutions which I drew up, and which, or the substance of which, I think, would do much good if introduced and unanimously supported by our friends. They do not touch the territorial question. Mr. Weed goes to Washington with them; and says that he will first of all confer with you and Mr. Hamlin. I think it would be best for Mr. Seward to introduce them, and Mr. Weed will let him know I think so. Show this to Mr. Hamlin, but beyond him do not let my name be known in the matter.
Yours as ever,
A. Lincoln.

South Carolina having seceded on December 20th, Mr. Lincoln wrote as follows on the 24th to Lyman Trumbull: "Despatches have come here, two days in succession, that the Forts in South Carolina will be surrendered by the order, or consent at least, of the President. I can scarcely believe this; but if it prove true, I will, if our friends at Washington concur, announce publicly at once that they are to be retaken after the inauguration. This will give the Union men a rallying cry, and preparation will proceed somewhat on their side, as well as on the other."

William Cullen Bryant, who edited the New York *Evening Post,* had written protesting against the choice of Seward for Secretary of State. Replying to him, Mr. Lincoln wrote: "Yours of the 25th is duly received. The 'well-known politician' to whom I understand you to allude . . . . did not press upon me any such compromise as you seem to suppose or, in fact, any compromise at all. As to the matter of the Cabinet mentioned by you, I can only say I shall have a great deal of trouble, do the best I can. I promise you that I shall unselfishly try to deal fairly with all men and all shades of opinion among our friends."

On December 31st the following note was sent from Springfield:

Hon. Salmon P. Chase.
My Dear Sir:
    In these troublous times I would much like a conference with you. Please visit me here at once.
                Yours very truly,
                        A. Lincoln.

A week later, writing a letter to Lyman Trumball marked *"Very Confidential."* Mr. Lincoln said: "It seems to me not only highly proper, but a *necessity* that Governor Chase shall take that place [the Treasury]. His ability, firmness and purity of character produce this propriety; and that he alone can reconcile Mr. Bryant and his class to the appointment of S[eward] to the State Department produces the necessity. But then comes the danger that the protectionists of Pennsylvania will be dissatisfied; and to clear this difficulty General C[ameron] must be brought to co-operate. He would readily do this for the War Department. But then comes

HORACE IS SICK!
"Poor boy! Well, give him his Seward's gruel and his Weed's elixir. He'll soon be up and around, and as saucy as ever!"

Horace Greeley had played an important part in the campaign that elected Lincoln, as earlier chapters in this volume have shown; but Senator Seward and Thurlow Weed became the President-elect's political advisers from New York in the period of cabinet-making.

the fierce opposition to his having any Department, threatening even to send charges in to the Senate to procure his rejection by that body. Now, what I would most like, and what I think he would prefer too, under the circumstances, would be to retain his place in the Senate, and if that place has been promised to another, let that other take a respectable and reasonably lucrative place abroad. Also, let General C.'s friends be, with entire fairness, cared for in Pennsylvania and elsewhere. I may mention before closing that besides the very fixed opposition to General C. he is more amply recommended for a place in the Cabinet than any other man.''

During November and December, Governor Chase had not been in direct communication with Mr. Lincoln regarding policies or appointments, and it was not until December 31st that the President summoned him to Springfield in the telegram already quoted. The visit lasted two days, and the President-elect had full opportunity to form a careful and revised estimate of the ambitious but sincere gentleman of the transplanted New England type so prominent in northern Ohio as in other parts of the Northwest, notably the new State of Iowa. This type was neither better nor worse than that which was more prevalent in southern Ohio, Kentucky, and the southern halves of Indiana and Illinois, to which Lincoln himself belonged, with Pennsylvania and Virginia rather than New England as the background of origin and tradition. In the New England stock the Puritan strain was persistent, and it carried with it a sense of moral and intellectual superiority that had become more tolerant and genial in the West, though still distinct.

Lincoln did not treat Chase as he had treated Seward and Cameron. That is to say, he did not make a direct and unqualified offer of a Cabinet position. Instead, he asked him if he would be free to accept in case Lincoln should find that he could make the appointment fit into his scheme as a whole; and the only position that he mentioned was that of the Treasury. This was the place that the Pennsylvania friends of Cameron were demanding for their own man. It was at this juncture, on the turn of the year, that Lincoln came suddenly and sharply to the conclusion that he must hold definite appointments in abeyance, consult widely, have tentative understandings, but allow the country to find out about the Cabinet group when the names were sent to the Senate for confirmation. Seward had waited to know something about Administration policies and had not sent his acceptance until December 28th. Lincoln was waiting to have Seward's answer before he could do business with so important a Republican as Governor Chase.

Afterward Mr. Lincoln told someone that he had always, from the beginning, had it in mind that both of these leaders would be invited to take Cabinet places. If Seward had concluded to stay in the Senate, Chase would probably have been made Secretary of State, which was the place he clearly preferred. It was not until Lincoln was in Washington just before inauguration that Chase knew definitely of his appointment. There had come to be a general impression that all the final decisions were reserved.

Lincoln had simply decided not to tie his own hands. Among the letters of Salmon P. Chase brought to light by the Manuscripts Commission of the American Historical Association, is one written to Hon. Thaddeus Stevens of Pennsylvania, a radical Republican leader of the House, as follows:

COLUMBUS, O., January 9.

My Dear Sir:

Your note came when I was in Springfield at Mr. Lincoln's request. I arrived after your Pennsylvanians had all gone. Mr. Lincoln conversed frankly and fully. He is a man to be depended on. He may, as all men may, make mistakes; but the cause will be want of sufficient information, not unsoundness of judgment or of devotion to principle. It is the business of Republicans occupying responsible positions, or possessing in private stations the confidence of their fellow-citizens, to give him that information which is indispensable to right conclusions. I am glad to find your course in opposing concession to principle approved throughout the Northwest. Why can't Republicans await the coming in of their own Administration, and then act generously as well as justly?

Mr. Lincoln was realizing that different things, seemingly contradictory, may be true at the same time. Governor Chase, Gideon Welles, Thaddeus Stevens, Senator Sumner, to mention only a few names, were suffering anguish because what they called "treason" was flaunting itself at Washington as well as in the lower South. Doubtless Mr. Lincoln took some courage from their unyielding Unionism. But he had no desire to precipitate a war, and he was not ready to doubt the loyalty of men like Seward and Weed who were now seeking to find some basis upon which to erect a *modus vivendi*. At Washington there was a tendency to see details, while at Springfield there was better perspective upon the main situation.

CHAPTER XXIII

Cameron — An Episode in Cabinet Making

A Pennsylvanian who led his State—An offer made, cancelled, and finally renewed—Personal and political rivalries exhibited—Difficulties in making up the Cabinet list—Lincoln learns caution

I THINK THAT MOST READERS may learn more from Lincoln's own words, as I am quoting letters not familiar to them, than from much discourse by others regarding his method of dealing with conflicting views and with rival political elements. He had made no embarrassing promises, but his friends in the Chicago convention had undoubtedly held out inducements to the Pennsylvania and Indiana delegations, both of which were working for the defeat of Seward.

Simon Cameron had in 1845 succeeded Buchanan in the Senate, and was then acting with the Democratic party. In 1856 he had supported the Republican ticket headed by General Frémont and had gone to the Senate again, this time as a Republican. He had been a presidential candidate at Chicago, as had Seward, Chase, and Bates. The demand from Pennsylvania for his appointment to the Cabinet was so insistent that (to anticipate) Lincoln actually made him Secretary of War, although, at the age of sixty-two, he was not well fitted to bear the burdens that were suddenly imposed upon the War Department. He remained in the Cabinet for ten months, when he resigned to represent us at the Russian court.

Lincoln was building his Cabinet with the most careful consideration, having in mind above all things the strength and efficiency of the federal Government, and the support of as many factors of public opinion as possible. He had already, on December 31st, written a note, informing Mr. Cameron of his intention to name him for a Cabinet post. The letter to Trumbull shows that after having made the offer he was hoping that the Pennsylvania leader would prefer some other position, and would decline.

If I should omit further reference to the Cameron controversy I should fall short of

SIMON CAMERON, OF PENNSYLVANIA

doing justice to an affair that was accounted by Lincoln himself as of exceptional importance. Pennsylvania, the home State of President Buchanan and the banner State of the northern Democracy in times past, had now turned a sensational somersault and was the foremost State of Lincoln's party. The delegation from Pennsylvania had gone to Chicago with instructions to support General Cameron as a presidential candidate. We have already given an account of the circumstances under which that delegation had made Lincoln's nomination possible. But the party was so new in Pennsylvania that it was not until the election was won that the Lincoln voters of the Keystone State were ready to call themselves Republicans. There were intense rivalries among their leaders, inherited from many bygone contests.

On the face of things the political arguments for inviting General Cameron to a place in the Cabinet were obvious. But the opponents of Cameron in Pennsylvania, like the opponents of Seward in New York, regarded themselves as more high-minded and sincere and far better entitled to Mr. Lincoln's private ear, than the politicians charged with corrupt practices who made up the personal machine of the chief boss. Cameron had visited Springfield at the end of December at the President's invitation; and the note offering him a seat in the Cabinet was handed to him as he took his departure on the last day of the year. "I think fit to notify you now," read this missive, "that by your permission I shall at the proper time nominate you to the United States Senate for confirmation as Secretary of the Treasury, or as Secretary of War—which of the two I have not yet definitely decided."

Returning to Pennsylvania, Cameron had given out the news of this offer; whereupon, the anti-Cameron men lost not a moment in making vehement protest. Among these were some of the ablest and best Republicans of the State, including Governor Curtin, Thaddeus Stevens, and Col. A. K. McClure. As the emissary of this group, McClure hastened to Springfield. Only a week earlier than Cameron's visit, David Wilmot himself, having received from Lincoln more than a mere intimation that he would probably be asked to enter the Cabinet, had also visited Springfield on invitation, and had been warmly received. A series of letters from Wilmot's files somehow disappeared in later years, and nobody now knows exactly what happened. Seemingly, Judge Wilmot thought he could be of more use in the Senate; and he expected to be at once chosen to fill the place about to be vacated by William Bigler, Buchanan's friend.

Col. McClure's visit to Springfield had an immediate result, of extraordinary character. On January 3rd, Mr. Lincoln addressed the following letter marked "Private" to "Hon. Simon Cameron": "My dear Sir: Since seeing you things have developed which make it impossible for me to take you into the Cabinet. You will say this comes of an interview with McClure; and this is partly, but not wholly,

true. The more potent matter is wholly outside of Pennsylvania; and yet I am not at liberty to specify it. Enough that it appears to me to be sufficient. And now I suggest that you write me, declining the appointment, in which case I do not object to its being known that it was tendered you. Better do this at once, before things so change that you cannot honorably decline, and I be compelled to openly recall the tender. No person living knows or has an intimation that I write this letter. Yours truly, A. Lincoln. P. S.—Telegraph me instantly on receipt of this saying 'All right.' A. L."

Instead, however, of sending the expected telegram, Mr. Cameron preferred to face the possible alternative of having Lincoln openly withdraw the Cabinet offer. Evidently the offer itself had been made quite prematurely; and Lincoln now meant to save embarrassment on both sides by the earliest possible rectification of his mistake. His action on December 31st had been due, undoubtedly, to the fact that the Pennsylvania legislature was at that time occupied with a contest over the Senate seat, for which Mr. Wilmot was a candidate. If Mr. Cameron were leaving the Senate for the Cabinet, his vacant seat would also have to be filled.

Although Col. McClure in his later reminiscences mentions Judge Wilmot as among the men protesting to Lincoln against Cameron's appointment, I think it more likely that Wilmot's objections had been natural inferences rather than open expressions. The contest in the legislative caucus for the full Senate term lay between David Wilmot and Edgar Cowan, with the chances in favor of Wilmot, who expected the support of the Cameron influence. But Cameron received this recall letter from Lincoln, dated January 3rd, just in time to exhibit at once his wrath and his power by seeing that Cowan secured the nomination by a very large majority over Wilmot. With or without evidence, he had associated Wilmot with Curtin, Stevens, McClure, and others, as having influenced Lincoln's mortifying and astonishing reversal.

As against the anti-Cameron charges that had been brought to Lincoln's attention, there

CAMERON AT SPRINGFIELD

Alarming Appearance of the Winnebago Chief

CAMERON: "You have sent for me, and I have come. If you don't want me, I'll go back to my wigwam."

From *Vanity Fair*, February 2, 1861.

began to pour in upon Springfield floods of pro-Cameron telegrams, letters and visiting emissaries. And now comes to Harrisburg another letter from Lincoln, written January 13th. Referring to the recall letter of the 3rd, Mr. Lincoln says: "I wrote that letter under great anxiety, and perhaps I was not so guarded in its terms as I should have been; but I beg you to be assured I intended no offense. My great object was to have you act quickly, if possible before the matter should be complicated with the Pennsylvania senatorial election. Destroy the offensive letter or return it to me. I say to you now I have not doubted that you would perform the duties of a Department ably and faithfully. Nor have I, for a moment, intended to ostracize your friends. If I should make a Cabinet appointment from Pennsylvania before I reach Washington, I will not do so without consulting you, and giving all the weight to your views and wishes which I consistently can. This I have always intended."

Not content with this explanation, made in a letter marked "Private and Confidential," Mr. Lincoln enclosed a formal letter that could be shown or published, bearing the date of January 3rd, as a substitute for the now repudiated letter actually written on that earlier date. This public letter faithfully records the fact that Cameron had visited Springfield at Lincoln's own invitation; that he had been given a letter proffering a Cabinet seat; that he had not yet signified his acceptance, and that with much pain the President asks to be relieved from great embarrassment by being allowed to recall the offer. "This springs" (to quote the letter in direct terms) "from an unexpected complication, and not from any change of my view as to the ability or faithfulness with which you would discharge the duties of the place. I now think I will not definitely fix upon any appointment for Pennsylvania until I reach Washington."

Mr. Lincoln actually waited until he had been in Washington several days before making the Pennsylvania appointment, and he vindicated the sincerity of his kindly expressions in the letters I have quoted by giving the place to Cameron himself, about March 1st. Later in the same month, the Republicans of the Pennsylvania Legislature chose David Wilmot to fill the Senate vacancy by a great majority and with very little opposition. Everything was working out, with exemplary neatness, in due time. Mr. Lincoln had been obliged to deal with groups of men seriously at variance with each other in Pennsylvania. He was trying to shape his course in such a way as to hold all the factions in support of his Administration, and to keep them from squandering energy, such as the public interest required for greater things, in unworthy political strife at home.

The charges against Cameron had reflected seriously upon his political and personal character. But when Lincoln tried to sift them, he could find nothing but hearsay, and defensive excuses that mentioned one matter or another that had been said at some time in anonymous newspaper articles.

Since Col. McClure had made himself the chief spokesman of the anti-Cameronians, it is well worth while to have his revised estimate as he gives it to us in a volume written long afterwards. Says Col. McClure: "Looking back upon that contest with the clearer insight that the lapse of thirty years must give, I do not see how Lincoln could have done otherwise than appoint Cameron as a member of his Cabinet, viewed from the standpoint he had assumed. He desired to reconcile party differences by calling his presidential competitors around him, and that opened the way for Cameron. He acted with entire sincerity, and in addition to the powerful pressure for Cameron's appointment, made by many who were entitled to respect, he felt he was not free from the obligation made in his name by Davis at Chicago to make Cameron a member of his Cabinet. The appointment was not made wholly for that reason, but that pledge probably resolved Lincoln's doubts in Cameron's favor, and he was accepted as Secretary of War."

In the light of the facts that I have presented in the preceding chapter relating to Governor Chase and his visit to Springfield, it would seem almost certain that the "more potent matter wholly outside of Pennsylvania," to which the President-elect referred in his letter to Cameron of January 3rd, was essentially connected with the conclusion that now formed itself in Mr. Lincoln's mind that Chase would have to be made Secretary of the Treasury. The President-elect had doubtless learned from Chase, as well as from many others, that the opposition to Cameron was far more widespread and intense outside of Pennsylvania than within that State. Col. McClure was a departing guest as the Chase visit began; and the cumulative assaults upon Cameron's reputation gave Mr. Lincoln an intense desire to be released from a definite offer that he had made and which had not as yet been definitely accepted.

His recall of one letter and substitution of another with a false date was awkward and infelicitous, as regards the mere method of dealing with an embarrassing situation. He was intent upon saving General Cameron's dignity; and the second letter was truthful in letter and in spirit. There was no fault on the President-elect's part except the predating; and this, as will be readily understood by members of the legal profession, was in consequence of certain accepted practices.

It is hardly necessary to remark that no public office—certainly not so responsible a place as a Cabinet position—is a private perquisite.

An appointment is made when the President sends the name to the Senate, and not before. If, for reasons seeming to bear upon his own sole accountability for the executive branch of the government, a President-elect changes his mind, after he has mentioned privately to one man or another that he expects to place him in the Cabinet, the personal embarrassment should not weigh much as against the higher obligation to serve public interests rather than to gratify individuals.

This experience with General Cameron quite distinctly clarified Abraham Lincoln's views as to the exercise of the appointing power. In consequence, surprising as it may seem, no man who was destined to occupy a chair in the Cabinet council knew until the last moment what other men would be found at the same table. Upon this point I find some interesting testimony in "Recollections of War Times," by Albert G. Riddle, a member of Congress from northern Ohio, and one of Mr. Chase's closest personal and political friends. Mr. Riddle, exceedingly prominent and active in northern Ohio, was at this time a Congressman-elect, making his first visit to Washington a few days before the end of the Buchanan

A HINT TO OFFICE-HOLDERS
The Democrats had been in power for eight years, during the terms of Pierce and Buchanan. It was, indeed, the first time that the Republican party had patronage to distribute; and many federal "heads" were expected to fall.

Administration and remaining for several weeks. Writing of a call on Mr. Chase at his hotel he informs us that even at that late date, having been offered the Treasury portfolio, Chase "was in the sorest straits as to his duty in the premises. He had just been returned to the Senate, and the intensely radical among us were very anxious to have him remain there. Where the choice of the President for his Cabinet would fall was the greatest of problems up to the all-revealing 4th of March. While I was very desirous that he should remain in the Senate, I was very clear it was his duty to accept the Treasury portfolio; I found that one of his objections was his utter want of knowledge as to the man selected for the State Department." This would seem almost incredible, yet Mr. Riddle was an intimate friend of Chase, and his testimony is valuable.

The following paragraph, also from Mr. Riddle, gives us a side light upon Mr. Lincoln's now cautious mode of proceeding that I think

OLD ABE INVOKES THE SPIRIT OF ST. PATRICK
He begs to be rid of the reptiles that destroy his peace— the office-seekers.

From the *Phunny Phellow*, New York.

well worth presenting here: "A thing much talked of at the time in the capital was that Mr. Lincoln, on Sunday the 3rd, gave a dinner to seven gentlemen, and they happened to be those whose names were sent to the Senate the next day. Yet it was said that several of them at that dinner party were not informed of their intended associates. I was enabled, on the Thursday or Friday of that week, to inform Mr. Chase that Mr. Seward was to be the Chief of the Cabinet, which was to him a great relief. I did not, however, know the name of any of the others, except Mr. Seward, selected by the President-elect, nor did anyone save Mr. Chase learn from me the source of my information, nor what it was."

In his life of Chase, Albert Bushnell Hart tells us that "to the last moment Chase had no positive assurance that he would be appointed, and he was not consulted about the rest of the Cabinet slate; hence he could truthfully say that the sending his nomination to the Senate was a surprise to him."

There is ample evidence, along the line of Riddle's allusion and Hart's statement, to the effect that Chase was anxious to work well with Seward. He was exercising his mind in realms far above personal jealousies, remote from the pettiness of the patronage squabbles that were so prevalent.

The appointment of Hon. Caleb B. Smith of Indiana to be Secretary of the Interior followed somewhat naturally upon the political events that culminated in the Chicago convention. The Indiana delegation had supported Illinois with genuine enthusiasm for the "Rail-splitter," and Mr. Smith was regarded as trustworthy and competent. After two years in the Cabinet he retired to a federal judgeship and died in 1864.

The selection of Gideon Welles of Connecticut for the Navy Department followed a careful consideration of available New England men, and subsequent events proved the wisdom of this designation. Mr. Lincoln had thought it suitable and courteous to consult the Vice-President-elect, Hannibal Hamlin of Maine, regarding the appointment of a New England man, preferably a former Democrat;

and Mr. Lincoln was satisfied to accept the preference expressed by Mr. Hamlin.

Mr. Welles belonged to one of the oldest Connecticut families, had studied law after full academic training, and at the age of twenty-four had become director and editor of the Hartford *Times,* a Democratic paper that staunchly supported Andrew Jackson. In Van Buren's term he was postmaster at Hartford, while continuing his editorial career; but with the emergence of the slavery issue he became a Republican, refusing to support Pierce and Buchanan. In 1856 he was the unsuccessful Republican candidate for Governor of Connecticut, and in 1860 he was chairman of the Connecticut delegation at the Chicago convention that nominated Lincoln.

Mr. Morse in his introduction to the invaluable "Diary of Gideon Welles," makes it plain that the inclusion of this Connecticut leader in the Cabinet group was in every way congenial to Mr. Lincoln. "Wanting a man from New England, Lincoln took an ex-Democrat trained in public business, who had manifested his courage and the earnestness of his conviction by casting loose from his old associates on the question of slavery; and who also, it may be noted, had shown a natural aptitude for politics, a quality which Mr. Lincoln, possessing it himself in a high degree, did not undervalue in others."

Thus Mr. Lincoln was dealing at once with measures and with men. He was welding together the elements throughout the country that had supported Republican presidential electors. He was testing himself, moreover, as he met one after another of the preliminary problems. He was rapidly learning the lesson that he could not permit himself to exercise his responsibilities vicariously. By the time he was ready to go to Washington, he had begun to acquire the presidential habit of mind. However he might have felt a dozen years earlier, he had now wholly ceased to stand in awe of any other living statesman, whether the austere Sumner of Massachusetts, the vain, philosophic and temperamental Seward of New York, or the able, earnest, and perhaps over-consecrated Chase of Ohio.

CHAPTER XXIV

Seward – Principal or Under-Study?

Activities of the first-named member of Lincoln's Cabinet—His compromising Senate speech—Sumner, Chase and Schurz worried over Seward's assumptions—Lincoln undisturbed and in full control

HAVING AT LENGTH ACCEPTED the offer of the ranking position in Lincoln's official family, Senator William H. Seward became exceedingly active behind the scenes at Washington. He was given confidential reports of all that was taking place in the Buchanan Cabinet, being on intimate terms with Mr. Stanton, and also with John A. Dix. Through certain friends acting as intermediaries, he was in communication with Southern leaders.

Even after the secession of Mr. Davis's own State, his return to the South, and his election as President of the Confederacy, Mr. Seward managed to keep in touch. Seward had spoken seldom on the Senate floor for a month, and every one at Washington was waiting in suspense for some great utterance. The foremost figure in the coming Republican Cabinet was expected to pronounce momentous conclusions and verdicts on behalf of the President-elect. It was still supposed at Washington that Seward, rather than Lincoln, was to be the authoritative spokesman of the new party that was about to assume full power.

Seward chose his moment carefully, keeping silence until Mississippi on January 9th, Florida the next day, and Alabama on the 11th, had joined South Carolina in official secession from the Union. On the following day, January 12th, came the prepared and elaborate oration that had been awaited. The stage was set and the occasion was duly heralded. The desire to hear Seward crowded the Senate Chamber with the largest audience that had ever been gathered within its walls.

He proposed a truce from arguments, and an appeal to all parts of the country to save the Union in its integrity. There was no way to dissolve the Union, he held, except by Constitutional amendment, and Congress should go as far as it could to meet any real griev-

LET IT BE EVER THUS WITH TRAITORS

Columbia, with her sword of Liberty and Union, is astride the figure of Secession. Senator Seward spoke for conciliation, and declared that the Union "would rise again tomorrow." But others in the North held the opinion expressed in this New York cartoon, that incidents at Charleston, New Orleans, and elsewhere, were nothing less than treason.

ances, and should then see that the President was fully authorized, and provided with ample means, to defend the Union. He declared that he could "afford to meet prejudice with conciliation, exaction with concession which surrenders no principle, and violence with the right hand of peace.'"

Beginning first with the fugitive slave question, his tone was intended to conciliate the South. Second, he said that he was willing to amend the Constitution in order to give added assurance against future interference by Con-

221

THE LAST PORTRAIT OF THE
BEARDLESS LINCOLN

It was not generally known that the President-elect was
allowing his beard to grow. *Frank Leslie's Illustrated
Newspaper* printed this portrait in its issue for inauguration week, a wood engraving as large as a newspaper page.

gress with slavery in the States. Third, with
Kansas admitted as a Free State, he would
support the plan of consolidating all remaining
territory into two States without restriction as
to slavery, with some provision for future sub-
division. He was prepared to support the idea
of a Constitutional convention in the early
future, to work out compromises. Fourth, he
was in favor of laws to prevent the invasion
of any State by citizens from outside, evidently
having reference to the John Brown raid. As
a fifth consideration he proposed a southern
transcontinental railroad to the Pacific as well
as a northern one.

The concluding portion of the speech was
in Seward's best vein of patriotic oratory. If
the Union were cast down by faction today, it
would rise again and reappear in all its majestic proportions tomorrow. "It shall continue and endure, and men in after times shall
declare that this generation, which saved the

Union from such sudden and unlooked-for
dangers, surpassed in magnanimity even that
one which laid its foundations in the eternal
principles of liberty, justice, and humanity."
It was a speech that aroused much controversy.
The wild fanaticism of the lower South had
now reacted upon the more radical elements of
the Republican party, and there had resulted a
rigid attitude against compromise that went
far beyond the position that Lincoln had taken.

The admirers of Mr. Seward have always
held that this speech was valuable in helping
to keep the Border Slave States in a hesitant
mood. Mr. Seward felt that, in the very fact
of the election of a Republican President, the
prestige of the lower South was broken at
Washington, and that the North could afford
to be so conciliatory that further rebellion
would be checked. His optimism was not justified by any careful survey of existing facts.
I have no desire to make out a case against
Mr. Seward as a wise and discerning statesman. There is sufficient evidence of contrast
between his self-esteem with its tinge of vanity
and Mr. Lincoln's humility and modesty. With
something of the poise and the patience
of Washington, Lincoln was able to take the
leading men of the day for what was best in
them, without being unduly disturbed by
their displays of egotism, or impatience, or
bad judgment.

In commenting upon the Seward speech of
January 12th, his biographer, Mr. Bancroft,
says: "Considering the actual conditions and
what was most urgent at that time, there is reason to believe that this was as wise, as patriotic,
and as important a speech as has ever been delivered within the walls of the Capitol. If
Seward had spoken as most of the Republicans
had done, or if he had gone no farther than
Lincoln had even confidentially expressed a
willingness to go, by March 4th there would
have been no Union that anyone could have
summoned sufficient force to save or to re-
establish . . . . Nearly everyone demanded a
comprehensive declaration, either for compromise and peace, or for coercion and war.
The zeal of the abolitionists and of the secessionists had bred a fanaticism that made the
importance of preserving the Union seem small

indeed. While Garrison attacked Seward, he called upon the North to 'recognize the fact that the Union is dissolved.' Sumner and Chase had protested in advance against Seward's sentiments, and they deplored them afterwards."

Senator Sumner of Massachusetts was indeed greatly disturbed. On January 17th, five days after the Seward speech, writing to Dr. Howe, the husband of Julia Ward Howe, he declared: "My solicitude is so great that it has touched my health, but I cannot help it. Seward read me his speech four days before its delivery. When he came to his propositions I protested with my whole soul, for the sake of our cause, our country, and his own good name, and I supplicated him to say no such thing. I do not speak, for such a speech as I should make would be seized by the conservative press and be made the apology for the conduct of the Slave States. To a member of the House who inquired what concession I was willing to make, I said, 'There is one: I will consent to be silent yet a little longer'."

Perhaps a majority of the Republicans at Washington were now as uncompromising in their attitude as were Senators Sumner and Wilson of Massachusetts. On January 21st Seward delivered himself of his feeling about the state of the country and about himself as the man of the hour in the following sentences that I quote from a letter afterwards published in his edited correspondence: "Mad men North and mad men South are working together to produce a dissolution of the Union by civil war. The present Administration and the incoming one unite in devolving on me the responsibility of averting those disasters. My own party trusts me, but not without reservation. All the other parties, North and South, cast themselves upon me."

It is assumed by writers who yield to the natural temptation to exaggerate for the sake of strong dramatic effects, that Seward and Lincoln were working at cross purposes. But a letter from Lincoln found in the Seward manuscripts, dated January 19th, contains the following sentence: "Your recent speech is well received here, and, I think, is doing good all over the country."

CHARLES SUMNER, OF MASSACHUSETTS
Who implored Seward not to deliver his speech of January 12, 1861. In March, Sumner became chairman of the Senate Committee on Foreign Relations, and he held that post during the administration of President Lincoln and for six years thereafter.

It should be remembered that when Sumner was begging Seward not to suggest concessions, there remained two months of the Buchanan Administration, and the crisis was at one of its most acute junctures. After all, the speech was rather hazy in its proposals, and its importance lay in its tone and manner. For years the South had regarded Seward as its most dangerous enemy, and if he had been nominated at Chicago, as he and his friends had expected that he would be, the secessionist agitation would have been decidedly more active and widespread than Lincoln's selection occasioned. Seward was now merely trying to pour some oil on the troubled waves. He had not consulted Lincoln about his speeches, and this gave the President-elect the opportunity, which he did not hesitate to utilize when convenient, to declare that the eminent New York Senator was speaking for himself, as he had a right to do, and was in no sense expressing himself in his capacity as a future member of Lincoln's Administration.

On the very day before the Seward speech, Lincoln, in a letter to Hon. J. P. Hale, had pronounced it utterly futile to "surrender to those we have beaten before we take the offices." He proceeded as follows: "In this they are either attempting to play upon us or they are in dead earnest. Either way, if we surrender, it is the end of us and of the Government. They will repeat the experiment upon us *ad libitum*. A year will not pass till we shall have to take Cuba, as a condition upon which they will stay in the Union. They now have the Constitution under which we have lived over seventy years and Acts of Congress of their own framing, with no prospect of their being changed; and they can never have a more shallow pretext for breaking up the government, for extorting a compromise, than now. There is in my judgment but one compromise

COLUMBIA'S TRIBUTE TO MAJOR ANDERSON
Bob Anderson, my beau, Bob, when we were first acquent,
You were in Mex-i-co, Bob, because by order sent;
But now you are in Sumter, Bob, because you chose to go;
And blessings on you, anyhow, Bob Anderson, my beau!

Bob Anderson, my beau, Bob, I really don't know whether
I ought to like you so, Bob, considering that feather,
I don't like standing armies, Bob, as very well you know;
But I love a *man that dares to act,* Bob Anderson, my beau!

which would really settle the slavery question, and that would be a prohibition against acquiring any more territory."

On January 12th, the very day of the Seward speech, Mr. Lincoln had written to that gentleman as follows: "Your selection for the State Department having become public, I am happy to find scarcely any objection to it. I shall have trouble with every other Northern Cabinet appointment, so much so that I shall have to defer them as long as possible to avoid being teased to insanity to make changes." There is no evidence whatsoever that Mr. Lincoln would have altered the tone of his letter if he had known what Seward was then saying on the Senate floor.

In a letter marked "private and confidential," dated February 1st, the President-elect wrote again to his designated Secretary of State, and in that letter occur the following sentences that summarize the Lincoln position:

"On the territorial question—that is the question of extending slavery under the national auspices—I am inflexible. I am for no compromise which assists or permits the extension of the institution on soil owned by the nation. And any trick by which the nation is to acquire territory, and then allow some local authority to spread slavery over it, is as obnoxious as any other. I take it that to effect some such result as this, and to put us again on the high road to a Slave Empire, is the object of all these proposed compromises. I am against it. As to fugitive slaves, District of Columbia, slave trade among the slave States, and whatever springs of necessity from the fact that the institution is amongst us, I care but little, so that what is done be comely and not altogether outrageous. Nor do I care much about New Mexico if further extension were hedged against."

The reader will, I am confident, never find Mr. Lincoln's own words tedious; and I am far from offering apologies for quoting so freely from some of the many important letters that he wrote during this period of waiting at Springfield. If they were hasty in form or phrase, they were deliberate in their basic thought. He was using the Governor's room in the State House, where he was receiving delegations from near and far. He was holding some of his more private and exclusive conferences with prominent members of the party, or their emissaries, in his comfortable home. When the session of the Legislature was opening and the Governor was in need of his office, Mr. Lincoln was transferred to rooms in a new business building across the street. His intelligent secretary, John G. Nicolay, was on constant duty as a political aide, but there seems to have been little system about the keeping of the records, and even less about correspondence files and the copying of Mr. Lincoln's letters to men in all parts of the country. Many such letters have come to light in subsequent years among the papers of their recipients. Most of them

DR. LINCOLN'S HOMEOPATHIC TREATMENT

"Now, Miss Columbia, if you will follow my prescriptions, which are of an extremely mild character, but which your old nurse, Mrs. Buchanan, seems to have been so averse to, I have no doubt but that the Union will be restored to position, health, and vigor."

From *Yankee Notions,* New York.

were destroyed, others hopelessly lost, and a few may yet come to light, the quest being subject to the law of diminishing returns. Fortunately, enough of these letters are available to reveal the consistency of Lincoln's position, as he faced the prospects of an administration fraught with anxieties and trials greater by far than those of any possible foreign war.

It becomes clear, therefore, that while Lincoln was following the course of events, eagerly reading the newspapers, and obtaining confidential reports through letters and by word of mouth, he was settling his own views of policy, and was quietly but firmly impressing them upon the leaders, of all shades of opinion, who were opposed to Secession.

In the vast bombardment of oratory to which the country had been subjected during the campaign of 1860, the most impressive among the newer men who had come forward, was a young German named Carl Schurz. As a youth not yet of age in the Revolution of 1848, he had made a reputation as a bold par-

ticipant in the Liberal movement. He lived as an exile for several years in Switzerland, France, and England, and came to the United States in the summer of 1852, when he was only twenty-three years old. A marvelous linguist, an excellent scholar, and an accomplished man of letters, he was at once in demand as an editor of German newspapers and a leader of the scholarly and idealistic element among the recent German immigrants, who were becoming so numerous and influential in Cincinnati, St. Louis, Milwaukee, and many other communities. These men were instinctively opposed to slavery, and were in ready sympathy, as a rule, with the more pronounced leaders of the new Republican party. Mr. Schurz had gone to Wisconsin to make his home in 1856. He was at once accounted among the leading men of the State. He was the most prominent and influential member of the Wisconsin delegation (being its chairman and a member of the platform committee) at the convention that nominated Lincoln.

He had acquiesced with good-will in the nomination of Mr. Lincoln, but had spoken in the convention a last word of regret for the defeat of Seward while promising support of the nominee. We have Lincoln's own words of appreciation, and the statement of his belief that Schurz was the most effective of all the Republican campaign speakers. Coming to this country without money, and without friends except among his fellow German immigrants, this young man in less than ten years had made himself known throughout the entire country, and had taken equal rank with political leaders of twice his age. I am mentioning the unique position he had attained in order to give significance to certain quotations from his letters of that precise period. We have much that is of historical value in his volumes of reminiscence written later in life. But, beside many letters published previously, we have a volume, issued in 1929 by the

SCHURZ AS MINISTER TO SARDINIA
Horace Greeley is presenting Schurz as deserving of reward for his campaign speeches. He suggests the post of Minister to Sardinia. Mr. Schurz was subsequently appointed Minister to Spain, but he served less than a year and entered the army in time to command a division at the Second Bull Run and as Major-General to lead a corps at Chancellorsville. After the War he was a Senator from Missouri and was in the Cabinet of President Hayes.

State Historical Society of Wisconsin, comprising a large number of "Intimate Letters of Carl Schurz." His letters to his wife, written from various places while he was making an extended lecture tour, show remarkable foresight, and I shall quote from them.

By Christmas time, 1860, Schurz had no doubt as to the practical certainty of a "struggle between the North and the South whose duration will depend upon the determination with which it is conducted." Writing from Boston, December 27th, he said: "The reports from Washington are excellent as respects the firmness of our men. Lincoln has sent letters which have given a new spirit to even the most timorous. 'Old Abe' so far is splendid, and it would not surprise me if his Administration were to determine the future development of the Republic. The Secessionists are proceeding further and further down their mad path, and it almost seems as if plans were being developed in the South which must soon lead to a direct conflict. The Secessionists are trying to draw Virginia and Maryland into the movement. Should that be accomplished, their next step will be to seize Washington, which is chinked in between Virginia and Maryland. This would take place during Buchanan's Administration, or on the 4th of March."

With his wide historical knowledge and his background of European experience, Schurz looked without self-deception at the hard facts. He favored the most rapid possible arming of the North, and wrote his views in full to Lincoln. In a letter to his wife he wrote:

"What do you think of Seward? Have you read or heard about his last speech? The mighty is fallen. He bows before the slave power. He has trodden the way of compromise and concession, and I do not see where he can take his stand on this back track. This star also paled! That is hard. We believed in him so firmly and were so affectionately attached to him. This is the time that tries men's souls and many probably will be found wanting. Lincoln still stands like a stone wall. Every report from Springfield confirms my faith in him. . . . Between us it would not surprise me if Lincoln should recall his invitation to Seward to head the Cabinet. It would be a

LINCOLN'S POLITICAL INDEBTEDNESS TO CARL SCHURZ

Senator Seward stands at the left of the cartoon, next to Lincoln, who is supported by the American Eagle. The man with the high hat is the Uncle Sam of that day. At the right is a group of "adopted fellow-citizens"—Italian, French, Irish, German, and Negro. The German, with a stein around his neck and a huge pipe in his hand, is Carl Schurz. Mr. Lincoln addresses the group: "My dear friends, I cannot express to you in words how deeply I am obliged to you for your generous votes. They have made me what I am. Without you I should have remained what I was —nothing. My emotions overpower me, as you can easily perceive. Be assured that I will do for you whatever *lies in my power!*"

From the *Budget of Fun*, New York.

sharp, perhaps a dangerous, stroke, but a just one; for Seward, whatever he may think privately, has no right on his own responsibility to compromise the President's future policies against his will. What has now become of our Chicago-convention Seward enthusiasm? Where are the lovely oratorical bouquets with which we covered his defeat?"

This letter fully reflects the views entertained in January and February by large numbers of influential Republicans, probably a majority of those who had taken part in the Chicago nominating convention. No one was better aware than Lincoln himself of the impatience of these men, who were fully convinced that they ought to lay violent hands upon the drifting course of events in order that history might proceed upon right lines.

Lincoln was able to see that it was to his advantage to allow the debate to proceed as it would, for several months at least. Seward's record as an anti-slavery spokesman and a defender of the Union had behind it several decades of conspicuous leadership; and no possible harm could come to the country, in Lincoln's opinion, from these belated oratorical efforts to reassure troubled minds below Mason and Dixon's Line. On the other hand, Lincoln fully understood the Puritan sternness of New England men of the Sumner type, and the crusading and prophesying zeal of Governor Chase of Ohio, who in February led the uncompromising element in the Peace Convention. The militant ardor of a young idealist like Carl Schurz found its natural justification in the corresponding ardor of young

OLD ABE'S UNCOMFORTABLE POSITION

"Oh, it's all well enough to say that I must support the dignity of my high office by force—but it's darned uncomfortable sitting."

From *Frank Leslie's Illustrated Newspaper.*

Secessionist orators in the South. Lincoln was firm, but he was also patient; and he was determined to be as conciliatory as might be possible up to the point of making concessions that would harm rather than alleviate the ills of the body politic.

Mr. Schurz went on to write as follows: "Governor Chase stands firm and true upon his old principles. I wrote him yesterday and urged him strongly not to decline the proffered place in the Cabinet. He will be our staff and support there. . . . I shall see Lincoln next Saturday, and will disclose to him in the fullest manner my views relative to the public interest. I do not believe that his own views will be withheld from me."

Meanwhile Schurz was advising the Governor of Wisconsin to send delegates to the Peace Convention—himself among the number—although he did not believe it could have any decisive results. "It will have no influence," he wrote, "upon the Cotton States, and in the end the war of Secession will have to

be waged. You may ask, why then go to the Peace Conference? It shows the South our desire to meet its complaints. It enables us to cultivate good relationships with the Border Slave States—Virginia, Kentucky, Tennessee, etc.—to quietly discuss the causes of dispute, tell them the truth, prolong the debate, and, what on our side is of critical importance, *gain time*. Let Lincoln once be inaugurated and things will look different. Talk will end and action begin. The Peace Conference will probably prevent uprisings in Maryland and Virginia, and the 4th of March will be here before we know it."

A few days later, on February 9th, Schurz wrote from Springfield, the last paragraph of his letter being as follows: "I had a conversation with Lincoln before my lecture, and he said he would visit me at my room tomorrow when we would discuss everything. He is a whole man, firm as a stone wall, and clear as crystal. He told me that Seward made all his speeches without consulting him. He himself will not hear of concessions and compromises, and says so openly to every one who asks."

Lincoln realized that everybody, North and South, except for certain extremists and fire-eaters in both sections, was trying to "gain time" in order to avoid the horrors of a civil war. Even Buchanan, so greatly blamed for gentle and dilatory proceedings, had this one dominant motive. A few days after the secession of South Carolina, which had carried with it all the federal functionaries in that State, Mr. Buchanan had sent to the Senate the name of a new Collector of the Port of Charleston. In a subsequent letter, after his retirement, Buchanan explained that if the Senate had confirmed this appointment, civil war would have been precipitated at once.

There might have been weaker men than Buchanan. There were leading northern Republicans who would have left the post of Charleston customs collector vacant rather than provoke a clash that could not fail to set the whole South on fire. Mr. Lincoln, also, was doing what he could to keep the fire from spreading all the way to the Potomac or to the Pennsylvania line in the East, and to the Ohio River and the Iowa line in the West.

CHAPTER XXV

Lincolns and Todds – A Family Chapter

Genealogists study the Lincoln and Hanks families—Searching for lost grandmothers—Mary Todd and her Confederate brothers—A worthy mistress of the White House—Origin of lingering prejudices

ENOUGH has been said in the three preceding chapters to convey an idea of the activities of Abraham Lincoln as President-elect. Many political leaders from various States, with numerous editors, writers, artists and hopeful claimants for appointive office, had made their way by various routes to the capital city of Illinois. It was arranged that the presidential party should leave Springfield as early as February 11th, three weeks before the date of inauguration. This would allow time to accept the hospitality of a number of important cities on the eastward journey, and a week for consultations in Washington. Seeing the visitors who came singly and in delegations; keeping the newspaper correspondents friendly and discreet; juggling with names on the patronage checker-board; watching the course of events in the South and at Washington—all these things belonged to the daily routine of a public man soon to assume the most important office in the world, at an ominous hour in the nation's history.

Highly responsible duties of almost any kind present an ordeal that may at times test physical endurance and power of self-control. Political place especially exposes the official personage to observation and criticism. But whatever the occupation, public or private, that brings men into relationship with their fellows, it requires constant obedience to the demands of time and place. Those who

cannot keep appointments and face emergencies, who cannot "endure unto the end," fall by the wayside and are very soon forgotten There is always a distinction to be made between the external or work-a-day life, and the intimate and personal affairs of private life. But, also, there is some blending of the two aspects that might fairly be urged to justify invasions of privacy, in the effort to understand public men of established fame.

In the case of Lincoln, it is evident that readers of our generation are peculiarly interested in knowing all that can be learned about the circumstances of his early life, about his heredity, about his domestic relations, and about everything pertaining in any way to his individuality, apart from his career as a public man. In the chapters here presented, and in those that are to follow these in due sequence, I am endeavoring to analyze and recount movements in the field of American his-

THE LINCOLN HOME IN SPRINGFIELD
The crowd was there to congratulate a neighbor upon his election to the Presidency. It was the morning of November 7, 1860, when the result of the voting was known.

tory from the standpoint of Lincoln as a political leader. But I am aware that the tendencies of Lincoln biography in recent years have been predominantly personal. Those who, like myself, find in the public life of Lincoln an intelligible and satisfactory index to his qualities of character and mind are, nevertheless, indebted to the researches of recent scholars who have given us much firm and satisfactory ground for what we were already disposed to believe from reasonable inference.

In the thick of a presidential campaign, the sort of personal attack known as "mud-slinging" is seldom altogether avoided. There was, of course, some belittling gossip and some mendacious scandal on the tongues of people whose prejudices made it easy for them to believe anything against Lincoln. This was of no great consequence in 1860, because voters were not choosing their favorite on the ground of lineage or manners, but on account of the political issues involved. When, however, the campaign was over and it was known that Mr. and Mrs. Lincoln were to become occupants of the White House, curiosity was freshly aroused as to these two people, recently obscure but now prominent. Prejudice and slander now found fresh opportunity. Some vestiges of those prevalent misunderstandings have lingered in the popular mind for more than half a century. Now, in 1861, that the home of long years at Springfield was to be dismantled, never again to welcome a returning Lincoln family, the purely personal aspects of Abraham Lincoln's altered status were touching his feelings deeply, as also they were profoundly affecting the anxious mind of Mrs. Lincoln.

It is to be remembered that many earlier writers about Lincoln, most of them eulogistic in tone and purpose, had joined in creating an artificial person, bolstered up by unverified reports and rumors. It was difficult to reconcile their pictures of Lincoln's private life with the more obvious, and therefore less distorted, facts of his public career. It has been the main object of the scientific and painstaking students of recent date to delve more deeply, to reject irrelevant and idle tales, to find as many definite facts as possible, and to set these facts in relation to one another. I have referred more frequently to the work of the late Senator Beveridge than to that of some other Lincoln biographers, more especially because Mr. Beveridge was engaged in the study of Lincoln as a public man, developed and matured in the varied exigencies of western pioneer life. Many of us, like Mr. Beveridge, have known through ancestral and personal experience the advantages as well as the disadvantages of such participation in the making of Western States and communities. To have had this familiar acquaintance with the life of the frontier, leaves less room for mystery in the emergence of a leader like Abraham Lincoln.

But when Lincoln came to the center of the stage, he encountered most extraordinary misunderstandings of several different origins. He was encompassed by invisible walls of prejudice and animosity. These proved even harder to break down than the defenses of Southern strongholds in the War. Andrew Jackson had encountered prejudices of a similar kind, as he had come to the Presidency with all the bold assertiveness of the lower Mississippi Valley. But Jackson was a world-famed military hero, besides being a masterful politician. He throve in an atmosphere of controversy. The bitterness of his opponents, however, had encouraged malicious gossip; and it is only within recent years that the persistent calumnies affecting the personal and domestic affairs of Andrew Jackson have been cleared away by impartial and thorough students.

Abraham Lincoln was far more seriously the victim of Eastern prejudice than Andrew Jackson had been. The masterful Southerner, accustomed to ride his horse over an extensive plantation cultivated by slave labor, who had organized raw militia and defeated the veterans of Wellington's army, might be hated in the circles of culture and wealth in Philadelphia, New York and Boston. But he would not be treated with contempt, as a despised inferior. Lincoln's type was not that of the warrior bold, nor that of the absolute ruler of a little principality, like a Southern plantation. The families that had gone northwestward,

THE SITTING-ROOM IN THE HOME OF THE LINCOLNS
AT SPRINGFIELD, ILLINOIS

Leslie's, in New York, sent an artist to the house of the President-elect, to make the two drawings reproduced on this page. It also printed the following comment: "The house in which a man of mark dwells is interesting, as to a certain degree indicating his character. The sitting-room and parlor of Abraham Lincoln are, as the reader may observe, simply and plainly fitted up, but are not without indications of taste and refinement.

pushing the frontier before them, and migrating from place to place, had cut themselves off from the homes of their forefathers on the Atlantic seaboard. Such pioneering meant

poverty, though not of the humiliating kind. There was little looking backward; letters were few, and travel to the eastward was strictly limited. Movement on the new Erie

THE FRONT PARLOR OF THE LINCOLN HOME

Sofa, rocking chairs, and hassocks; the ornamental stove, and two whatnots holding books and bric-a-brac—all had their place in the home of "a gentleman in comfortable circumstances," to use an expression of *Leslie's.*

Canal was mostly that of people migrating to the West.

Today the conditions of culture and of civilization are almost precisely alike in every one of the forty-eight States. In 1860 there were marked differences. But of more consequence than the differences themselves was the exaggerated notion in the East of the significance of such disparities. Generous and discerning men of the Eastern States had quickly discovered Lincoln's great qualities. Few people, however, could overcome the feeling that Lincoln was merely the glorified "rail-splitter," who had come to the front through inherent force of character, through political shrewdness, but most of all, through those party exigencies that had deprived Seward of the nomination.

Far more intense and more penetrating, however, was the sectional prejudice due, not to the contrast between East and West, but rather to the cleavage between North and South. Everywhere in the South there was hatred of the Republican party as essentially Abolitionist. And this hatred came to be personified in the man chosen by the Republican party to win a presidential campaign, followed by a crushing and devastating war against the South. The nation's capital city, always a hotbed of malicious gossip, was dominated in the social sense by Southern sympathizers. The District of Columbia, wedged in between Virginia and Maryland, was sullenly hostile to the idea of having the Lincoln family in the White House.

Thus, the reputation of Abraham Lincoln had to rise by sheer merit above the prejudices of the East and the hatreds of the South. Every conceivable kind of disparagement and misrepresentation was spread abroad throughout the country. Evil reports came from all directions. The extreme anti-slavery elements —and these became increasingly large—grew deeply suspicious because Mrs. Lincoln had come from Kentucky. It was enough for the censorious fanatics that her own brothers and other relatives were living in the South, and were serving in the Confederate army. Some people have believed until this day that Mrs. Lincoln was a Southern spy in the White House. The extreme elements in the South, on the other hand, hated Mrs. Lincoln because in point of fact she was intensely loyal to her husband and to the Union cause, although of Southern origin. People in the back districts of all the Southern States were told that Mrs. Lincoln had negro blood in her veins, and was profligate in her personal life; though precisely how they differentiated her ancestry from that of her brothers and noble kinsmen, greatly esteemed, who were fighting chivalrously for the Southern cause, was a point never quite cleared up.

By common consent, the name of Abraham Lincoln is regarded as that of one of the world's greatest men of all time. This being the case, it is a worthy pursuit to clear away myths, to dissipate false traditions even though harmless, and, in short, to set Lincoln biography upon solid foundations, and to build it with true and symmetrical lines. It has been no easy task that some of these biographers have undertaken. For example there appeared in 1929 the latest volume of a series on Lincoln written by Dr. William E. Barton. This one is entitled "The Lineage of Lincoln," and its preparation involved more protracted and thorough research, so far as I am aware, than any other study in the genealogy of an American public man. One can imagine the amazement with which Lincoln himself might have read this remarkable volume. Its appearance one hundred and twenty years after Lincoln's birth, and sixty-nine years after his presidential campaign, represented much travel and labor and the conquest of almost insurmountable difficulties.

Samuel Lincoln of Hingham, England, came to Massachusetts in 1637 and lived to a great age. Four or five previous generations in England seem to be distinctly traced. Although there may be doubts, it is probably true that the Hingham lineage of Lincoln is now as well established as the Sulgrave lineage of Washington. The grandson of Samuel Lincoln removed to Berks County, Pennsylvania, where he died in 1736. His son, John Lincoln, born in Berks County, removed to the Shenandoah Valley in Virginia, and died there in 1788. His son, Capt. Abraham Lincoln

THE LINCOLN FAMILY IN 1861
Robert, the eldest son, is standing. He was then a student at Harvard. At Mr. Lincoln's side is
Thomas, familiarly known as "Tad," nine years old. Near the mother is William, eleven, who died
in the White House in February, 1862.

(the President's grandfather) was born in Virginia, in 1744, and was killed by an Indian in Kentucky in 1786. The youngest son of Capt. Abraham was Thomas Lincoln, father of the President, born in Virginia in 1778. He removed with his family to Indiana, and afterwards to Illinois as we have stated in previous chapters, and his death occurred in 1851.

One of the principal achievements of Dr. Barton has been to clear away many doubts and mistakes about Capt. Abraham Lincoln. But especially Dr. Barton is to be credited with having clearly discovered Lincoln's paternal grandmother, whose maiden name was Bathsheba Herring, and who lived until 1836.

A host of our fellow-Americans, who have attained sufficient leisure to take up the study of their own ancestry, show a marked patronymic preference. They sometimes forget

that they also have mothers, who in turn have pedigrees to find or invent. Lincoln's mother was named Nancy Hanks. People who bear that family name are not a dwindling tribe, and they, on their part, have never forgotten that Abraham Lincoln's mother was a Hanks. But it has remained for Dr. Barton to make a serious and protracted effort, in England as well as in America, to trace Lincoln's ancestry on his mother's side. He finds the Hanks family an ancient one at Malmesbury, and also discovers that this old English town is aware that Lincoln's mother's family went from that place to America.

It is no part of my task to deal in detail with this Hanks lineage. All Americans have the proper number of ancestors, who came at one time or another from some European place or places, where they were likely to have lived for many generations, because in feudal times people seldom crossed the borders of their own parishes. It is not to add anything to the stature of Abraham Lincoln that Dr. Barton has spent years in these inquiries. It is, rather, to show by way of a distinguished example the nature of those migrations that have created our American nationality, while—in the sheer necessities of the epoch—their family records have become obscured or lost. The stern privations of the stupendous enterprise of taming the wilderness have resulted in thousands of lost grandmothers. Incidentally, it is well enough to know—not merely on presumption, but with a recovery of hundreds of specific facts—that Abraham Lincoln was descended on both sides, through long generations, from reputable English and American stock. If these facts had been known, even to Lincoln himself, the biographers in 1860 would have told a different story, and certain typical forms of disparagement would have been less current.

Another investigator, whose valuable studies of Lincoln's parentage and early life are recognized by Dr. Barton, is Mr. Louis A. Warren, who for some time edited a newspaper at Hodgenville, near Lincoln's birthplace, and who investigated records in many places, particularly in Kentucky court-houses. Mr. Warren throws much light upon the early surroundings of Abraham Lincoln and his family in Kentucky. As illustrating the pioneer instinct that affected thousands of families, Mr. Warren remarks, in an article (1929) in the *Wisconsin Magazine of History*: "In 1637 the Samuel Lincoln before mentioned arrived in Old Salem, Massachusetts. In 1837, just two hundred years later, Abraham Lincoln left New Salem, Illinois, for Springfield. Seven generations of these Lincolns participated in this covered-wagon enterprise. Five of the seven men who were heads of these migrating families had the experience of being born in one State, marrying in another, and dying in still another. Massachusetts, New Jersey, Pennsylvania, Virginia, Kentucky, Indiana, and Illinois form the panorama for this pageant of Lincoln frontiersmen."

Lincoln had once said in a letter, "I am naturally anti-slavery. If slavery is not wrong,

nothing is wrong. I cannot remember when I did not so think and feel." How this came to be true is explained for us by Mr. Warren. Lincoln's father and mother were living in Kentucky near one of the oldest of Western churches; and "this Severns Valley Baptist Church was one of the first organizations to raise the question about slavery." Preachers at that place were "credited with organizing the first Emancipation church in the country." Bitter divisions arose in several neighboring Baptist churches, resulting in the closing of some of them, the slavery question being always in the forefront.

It will be remembered that in one of his brief autobiographies Lincoln, speaking of the removal of his father and the family from Kentucky to Indiana, wrote that "it was partly on account of slavery." Mr. Warren's researches have satisfied him that Thomas and Nancy Lincoln belonged to the anti-slavery faction of one of these Baptist churches, and that their antipathy to slavery formed one of the early influences affecting the future President.

Mr. Warren has made a parallel study of the LaFollette family. The LaFollettes were immediate Kentucky neighbors of the Lincolns. We may quote the following from Mr. Warren's study of these families: "Defective land titles and slavery were doubtless both contributing factors in the removal of the Lincolns and most of the LaFollettes to the great Northwest. The destination of these families was Indiana. This called for the crossing of the Ohio. The Lincolns chose to ferry at a point near the mouth of Anderson Creek, which was but sixteen miles from their destination in the new State. They settled in what was then Perry County; but later, because of the establishment of the new boundaries, their home was just over the line in Spencer County. Here they settled near the family of Austin Lincoln, and the Hankses had also located in the same community. They remained in this Hoosier home until 1830."

It was natural that Lincoln's mind should revert to his early associations, and that he should feel the claims of kinship and of former friends, before making the final change of scene. He was deeply attached to his step-

MRS. LINCOLN WITH HER TWO YOUNGER SONS, WILLIE AND TAD
From a photograph by Brady, in 1861, in the collection of the author.

mother, who continued to live in the home that Lincoln had established for his father and the family in Coles County. His father had died in 1851, at the age of 73. There have been attempts to show estrangement between Lincoln and his father, and neglect of the family on Lincoln's part. Conditions of travel were difficult, and Lincoln as a lawyer and politician at Springfield had his own life to live. His father, like all members of the Lincoln family, was of highly independent mind and spirit. Sarah Lincoln, the step-mother had kept in much closer and more sympathetic touch with the absent but devoted son who, being more responsible than other members of the family, never ceased to show his solicitude and his affection in practical ways. She lived until April, 1869, and was buried beside the grave of her husband, where Abraham Lincoln had provided for a tombstone.

It was early in February, a few days before the presidential party left Springfield, that Lincoln made his visit to these kinsfolk in Coles County. There were Hanks cousins, besides Mrs. Thomas Lincoln and her daughter, Lincoln's step-sister.

UNDER THE VEIL

Mr. Lincoln is seen to be a Negro when the veil is lifted.
This is a hitherto unpublished caricature by Adalbert
Volck of Baltimore, made at the time of the Emancipation Proclamation. It represents the unfounded rumors
then in circulation concerning the lineage of the President.

The Hanks family was indeed so ramified
and so inter-related that Abraham Lincoln,
having left early scenes and neighbors while
a mere child, could never have kept track of
his relatives on his mother's side, more especially of the scores or even hundreds of them
remaining in Kentucky. Nancy was a favorite
name in this Hanks tribe; and there were several contemporary Nancy Hankses besides
Lincoln's mother.

A part of the network of scandal and unfriendly gossip that accompanied Lincoln to
the White House had to do with his mother
and the Hanks family. There is ample testimony that Nancy Hanks who married Thomas
Lincoln and died while Abraham was a mere

lad, was a young woman of exemplary character and idealistic qualities of mind and sentiment. Her mother, Lucy Hanks, is said to
have been a young girl in lower Virginia, living not far from the Potomac-River home of
Washington when the Revolutionary War
ended in 1783. Nancy was born probably in
1784, her mother Lucy being eighteen years of
age. There is dispute about Nancy's paternity.
Dr. Barton, in a chapter included in his volume entitled "The Women Lincoln Loved"
comes to the defense of Lucy Hanks with fine
understanding of life and human nature. With
her father's family and the infant Nancy she
went to Kentucky, and there, in due time, she
was married to a certain Henry Sparrow,
about whom all reports are most favorable.
The average Kentucky family was large in
those days; and Lucy's nine young Sparrows,
together with Nancy, making ten in all, fell
below the average then prevailing of a dozen
children to the household.

Dr. Barton does not lose sight of what he
regards as an established fact. But he also
uses sympathetic imagination to make a romantic story. Mr. Sandburg does not avoid
this subject, and gives us certain descriptive
personal details about Lucy Hanks and her
daughter Nancy. Senator Beveridge avers
that these have never been verified; and Mr.
Beveridge's researches fully agree with Dr.
Barton's. Herndon declared that Lincoln once,
in a burst of confidence, had said to him that
his maternal grandfather was a Virginia
planter of substantial position, at the same
moment pledging Herndon to keep this fact
secret while Lincoln lived.

Nicolay and Hay avoid discussion of this
question, merely remarking that "the child-
hood of Nancy was passed with the Sparrows,
and she was oftener called by their name than
by her own." Miss Tarbell, writing of Lincoln's mother in early editions, does not mention Lucy Hanks as Lincoln's grandmother.
In her later revisions she questions the Herndon views. Dennis Hanks, a cousin of Lincoln's mother, in order to avoid embarrassment
when the future President had risen to national
fame, insisted that Nancy's maiden name was
Sparrow, and that she was the daughter of

BEHIND THE SCENES: LINCOLN AS "OTHELLO"

The principal character in Shakespeare's "Othello" is a Moor, described in the play as "black" and "sooty." Lincoln is rehearsing the lines: "O, that the slave had forty thousand lives!" and "Why should honor outlive honesty?" At the right are three members of his Cabinet—Seward, at the table; Welles, asleep in his chair; and Stanton, warning the others to be ready to go on "in the first act." This is a poster caricature, of unknown origin.

Thomas and Betsy Hanks Sparrow, rather than the daughter of Lucy, who married Henry Sparrow. Professor Stephenson, a recognized authority, who has written the comprehensive chapter on Lincoln that appears in the 1929 edition of the Encyclopedia Britannica, accepts without question the view that Lucy Hanks was Lincoln's grandmother, and that the father of Nancy Hanks is unknown. Mr. Warren, on the other hand, still believes that the legitimacy of Lincoln's mother can be established by further research, and he is not alone in finding Herndon a doubtful authority on some points. Henry B. Rankin's "Personal Recollections of Abraham Lincoln" dispose of various myths and morbid tales. Dr. Barton especially is to be praised for having had the patience to clear away numerous conflicting stories, in seeking to bring the truth to light.

My object in this chapter is simply to emphasize the fact that Abraham Lincoln holds so high a place in the roll of immortal names that his life history will be read with unflagging interest during centuries yet to come.

There is nothing in the truth, in so far as it can be ascertained, that would justify a conspiracy of silence on the part of those who cherish the honor and fame of Abraham Lincoln, as regards his maternal grandmother.

Several writers have come to the rescue of the fair name of Mary Todd, Lincoln's wife, who had been more unpleasantly criticised, from various standpoints private and public, than any other woman in the long succession of mistresses of the White House. Dr. Barton does not deny that Mrs. Lincoln had a quick temper, and that she sometimes made regrettable mistakes of judgment. But he finds her intelligent, attractive, and loyal. All who have written with knowledge, even those who are grudging in their treatment of her, admit that it was she, more than anyone else, who believed in Lincoln's ability and in his great capacity for high public position. Her aspiration for him spurred him on at times when he would, perhaps, have allowed the fires of ambition to die out. In a volume published in 1928, Mrs. Honoré Willsie Morrow presents an appreciative biography of Mary Todd Lincoln. It is popular in manner, and apparently an argumentative defense rather than an impartial study. It rests, however, upon firm foundations, resulting from sincere and intelligent inquiry.

Still more important, because of unusual sources of information, is the biography of "Mary, Wife of Lincoln" published in the same year, 1928, and written by Mrs. Lincoln's niece, Katherine Helm. The father of Mrs. Lincoln was Robert Smith Todd of Lexington, Kentucky. He was the son of General Levi Todd, who was born in Pennsylvania in 1756, and who went to Kentucky in 1781, where he filled various posts of responsibility. In 1791 Robert Smith Todd was born near Lexington. He was a local bank president, a State senator, and a citizen of excellent standing in Lexington and in the State at large. He was married twice, and had seven children by his first wife, of whom Mary was the fourth. There were nine children by the second marriage. Members of the Todd family had held appointive office in the territorial days of the Illinois country, and one of Mrs. Lincoln's sisters was married to the son of an early Governor of Illinois, Ninian Edwards. Lincoln's acquaintance with her was formed during her protracted visits at the home of her sister. The numerous Todd relatives remaining in Kentucky were intermarried with most of the leading families of the Blue Grass region.

Speaking at large, the Todd connection was in favor of gradual emancipation and supported the Union. But three of Mary's half-brothers were living in New Orleans at the time with which we are now concerned, and two of her married half-sisters were living in Selma, Alabama. Louisiana and Alabama had seceded in January; and Mrs. Lincoln's brothers and brothers-in-law were swept into the Confederate movement along with their adopted States. To anticipate somewhat, it may be noted that Samuel Todd was killed in the battle of Shiloh; David died from wounds received at Vicksburg, and Alexander was killed at Baton Rouge.

Mrs. Lincoln had always read Kentucky newspapers, and in the winter of 1860-61 she was following the course of political events with keen insight and great anxiety. Mrs. Helm, with her accumulations of knowledge based upon letters, diaries, and personal intercourse with members of the extensive Todd family to which she herself belonged, has given us a volume about Mrs. Lincoln that is conclusive as to many things that had been popularly misunderstood. We are now assured that Mrs. Lincoln belonged to a type of Kentucky womanhood that has not been unduly praised for grace, charm, quick wit, social adaptability, and fine loyalty in all the relationships of life. She was impulsive, and therefore at times her quick temper was in evidence. Her faith in Abraham Lincoln had been unwavering. She had come from an environment of wealth and culture, in sharp contrast with the humble origins and laborious youth of her husband. With such limited means as were at her disposal, she had made the Springfield home as nearly like those of her Kentucky friends as she could. Future generations will be glad to study the reproductions that show the furnishings of the living rooms at Springfield, as drawn in 1860.

For a number of years, with his junior partner Herndon carrying on the business of the firm in the Springfield law office, Lincoln had chosen the more important professional duty of trying cases in court, at the county-seats comprised within the judicial circuit. This gave him wide acquaintance, strengthened his political influence, and steadily increased his modest income. He was handling larger and more lucrative cases from year to year, and had become one of the group known as "railroad lawyers" in the period of rapid railroad building, during the decade preceding his election as President. The persistent idea that Lincoln spent months of every year away from home on the circuit because of domestic unhappiness may be dismissed as absurdly lacking in justification. He was fond of his home surroundings and devoted to his children; and he shared with Mrs. Lincoln her profound grief in the early death of two of their sons, Edward, the second son, having died on February 1, 1850, at the age of four years, and Willie on February 20, 1862, at twelve years of age. Another son, Thomas ("Tad") who survived his father, and who had been a White House favorite, died July 15, 1871.

I am not attempting at this point to write of the experiences of Mrs. Lincoln as mistress of the White House, but rather of her qualities and personality, as her life at Springfield was drawing to an end. She was facing the new and momentous problems that lay before her, as wife of the President in a period of national disruption that affected her deeply in her personal and private relationships.

The day for departure grew near. Household furniture was sold, and the Lincoln family went to a local hotel as their comfortable home was dismantled. Sunday night, February 10th, the strong and self-reliant President-elect, with his own hands "roped" the family trunks at the hotel, in preparation for an early start the next morning.

Under a lowering sky in a drizzling rain the hotel omnibus carried them on Monday morning to the railroad car on a side-track, that had been reserved for the journey of the presidential party. Many neighbors and friends, braving the dismal February weather, were gathered at the railroad station. Lincoln's farewell speech from the platform of his car has often and justly been quoted as one of the best examples of his power to express thought and feeling in English sentences of rare and haunting quality. We may here repeat this familiar address as he left his home town never to see it again:

"My friends: no one, not in my situation, can appreciate my feeling of sadness at this parting. To this place, and the kindness of these people, I owe everything. Here I have lived a quarter of a century, and have passed from a young to an old man. Here my children have been born, and one is buried. I now leave, not knowing when or whether ever I may return, with a task before me greater than that which rested upon Washington. Without the assistance of that Divine Being who ever attended him, I cannot succeed. With that assistance, I cannot fail. Trusting in Him, who can go with me, and remain with you, and be everywhere for good, let us confidently hope that all will yet be well.

"I BID YOU AN AFFECTIONATE FAREWELL"

It was a dismal February morning when Mr. Lincoln left Springfield for his inauguration, and a light rain was falling. From the platform of his car he delivered a farewell address to the neighbors and friends who had gathered. The illustration is from the original edition of "The Every-Day Life of Lincoln," by F. F. Browne.

To His care commending you, as I hope in your prayers you will commend me, I bid you an affectionate farewell."

I have referred to this brief speech as one that has "often and justly been quoted as one of the best examples of Lincoln's power to express thought and feeling in English sentences of rare and haunting quality." If we are to treasure it for its revelation of deep feeling, we may not be particular about its exact words and phrases. If at the same time, however, it is to be preserved as a literary specimen, we may well prefer to have Lincoln's own report as he afterwards phrased it. Mr. Nicolay, who was with him as his private secretary, tells us that immediately after the train started from Springfield, Lincoln set down with his own hand a part of the speech (as he remembered it) and dictated the remainder to Nicolay himself. As the listening correspondents reported the speech and sent it to their newspapers, there are differences in virtually every sentence. Mr. Barrett says that there were published a "score of variants"; and he gives a version quite different from that of Mr. Nicolay, asserting that his is an accurate, verbatim report of the speech as delivered. He does not, however, give us his authority for the assertion.

A number of versions which are at hand as these sentences are written differ materially from one another. No two are the same. Some of them include entire sentences that are not present in others. Yet each of them taken alone would seem authentic; and the same spirit is present in them all. Probably the words that the newspaper men took down as Lincoln was speaking bring us fairly close to his extemporaneous speech. I prefer to print the Nicolay report, because as it stands it is Lincoln's own memorandum word for word. This is the view that was accepted by his fellow-citizens of Springfield in the year 1918, when they erected a new Lincoln statue. Upon the great block of granite at the back of this bronze statue, the farewell speech is deeply carved in capital letters; and the version used is that which Mr. Nicolay has given us in phrases that we know to have been of Lincoln's own composition. A photograph of the statue is reproduced on page 203 of the companion volume of the present work.

AN ANXIOUS MAMMA AND A FRACTIOUS CHILD

THE INFANT SOUTHERN REPUBLIC: "Boo hoo-hoo! I want Fort Sumter."
MRS. BUCHANAN: "Now, Baby, you can't have it. You've got two or three forts and a number of ships and arsenals already; and you won't be allowed to keep even them, for here comes Honest Old Abe to take them all away from you!"

From the *Phunny Phellow*, New York.

MR. LINCOLN ADDRESSES THE MEMBERS OF THE OHIO
LEGISLATURE AND THEIR GUESTS

The official reception at Columbus by Governor Dennison and both Houses of the Legislature was
remarkable for its enthusiasm and its non-partisan character. The drawing reproduced above was
one of many by the special artist for *Leslie's,* several of which are presented in this chapter.

CHAPTER XXVI

A Triumphal Tour, with Its Anti-Climax

Lincoln accepts official invitations, and enters upon a two-weeks' pil-
grimage—He breaks long silence, minimizing public danger—Honored
as guest in many States—Enters Washington secretly by night

THERE ARE NO conventional rules
providing for the escort of Presidents-
elect to the nation's capital. They may
take the oath of office at their own homes if
they like, and travel to Washington at their
convenience. But Congress provides for a
ceremonial installation as each new President enters upon his duties, and no President-
elect would intentionally disregard the customs that have given dignity and character to
the celebration of Inauguration Day.

George Washington journeyed from Mount
Vernon to New York in 1789 through
admiring throngs of his fellow-citizens as he
passed from Virginia to Maryland and thence
across Delaware and New Jersey. Thomas
Jefferson chose to assume a rôle of the utmost
republican simplicity. Andrew Jackson was

in mourning for his wife who had recently
died; but his journey from Nashville to Washington was attended by public enthusiasm and
by official welcomes from point to point that
he did not seek to avoid. He traveled by
steamboat from Louisville up the Ohio with
stops *en route,* as at Cincinnati, for example.
He proceeded overland from Pittsburgh,
declining the escort of a great cavalcade that
had been planned. In short, the successors of
Washington have one after another found
their own way to the capital, and they have,
as a rule, carefully maintained the status of
private citizenship until inaugurated.

Abraham Lincoln's journey to Washington
stands out as altogether exceptional. It was
leisurely, and it took on official aspects.
Leaving Springfield early in the morning of

241

Monday, February 11th, Lincoln had three weeks in which to dispose of his time before taking up his residence in the White House. From his own State of Illinois, he was to pass through Indiana, Ohio, Pennsylvania, New York, New Jersey, Delaware and Maryland before reaching the District of Columbia. He had received official invitations from the Legislatures and Governors of all these States (Delaware and Maryland excepted), and also from Massachusetts, to break journey and attend welcoming receptions. It was not feasible to go as far out of the way as Boston; but the other invitations were all duly accepted. No other President-elect, while on his way to the nation's capital, has ever thus been officially received and honored, although most of the Presidents have while in office accepted attentions from State governments.

Nothing could have been more remote from Lincoln's thought or preference than the desire to be seen and applauded by multitudes, or flattered by State officials. But he had owed his nomination to the support of several of these States, especially Indiana and Pennsylvania; and all of them had given him their electoral votes, the State of New York having turned the scales and "made his calling and election sure." The time was one of political confusion and intense anxiety. Buchanan was trying in vain to find ways to cope with conditions over which he had lost all control, and he had retained not the slightest vestige of influence. The Peace Conference was debating Constitutional amendments with a view to saving the Union. But such amendments would have required months if not years for adoption, and meanwhile the Union was already dissolved. To recall dates heretofore presented, South Carolina had seceded on November 17th; Mississippi, January 9th; Florida, January 10th; Alabama, January 11th; Georgia, January 19th; Louisiana, January 25th, and Texas, February 1st.

Lincoln had learned by long experience that he could rely upon personal intercourse to bring him additional friends and support. He had the gift of inspiring confidence. He could count upon the new Northwest and upon New England; and he was now especially anxious to strengthen the support that had come to him on election day in Ohio, Pennsylvania and New York, as head of the Republican ticket. He had been elected as representing a cause; he now wished to be known personally. It was a remarkable tour, well planned for its purpose of strengthening faith in the intelligence, calmness and wisdom of the man upon whom the fate of the nation was henceforth so greatly to depend.

There was, then, nothing hidden or obscure about the Lincoln pilgrimage of February, except for its very last stage. It opened impressively with the scene that I have described at the end of the preceding chapter. It continued in a blaze of publicity, with newspaper reporters and the special artists of illustrated weeklies constantly present, besides groups of local officials, politicians and friends who joined the Lincoln train and accompanied the party from point to point. At the very end there was rumor of trouble in Baltimore, and plans were accordingly changed with the utmost secrecy. Separating himself from his larger party and accompanied only by a single friend he took an evening train from Harrisburg to Philadelphia, made connection with the night train from New York, and arrived at Washington at six o'clock Saturday morning, the twenty-third, where he was met by Senator Seward and the Hon. Elihu B. Washburne, and taken to Willard's Hotel. I shall revert in a later paragraph to this much discussed "anti-climax"—the secret and mysterious ending of a journey that for almost two weeks had out-rivalled in publicity the simultaneous scenes in Washington and the doings of the new Confederate Government at Montgomery.

Lincoln was carrying with him, in a personal hand-bag, the preliminary draft of his inaugural address. He meant to make it tell impressively for conciliation. He knew that both North and South were dangerously affected by what we would term "mob mania." His newspapers acquainted him with Southern as well as Northern speeches and activities. The New York illustrated weeklies, whose correspondents and illustrators were with him, also had other correspondents and illustrators

Kelloggs & Thayer 144 Fulton St, N.Y.   E.B.& E.C. Kellogg 130 Main St. Hartford Conn.   D. Needham 223 Main St. Buffalo

WASHINGTON'S RECEPTION BY THE LADIES AT TRENTON. N. J. APRIL 1789.

ON HIS WAY TO NEW-YORK TO BE. INAUGURATED FIRST PRESIDENT OF THE UNITED STATES.

The new government machinery moved slowly when the First Congress met. Washington was not officially notified until the middle of April, and on the 16th he set out for New York, arriving in time to be inaugurated on the 30th. Referring to his journey from Mount Vernon as "one long ovation," Mr. Muzzey says: "The streets were strewn with flowers. Triumphal arches, dinners, speeches, cheers and songs gave him the grateful assurance that his inestimable services in war and peace were appreciated by his countrymen." The lithographed scene here reproduced, while drawn many years later, suggests the enthusiasm with which Washington was greeted on his entire journey.

at Charleston, Montgomery, New Orleans, and elsewhere in the South. Secession had not interrupted the interchange of telegraphic news. Just as Lincoln, on his train, was reading the words of Davis, Toombs, Stephens, Benjamin and other secession leaders, even so, as he was fully aware, these same men in their Southern papers were reading every morning the reports of his brief speeches, and the accounts of his enthusiastic receptions.

It was this consciousness on his part that made Lincoln careful not to add fuel to the flames. Many of his more radical friends and supporters in the North were disappointed with his speeches. He had been silent on public questions for almost a year. Meanwhile, Southern defiance and actual secession had

changed the tone and temper of the North. The Douglas Democrats and the Bell Unionists were now almost, if not quite, as angry and outspoken as the more extreme leaders of Lincoln's own party. The Lincoln-Douglas debates and the Cooper Union speech were remote. They seemed to the militant anti-secession men of 1861 to belong to an early period of mild academic exchange of civilities.

But Lincoln studiously avoided the Jacksonian tone of challenge and of autocratic assertion. Undoubtedly his soothing words to some extent belied his feelings. If soft answers could help to check precipitate action in North Carolina, Tennessee, Virginia and Missouri, he meant to withhold the note of coercion that would only have helped Mr. Davis's agents to win more States. It was undoubtedly his object to have the South realize the overwhelming strength of Union sentiment in the States through which he passed. At the same time he was letting the Border Slave States know that he himself was not excited, that he regarded secession as artificial and temporary, and that he felt an equal concern for the welfare of the American people in all parts of the land. To have been denunciatory might have thrilled local audiences; but it would have shown that Lincoln had lost sight of the fact that as Chief Executive he meant first of all to announce conciliatory policies. Blustering words more often go with weakness and lack of self-restraint than with strength and wise plans of action.

The day trip across Illinois and Indiana brought cheering crowds to every station, with greetings from the rear platform, but no important speeches until Indianapolis was reached. Oliver P.

"LINCOLN'S COMING!"

Morton, one of the great public characters of the ensuing war period, was Governor of Indiana. The reception was on an elaborate scale, quite beyond anything in the previous history of the Indiana capital. There were no differing reports of Lincoln's principal speech at Indianapolis, because it had been carefully written out. His informal remarks replying to Governor Morton's welcome emphasized the point that the problems then before the country were those of the people rather than of the President. "If the Union of these States and the liberties of this people shall be lost, it is but little to any one man of fifty-two years of age, but a great deal to the thirty millions of people who inhabit these United States, and to their posterity in all coming time . . . I appeal to you again to constantly bear in mind that not with politicians, not with Presidents, not with office-seekers, but with you, is the question, Shall the Union and shall the liberties of this country be preserved to the latest generations?"

In the prepared address he dwelt upon the meaning of the words "coercion and invasion." "Would the marching of an army into South Carolina," he asked, "without the consent of her people, and with hostile intent towards them, be 'invasion'? I certainly think it would; and it would be 'coercion' also if the South Carolinians were forced to submit. But if the United States should merely hold and retake its own forts and other property, and collect the duties on foreign importations, or even withhold the mails from places where they were habitually violated, would any or all of these be 'invasion' or 'coercion'?" This was regarded as foreshadowing the policy upon which Lincoln would act as President. The speech was brief, and he ended it by asking this question: "By the way, in what consists the special sacredness of a State?" He explained that he was not questioning the position of the States as provided by the Constitution, and then proceeded as follows: "I speak of that assumed primary right of a State to rule all which is less than itself, and ruin all which is larger than itself." He compared States with counties, and asked why, if one should be equal in population and extent to the other, it could not claim equality of rights.

He ended with these words: "What mysterious right to play tyrant is conferred on a district of country with its people, by merely calling it a State? Fellow citizens, I am not asserting anything; I am merely asking questions for you to consider." This, of course, was to shock the medieval mentality of those who regarded "States rights" as issues to be solved by abstract reasoning. Lincoln, with his modern mind, was merely asking people to learn to think in terms of history and political science.

Spending the night at Indianapolis, Mr. Lincoln and his party renewed their journey on the morning of his birthday, February 12th, arriving at Cincinnati in the afternoon, where he was escorted through the streets by a civic and military parade, and where he spoke from the balcony of the Burnet House to a great throng who disregarded the harsh February weather. Referring to his Cincinnati speech of 1859, when he had addressed himself particularly to the Kentuckians, he took occasion again to give them a direct message of friendly regard and reassurance.

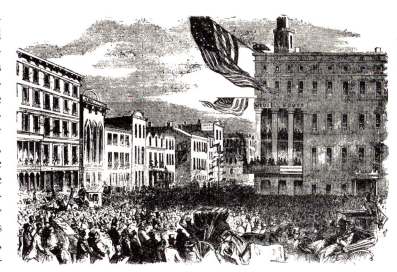

THE PRESIDENT-ELECT ADDRESSES THE PEOPLE OF CLEVELAND
From the balcony of the Weddell House, February 15, 1861.

Certain informal speeches, not on the schedule, were remarkable for their high spirit as well as their tact. A five-hour ride on the following day brought him to the State capital, Columbus, early in the afternoon, where he was officially received by the Governor and the Legislature.

At Columbus he defended himself from the charge of having been unduly silent in a time of doubt and anxiety. He had thought it best to have gained a view of the whole field before expressing himself too freely. He took the philosophical position that nothing thus far had happened which was irreparable or which had caused much actual damage. He was criticised for seeming in this speech to come short of understanding the seriousness of the crisis; but it was precisely because he understood it so well that he was seeking to keep from making matters worse by sounding alarms and changing foreboding into panic.

He spoke at Steubenville with particular reference to Virginians who were living on the opposite side of the Ohio River. He thought the devotion to the Constitution equally great on both sides; but he also held that where there were differences of opinion the majority must rule. He had been chosen by the voice of the majority, and the time to condemn him would occur after four years, at the next election.

At Pittsburgh again he made an appeal to the Virginians. "If the great American people will only keep their temper on both sides of the line, the trouble will come to an end, and the question

ARRIVAL OF THE PRESIDENTIAL PARTY AT BUFFALO
From Saturday evening until Monday morning Mr. Lincoln rested at Buffalo, staying at the American Hotel, at the right in the picture.

which now distracts the country will be settled just as surely as all other difficulties of like character which have originated in this government have been adjusted. Let the people on both sides keep their self-possession, and just as other clouds have cleared away in due time, so will this, and this great nation will continue to prosper as heretofore." If these mild phrases sounded somewhat like the soothing platitudes that Buchanan had been uttering, Lincoln made it plain that he was not yet ready to speak "fully and definitely." "My intention," he declared, "is to give this subject all the consideration which I possibly can. . . . so that when I do speak, I may be as nearly right as possible." The Morrill tariff bill was pending, and Mr. Lincoln spoke favorably to Pittsburgh men of the protective policy, and favored a measure "looking to all the varied interests of the common country, so that when the time for action arrives adequate protection shall be extended to the coal and iron of Pennsylvania and the corn of Illinois."

The Lincoln train arrived at Buffalo Saturday evening, where the President-elect was received by a former President, Millard Fillmore, heading a committee of leading citizens.

In a speech replying to Mayor Bemis, Mr. Lincoln referred to the "fortunate and agreeable journey" of the past week, with "nothing thus far to mar the trip." He had been met all along the way not merely by his own political supporters, but by the general population. This he thought was as it should be, the people honoring the office rather than the particular individual. "These demonstrations," he said, "are tendered to the country, to the institutions of the country, and to the perpetuity of the liberties of the country for which these institutions were made and created." As regards the particular situation (referring, of course, to the fact of secession), he deemed it proper to await developments and get all the light possible. He remained at Buffalo from Saturday until Monday morning.

As the journey proceeded, there was no loss of popular interest, and Lincoln seemed to grow and mature as a man destined for leadership. A year of quiet thought had prepared him for these days of cautious expression and of valuable contacts with men whose support was to be necessary in the months to come. He had been in conference, the very day before leaving Illinois, with Governor Bross of that State. The next day he was not merely meeting throngs in Indiana and making brief speeches, but was in private conferences with Governor Morton and others. Such experiences at Cincinnati, Columbus and Cleveland gave him a thorough understanding of the sentiment and the politics of Ohio.

Proceeding on Monday to Albany, he recognized the fact that he was at the most influential of the Eastern State capitals; and his addresses in response to the welcoming words of Governor Morgan, and in the legislative halls of the old State House, were frank, dignified and reassuring. He justified parties as an instrument of popular self-government, but held that the man elected by the majority belonged,

MR. LINCOLN MAKES A SPEECH

"He said he jest cum out to see and be seen, and didn't intend to blab anything about public affairs."

The illustration is from a book entitled "The Letters of Major Jack Downing," a satiric treatment of Lincoln by Charles A. Davis, modeled upon an earlier satire on Andrew Jackson with the same title.

LINCOLN'S ARRIVAL AT A FORMER TERMINAL OF THE HUDSON RIVER
RAILROAD IN NEW YORK

The illustration presents a scene at the railroad station when Lincoln's special train was arriving and
he was about to be escorted through the streets in an open carriage drawn by six horses, and accompanied by the city officials with parading police and civic bodies.

while in office, not to a party, but to the whole country. Speaking before the Legislature he said: "It is true that, while I hold myself, without mock-modesty, the humblest of all the individuals who have ever been elected President of the United States, I yet have a more difficult task to perform than any of them has ever encountered. You have here generously tendered me the support, the united support, of the great Empire State. For this, in behalf of the nation—in behalf of the present and the future of the nation—in behalf of the cause of civil liberty in all time to come—I most gratefully thank you. I do not propose now to enter upon any expression as to the particular line of policy to be adopted with reference to the difficulties that stand before us in the opening of the incoming Administration. I deem that it is just to the country, to myself, to you, that I should see everything, hear everything, and have every light that can possibly be brought within my reach to aid me before I shall speak officially, in order that, when I do speak, I may have the best possible means of taking correct and true ground. For this reason, I do not now announce anything in the way of policy for the new Administration. When the time comes, according to the custom of Government, I shall speak, and speak as well as I am able for the good of the present and of the future of this country—for the good of the North and of the South—for the

good of one and of the other, and of all sections."

I have made this somewhat extended quotation in order to give a clear idea of the non-committal character of the numerous speeches, perhaps forty or fifty in all, that Mr. Lincoln made on his way to Washington. At another time, these brief addresses might have seemed lacking in flavor and force. But their non-partisan tone, their broad patriotism, their faith in the future of America, were well suited to the circumstances, and it is to be remembered that Lincoln's unusual and strikingly interesting personality gave a living quality to his utterances that is not to be found in the printed words.

A local individual then of wide celebrity, Fernando Wood, was Mayor of New York City. He was a factional Democratic leader, sometimes in Tammany favor and sometimes out of it, and he had been conspicuous among the New York groups who attended the Charleston convention. Though not in sympathy with Lincoln's views, he made every effort to receive the President-elect with metropolitan hospitality. City officials escorted the Lincoln party from Albany southward. Crowds were gathered everywhere at the stations along the Hudson River Railroad, and the arrival at the old terminal of the railway at Thirtieth Street and Eleventh Avenue was the beginning of a typical demonstration. Places of business were closed for a day. This great Democratic town, with an open-mindedness and a friendliness that are its tradition, gave greeting to the man whose Presidential Electors it had tried so hard to beat in November.

This is the story of Abraham Lincoln, and not that of a lesser man like Fernando Wood. It is enough to say that the Mayor of New York was a picturesque character, with a bold imagination and with the courage to speak his mind and act on his own convictions. It was only a few months later that he was proposing the withdrawal of New York City from the Union, and its establishment as a free port of entry and a neutral in the war between the North and South. In his address of welcome to Mr. Lincoln he reminded the President-elect of his grave responsibilities in the following terms: "Coming into office with a dismembered government to reconstruct, and a disconnected and hostile people to reconcile, it will require a high patriotism and an elevated comprehension of the whole country and its varied interests, opinions, and prejudices to so conduct public affairs as to bring it back again to its former harmonious, consolidated and prosperous condition." He went on to speak

for New York City as deeply afflicted, with her material interests paralyzed and her commercial greatness endangered.

Mr. Lincoln did not try to comfort or reassure Fernando Wood. But as regards the difficulties to which the Mayor had referred and "of which your Honor has thought fit to speak so becomingly and so justly, as I suppose, I can only say that I agree in the sentiments expressed." He said that he hoped to save the ship, and also to save the cargo. In short, his reply to the Mayor was perfect in tone, temper and sentiment.

Local readers will find in no book an explicit account of Mr. Lincoln's stay in New York, and may like to know that he was escorted to the old Astor House at City Hall Park by the Common Council riding in carriages, proceeding down Ninth Avenue, to Twenty-third Street, through to Fifth Avenue, and from Fourteenth Street down Broadway to the hotel. The spectacle imitated somewhat the recent pageants in honor of the Prince of Wales and the Japanese delegation. At an ovation given by Republican clubs that evening, Lincoln asked to be allowed to make excuses for avoiding discourse upon the issues of the day. He admitted that he might easily talk upon the matters that were in the public mind, and added, "I am brought before you now to make a speech, while you all approve, more than anything else, that I have been keeping silence." He intimated plainly that he was reserving his utterance for Inauguration Day.

It was on Wednesday, the twentieth, that his reception occurred at the City Hall, and on the following morning he went to Trenton, New Jersey, where he spoke briefly before each branch of the Legislature. It was in one of these addresses that he made the remark that was most widely noted as indicative of his inner state of mind. "I

MR. LINCOLN AT THE CITY HALL IN NEW YORK
Fernando Wood, Mayor of the city, is shown making a speech of welcome to the distinguished guest.

ARRIVAL OF MR. LINCOLN AT THE ASTOR HOUSE, NEW YORK
The trees of City Hall Park are seen at the right. Here the President-elect remained two nights
and the intervening day.

shall endeavor to take the ground," he said, "I deem most just to the North, the East, the West, the South, and the whole country. I take it, I hope, in good temper, certainly in no malice toward any section. I shall do all that may be in my power to promote a peaceful settlement of all our difficulties. The man does not live who is more devoted to peace than I am—none who would do more to preserve it; *but it may be necessary to put the foot down firmly.*" The applause that followed this remark was so prolonged that it brought the speech to an end, except for a sentence or two in conclusion.

In the State Senate at Trenton, he spoke in a charming way of the intense interest he had felt as a child in reading in Weems's "Life of Washington" the story of the crossing of the Delaware by Washington and his troops. "Boy even though I was," he said, "I recollect thinking then that there must have been something more than common that those men struggled for." It was "something more than national independence—something that held out a great promise to all the people of the world in all time to come." And it was his hope that he might be "an humble instrument in the hands of the Almighty, and of this his almost chosen people, for perpetuating the object of that great struggle."

Abraham Lincoln was about to assume the most difficult and at the same time the most authoritative position of any governmental official in the world. His progress from point to point, as he was making these public appearances as President-elect, had the double purpose of having the public know him as never before, while he himself was sensing public opinion in the most populous and influential portion of the country. When he left Springfield on the 11th of February he was still for most people the rising Illinois attorney, with a talent for politics, and a bias against slavery, who had been picked as the compromise candidate at Chicago, largely because, being little known, he was without enemies. When he arrived at Philadelphia to take part on Washington's Birthday in the celebration at Independence Hall, he had so managed the tour as to have emerged entirely from obscurity. He had made countless friends. If he had once been too inconspicuous to have aroused personal enmity, he was still without enemies, for the opposite reason that he had been able to become well-known without giving offense.

The population of Philadelphia, unlike that of New York City, was predominantly Republican in the election of 1860. I shall not quote from speeches of welcome and fitting replies, as Lincoln was greeted with enthusiasm after leaving Trenton. On the following morning, Friday, the twenty-second, he raised the flag over Independence Hall, and, being called upon unexpectedly to speak, paid a fine tribute to the spirit of the Revolution, saying: "I have never had a feeling, politically, that did not spring from the sentiments embodied in the Declaration of Independence." It was upon this principle that the country must now be saved. "But if this country cannot be saved without giving up that principle [of liberty] I was about to say I would rather be assassinated on this spot than surrender it."

After these ceremonies, which evoked two or three brief speeches from Mr. Lincoln, the journey was quickly made to Harrisburg, where the Legislature was waiting to receive the President-elect. State troops were in evidence, and this gave Lincoln the opportunity to express the hope that it would never become their duty to shed fraternal blood. "I promise," he said, "that so far as I may have wisdom to direct, if so painful a result shall in any wise be brought about, it shall be through no fault of mine."

After a busy day at the capital of Pennsylvania, with its citizens thronging to his hotel, the wearied subject of so much public attention was preparing for a good night's rest, in order to complete his

pilgrimage on the following day. His train was to leave Harrisburg Saturday morning, arriving at noon in Baltimore, where the Republican clubs were expecting to make a demonstration in his honor, in spite of the fact that the unfriendly Democratic clubs were much more numerous in membership. After this stop at Baltimore, he was to proceed to Washington early Saturday evening.

His plans were changed, however, and he arrived at Washington unexpectedly and quite secretly at six o'clock Saturday morning. There was much conjecture about the reasons, and it was rumored that he had been summoned to confer with members of the Peace Convention then in session, or for some other kind of political conference.

In point of fact he had received warnings from two different sources that there was danger of trouble in Baltimore, and that there was a plot to do him bodily harm. Without his previous knowledge some of his friends had employed Allan Pinkerton, who afterwards became the most famous of our secret service men, to look into rumors that seemed to indicate a plot with its center at Baltimore. From another standpoint, General Scott and army officers had been planning for a safe arrival and a quiet inauguration week.

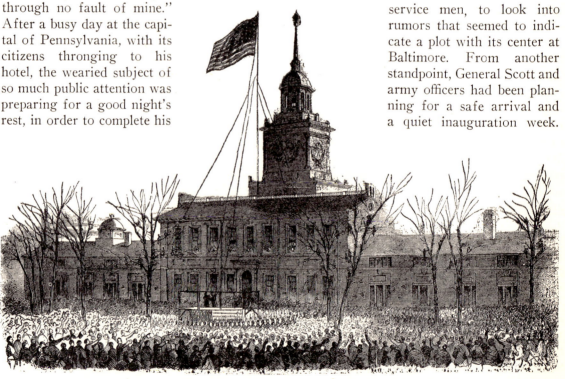

RAISING THE STARS AND STRIPES OVER INDEPENDENCE HALL IN PHILADELPHIA
It was Washington's Birthday, and the citizens were celebrating the past and the present at the same time. Mr. Lincoln himself pulls the rope that hoists the flag to its place.

THE FAMOUS EPISODE OF THE PASSAGE THROUGH BALTIMORE

Thomas Nast was with the presidential party after it left New York, to make sketches of inauguration scenes for the *Illustrated News*. He drew an accurate picture of the scene at Camden Station
in Baltimore; but when his sketch arrived in the editorial rooms of the paper, it was altered to
accord with a story then widely accepted. Text accompanying the drawing referred to Mr. Lincoln's
"rapid flight" during the night, wearing "a Scotch cap and heavy military cloak."

They had advised Senator Seward that it
would not be well for Mr. Lincoln to make the
expected stop at Baltimore. Mr. Pinkerton
had reported to Mr. Felton, president of the
railroad, and to Mr. Judd, who was traveling
in the presidential party. While Mr. Felton
and Mr. Judd were making plans for a night
trip to Washington, an additional warning
came from Senator Seward. General Scott
and Colonel Stone had made an investigation,
quite independently of that of Allan Pinkerton. They had reported to Seward, and he had
sent a note to Lincoln by his son, Frederick W.
Seward, who arrived at Harrisburg early Friday evening, and conferred with Mr. Lincoln.

A readable account of this experience is
contained in the book "Reminiscences of a
Wartime Statesman and Diplomat, 1830-1915,
by Frederick W. Seward." The younger
Seward was then his father's secretary, and
soon afterwards became Assistant Secretary
of State. It is needless to repeat the details of
the plan by which Mr. Lincoln, accompanied

solely by his friend, Colonel Ward H. Lamon,
was taken by special train to Philadelphia,
where the two were transferred to the regular
night train from New York to Washington.

The secession movement had many sympathizers in the District of Columbia, and in the
adjacent States of Maryland and Virginia. At
that time there were rowdy elements in Baltimore, who were, within a few weeks, to show
their capacity for street violence when a Massachusetts regiment passed through their city.

All things considered, it was wise and pru-
dent for Mr. Lincoln not to stop at Baltimore.
He had received no official invitations from
the Governor or the Mayor, and was breaking
no very definite engagements. There were no
plots against his life that had the connivance
of any men in official position, or of any citizens of prominence, no matter how strong
might have been their Southern sympathies.

It was indicative of the peculiar state of
opinion at that time that important periodicals
should have published cartoons holding up

THE MacLINCOLN HARRISBURG
HIGHLAND FLING

Mr. Lincoln to ridicule for this change of his
plans, involving the night journey. The persistent story that he traveled in disguise was
incorrect, though not intentionally so. It is
probably true that he wore a Scotch cap as a
matter of comfort on the train, and that, in
accord with what was an almost universal
custom of that day among gentlemen, he
threw a plaid shawl across his shoulders in
the chill of the evening. The incident has had
undue importance in some of the biographies
of Lincoln; but since in this work I am especially emphasizing the manner in which current opinion was expressed by the cartoonists,
it must claim some prominence.

It may be well to make note of the personages who were traveling as members of
the presidential party. With Mr. Lincoln were
Mrs. Lincoln and their three sons, Robert T.,
William and Thomas. Lockwood Todd represented Mrs. Lincoln's family, and Dr. W. S.

Wallace was friend and physician. John G.
Nicolay and John Hay were secretaries. Hon.
N. B. Judd and Hon. David Davis were
political intimates. Colonel E. V. Sumner and
Major David Hunter, Captain George W.
Hazard and Captain John Pope were military
representatives. Colonel Ward H. Lamon was
a former partner and a Springfield friend,
while Colonel E. E. Ellsworth of Chicago was
a personal favorite. J. M. Burgess, George C.
Latham, W. S. Wood, and B. Forbes were in
general attendance. To these original members of the group there were added from time
to time friends and officials who traveled for
portions of the way, not to mention representatives of the press.

In the published letters and reminiscences
of various people are exceedingly interesting
side-lights on this famous Lincoln pilgrimage.
I cannot take space to mention them, but readers will have no difficulty in discovering them
with the help of public librarians. When Mr.
Lincoln and Mr. Lamon left the party at
Harrisburg, there were additions to the main
body which followed on
Saturday morning. A
veteran Pennsylvania
Republican, Thomas
Williams, had been
prominent in the festivi-
ties at Harrisburg. His
two daughters had met
Mrs. Lincoln and she
had asked him to allow
them to accompany her
to Washington. Mr.
Williams and these
young ladies remained
as Mr. Lincoln's per-
sonal guests during the
following days and un-
til after inauguration.
Both of the young
ladies were included in
the opening quadrille at
the Inauguration Ball.
Mr. Seward had met
Mrs. Lincoln at the
Washington station, and
had taken her and the

THE NEW
PRESIDENT

Vanity Fair adds that this
is "a fugitive sketch."
Both cartoons on this
page are from that
periodical.

THE PASSAGE THROUGH BALTIMORE

The cartoon is by Adalbert Volck, himself a resident of Baltimore. It accepts the story of the Scotch cap, and adds the disguise of a freight car. Volck published a portfolio of his copper-plate engravings during the War, giving it a false London imprint and the signature of "V. Blada" (his own name, reversed). He did this to avoid detection and confiscation of the plates by Federal authorities.

Misses Williams in his carriage to the hotel where Mr. Lincoln had been established since morning. Glimpses of an intimate kind are given in "The Life and Speeches of Thomas Williams." Passing through Baltimore was not a wholly pleasant experience for the main party. The Williams girls thought young "Bob" Lincoln quite courageous, when he presented himself on the platform at Baltimore, answering the call of unfriendly-looking crowds. Mr. Nicolay writes of the Baltimore episode with intimate knowledge.

(1.) THE ALARM

"On Thursday night Mr. Lincoln was aroused, and informed that a stranger desired to see him on a matter of life and death. * * * A conversation elicited the fact that an organized body of men had determined that Mr. Lincoln should never leave Baltimore alive. * * * Statesmen laid the plan and bankers indorsed it."

(2.) THE COUNCIL

"Mr. Lincoln did not want to yield, and his friends cried with indignation. But they insisted, and he left."

(3.) THE SPECIAL TRAIN

"He wore a Scotch plaid cap and a very long military cloak, so that he was entirely unrecognizable."

(4.) THE OLD COMPLAINT

"Mr. Lincoln, accompanied by Mr. Seward, paid his respects to President Buchanan."

THE FLIGHT OF ABRAHAM
(As Reported by a Modern Paper)

This series of cartoons appeared in *Harper's Weekly* at the very moment of Lincoln's inauguration. The paper enjoyed a large circulation, widely distributed. The contrast between the secret trip through Baltimore, and the public reception that had been planned, was a subject of anxious comment throughout the country.

THE SUDDEN APPEARANCE OF MR. LINCOLN
"And the Awful Consternation of the Old Party
at the White House."

Mr. Seward, at the left, plays the part of Chief Magician, producing Mr.
Lincoln out of a cloud of smoke. The retiring President, Mr. Buchanan, is
described by the *Illustrated News* as "the old party at the White House."

CHAPTER XXVII

Scenes of a Well-Ordered Inauguration

*Each President-elect arrives at Washington as he will—Lincoln's week
of courtesies and conferences—Notes on men and manners—Two
inaugural addresses: one remembered, one forgotten*

THOSE WRITERS ABOUT Lincoln whose method is that of psycho-analysis are not pleased with the Illinois statesman as he revealed himself on his way to Washington after almost a year of silence. For the purposes of the dramatic poet, Lincoln at this stage is negligible. One of the ablest of his biographical interpreters says that "he entered this period a literary man who had been elevated almost by accident to the position of a leader in politics. After many blunders, after doubt, hesitation and pain, he came forth from his stern ordeal a powerful man of action."

The same writer, further developing his thought, remarks: "The very power that had hitherto been the making of him—the literary power, revealing to men in wonderfully convincing form the ideas which they felt within them but could not utter—this had deserted him. Explain the psychology of it any way you will, there is the fact! The speeches Lincoln made on the way to Washington during the latter part of February were appallingly unlike himself. His mind had suddenly fallen dumb. He had nothing to say. The gloom, the desolation that had penetrated his soul, somehow, for the moment, made him commonplace. When he talked—as convention required him to do at all his stopping places—his words were but faint echoes of the great political exponent he once had been."

Nobody could have answered this kind of comment, which indeed prevailed extensively at the moment in certain circles, as well as Lincoln himself. The biographical critic has access to printed material in abundance; but in the pleasant warmth and comfort of the library alcove he may not make proper allowance for the fact that the subject of his study was living and speaking in the out-of-door weather of actual political turmoil. Lincoln's reply would have been to the effect that the Cooper Union speech, delivered exactly one year earlier, had been adapted to the occasion and the times. He would have added that the dozens of brief talks on his way to Washington were similarly intended to meet the exigencies of a situation that had become completely changed, both as regards the state of the country, and also in respect to his own responsibilities.

In all the records of political speech-making, it would be difficult to find more appropriate or tactful utterances than those of the President-elect in February, 1861. He could not have formulated policies, because he had not been put in the position of a dictator or an absolute ruler. He, at least, did not forget that thousands of other people besides himself were taking part in the current business of making American history. His newspapers kept him informed, day by day, as he made his progress from city to city. Momentous things were happening, in which Lincoln was having no direct or immediate part.

On Washington's Birthday, with Lincoln raising the flag over Independence Hall at Philadelphia early in the morning, and addressing the Legislature at Harrisburg later in the day, there was also a Washington's Birthday parade in the streets of the national capital, as elsewhere throughout the country. President Buchanan had been taken to task by a former President, John Tyler, for allowing federal troops to participate in the celebration. Mr. Tyler had come to Washington as head of the Virginia delegation in the Peace

OFFICE SEEKERS AT WASHINGTON DURING THE INAUGURATION
"These gentlemen, who are ready, like good patriots, to serve their country, are all *original Lincoln men*. It is true that they voted for Pierce and Buchanan; but that was a deep game to secure the election of Lincoln."

From *Harper's Weekly*, March, 1861.

THE PEACE CONVENTION IN SESSION AT WASHINGTON
Delegates were present from twenty-one States, with John Tyler of Virginia, former President of the United States, serving as chairman. The convention was in session from February 4 until February 27, 1861, when it adopted and referred to Congress a proposed Constitutional amendment. The delegates, in a body, called upon President-elect Lincoln at his hotel.

Convention that was then meeting. As presiding officer of that important body he was not hesitating to assume a tone more sharply authoritative than was becoming even in a Nestor of the Democratic party.

And so, on this February 22nd, President Buchanan was writing an explanatory and somewhat apologetic letter to Mr. Tyler, declaring that only two or three companies of Federal troops were appearing in the parade, along with local militia, and that this had been arranged without the President's knowledge, and with no purpose of provoking ill-feeling in the South by making a show of federal militarism.

When Lincoln, under Seward's escort, took possession of his rooms at Willard's Hotel, he found many distinguished members of the peace conference also lodged there, with

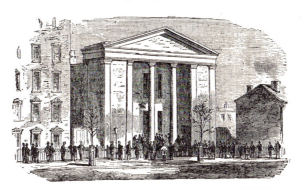

THE CONCERT HALL OF WILLARD'S HOTEL
Where the Peace Convention was holding its sessions when Mr. Lincoln reached Washington.

the conference itself holding its meeting in an annex of the hotel known as Willard's Hall. Early in the day, this being Saturday, February 23rd, Senator Seward took the President-elect to the White House to pay his respects to President Buchanan. Writers have been fond of setting these two men in contrast. Buchanan, during his last year, had seen himself constantly caricatured in the illustrated press, particularly by Stephens of *Vanity Fair*. He had been reprobated in the Northern newspapers, and in recent weeks he had been ferociously assailed in the Southern press because of his repudiation of the South Carolina commissioners. But Lincoln was also the victim of ridicule and belittling caricatures; and such attacks upon him during the year to come were to be even more unsparing than those that Buchanan had encountered. Lincoln bore insult with similar lack of resentment.

In point of fact, with obvious differences conceded, the two men had many resemblances. In spirit both were modest, kindly and unselfish. In their manner toward others both were courteous and considerate. They were alike in the quality of patience; but both could show due dignity and could act firmly toward persons giving offense, when patience was no longer a virtue. Each of these two men saw the country as a whole, and was intensely patriotic. Both sought to avert civil war, Buchanan having even a keener realization than Lincoln of the disasters that must follow such a conflict.

On this very Saturday of Lincoln's call at the White House, Buchanan was sending a brief message to the House of Representatives concerning the seizure of the Branch Mint at New Orleans by secessionists. He explained that all the facts in possession of the Government had already been sent to the House by the Secretary of the Treasury. This is an

JEFFERSON DAVIS—AN INAUGURATION
PORTRAIT

This is not an idealized, emblematic drawing of Southern origin. It occupied the front page of a New York illustrated weekly, in the same issue which carried inside—though larger, it is true—a similar portrait of Abraham Lincoln. Davis was inaugurated as President of the Southern Confederacy on February 18, 1861, just two weeks before Lincoln entered the White House.

instance of the extraordinary affairs that were filling newspapers and occupying the attention of Congress as Lincoln was spending his last week as a private citizen, and preparing to relieve his predecessor of the load that was growing heavier every day. There has remained, it may be remarked parenthetically, a somewhat unfounded impression that Mr. Buchanan was in a broken, tottering state, mentally and physically impaired to the point of helplessness. But at this juncture he had written a letter to his friend James Gordon Bennett of the New York *Herald,* declaring that nothing in the situation had cost him an hour's sleep, and that he was neither despondent in mind nor broken in body. Buchanan was a man of placid and serene temperament, who has been unduly neglected by the psycho-analysts of our later school of writers about public characters.

On the following Friday, Mr. Buchanan sent a self-justifying message to the House of Representatives in answer to a resolution that had been passed some days earlier, calling upon him for information regarding the concentration of federal troops in the city of Washington. There had been wild rumors that secessionists in Washington, joined by sympathizers from Maryland and Virginia, were planning to seize public buildings, assume control of the city, and prevent the inauguration of Mr. Lincoln. An opposing set of rumors had spread across the country, with especial currency in the South, to the effect that General Scott, under direction of President Buchanan and the new Secretary of War, had been gathering available troops in readiness to put down mobs and uprisings, and to keep the peace on Inauguration Day.

Of all these things, Mr. Lincoln in his quarters at Willard's Hotel, was fully apprized. Mr. Buchanan reported that the total number of Federal troops at Washington, including infantry, cavalry and artillery amounted to 653 officers and men. This, he explained, was exclusive of a certain number of marines who were always regularly stationed at the Navy Yard. He spoke of the importance of the great aggregation of public property in Washington, and the need of protection in a

UNITED STATES ARTILLERY DRILLING NEAR THE WASHINGTON MONUMENT
The drawing was made by Thomas Nast, in the last days of the Buchanan administration. It shows
the Washington Monument in an unfinished state, as it remained from 1855 to 1877.

turbulent period. He also gave assurance that what had seemed a menacing situation some days earlier was no longer giving anxiety to the Administration. The message was one of dignity and spirit.

It is well to know that there was nothing offensive to the Buchanan Administration in Lincoln's presence at Washington, nor in anything said or done on his behalf at that time. Mr. Seward was in confidential relations with two or three members of the outgoing Cabinet, and such information as the War Department possessed regarding occurrences in the South was placed without limit at the disposal of the new Administration.

The reader who chooses to compare various accounts of Mr. Lincoln's lack of drawing-room manners—as disclosed by many incidents and episodes in the months of February and March, 1861—must fit these things into his picture of Lincoln in accordance with his own preferences. Those black gloves that he wore at the opera in New York are still precious to the writers whose theme is the "Soul of Lincoln." They are intent upon finding the essential greatness of their hero as something the more strange and mysterious because of the contrast afforded by all this accumulated testimony regarding his external uncouthness.

Mr. Lincoln was not, indeed, a fashion-plate; although the photographs show him to have been quite well enough dressed for the less artificial standards of later times. As for manners, they are the expression of the real man. Mr. Buchanan, who had been familiar with European courts, had no fault to find with Mr. Lincoln as a gentleman of courtesy. Senator Crittenden, who was at this moment the foremost figure in Washington, in his earnest and prophetic appeals for compromise on the basis of the work of the Peace Convention, could never have thought of his friend, Abraham Lincoln, as otherwise than a man always considerate and deferential. In the halls of Congress, where Mr. Lincoln was informally received during these days of waiting, he was conversing amiably with men of fastidious appearance and attractive personality like Vice-President Breckinridge, Senator Sumner, the Speaker of the House, and many others. To these gentlemen he was no mountebank, or grotesque figure obviously ill at ease, but rather, one of themselves—a typical Western public man, who had known Henry Clay, Daniel Webster, and John Quincy Adams, and who had his own memories of service in Congress.

Andrew Jackson, in 1829, had arrived at Washington on the day when the Electoral vote was counted, just three weeks before his inauguration. His hotel was thronged with office-seekers, and he was the center of attention, a lordly personage, with the self-confidence of a man who had won great victories as a Major-General, who had served in the Senate and other civil offices, and who had

THE CAPITOL ON INAUGURATION DAY

Wings were being added at each end of the original building, and the existing dome was being erected. These alterations were not completed until 1863. The illustration is from a wood-cut based upon a photograph.

been the potentate of a domain populated by humble folk accustomed to obey his slightest wish. In the White House was John Quincy Adams, without superior as an accomplished statesman and diplomat of international reputation. But Jackson held his court at the hotel; and never once approached the White House. Adams in turn ignored the man who had stood in the way of his coveted second term; and he vacated the presidential mansion one day ahead of time, to avoid contact with his successor. These two were men of vast experience, who would not have brooked criticism on the score of manners or personal conduct. Yet there are those who would prefer the gracious, modest and unselfish qualities of Lincoln and Buchanan. These two men were thinking little of themselves but much of the country's welfare.

Messrs. Nicolay and Hay, both of whom were present and in constant attendance as aides to Mr. Lincoln, speak of his visits "to the outgoing President and Cabinet, where Mr. Buchanan and his councillors received him with cordial politeness; to the two Houses of Congress, where he was enthusiastically welcomed by friends and somewhat sullenly greeted by opponents; and to the Supreme Court of the United States, whose venerable Chief and Associate Justices extended to him an affable recognition as the lawful successor in Constitutional rulership."

In an additional paragraph, these chroniclers give us a well-rounded statement of the official courtesies shown to Mr. Lincoln in returning his polite approaches: "In his own parlors, also, the President-elect received numerous demonstrations of respect. President Buchanan and his Cabinet officially returned his visit. The Peace Conference, embracing distinguished delegates from all the Free States and the Border Slave States, and headed by their Chairman, ex-President Tyler, waited upon him in a body, in pursuance of a formal and unanimous resolution. His presidential rivals, Douglas and Breckinridge, each made him a call of courtesy. The Mayor and the Municipal Council came in an official visit of welcome. Several delegations and many high functionaries repeated these ceremonial calls,

MR. LINCOLN PAYS A VISIT TO THE HOUSE OF REPRESENTATIVES

The reception, on February 25th, was quite informal. The President-elect entered the Senate
chamber first, accompanied by Mr. Seward, and later proceeded to the House. In both chambers
members of all parties came forward to greet him. The sketch we reproduce is by Thomas Nast.

which again were supplemented by numerous cordial invitations to private hospitality."

He was taking counsel with Republican leaders who were either in Congress or attending the Peace Conference, and was making final decisions about Cabinet appointments and other selections, no public notice of any of these choices having yet been made. Mr. Nicolay tells us that from the day of his arrival to the time of his inauguration, every moment of the day and many hours of the night were thus occupied. So far as we know, nothing in his plans and arrangements was changed by these conferences, but it was valuable to Mr. Lincoln to have reached the point where he could say, if he chose, that no Republican in the country was as widely informed, or as intimately acquainted with the opinions of other prominent men, as he was himself.

In the reminiscences of various writers we find incidents that help us to understand the situation at Washington in those perplexing days. One of these is an Ohio Congressman-elect from the Cleveland district, Albert Gallatin Riddle, an active Republican in the "Western Reserve," who had been one of Lincoln's companions on part of the eastward journey. He tells of the men whom he heard and met as the session of Congress was closing, with the seats of most of the men from the Slave States now vacant. "The Peace Congress," says Mr. Riddle, "originating with Virginia, and presided over by John Tyler—the "Tyler Too" of 1840—had done its work and gone. [The convention had adjourned on the twenty-seventh]. Its seven propositions were under debate in the Senate, and I heard upon them Douglas, Baker, Mason, Wade, Greene, and others . . . . The work of that body consisted of seven propositions to amend the Constitution in the interests of slavery, which already had a Confederacy of seven States, a President, a Congress, an Army, and a Capital of its own."

Mr. Riddle being a man of active mind, sets down for us some impressions of Washington as he saw it on this first visit. Since this was

GENERAL WINFIELD SCOTT

General Scott, anxious and responsible, was still in 1861 head of the American army, at the age of 75. Though a Virginian who had lived further South, he was intensely loyal to the Union. He retired in November, 1861, and died at West Point in 1866.

to be the scene of Lincoln's labors for the next four years, and a focus of intense interest for the whole civilized world, a few sentences from Mr. Riddle's "Recollections of War Times" may well be quoted. "The President's house, the little dingy State Department, set squat on the ground now occupied by the north wing of the Treasury building, the War and Navy on Seventeenth Street, the Post Office Department, and the Interior, were the only completed public edifices of the Capital. The Washington Monument, the Capitol and the Treasury building were melchancholy specimens of arrested development."

Many changes have been made in the Capitol building and its surroundings, and still others continue to be made. A description of the Capitol as it then was, and as the crowds saw it who were gathered from far and near on Inauguration Day, is pertinent. "The walls of the two wings of the Capitol had not been perfected and the little old jug-like dome of the old central structure still occupied its place, utterly lost in the expanse of the acres of roof that it could not dominate. The building was placed at the west margin of a table-land that sloped westward, facing the east, with the surface rising several feet in the distance of one hundred and fifty yards. This was a fenced square filled with a heavy growth of forest trees, mostly the short-lived Southern maple. The west approach was upon an earthen terrace, which sloped down into another timbered enclosure. North and South "A" Streets were then in place, and each was built up compactly on the sides facing the Capitol, with low, mean structures. Pennsylvania Avenue passed around the north wing of the Capitol on its eastern way, and all that open ground was covered with the remains of building stone, lumber, and timber, and loaded over at every place of access with the huge iron plates for the great Capitol dome doomed in the councils of the slavery hosts never to be set in place."

OUR PRESIDENTIAL MERRYMAN

"The Presidential party was engaged in a lively exchange of wit and humor. The President-elect was the merriest among the merry, and kept those around him in a continual roar."—Daily Paper.

From *Harper's Weekly*, March 2, 1861.

"Nothing more conclusively showed the pre-determined destruction of the Republic than this deliberate suspension of the completion of the Capitol, and of the Treasury building—then limited to the portion represented by the colonnade fronting Fifteenth Street. The Capitol was unfinished on the inside. All during the Thirty-seventh Congress the old hall of the House was a mere lumber room, unsightly and offensive."

Mr. Riddle called on the President-elect and found him holding an informal reception in an open hallway on the second floor. "He was in wonderful spirits, surrounded by twenty or thirty admiring adherents, standing at his full height, which, from his lack of breadth, always seemed exaggerated. His face was fairly radiant, his wit and humor at flood-tide. His marvelous faculty of improvising illustrated stories was at its best. They followed each other with great rapidity. In the midst of the flow, the majestic form of General Scott was seen grandly rising in the open stairway, steady and unswerving, as if solemnly lifted by noiseless machinery." Mr. Riddle refers to the magnificent uniform in which General Scott then shone, and tells us that it was the first meeting of these remarkable men since Mr. Lincoln's election. "The General advanced a stride and awaited the presentation by Colonel Sumner, who in undress uniform, made it in the simplest manner. It would do the drawing-room dudes of today good, with whom the gentlemanly art of bowing is a lost one, to have witnessed the profound grace of the old hero's acknowledgment of the presence of the President-elect, as he swept his instep with the golden plumes of his chapeau."

It is Mr. Riddle who tells us that on Sunday, the third, the day before inauguration,

THE MEMBERS OF PRESIDENT LINCOLN'S CABINET
Top row: Caleb B. Smith, Simon Cameron, Edward Bates. *Center*: Wm. H. Seward. *Bottom row*: Montgomery Blair, Gideon Welles, Salmon P. Chase.

Mr. Lincoln "gave a dinner to seven gentlemen, and they happened to be those whose names were sent to the Senate the next day." This paragraph has been quoted in an earlier chapter, on Lincoln's preliminary efforts to select his Cabinet. Although these were the men actually chosen, several of them, at least, had not been told the names of their colleagues. The seven were William H. Seward of New York, Secretary of State; Salmon P. Chase of Ohio, Secretary of the Treasury; Simon Cameron of Pennsylvania, Secretary of War; Montgomery Blair of Maryland, Postmaster-General, Gideon Welles of Connecticut, Secretary of the Navy; Caleb B. Smith of Indiana, Secretary of the Interior; Edward Bates of Missouri, Attorney-General.

Mr. Bates of Missouri represented a Slave State, but it had been thought best to avoid the charge of sectionalism by placing a Maryland man in the Cabinet. Montgomery Blair had been a prominent Democrat, while Henry

ABRAHAM LINCOLN IN 1861
From a photograph made at Springfield, Illinois, before the President-elect
started on his journey to Washington.

MR. LINCOLN ON HIS WAY TO THE CAPITOL, TO BE INAUGURATED
He is saluting the crowds along Pennsylvania Avenue, with hat in hand, from the carriage in which
he rides with President Buchanan. The unfinished dome of the Capitol looms in the distance.

Winter Davis, a younger man and a brilliant figure, had been a Maryland Whig previously to his joining the new Republican party. Lincoln was told that with Blair named, there would be four Democrats and only three Whigs in the Cabinet, to which he replied that he would be there himself to make the parties even. The Blair-Davis quarrel was furious

This controversy finally involved the supposed rivalry of Seward and Chase. Men of less importance but of more vehemence were going back and forth creating misunderstandings. One effect of the plotting and counter-plotting was a note from Seward on Saturday, March 2nd, saying: "Circumstances which have occurred since I expressed to you in December last my willingness to accept the office of Secretary of State, seem to me to render it my duty to ask leave to withdraw that consent." Mr. Seward had been in the confidence of the President-elect, and had spent the previous Sunday in making suggested changes in the forthcoming inaugural address. Under the circumstances, to have sent such a note was to behave like a pouting opera-singer, who refuses at the last moment to go on the stage,

with no time left to notify her under-study.

Mr. Lincoln took his time and pondered the situation until the inaugural procession was forming on Monday morning. He then wrote a note, dating it the "Executive Mansion, March 4, 1861," although it was actually written at Willard's Hotel. After acknowledgment of the letter Mr. Lincoln proceeded: "It is the subject of the most painful solicitude with me: and I feel constrained to beg that you will countermand the withdrawal. The public interest, I think, demands that you should; and my personal feelings are deeply enlisted in the same direction." He was not attempting to force Seward to an instant reversal, but asked for an answer by nine o'clock the following morning.

In the afternoon of Monday, with the pageantry and the hand-shaking ended, Mr. Seward called upon the President and they had a long and evidently a satisfactory conference. On the following morning, Mr. Seward sent a note withdrawing his letter of Saturday, and at noon on that day, the Senate—which was convened in extra session to confirm appointments—received from the President

MR. LINCOLN ENTERING THE SENATE CHAMBER, ACCOMPANIED BY
PRESIDENT BUCHANAN—From *Harper's Weekly.*

the Cabinet list that I have already mentioned, and they were confirmed without delay.

In order to leave that episode quite complete, I have somewhat anticipated events. The weather proved agreeable on March 4, 1861, which was fortunate for the assembled crowds as well as for the participants in a parade that was colorful beyond present-day customs. With a military escort lined up at the hotel, Mr. Buchanan, in the state carriage with liveried servants, called at the entrance and went in person to Mr. Lincoln's room. The band played "Hail, Columbia!" and Senators Baker and Pearce joined the President and the President-elect in their carriage. Surrounded by soldiers, they proceeded up Pennsylvania Avenue. Mr. Hamlin, who was to succeed Mr. Breckinridge as Vice-President, had walked to the Senate Chamber unattended, and at exactly twelve o'clock, Mr. Breckinridge administered the oath of office to his successor.

The diplomatic corps now arrived, and the Judges of the Supreme Court entered, with Chief Justice Taney leading the way. At ten minutes past one, the Marshal-in-Chief ushered in Messrs. Buchanan and Lincoln. The dignitaries proceeded to the platform on the east side of the Capitol, where Senator Baker introduced Mr. Lincoln to the assembled multitudes. Thereupon, the President-elect found his spectacles, produced the manuscript of his inaugural address, handed his hat to Senator Douglas, and read the famous document which stands among the foremost state papers of our national annals. It is to be noted that it was after the address, and not before, that Chief Justice Taney, who had sworn in seven of Lincoln's predecessors, administered the oath of office. The procession made its formal way down Pennsylvania Avenue to the White House, where Mr. Buchanan, after courteously entering with his successor, bade him Godspeed with affecting and sincere words of parting.

Men who represented in the most conspicuous way the history of a great political year were to be seen closely associated on the platform as Lincoln had taken the oath. By

ABRAHAM LINCOLN TAKING THE OATH OF OFFICE

Chief Justice Taney is administering the oath. To the left of Mr. Lincoln is the retiring President, Mr. Buchanan. The illustration is from a drawing made at the time, by Thomas Nast.

reason of the Dred Scott Decision the Chief Justice had done much to shape the issues. Mr. Douglas and Mr. Breckinridge had been rival candidates, representing the Northern and Southern divisions of the Democratic party. President Buchanan had been mistaken in his Kansas record, but had grown wiser at the end.

I shall not make extended reference to the address itself. It avers, quoting the Chicago platform, that the Republican Administration had no intention to interfere with the domestic institutions of the South, or with any of the safeguards of the Constitution. Mr. Lincoln proceeded to declare his belief in the perpetuity of the Union, as intended in the very nature of its creation. By his reasoning it followed that secession ordinances were legally void, and that acts of violence against the authority of the United States were insurrections or, if on a larger scale, were revolutions. He announced his purpose, therefore, to see that the laws of the Union were faithfully executed in all the States. This declaration was expanded with some detail.

There follows a logical analysis of the anarchical character of the secession doctrine. The only substantial dispute, continues the address, lies in the fact that "one section of our country believes slavery is *right,* and ought to be extended, while the other believes it is *wrong,* and ought not to be extended." The physical difficulties of running two separate governments side by side, one on a free basis, the other on a slave basis, are set forth in impressive sentences. Mr. Lincoln's countrymen are asked to think calmly and not to be in haste. Some of the more soothing paragraphs of the address were due to the acceptance by Mr. Lincoln of Seward's advice.

"In *your* hands, my dissatisfied fellow-countrymen," said Mr. Lincoln in his appeal to the South, "and not in *mine,* is the momentous issue of civil war. The Government will not assail *you.* You can have no conflict without being yourselves the aggressors. *You* have no oath registered in Heaven to destroy the Government, while *I* shall have the most solemn one to 'preserve, protect and defend it'."

In his original draft Mr. Lincoln had concluded with the words, "You can forbear the assault upon it, I cannot shrink from the defense of it. With you, and not with me, is the solemn question, Shall it be peace or a sword?" Mr. Seward preferred a peroration much less painful in its suggestions. He wrote two that he offered as alternatives. The second

I am glad, I am out   Just in time!   Now or never.   This is the way   I'm ready!
of the scrape!   we serve all Traitors!   Copy right secured.

MR. LINCOLN ARRIVES JUST IN TIME

President Buchanan, at the left, retires from the fight to preserve the Union, declaring: "I am glad I am out of the scrape." General Scott, and his troops, at the right, have succeeded (in this poster cartoon) in routing the Southern forces. Jefferson Davis, with drawn sword, remains to fight President Lincoln, who carries the typical rail,

This is the way the
North received it

This is the way the
South received it

PRESIDENT LINCOLN'S INAUGURAL
Thomas Nast made this drawing for the *Illustrated News*. It may be regarded as his first political
cartoon. He was then twenty-one years old, and had recently returned from his European
experiences as a news illustrator.

of these had a literary quality that pleased
Mr. Lincoln, who accepted it, but improved it
by making his own revision.

It is numbered among the best-known and
most often quoted of Lincoln's utterances: "I
am loath to close. We are not enemies, but
friends. We must not be enemies. Though
passion may have strained, it must not break,
our bonds of affection. The mystic chords of
memory, stretching from every battle-field
and patriotic grave, to every living heart and
hearth-stone all over this broad land, will yet
swell the chorus of the Union, when again
touched, as surely they will be, by the better
angels of our nature."

This was indeed a touching appeal. It was
in keeping with the remarks Lincoln had made
at Trenton on the Revolutionary heroes, and
again as he raised the flag on Washington's

Birthday at Philadelphia. But, they had also
observed Washington's Birthday, as equally
belonging to themselves, in the States of the
Confederacy; and the Confederate Congress
was then in session at Montgomery, in a hall
where portraits of Washington were hanging
along with those of other heroes, earlier and
later, including Andrew Jackson and Henry
Clay. There Jefferson Davis had been
inaugurated as President on February 18th.
He had, in his inaugural statement, argued as
strongly for the right of States to secede as
Lincoln two weeks later was arguing against
it. Both men spoke sincerely; and evidently
the issue was one that was not now to be
determined by long-distance debating.

The Confederacy was no longer a thing that
might be brought into being and justified on
Constitutional grounds, but it was an ob-

"THE SCHOOLMASTER ABROAD" AT LAST

Lincoln appears at the Secession pool, where some of his pupils are playing truant, and setting a bad
example for the others. He promises to forgive them if they will try to do better in the future. The
urchin representing South Carolina evidently awaits special attention from the schoolmaster. His
palmetto flag and soldier's hat lie on the ground.

jective entity, formed by the agreement of
seven consenting and well-organized States.
"We have entered upon a career of independence," said Mr. Davis, "and it must be
inflexibly pursued. Through many years of
controversy with our late associates of the
Northern States, we have vainly endeavored to
secure tranquillity and obtain respect for the
rights to which we were entitled. As a necessity, not a choice, we have resorted to the
remedy of separation, and henceforth our
energies must be directed to the conduct of
our own affairs, and the perpetuity of the
Confederacy which we have formed."

Mr. Davis declared that the separation of
the Confederate States had been marked by
no aggression upon others, and followed by
no domestic convulsion. He held that if they
should be involved in war, they could continue
to produce their staple crops and export them,
with the confidence that foreign countries
would not wish to see such trade intercepted.
There was no appeal to the people of the
North, but rather a stern warning against
"the folly and wickedness" of aggressive interference with the course that the South had
chosen to pursue. Mr. Lincoln's address, therefore, while familiar to later admiring generations, made no impression upon the South in
March, 1861. The inaugural address of
Mr. Davis, now forgotten, had strengthened
the cause of separation, and Mr. Lincoln was
soon to find that the long period of arguments
on the sectional issue was at an end.

INDEX

INDEX